A HISTORY OF ANCIENT EGYPT

Egyptian Civilization in Context

Donald B. Redford
Penn State University

KENDALL/HUNT PUBLISHING COMPANY
4050 Westmark Drive Dubuque, Iowa 52002

Cover images from Corel.

ISBN 13: 978-0-7575-2276-5
ISBN 10: 0-7575-2276-9

Printed in the United States of America
10 9 8 7 6 5 4 3 2 1

CONTENTS

PREFACE ....**XI**

INTRODUCTION ....**XIII**

CHAPTER ONE
The Geography of Egypt 1
The River 1
The Annual Inundation 3
Arable Land and Agriculture 4
Foodstocks 5
Demography 6
Eastern and Western Deserts 7
The Coast East and West of the Delta 8
Further Readings 9

CHAPTER TWO
The Foundations: The Prehistory of Egypt 11
The Appearance of Man 11
The Agricultural Revolution 13
The Sedentary Community in Ancient Egypt 15
Belief Systems in Prehistoric Egypt 17
A Selection of Egyptian Towns and Deities 22
Understanding the World: Mythic Narrative 24
Further Readings 29

CHAPTER THREE
The Advent of Complex Society and the Rise of the Pharaonic State 31
The Naqada II Period and the End of the Neolithic 32

Egypt and the "Uruk Phenomenon" 34

The Rise of the First Dynasty 36

The Creation of a Civil Service and the Mechanisms of Government 39

Government Archives 42

"The Hermeneutic of Horus": the Creation of a Royal Mythology 47

The Nascent State: Expansion and Reaction 51

Further Reading 53

CHAPTER FOUR

The Third and Fourth Dynasties: The High Old Kingdom 55

The Worship of the Ancestors and Mortuary Economics 56

The Evolution of the Tomb and the Monument of Djoser 59

Advances in Pyramid Construction 61

The Fourth Dynasty: the Apogee of Royal Power 63

Pharaoh's Government 67

Social Class and the Reward System 68

Pharaoh's Sphere of Foreign Influence 69

Artificial Consistency in the Belief System: Syncretism 70

The King as Perfect God and Man 72

The Cult of the Sun-god Re 74

The Royal Mortuary Temple 75

The Pyramid Texts 77

Further Readings 78

CHAPTER FIVE

The Collapse of the Old Kingdom and the Regime of Herakleopolis 81

Township and Manor 82

The Downsizing of the State 84

The Collapse 85

The Social Phenomenon of the "Common Man" 86

Magic and the Coffin Texts 87

Osiris, the Hypostasis of Fertility and Salvation 90

The Civil War 93

The Theban Eleventh Dynasty 95

Further Reading 95

CHAPTER SIX

The Middle Kingdom 97

Amenemhet I: the Beginnings of Reform 98

The Writing-School 99

The Literature of Persuasion 100

The Reorganization of Egypt 102

The Reign of Amenemhet III 104

The Twelfth Dynasty and the External World 106

Further Reading 110

CHAPTER SEVEN

The Decline of the Middle Kingdom and the Hyksos Conquest 111

The Downsizing of the State 111

Relations with Western Asia 112

The Hyksos 114

The Hyksos in Later Tradition 118

Further Readings 119

CHAPTER EIGHT

". . . With Their Tribute on Their Backs" The Rise of the Egyptian Empire . .121

The War of Liberation: The Seventeenth Dynasty 122

The Early Eighteenth Dynasty: Spiritual Heirs to the Middle Kingdom 124

The Coming of the Indo-Europeans 124

Empire or Retrenchment? 126

The Matriarchal Regency of Hatshepsut 127

The Conquests of Thutmose III 129

The Annihilation of Kush and the Creation of an African Empire 132

The Provinces of Asia and Kush: A Contrast in Administration 133

Cultural Exchange during the Empire of the Eighteenth Dynasty 135

Further Readings 137

CHAPTER NINE

Monarchy in Crisis 139

The Reign of Amenophis III 140

The God Amun and His Cult 143

Akhenaten: the Man 146

The Early Years at Thebes 149

The New City of Amarna: "The Horizon of the Sun-disc" 151

Further Readings 155

CHAPTER TEN
The Reaction against Egypt and the Hittite War 157

The Hittite Threat to Syria 158

The End of the Eighteenth Dynasty 159

The Army Assumes Power 162

The Accession of Ramesses II, "The Great" 164

The Resumption of Hostilities with the Hittites 165

The Egypto-Hittite Entente 167

Further Readings 170

CHAPTER ELEVEN
The Life and Times of Ramesses the Great 171

The Royal House of the Nineteenth Dynasty 171

Government Officials and the Grandees of the Realm (L–M) 174

The Professional Scribes 176

The Professional Priesthood (N–O) 177

The Army 179

Workers, Peasants, and P.O.W.s: the Demographics of Empire 181

Land-holding and Taxation 183

Law during the New Kingdom 184

Family Life 186

A Day in the Life of 187

The "Literature" of the New Kingdom 188

Further Readings 189

CHAPTER TWELVE
The Decline of the New Kingdom (Dyn. 20–21) 191

Keftiu and the Hau-nebu 192

International Trade and Exchange 193

The End of the Nineteenth Dynasty 195

Piracy and the "Sea Peoples" 195

Economic Hardship and Social Protest 199

The Dynastic Succession of the Twentieth Dynasty 200

The Priesthood of Amun and the Army 201

The Tanite Period: the *De Facto* Division of Egypt 202

Further Readings 204

CHAPTER THIRTEEN

The Libyan Kings (Dyn. 22–24) 205

The Meshwesh 205

Egypt and Asia in the Iron Age 207

The Revolt of Thebes 208

The Decline of Libyan Hegemony 209

Egyptian Society in the 8th Century B.C. 210

Further Readings 212

CHAPTER FOURTEEN

The Evolution of the Belief System of Egypt from the End of the New Kingdom to Christian Times 213

The Syncretism of the Amun Theology 213

Animal Worship 215

The Personal Piety of the Masses 216

Sickness and Prophylactic 217

Trial after Death 217

The Afterlife: a Pessimistic View 221

Reward and Punishment 222

The Invention of Heaven and Hell 224

The Island with No Name 227

Further Readings 228

CHAPTER FIFTEEN

Kush, Assyria, and the Struggle for Egypt 229

The Rise of Independent Kush 230

The Assyrian Threat and the Consolidation of the Delta 232

The Kushite Hold on Egypt (712–664 B.C.) 234

The Twenty-fifth Dynasty and Assyrian Expansion 236

Further Readings 238

CHAPTER SIXTEEN

The Spirit of Sais: The Twenty-sixth Dynasty. 239

A Note on Sources for Saïte History 240

The Triumph of Psamtek 240

The Re-unification of the Two Lands 241

The Central Government and the Saïte Court 242

The Restoration of Provincial Administration 244

The Reorganization of the Armed Forces 245

Fiscal Controls and Commerce 248

The Reassurance of Antiquity 250

The Community of Proto-philosophic Thought 252

Further Readings 255

CHAPTER SEVENTEEN

Egypt in the World of the Persian Empire 257

The Persian Conquest of 525 B.C. 258

Egypt under Cambyses and Darius I 259

Persian Administration 260

The Denigration of the Monarch and the Folklore of Deliverance 262

The Last Period of Political Independence: Dyn. 28–30 263

The Last Persian Conquest of Egypt 266

Further Readings 268

CHAPTER EIGHTEEN

"No Longer Masters of Their Own House": Egypt under the Ptolemies 269

The Arrival in Egypt of Alexander the Great 269

A Note on Sources 271

The Government of the Ptolemies 271

The Ideology of Kingship 272

The Egyptian Temples under the Ptolemies 274

Race Relations between Egyptian and Greeks 276

Egypt under the Roman Empire 278

Egypt's Spiritual Bequest to the Roman World 279

Ancient Egypt in the Writings of Classical Authors 281

The Impact of Christianity 282

APPENDIX I

Textual Sources for Egyptian History 285

Our Sources for the Old Kingdom 285

Our Sources for the First Intermediate Period 288

The Middle Kingdom 289

The New Kingdom 292

The Period of Libyan Hegemony 298

The Kushite, Saïte, and Persian Periods 299

APPENDIX II

Basis of Our Chronology 301

APPENDIX III

The King List 307

INDEX 311

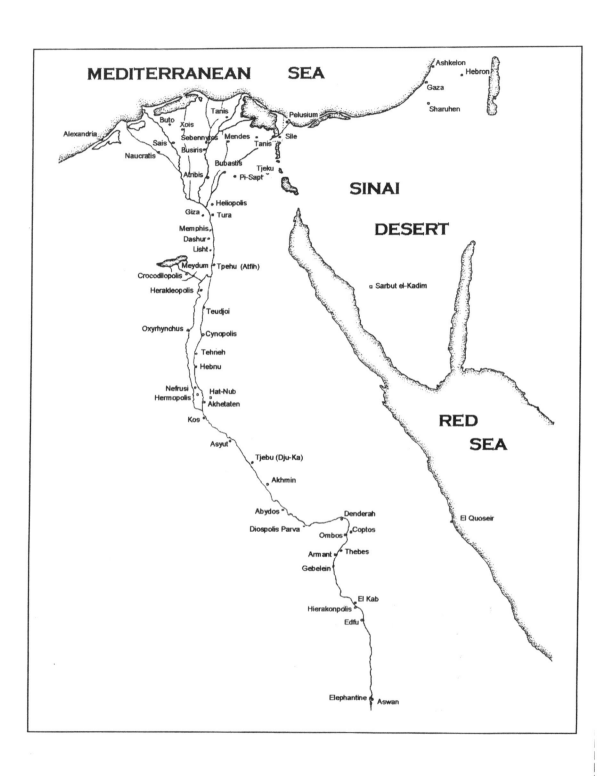

MEDITERRANEAN   SEA

Ashkelon
Hebron
Gaza
Sharuhen

Tanis
Buto
Xois
Pelusium
Sebennytos
Mendes
Sile
Alexandria
Sais
Tanis
Busiris
Naucratis
Bubastis
Atribis
Tjeku
Pi-Sapt

SINAI

Heliopolis
Giza
Tura

DESERT

Memphis
Dashur
Lisht
Meydum
Tpehu (Atfih)
Crocodilopolis
Herakleopolis

Sarbut el-Kadim

Teudjoi
Oxyrhynchus
Cynopolis
Tehneh
Hebnu

Nefrusi
Hat-Nub
Hermopolis
Akhetaten
Kos

RED

Asyut
Tjebu (Dju-Ka)

SEA

Akhmin

Abydos
Denderah
El Quoseir
Diospolis Parva
Coptos
Ombos
Armant
Thebes
Gebelein

El Kab
Hierakonpolis
Edfu

Elephantine
Aswan

PREFACE

This work is a distillation of the author's notes collected and augmented over 40 years in the context of teaching courses on Egyptian history at the University of Toronto, the University of Pennsylvania, and Pennsylvania State University. In addition, I have been privileged to "test" certain ideas in guest lectures at many universities, including Ben Gurion University of the Negeb, Cambridge University, the University of Heidelberg, the Johns Hopkins University, and McGill University. The book follows in its main lines the profile of a major history of Egypt in three volumes being currently prepared, to be accompanied by a volume (or volumes) of translation of sources. Most illustrations are drawn from the author's own slide collection, here reduced to an accompanying CD. Most of the dynasties with their putative dates are listed at the place appropriate to the discussion in the body of the text; only dynasties 8–10, 13, 14, and 16 are omitted (for reasons which will become evident). For ease of student comprehension some of the italicized transliterations are vocalized. Each chapter is followed by a list of suggested readings, which, in view of the monolingual handicap of the expected readership, has been confined to works in the English language.

I owe a debt of gratitude to so many that it is difficult to know where to begin. My wife has always listened to me and offered excellent advice, and was always polite enough not to indicate her boredom. My four sons have exercised a laudable restraint on their father's tendency toward immature flights of fancy. My academic colleagues have long tolerated my half-baked ideas and naïveté, for four decades in fact, and I thank them all for setting me straight upon occasion (though not for their discreet silences). The notes were put together and repeatedly modified within the context of the classroom or seminar, and, whether they know it or not, my students have had a hand in shaping my thinking. I am proud of the dissertations they were gracious enough to write under my supervision. The following have contributed greatly to my work in history: the late Professors John Wilson, Gilbert Bagnani, and Fritz Heichelheim taught me a great deal about what it means to write history and maintain sound judgment. The late Professor Ricardo Caminos inculcated a feeling for thoroughness in data collection, and the late Dame Kathleen Kenyon taught me how to dig and use archeological evidence. Others, still living, may not realize how much they have influenced me. I mention, among many others, Professors Jan Assmann, B. Halpern, Gerald Kadish, Gary Knoppers, John Ray, William Kelly Simpson, Hayim Tadmor, and Edward Wente.

In the preparation of this book my wife, Dr. Susan Redford, and my student Ashley Irminger have contributed the maps and line drawings; my graduate student Kyle Long has done the word processing and preliminary editing. My PhD candidate, Matt Adams, has been always ready with advice and help with the computer; and he and my teaching assistants have lifted a burden from my shoulders in addressing classroom problems. Earlier versions of some chapters were prepared by my former student Rosa Frei.

It should be noted that, in the thorny debate over New Kingdom chronology, the author has chosen to follow the "high" chronology, although this does not represent or reflect a dogmatic adherence. Future discovery will undoubtedly modify the picture to the benefit of everyone.

INTRODUCTION

The Recovery of Ancient Egypt

At the beginning of the 19th century A.D., when Western scholarship was beginning to take a serious interest in Egypt, two sources of information were available to the European scholar: (1) the texts (inscriptions and papyri) left behind by the ancient Egyptians themselves, and (2) the writings in Greek, Hebrew, and Latin by classical visitors to Egypt and by biblical writers. Hebrew, Greek, and Latin had never been lost to the memory of man, but the ancient Egyptian language had long since passed into oblivion. The explanation of these curious facts lies partly in the checkered history of northeast Africa from the 7th century B.C. to Roman times, and partly in the triumph of Europe at the expense of Africa in the early centuries of the Christian era.

From 671 B.C., Egypt suffered six grievous invasions of her territory (and as many unsuccessful attempts) by foreign armies bent on subjugating the lower Nile and Delta. Although traumatic to the Egyptian psyche and momentarily destructive to aspects of the nation's culture, the Assyrian occupation of Egypt (671 to c. 660 B.C.) was too brief to establish any pattern of systematic subversion. This cannot be said, however, of the aftermath of the overwhelming defeat Egypt suffered at the hands of the Persians in 525 B.C., when the entire country lost its independence and found itself for 120 years a mere province of a world empire. Although for most of the period of occupation the Persian authorities proved admirably tolerant of Egyptian customs and beliefs, official business touching upon Egyptian administration and the position of Egypt within the empire was carried on in Aramaic, the language everywhere employed by the Persians in the running of their universal regime. The favoring of a foreign tongue and script in no way discouraged the use of the Egyptian language and script for internal affairs; but it did point up how isolated Egyptian culture had become in the new Mediterranean world. The fact was underscored by Alexander's arrival in Egypt in 332 B.C. Egypt now found itself not only run by foreigners, but also occupied in increasing numbers by those foreigners. Moreover, unlike the Persians, the incoming Greeks showed little respect and less admiration for the language of the natives; and while as time wore on they fell under the spell of Egyptian culture and religion, the native lore was universally communicated and transmitted in the Greek language. The administration everywhere used Greek as the language of communication, official business, judicial matters, and even local commerce. Egyptian might be used by the natives among themselves, in their own marketplaces and temples, but should a Greek be involved, the transaction had to be recorded in *his* language and script.

The Ancient Ruins and Inscriptions

Throughout the Late Roman Empire and the Middle Ages the Christian Church perpetuated the misinterpretation of Ancient Egypt and its scripts. The church's contempt for pagan antiquity led to priority being given to the biblical record of Egypt, which in fact is at best spotty and often wholly inaccurate. The pyramids for Christians became Joseph's granaries, and the "Land of Ramses" was sought in the environs of Heroonpolis. Christianity took the Hermetica, a hodgepodge of magical/mystical writings in Greek put together in Alexandria in the Roman period, as genuine "Egyptian" wisdom. Church fathers indeed succumbed to the danger of identifying anything of Alexandrian origin, and a manifestation of purely Greek culture, as genuinely Egyptian: and so astrology, since it had been given a pseudo-scientific basis by Claudius Ptolemy, was misconstrued by the church as *Egyptian wisdom*. But Egyptian wisdom was everywhere denigrated by the church as inferior to its own in that it was alleged to have been promulgated subsequent to biblical wisdom. St. Augustine, for example, advanced the most specious arguments in an attempt to date the wisdom of Egypt after the "wisdom of our prophets." Even Isis is made a daughter of Inachos of Argos and dated after Abraham or elsewhere turned into a "queen of the Egyptians." Hermes Trismegistos (in reality, the ancient Egyptian god Thoth, "thrice-great") is acknowledged as historical, but dated after Moses.

Apart from its nature as a brilliant burst of imaginative thought, the European Renaissance also represented the recovery of antiquity. Monuments and writings of the classical past were rediscovered in their Roman setting; and in the process it was found that many Egyptian objects purloined by the emperors had survived, too. The discovery of Horapollo's *Hieroglyphica* by a Florentine priest in 1419, and its subsequent publication in printed form, led to a revival of interest in things Egyptian. Travelers began to bring back tales of what Egypt was like, albeit at times lacking in scientific accuracy. Even Pope Alexander VI in 1492 had the Borgia apartments in the Vatican decorated with scenes showing incidents in the Osiris myth (as known through Plutarch) to enhance, in a quasi-allegorical way, the prestige of his ancestry; and sponsored an explanatory commentary by Pomponius Laetus.

Yet the total misunderstanding of the nature of the hieroglyphic script, enshrined in the prestigious writings of Plotinus and other classical authors, continued to be accepted as fact. No one seemed able to break away from the belief that the hieroglyphs were symbolic and allegorical. To scholars of the Renaissance, the works of Plato, Aristotle, Ptolemy, et al. were but a superficial reflection of the mass of Egyptian wisdom that had, for the most part, been lost—surviving to a limited extent in the Hermetica.

However, with the work of Athanasius Kircher, a Jesuit priest of the 16th century, a major stride was made that eventually would pave the way for the "cracking" of the hieroglyphic script. Kircher devoted himself to the study of Coptic, the latest stage in the ancient Egyptian language written in a modified Greek script. Though ousted as a vernacular by the Islamicization of Egypt in the 8th through 10th century A.D., Coptic had survived as a liturgical language used by the Coptic church; and by Kircher's day the Vatican library contained a rich collection of Coptic literature. Kircher's study of the language had advanced sufficiently by 1636 that he felt able to publish a grammar of the Coptic language, and this proved to be the first accurate, linguistic treatment of that tongue. And even though Kircher's attempts to decipher the hieroglyphs failed completely—he remained firmly committed to symbolical/allegorical theory—his Coptic grammar constituted a foundation on which future scholars would build.

The 17th and 18th centuries provided few, if any, advances toward deciphering the hieroglyphic script. All attempts had proceeded from the assumption that the signs were symbols, *idea-signs,* and the result was ludicrous: the "translation" of a given hieroglyphic text differed with each scholar assaying the task! By the 18th century a jaundiced skepticism had become faddish. Some even denied that the hieroglyphs were a script at all: perhaps they were merely a minor art of wall decoration.

Then came the great Napoleonic expedition to Egypt in July 1798. Designed as a blow against British trade, the expedition enjoyed limited success and was labeled by some as a fiasco. But as a *cultural* mission it was without parallel. For Napoleon had recruited a veritable corps of scholars, scientists, and artists to accompany his troops and subject the Nile landscape to the kind of encyclopedic investigation for which the times were famous. The scholarly army went everywhere in Egypt and recorded everything in painstaking detail, often under the most trying conditions of climate and combat. The result, published later from 1809 to 1822, was the nine-volume *Description de l'Egypte.* Now Europe had a scientific introduction to every aspect of Egypt, ancient and modern, which went far beyond the fantastic stories of medieval travelers. For the first time scholars were confronted by accurate renderings of the ancient ruins and inscriptions. But, more important, it was a chance discovery by French troops during their brief occupation of the country that led indirectly to the decipherment of the hieroglyphic script.

In the summer of 1799 an inscription on a basalt block was recovered at the site of Fort Julien, which was being built near Rosetta at the mouth of the westernmost branch of the Nile in the Delta. Upon closer inspection in Alexandria, the *Rosetta stone,* as it came to be called, was found to contain three bands of inscription in different scripts: the uppermost (of which only part was preserved) in hieroglyphs, the middle in cursive hieroglyphic called *Demotic,* and the lowermost in Greek. The latter was quickly translated and turned out to be a decree of King Ptolemy V issued in 197 B.C. It was a fair guess (and was eventually proved correct) that the hieroglyphic and Demotic bands were merely translations of the same Greek text. Although the stone was confiscated by the British troops when the French capitulated and was eventually consigned to the British Museum, the French savants had had the presence of mind to make copies, squeezes, and casts of the inscription before they were forced to give it up. In this way facsimiles of the Rosetta stone made their way both to the British Isles and continental Europe long before the Napoleonic wars came to an end, and scholars on both sides lost no time in subjecting the inscription to close examination.

Abetting attempts at decipherment was the fact that, both in the hieroglyphic and Demotic sections, individual groups of signs tended to recur at about the same positions that words were repeated in the Greek section. Early attempts fastened upon this discovery and tried to make capital out of it in the Demotic section. A Swedish diplomat, Akerblad, had succeeded by 1802 in identifying in Demotic many of the personal names in the Greek—the group of signs taken to be "Ptolemy" looked suspiciously phonetic in structure!—as well as postulating the Demotic for *temple* and *Greek.* Though it could not as yet be confirmed, Akerblad's suggestions that Demotic was in fact identical with Coptic, and that the script was largely phonetic, proved remarkably accurate. An Englishman named Thomas Young built on Akerblad's findings. A physicist who had already become renowned for his undulatory theory of light, Young approached the problem of the decipherment as a dilettante interested in the challenge of another conundrum. By 1814 Young was able provisionally to divide the hieroglyphic band of text into individual words, and to compile a glossary of 86 equivalences between Greek words and Demotic groups of signs. His article on "Egypt" for the 1819 edition of the *Encyclopaedia Britannica* showed several solid advances. He was now aware of the use and significance of signs that we today call *determinatives,* (i.e., signs placed at the ends of words that appear to "determine" their classification). He had also ferreted out the principle of *homophony*—that two or more separate signs might have the same sound value. It was clear that Demotic was simply a cursive form of hieroglyphic. Most important: he confirmed a suspicion that Akerblad had entertained that the glyphs within an oval (called a *cartouche* because of its resemblance to a French cartridge) in the hieroglyphic section constituted the writing of the name *Ptolemy* in Egyptian.

The work of Akerblad and Young attracted the attention of an erratic, volatile young genius named Jean François Champollion. Born in Figeac, France, in 1790, Champollion had as a mere child projected a vast program of future work on ancient Egypt, and had even begun a major history of the country under the title *Egypte sous les Pharaons.* A professor at the age of 19, he persevered with his research and was able in 1814 to publish the geographical sections of his history. Wild claims were made in the work regarding his decipherment of the hieroglyphs; but in fact he had done little more than to present Akerblad's findings as his own. However, when in 1819 he set about to study the Egyptian mortuary book dubbed today the *Book of the Dead,* he gravitated wildly to the conclusion, a retrogression as it turned out, that the Egyptian script was symbolic, not phonetic. Again, he reversed himself upon reading Young's encyclopedia article, and came to the realization that the ancient script must, after all, be a set of sound signs. It appeared now, however, that the investigation had reached an impasse: In spite of the presence of a trilingual text, the final clue remained elusive.

In 1815 an Englishman, W. J. Bankes, had recovered an obelisk from Elephantine at the First Cataract on the Nile that dated to the reign of Ptolemy VII (Physcon) and Kleopatra III (late 2nd century B.C.). Four years later he had his treasure shipped to London, where it was erected at Kensington. The unprepossessing monument offered little by way of artistic merit, but it did contain a bilingual inscription in Greek and hieroglyphic on the base. Moreover, unlike the Rosetta stone, whereon only the single cartouche provisionally understood as the hieroglyphic rendering of *Ptolemy* was preserved, the Bankes inscription mentioned both Ptolemy and Kleopatra, and where the latter would have occurred in the hieroglyphic section, a cartouche was to be found with new hieroglyphs different from those in the alleged Ptolemy cartouche **(fig. 1).**

When a copy of the Bankes texts came into Champollion's hands in 1822, he realized immediately its significance, and the hieroglyphic code was cracked. For, on the assumption of phonetic values for the signs, P, O, and L fell exactly where they were to be expected in both cartouches. Assigning values to the remaining glyphs as a working hypothesis, Champollion produced a list of about a dozen phonetic signs. Armed with this, he was able to identify an increasing number of names of Ptolemaic and Roman date and even earlier Pharaonic names (fig. 1).

The realization that the script was essentially phonetic opened the door to the exploration of grammar and syntax. Within two years Champollion had published a preliminary *Precis,* and

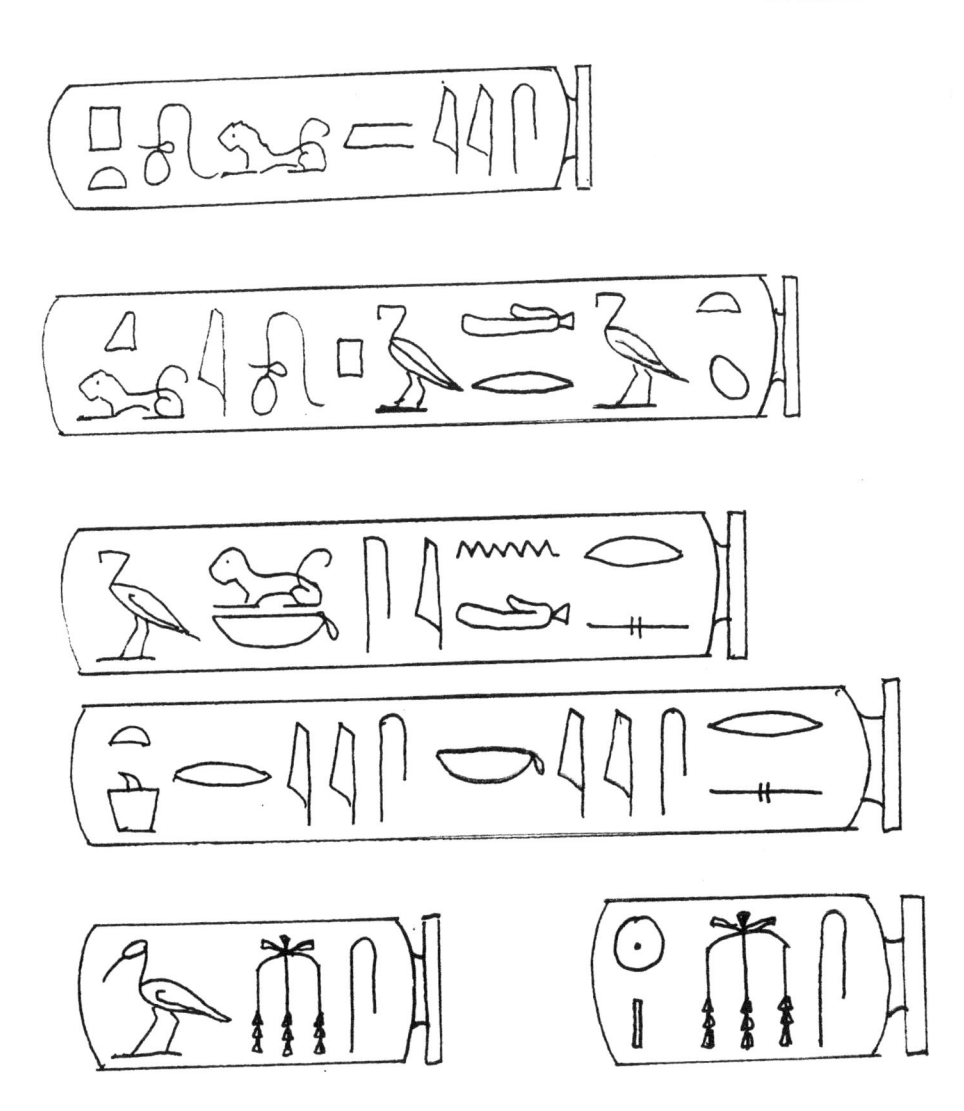

Figure 1 (1) Ptolemaios; (2) Kleopatra; (3) Aleksandros; (4) Tiberius Caesar; (5) Thutmose; (6) Ramess(u)

before his death in 1832 due to a stroke, he had completed a grammar (not published until 1838). Appreciation of the fact that Coptic represented the final stage in the language for which the hieroglyphic script had provided the vehicle helped greatly in eliciting grammar and lexikon. Scholars soon realized, however, that work on the language could only proceed if good copies of inscriptions were available. In 1828 Champollion himself led a scholarly team to Egypt to collect and copy inscriptions; and from 1842 to 1845 Richard Lepsius conducted a monumental epigraphic survey of Egypt, funded by the king of Prussia. By the close of the 19th century careful copies of every inscription known were filed away in Berlin, and in 1897 linguists had begun the daunting task of producing a hieroglyphic dictionary. By that time grammars had begun to appear, and through the 20th century there was no let-up in the appearance of scholarly grammars in Middle Egyptian (1927 to present), Old Egyptian (1964), Late Egyptian (1933, 2003), as well as Demotic and Coptic.

While linguistics and lexical studies have been well served to date, the same cannot be said of archeology. Throughout the 19th and the early 20th centuries what passes for archeology is nothing more than a treasure hunt undertaken at the behest of a museum or a private collector. The appointment of the Frenchman Auguste Mariette in 1858 as head of an antiquities service by the Egyptian government helped to regularize the recording and removal of finds. But it was not until the arrival of William Matthew Flinders Petrie a quarter-century later that scientific archeology was first developed in Egypt. Petrie trained a number of students in the meticulous methods of stratigraphy, pottery and artifact seriation, planning, and photography; but strangely, treasure hunting continued to such an extent that Egypt earned the reputation as the sphere of the private collector and interested amateur. I can cite several examples of scientific funding agencies turning down excavation proposals, not because the techniques employed were unscientific, but simply because the venue was Egypt!

Since World War II the picture has changed drastically. With the awareness of the importance of anthropological methods, a new refinement has informed archeological investigations in Egypt. Although sadly the treasure hunt persists as a model in some quarters, the work being done by major expeditions throughout the Valley, Delta, and the deserts equals the best excavations undertaken anywhere on earth. With the awareness of the importance of the holistic approach, and the admirable regulations of the Supreme Council of Antiquities of Egypt, the future is looking brighter than it ever has in the past.

Transliteration Alphabet

Transliteration Sign	Approximate Pronunciation
ꜣ	*aleph*, a glottal stop, as heard at the commencement of words beginning with vowels (not generally recognized in English)
i	*yodh*, usually as *y*, occasionally as ꜣ as the beginnings of words
y	*y*
ꜥ	*ayin*, a guttural unknown in English; pronounced as a short *a* for convenience
w	*w*
b	*b*
p	*p*
f	*f*
m	*m*
n	*n*
r	*r*
h	*h*, as in English
ḥ	emphatic *h*, as in *Ahmed*
ḫ	*heth*, as *ch* in Scottish *loch*
ẖ	uncertain, perhaps as *ch* in German *ich*
s	*s*
š	*shin*, as *sh*
ḳ	*qoph*, an emphatic *k*, as that found in Arabic and Hebrew
k	*k*
g	hard *g*
t	*t*
ṭ	*tjima*, as *tj*
d	*d*
ḏ	*djandja*, as *dj*

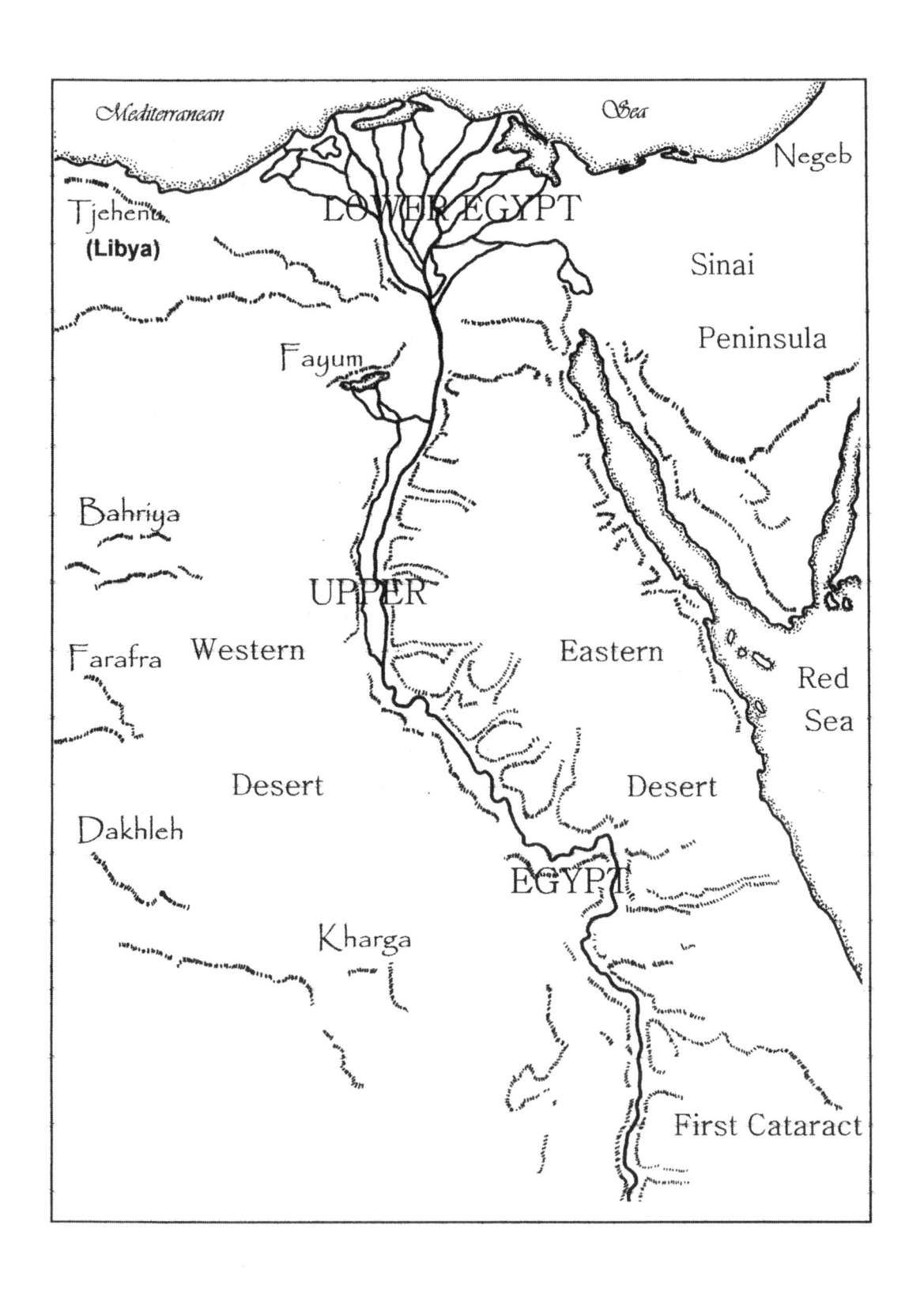

CHAPTER ONE
The Geography of Egypt

—— Ψ ——

Egypt past and present is constituted on an alluvial flood-plain, beyond the narrow limits of which settlement is scarcely feasible. Since complex society in north-east Africa could not have evolved but for the action of the river, Egypt can be construed, as Herodotus acutely observed, as "the gift of the Nile." And it is a perennial gift: for the river annually renews the flood-plain through the silt brought down by the Inundation.

The River

Measured along the course of the White Nile, from its most distant source east of Lake Tanganyeka, the Nile is over 4,100 miles long; but two other major streams contribute to the overall discharge. The Blue Nile, rising in the mountains of Abyssinia, joins the White Nile at Khartoum in the Sudan, while the Atbara, draining north-western Ethiopia, flows into the combined rivers 200 miles north of that city. For over one thousand miles north of Khartoum the Nile cuts a shallow bed across a desert plain with a thin ribbon of cultivable land on either bank. At intervals throughout this part of its journey the river must pass through six cataracts (numbered north-south), caused by the emergence at the surface of bands of granite strata. All six pose major obstacles for shipping, and none more than the second, the *batn el-haggar,* "the belly of rock," which the ancients termed "the capsizing place." In times of political strength and prosperity the Egyptian government for its own strategic purposes would attempt to canalize the first, and clear the second, so that its warships and merchant fleets could penetrate Nubia easily. Nonetheless, for any invader coming from the south, the cataracts proved virtually impassable, and thus they provided Egypt with a natural defence "in depth" on its African border.

Egypt, as it was conceived of in the historic period, began at the first cataract (A). Here a small town, Aswan, occupied the east bank, and a somewhat larger settlement, an emporium in fact, took shape on an adjacent island in the Nile. The island's name, "Elephantine" in

Greek, a translation of the Egyptian *Yeb,* "ivory," points to the commercial reason for the town's existence, i.e., trade with sub-Saharan Africa. The inhabitants of this barren region had a reputation for suffering deafness because of the noise of the water crashing over the cataract (B). They were also the butt of humor for their dialect, which was difficult to understand elsewhere in Egypt.

The stretch of the river from Aswan at the first cataract to the apex of the Delta, some 650 miles to the north, constitutes Upper Egypt. Here the Nile at first occupies the eastern side of the alluvial plain. The first forty miles, from Elephantine to Kom Ombo, finds desert conditions on both banks (C); then arable land begins to appear (D). On average throughout Upper Egypt the alluvial plain is six to nine miles wide, but at certain points it can attain a width of fifteen miles. The depth of the silt deposited by the annual floods again varies from place to place, and sometimes reaches 1,500 meters. From Esna to Naga Hammadi most of the arable land lies on the east bank until, as the massif of Kasr es-Sayyed approaches the bank, it is finally pinched off (E). From this point to Asyut the alluvium is evenly divided between the eastern and western sides of the valley; but from Asyut to Atfih the cliffs of the eastern desert border the river (F) and all arable land is on the western bank. In this reach, known commonly as Middle Egypt, the western cliffs have receded into a shelving desert edge, and the Nile spawns a parallel branch on the west, the Bahr Yussef, which leaves the main river just north of Asyut, and finally flows into the great lake in the Fayum depression. Approximately one hundred miles north of the Fayum the cliffs suddenly re-appear, the Mokattam hills on the east and the Giza plateau on the west, reducing the valley to half its average width.

North of Giza the cliffs retreat, both on the east and on the west, enabling the river to spread out and form a delta, Lower Egypt. The number of branches into which the Nile split at this point varied in antiquity—as many as nine are sometimes mentioned—but three in particular retained their strength throughout antiquity, viz. the "Western River" (modern Rosetta branch), the "Great River" (modern Damietta branch), and the "Eastern River" (the Pelusiac branch, now extinct). Until the 19th century A.D. extensive tracts of marshland were to be found in the Delta, especially along the coast, while here and there sand turtle-backs and levees of old river branches made human settlements possible. Before the construction of the Aswan dams, the silt deposits of the annual floods caused the Delta coast gradually to expand northward into the Mediterranean. This point has implications for political and economic history: 5,000 years ago such presently land-locked sites as Buto and Mendes were much closer to the sea and enjoyed a commercial lifestyle commensurate with a coastal location.

Much as sandy beaches attract us moderns (G), in antiquity the Egyptians viewed the Mediterranean coast as inimical to human activity. The presence of sand-bars and shoals off the mouths of the branches of the Nile, coupled with treacherous currents out to sea, combined to render navigation extremely risky, and only the most accomplished sailors could negotiate the Nile mouths. In historic times the Egyptians turned their backs on the Mediterranean, preferring for the most part to leave maritime commerce in the hands of Phoenicians and Greeks. But what acted as a deterrent to the Egyptians had a similar effect on foreigners: as the cataracts on the south had provided Egypt with natural defences, so the Delta coast acted as a barrier to invasion from the north (H).

The Annual Inundation

From the earliest times it was borne in upon the inhabitants of the Nile Valley and Delta that the fertility of the soil on which they depended was wholly due to the action of the river. How this realization impacted the ideology of fertility with Egypt's belief system we shall examine below. But that their situation differed from that of their Near Eastern neighbors, who received water from an unreliable "Nile in the sky," helped to reinforce the subconscious view that Egypt had been specially favored by the divine.

In Egypt, rainfall being negligible (only 150 mm per year in Alexandria), everything depends upon the annual flooding of the Nile. In the early spring the melting snows of the Abyssinian uplands cause the Blue Nile to flood, and by mid-May the crest has reached Khartoum. For Egypt the immediate impact of the inundation has changed because of the construction of two dams at Aswan which effectually hold back the flood each year, thus creating an artificial lake. But prior to the 20th century the annual drama of the river was enacted in the same way that it had been for millennia. By mid-June the inhabitants of Middle Egypt detected the rise of the waters, and on June 18 the festival of the "Night of the Drop" was celebrated in Cairo. (A romantic aetiology ascribed the flood to the tears of Isis grieving over her deceased husband, Osiris.) The height of the Nile was reached in July, and maintained itself until mid-October when the waters began to recede. Not only did the annual flood effectively "flush out" the Valley and Delta, but in antiquity it also deposited a film of fertile silt upon the valley floor, amounting to four inches per century.

It was all-important to the ancient economy that the Nile rise to an optimal level. Both too much and too little water could prove detrimental to irrigation. High and powerful floods carried the risk of destroying dykes and catchment basins; while lingering floods would delay the harvest and might foster parasites and even epidemics. Low inundations would not water marginal land and would thus adversely affect the food supply. In order to better control accurate prognostication, the Egyptians soon appreciated the value in setting up graduated scales or Nilometers by which to measure successive inundations. Records compiled over time would help to detect long range patterns. Since predictability and lead time were both necessary to enable farmers to make preparations by erecting dykes and digging channels and basins, it was imperative to measure the river's increasing height early in the spring and as far south as possible, before the flood reached Egypt proper; and thus Elephantine at the first cataract and later Semna at the second were chosen as sites for the placement of Nilometers whence precise information might be relayed quickly to the north.

Preparations for the annual inundation were made in the spring. Roads and settlements were already located on raised embankments or mounds, or flanked by protective walls; but dykes and catchment basins had to be built afresh or substantially repaired each year. The authorities had to have fairly accurate knowledge regarding the coming flood in order to raise the walls of the basins to a sufficient height to entrap the waters for use throughout the planting and growing season. When the inundation had reached its maximum height the dykes would be broken and the water would flow into the catchment areas. A network of artificially dug canals would enable fields far from the river to be worked.

Arable Land and Agriculture

The amount of farm-land under cultivation undoubtedly fluctuated over the three and one-half millennia with which this book is concerned. The figure 35,000 square kilometers, which reflects the fields under cultivation in the 1950s, may be slightly in excess of that of the peak imperial periods of Egyptian history. In times of prolonged drought considerable tracts would have been lost to irrigation and thus would have been reclaimed by the desert. On average, for most periods, it has been estimated on the basis of extant ancient records and educated guessing that c. 18,250 square kilometers corresponds to the total extent of worked arable land within the Nile Valley and Delta.

The ancient Egyptians were fully aware of the agricultural nature of their world, and their nomenclature arises directly from their environment. The Delta was the "Flooded Land" or the "Land of the Flood" (*T3-mhw*), the valley the "Land of the *shma*-plant" (*T3-šmʿw*), the entire land collectively the "Two Banks" (*idb.wy*), the fertile soil the "Black Land" (*Kmt*), the arid desert the "Sandy Cliffs" (*h3st*) (I). A complex classification of arable land was used, the criteria being location, history of cultivation or ownership; and the tax system could be adjusted to suit the particular type. Thus the best "ploughland" (*nhbw*) was taxed at the rate of ten measures per *arura* (⅔ acre), land which had been (over) worked, "tired land," at seven and one-half per *arura,* and "high ground" (*k3yt*), far from the river and irrigated artificially, at five measures per *arura.* "Riparian" land was the most fertile because of its location on the river bank, "elderly(?) land" less so, but for reasons unclear. Because, when the flood abated in early winter, the Nile frequently settled here and there into a new bed, it often left exposed levees and islands formerly submerged; and so the state was faced at any given time with a varying extent of "new land" which had to be put under cultivation. Both this "new land" and land which for some reason was ownerless (*khato*-land) became state property, to be worked without remuneration by neighboring owners.

The farmer's year in Egypt revolved around three seasons: inundation, planting, and harvest. Each involved necessary tasks which had to be carried out with skill and vigilance. During inundation repairs to the apparatus of irrigation was obligatory, and sluices had to be opened at exactly the right time. No one was permitted to act in such a self-serving manner that a neighbor up the canal, as it were, was deprived of water; and thus the phrase "to be on someone's water" came to denote co-operation and loyalty. Planting followed as the waters fell (J). The height of the Nile each year affected the human community in unsuspected areas of its activities. Toward the middle of January each year the state conducted a land survey to determine the amount of land inundated and the expected extent of the harvest. Contracts drawn up in the business community were adjusted in light of the predicted strength of the inundation; and a moratorium could be declared on rents and taxes if the flood were low that year. Even planting and salary assessment could undergo modification depending on the volume of water expected. "Now if a 'Great Nile' comes," says a farmer to his son (2015 B.C.), "then with barley shall you sow it (i.e. the field);" and again: "Now look! Assign us [our] rat[ions] specifically commensurate with a 'Painful Nile.' "

Foodstocks

Despite the remote possibility of famine because of low inundation, Egypt possessed the largest foodstocks in the ancient world. After its conquest by Augustus in 30 B.C. it was to become the bread-basket of the Roman world, but long before that it functioned as a reliable storehouse in time of want. The Biblical Joseph story is accurate at least insofar as it stresses this important fact: "there is corn in Egypt yet!"

The two staple cereals Egypt had to offer in antiquity were barley and emmer wheat (K). Their cultivation on a wide scale dates from the foundation of the state shortly before 3000 B.C., and they were to remain the principal source of taxation through Pharaonic times. The rate of the tax varied, but it was usually calculated on the "share-cropping" basis of two thirds to the farmer, one third to the state. Wheat and barley were extensively used to produce a weak sort of beer, akin in quality and texture to the *bouza* of rural Egypt today: indeed, so widespread was the production that beer jars and the multi-purpose mixing vats wherein the brew was concocted are among the most common vessels in the ceramic repertoire of ancient Egypt.

Of other plants native to Egypt mention may be made of flax and papyrus. The former was cultivated in prehistoric times, and by the time the country was unified and a Pharaonic state established, linen of the finest quality was being produced. At about the same time papyrus, which in ancient times grew in abundance in the marshes of the Delta, was found to be capable of producing a writing medium. Stalks of the plant could be laid side by side and topped by a second layer at right angles to the direction of the first. When watered, pressed, and polished, the result was a smooth, light-weight sheet of *paper*.

Other crops, cultivated mainly in the valley, were no less widespread than those passed in review above. Market gardens, of greater importance to the economy than has been realized heretofore, grew lettuce, lentils, onions, leeks, cucumber, garlic, beans, sesame, and castor. Flower gardens usually centered upon pools with aquatic plants including varieties of lotus and lilies, and produced blossoms for the bouquets and garlands the Egyptians loved, as well as the ingredients for perfumes. Orchards also abounded, with sycamores and date-palms predominating.

In spite of the erroneous claims of certain classical authors, vineyards were quite common from the earliest times (L). A large concentration of wine-producing estates lay on the Western River in the Delta (not far from the site of later Alexandria), and these manufactured a pleasant-tasting white wine. The area around Mendes and the land at the mouth of the Pelusiac branch produced red wine of quality. Further south, however, the excellence of the product rapidly diminished: the wines of Thebes were "thin" and of indifferent bouquet.

A keen awareness of animal life informs every aspect of the ancient Egyptian psyche. The country relied on animal husbandry as a mainstay of its economy. Cattle, both long- and short-horns, were of paramount importance, and in the Old Kingdom became the object of a biennial cattle census. Herds were to be found all over Egypt, but fens for cattle grazing were located mainly in the Delta. Flocks of sheep and goat also abounded, again especially in the Delta, and pigs were kept. From the earliest times ducks and geese inhabited the marshes, but were also kept on the farm. Chickens were not to appear until the 15th century B.C. as imports from western Asia. Ibises were sometimes domesticated and kept in households as surety against reptile life. The common beast of burden was the donkey; the horse makes its appearance, again from the north-east, no later than the 16th century B.C. Camels may have been known in the wild, although the evidence is equivocal, and enter Egypt as domesticates only after 1000 B.C. While the list of domesticated animals is impressive, wildlife and fishstocks remained sizeable throughout ancient times in both Valley and Delta. In contrast to the economies of other Near Eastern communities, fishing, fowling, and hunting continued to comprise an important strategy in food production, a curious fact which we shall attempt to explain in the next chapter. Predators were a constant menace throughout the land. Crocodiles, scorpions, and snakes are spoken of as ubiquitous; lions and wild bulls roamed the hither desert, and hippopotami were still to be found in the marshes of the Delta.

Demography

The population of Egypt at the time of writing is approximately 70 million, a dramatic increase over the 19 million of 1961. Neither figure, however, is in any way comparable to census figures for the ancient state (which, of course, we do not have but can reconstruct), even in its most prosperous and populous periods. For meaningful comparanda we must go back over two hundred years, to the eve of Napoleon's expedition of 1798, when the total population stood at slightly less than 3 million.

Ancient Egyptian archivists exhibited a great interest in listing things and arriving at totals, but their practical needs precluded counting for its own sake. A census of human beings made sense to them only as a means of ascertaining manpower available, and the resultant record would resemble a draft-list more than a true census. Those eligible for a call-up, or the total number of family dwellings in a town would be all that interested the scribe. Thus moderns are reduced to reliance upon population formulae and classical authors' statements, neither a foolproof basis for population estimates. If, as has been suggested, the population of a prosperous township in Middle Egypt in Roman times stood at approximately 125,000, we might make an educated guess that all forty-two townships combined would produce a total population of 5,250,000; and if the larger populations of Memphis and Thebes were taken into account, the total might exceed 6,000,000. Such a figure is not at odds with the 6–9 million posited by the historian Josephus in the first century A.D.

For earlier periods one suspects that estimates ought to be reduced somewhat. For the reign of Ramesses III (12th century B.C.) the Great Harris Papyrus, derived from official inventories, gives a figure of about 107,000 as total personnel employed by the temples, and if women, children, and the aged are estimated on a 1:4 ratio, we arrive at 428,000 for temple "population." On the assumption that the temple personnel represent between 10 percent and 15 percent of the total population of the land, we arrive at a figure between 3½ and just over 4 million for the probable population of late Ramesside Egypt. In times of famine and poverty, however, this figure will have to be drastically reduced, perhaps to as low as 1 million for the First Intermediate Period.

It is a fair guess that population distribution in Egypt today follows that of antiquity. The greatest concentration is to be found in the twenty-five-mile stretch just above the apex of the Delta, where Cairo is situated today, and Memphis, "the royal city of the Egyptians" as Strabo called it, in ancient times. For the rest there is an imbalance in favor of Lower Egypt, which now is home to two thirds of the overall population of Egypt. A similar situation must have obtained in Pharaonic times: the magnetic quality of the royal residence at Memphis will have ensured that the density of population increased in those parts lying close to the capital, viz. the Delta and the Fayum.

While the point will be taken up in greater detail throughout this book, it bears stressing that ancient Egypt was essentially an agricultural society. The activities, strategies, and mind-set of the farmer, shepherd, and fisherman inform all aspects of ancient ideology. In contradistinction to other societies in the ancient world, every Egyptian, even members of the elite, was close to the land; everyone had a village home, everyone was a townsman. In this light, it remains to be seen (and will be discussed in detail below) whether the term "urban" has any place in scholarly vocabulary relating to the ancient land.

Eastern and Western Deserts

Barren deserts hem the Nile Valley in on both east and west. The great Western Desert, which stretches virtually uninterrupted from the Nile to Morocco, comprises a massive plateau of sedimentary rock (M). The arid conditions of the region are nothing new, but date back to the very origins of the Nile Valley. The strip of wilderness closest to the valley of the Nile presents a tiresome prospect of slightly undulating, stony ground of little use to the human community. But at a point about 100 miles as one proceeds along the desert track from Asyut and Manfalut, there suddenly yawns at one's feet the bed of a vast prehistoric sea, the Khargeh depression. This is one of a string of oases (N), "the route of forty days" of mediaeval times, which stretches from north to south and provides a negotiable route between the Nile at the latitude of Memphis and the valley of the same river in Nubia. A much-used transit corridor in Pharaonic times, the route was early controlled by the Egyptians by placing governors in the oases; and the latter, because of their remote location, provided the government with convenient places of exile for dissidents. The oases themselves produce fruit of a remarkable quality, as well as the natron which the Egyptians required in all aspects of their society.

The Eastern Desert, between the Nile and the Red Sea, consists of a north-south chain of rugged mountains of igneous origin (O). A maze of wadys intersects and surrounds these mountains, and travellers at some seasons run the risk of flash floods if there is a cloud-burst. Quarries in the Wady Hammamat (P), accessible from Koptos, produced greywacke, schist, and diorite; while more remote mountains mainly south of Hammamat were early known for their gold deposits and extensively worked. Routes through the mountains from Nile to Red Sea coast are few, but not impassable. The shortest and most easily travelled was the 104-mile long corridor leading from Koptos through the aforementioned Wady Hammamat to Qoseir. Quarrying expeditions in quest of the stone described above frequently used this route; and it was also the route of choice for seafarers making for the coast to set out on a journey to Pwenet (Somaliland or East Africa). A rather longer route led from Koptos through the Wady Zeidun to Berenike on the Red Sea, and a more north-easterly track traversed the Wady Qena to Myos Hermos, also on the Red Sea coast. Much farther north a direct route, 150 miles long, led through the broad Wady Arabah from Atfih to the Gulf of Suez. This appears to have been favored by mining expeditions from Memphis, making for the short water-crossing to the west coast of the Sinai peninsula, where the turquoise mines were located.

The Coast East and West of the Delta

Though not part of the Eastern Desert, the Sinai peninsula forms a critical interface between Egypt and the Near East. Along 100 miles of its northern edge, from Gaza to the mouth of the Pelusiac branch, ran the only transit corridor connecting the two largest continents on earth, Africa and Asia. Although only eighty miles separates the Mediterranean coast from the Gulf of Suez, this "Suez frontier" is the threshold of the connecting corridor, and the only viable entry point into Egypt on any of its borders. Over countless millennia this threshold has witnessed the passing, in both directions, of peoples, trade goods, conquering armies, technologies, and ideas. Small wonder the Egyptians considered it a frontier to be guarded and controlled, and from a very early time sited fortresses (Q) at strategic points to intercept people seeking to enter the Delta. During the empire period the route to Gaza, sometimes dubbed by moderns the *Via Maris* (R), "the Way of the Sea," was fortified at intervals of about ten miles by block-houses and water holes, for the refreshment and protection of troops or caravans on the move.

But the Sinai peninsula offered Egypt more than a strategic location for defensive fortifications. As one proceeds southward in the peninsula the flat, dune-covered terrain of the northern coastal strip is left behind, and chains of rugged mountains arise, formed of volcanic rock; and in these rocks are veins of minerals. Some copper occurs here and there, in particular in the Arabah on the north-east, but more importantly for the Egyptians turquoise is readily accessible on the western side, not far inland from the Gulf of Suez. Here the Egyptians established seasonal stations, first at Wady Mughara and later (from the Middle Kingdom) at Sarbut el-Kadim, where a shrine was built and dedicated to the local goddess. Though local inhabitants of a sedentary nature were virtually non-existent, West Semitic speaking Canaanites would often drift down from the Negeb and interact with the Egyptian miners. Often they came for employment or demonstrations of loyalty; but occasionally, especially in the Old Kingdom, confrontations could be hostile. The large tableaux set up at Wady Mughara showing Pharaoh smiting a Bedouin were at one and the same time both records of clashes and apotropaic warnings of what an unruly Canaanite could expect.

Although a transit corridor ran along the North African coast west of the Delta as far as Cyrenaica if not beyond, it was never used as extensively as was the *Via Maris,* and very rarely did Egypt feel threatened in this sector. In the Ramesside Age a series of forts was built extending as far as Sollum and perhaps beyond, but these were called into existence by a perceived threat from the sea. The autochthonous population was relatively sparse, and not noted for being obstreperous: the occasional punitive raid proved sufficient to keep them in line. The principal tribe at the beginning of the Third Millennium B.C. was the *Tjehenu,* after whom the country took its original name (the term "Libya" derives from the *Labu,* a tribe which puts in an appearance rather later in New Kingdom times). These were transhumants possessed of flocks of sheep and goats, and able to produce a vegetable oil of high quality, all of which the Egyptians craved. Not all of the ethnic groups here were nomadic; the *Meshwesh* (Greek *Maxies*) lived in houses and kept cattle which were also highly prized by the Egyptians.

Thanks to its geographical location, ancient Egypt was able to live a charmed life. Deserts, cataracts, and a treacherous coast provided natural barriers against invasion from without; yet, should they wish, the Egyptians could with impunity venture outside their protected home and tap into transit corridors and the produce of others. The presence of a reliable river, abundant foodstocks, and copious mineral deposits made the country virtually self-sufficient. Stark contrasts, however, presented themselves at every turn: the desert and the alluvium, divided sharply from each other (I); mountain and arable field; the narrow Valley and the spreading Delta; low Nile and high Nile; the transhumant foreigner and the sedentary Egyptian farmer; cloudless sun-filled day and starry night. Small wonder then that, while the Egyptians developed an Egypto-centric view of the universe in which they were the master-race, a curious duality shows up in their mind-set in which opposites are constantly viewed in balance.

Further Readings

On Egyptian geography in general see J. Baines, J. Malek, *Atlas of Ancient Egypt*, London, 1980; J. Ball, *Egypt in the Classical Geographers*, Cairo, 1942; K. W. Butzer, *Early Hydraulic Civilization in Egypt: A Study in Cultural Ecology*, Chicago, 1976; J. Dumichen, *Zur Geographie des Alten Ägypten*, Wiesbaden, 1973; H. E. Hurst, *The Nile*, London, 1969; H. Kees, *Ancient Egypt: A Cultural Topography*, Chicago, 1961; B. J. Kemp, *Ancient Egypt: Anatomy of a Civilization*, London, 1991; A. Leahy, "Egyptian Geography and Settlement Patterns," in J. Bintliff (ed.), *Mycenaean Geography*, Cambridge, 1977, 94–97; B. Manley, *The Penguin Historical Atlas of Ancient Egypt*, London, 1996; W. J. Murnane, *The Penguin Guide to Ancient Egypt*, London, 1983; R. Said, *The Geology of Egypt*, Amsterdam-New York, 1962.

On arable land and agriculture, see A. K. Bowman, E. Rogan (eds.), *Agriculture in Egypt from Pharaonic to Modern Times*, Oxford, 1999; S. L. D. Katary, *Land Tenure in the Ramesside Period*, London, 1989.

On plants and animals, see D. J. Brewer, D. B. Redford, S. Redford, *Domestic Plants and Animals: The Egyptian Origins*, Warminster (n.d.); D. J. Brewer, R. F. Friedman, *Fish and Fishing in Ancient Egypt*, Warminster, 1989.

On foodstocks and diet, see W. Darby, *Food: The Gift of Osiris*, 2 vols., London, 1977; E. Endesfelder, "Die Nahrungsmittel der alten Ägypten und ihre Zubereitung," *Das Altertum 32* (1986), 18ff.; D. Faltings, *Die Keramik der Lebensmittelproduktion im Alten Reich*, Heidelberg, 1998; S. Ikram, "Diet," in D. B. Redford (ed.), *The Oxford Encyclopaedia of Ancient Egypt* (New York, 2001) I, 390–95.

On population and demography, see J. Champollion, *The World of the Egyptians*, Geneva, 1989; S. Donadoni (ed.), *The Egyptians*, Chicago, 1997; F. Hassan, *Demographic Archaeology*, New York, 1981; *idem*, in T. Shaw (ed.), *The Archaeology of Africa* (London, 1993), 560–64; T. G. H. James, *Pharaoh's People: Scenes from Life in Imperial Egypt*, London, 1984; J. Romer, *People of the Nile*, New York, 1982; N. Scott, *The Daily Life of the Ancient Egyptians*, New York, n.d.; E. Strouhal, *Life of the Ancient Egyptians*, Norman, OK, 1992.

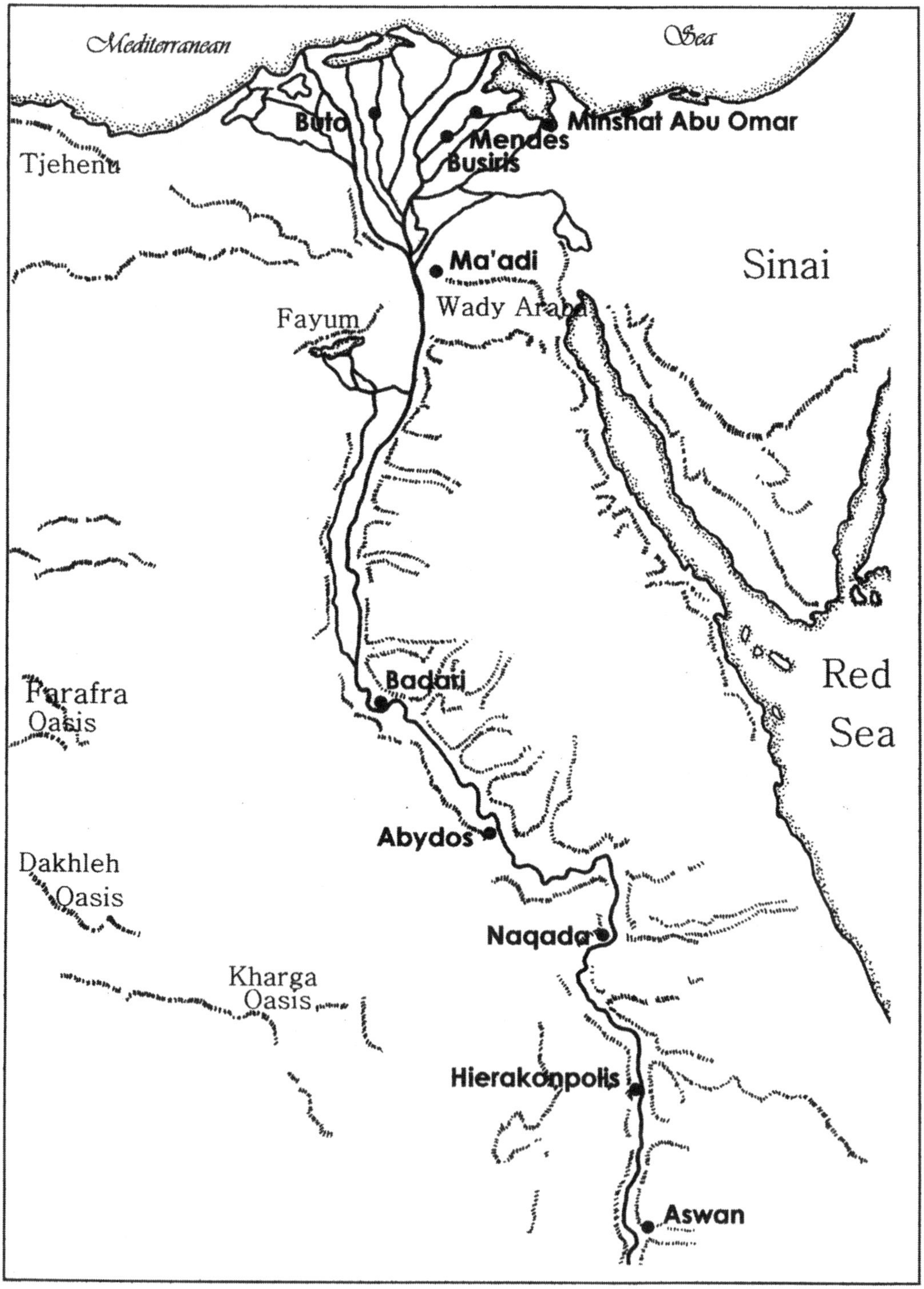

Mediterranean *Sea*

Buto

Minshat Abu Omar

Tjehenu

Mendes
Busiris

Sinai

Ma'adi

Wady Arab

Fayum

Red

Sea

Farafra
Oasis

Badari

Dakhleh
Oasis

Abydos

Naqada

Kharga
Oasis

Hierakonpolis

Aswan

CHAPTER TWO

The Foundations
The Prehistory of Egypt

———————— Ψ ————————

The Egypt of today which we have described in the last chapter is the last stage in a geological process that has been going on for over 40 million years. At the beginning of the Eocene the sea covered much of north-east Africa. By the end of that epoch, however, a tectonic shift had raised the level of the land, and created the conditions for a major drainage system. This, the Gilf System, featured far-flung tributaries and a powerful "Ur-Nile." It was succeeded in the early Miocene (c. 30 million years ago) by the Qena System which, because of further tectonic activity, flowed to the south. A drop in the level of the Mediterranean in the early Pliocene forced the flow to reverse itself, and thereafter the present Nile Valley was in process of being gouged out. A rising sea level in the late Pliocene turned the valley into an estuary: a primitive Delta is visible through satellite photography in the vicinity of Asyut. It is the gradual silting up of this estuary, at first on a course slightly west of the present bed, during the Pleistocene that constitutes the history of the modern river.

The Appearance of Man

While the old view that the Nile Valley, on the eve of the emergence of man, was a sluggish reed swamp, akin to the *sudd* in the Sudan has long been discredited, the river offered a prospect no less inimical to settlement. The discharge was strong, swamps rare, and the flood seasonal, as it is today. Levees and islands were covered with acacia, tamarisk, sycamore, and willow. Such an environment proved difficult for early man to control; but then he had no need to, given the other sources of food available.

The question as to whether the species *Homo erectus* originated in Africa and spread out from there, or appeared simultaneously in several parts of the world, has generated considerable debate, but would seem to have been decided in favor of the former alternative. *Australopithecus,* which stands in the direct line of descent of the genus *Homo,* is African not Asian; and it is not fortuitous that the earliest human remains in the world should have been found in Olduvai Gorge in East Africa. It will have been sometime before 1,200,000 years ago that *Homo erectus* appeared in Africa, and began to extend his habitat northward and eastward. By 800,000 B.P. he had reached the Far East, and was ensconced in Europe and the Near East before the first phase of the European Ice Age began.

At this point one must strike a cautionary note. Although occupying the same fault line as Olduvai, the Red Sea-Nile Valley corridor cannot help in the debate over the spread of *Homo erectus,* as no human remains from the early Ice Age or the Lower Palaeolithic have turned up there. Moreover, it would be wrong to imagine the spread of the species resulting in a substantial population with circumscribed location. In all probability we are dealing with no more than a few thousand for all north-east Africa and the Near East, grouped into small bands/family units for food-gathering, and on the move in a seasonal pattern. Finally: although by no means the well-forested landscape of romantic imagination, the eastern Sahara in Late Pliocene and Pleistocene times supported a savannah-like terrain, dotted with lakes (later to become oases). Over the vast time span we are here passing over so summarily, the climate changed many times from dry to pluvial to humid.

In Egypt and north-east Africa man signalled his presence only when he had developed the ability to manufacture artifacts and alter the environment according to his own will. This stage was reached about 350,000 years ago, after two successive glaciations had advanced and retreated in Europe and Western Asia. During this second interglacial the climate of Egypt had become semi-arid with seasonal precipitation. Artifacts in the form of Chellean and Acheulian hand axes (A) appear in numerous stations over the desert and on the cliffs bordering the Nile at the height of 24–30 meters above the present flood plain. These tools, showing slight local adaptation when compared with similar types elsewhere in Africa, Europe, and the Near East, reflect a rapid dispersal of a new technology from an east African center.

By the third interglacial period in Egypt, c. 100,000 to 50,000 years ago, a climate similar to that of the second had developed. Semi-aridity with moist/dry cycles (the Abassid Pluvial) had set in; lakes were in evidence in the hither desert, and the mean temperature was somewhat cooler. At this time, both scattered over the western desert and on the nine- to three-meter terrace along the edge of the valley, new artifactual assemblages appear replacing the Acheulian. The new "tool-kit" relies on bifacial tools, worked flakes rather than cores, fashioned into scrapers, awls, and projectile points. In some cases hand axes continue to be used, but there is a decided preference for long flakes with little secondary working. The flint used was often extracted by a process of "trenching" in the desert. The whole so resembles the Mousterian/Levalloisian of Europe, associated as they were with *Homo neanderthalensis* (a lateral sub-group of *Homo erectus*), that one is tempted to postulate the same species' presence along the banks of the Nile.

The Agricultural Revolution

As the last ice sheet began gradually to retreat after 40,000 B.P., momentous changes were occurring in Europe, Africa, and the Near East. Most likely it was at this time that *Homo sapiens sapiens* emerged by means of a sort of "punctuated equilibrium" within one group of *Homo erectus,* and spread outward from Africa. The Egyptian record, however, lacking as it is in human remains, cannot assist in solving the many knotty problems associated with the disappearance of *Homo neanderthalensis* and the advent of modern man. Compared with Europe, north-east Africa begins at this time to lag behind in terms of new technologies: Egypt did not share in the advancements betokened by "blade cultures" such as the Magdalenian or Aurignacian of western Europe (although this is not entirely true of adjacent regions such as Cyrenaica, Sinai, or the Negeb). Instead, increasing regionality becomes evident in the artifactual evidence. A sort of microlithic Levalloisian lingered on in the Nile Valley, especially around the Second Cataract ("Nubian Levallois": c. 40–30,000 B.P.); while an Aterian culture, characterized by miniature cores, invaded the eastern Sahara from the west between 20 and 15,000 B.P. By 12,000 B.P., in spite of the onset of the Holocene Wet Phase and the continued presence of lakes around Kubbaniya and in the desert, increasing desiccation west of the Nile began to force pastoralists and hunters toward the valley of the Nile. Here, in their new habitat, the hunting/gathering strategies of yore proved difficult to maintain.

Representative of the new lifestyle which was being forced upon the erstwhile Old Stone Age communities are three successive stages of culture, the Sebilian, the Arkinian, and the Elkabian. The first, the Sebilian (c. 19,000–13,000 B.P.), began as an intensive hunting/gathering economy in southern Upper Egypt, employing a tool-kit which was essentially a further degradation of the Levalloisian. Communities were semi-sedentary, using campsites beside the Nile on a seasonal basis, and subsisting on fish and riverine fauna. By the close of the period a few of the larger species of animal may have been in process of domestication. In terms of settlement pattern and type of economy the Arkinian of Nubia (c. 10,580–8860 B.P.) and the Elkabian of Upper Egypt (c. 8340–7885 B.P.) are essentially extensions of the Sebilian: fishing, plant and root collection, and hunting are the strategies employed. But there is no evidence of attempts *artificially* to produce food.

Environmental degradation, as the last ice sheet retreated, was not limited to north-east Africa. Western Asia too began to feel the impact of spreading desert conditions, reduced rainfall, and the disappearance of game. Foodstocks were diminishing, and in the absence of major rivers, they could not be replaced by fish and fowl.

The crisis which loomed forced a solution of truly revolutionary proportions. Of necessity man had to *produce* food, not simply *catch* or *gather* it. The human community had to learn how to cultivate those grasses it had randomly collected heretofore; how to domesticate those animals it had formerly hunted. The optimum core area within which these changes might be expected to occur would have to have variability in food plants, and these would have to be easily accessible and their seasonality predictable. Now the optimum habitat for the domestication of wheat and barley, sheep and cattle are the woodlands of the Levantine littoral and the coasts of Anatolia; and it is here in fact that the earliest evidence of the agricultural revolution has been found.

The Natufian culture (c. 12,000–10,000 B.P.), first encountered at the type site of Wady en-Natuf just north of Jerusalem and now identified from southern Syria to the Negeb, is the first sedentary community thus far discovered which sought to introduce artificial means of food production. Since farming, however rudimentary, requires the farmer to remain in one spot to tend the seeds he has planted, the camp-site or way-station had to be replaced by the permanent abode. Initially Natufian settlements were in caves—those in the Carmel range are a case in point—but later, and for the first time in man's development, free-standing *structures* were located in the open, near springs. Taking the form at first of curvilinear huts grouped in loose aggregations, domiciles came to be arranged within fortifications of field stone, and rectilinear walling systems were developed. We are here at the very beginning of the long, uninterrupted evolution of *urban* centers: such famous towns as Jericho (B) or Byblos had their origins in Natufian times. The artifact assemblage at first represents a half-way point between the standard tool bag of the Stone Age hunter and the microlithic industries derived from the Levalloisian; but by the end of the Natufian arrow heads and even polished stone axes had made their appearance. Indicative of a new economy and a new lifestyle are new tools: primitive hoes for breaking the soil, sickles made from animals' ribs and inset with flint "teeth," and rock-cut "basins" and grinding stones. Finally, to satisfy the need for a means of storing and transport in any community producing grain in bulk, the container was developed, at first out of natural forms such as gourds. In the post-Natufian period (c. 8,000 B.P.) the natural forms became the inspiration and the models for containers of a more durable material made of clay, either sun- or oven-baked: *pottery* is the natural concomitant of advanced farming techniques applied on an extended scale.

In spite of the sudden desiccation which set in in the Levant at the end of the Natufian period, the revolutionary developments just described made an indelible impact on surrounding regions. Knowledge of agriculture and experiments in animal husbandry spread to North Syria and Anatolia, and thence to northern Iraq. Wherever the revolution took hold it drastically changed the socio-economic basis of the community.

While the course of events in Western Asia seems on the whole to be clear enough, the picture in north-east Africa is complicated and paradoxical. In the oases of the western desert and in the Sudan there is definite indication of a knowledge of agriculture by 8000 B.P.: the ingredients are all present in the assemblages—grinding stones, axes, pottery. The Nile Valley, however, has yielded very little evidence at all. Why should this be? For one thing, since around

8000 B.P. the Nile discharge had slackened somewhat, settlements built along its bank would have been swept away and/or buried when later the river regained its strength. But there remains another, and perhaps more cogent explanation.

Food procurement strategy in the Nile Valley is, as we have seen, logistically straightforward. There are reliable and abundant foodstocks of fish, grasses, and roots, and a copious supply of riverine fauna, all available on a seasonal basis. After 20,000 B.P. procurement was enhanced with improvements in hunting and fishing techniques, and controlled burning of wetlands to increase root foods. These strategies, because they were admirably suited to the Nile Valley and Delta, perpetuated themselves over millennia and far outstripped other strategies, such as agriculture, in ease of application and results. With the fluctuations in Nile floods, however, which we have seen afflict north-east Africa in the Holocene, the resultant dry periods would have made it difficult for foragers. Late floods would have delayed catfish spawning, lingering floods would have created conditions for epidemics, and low floods would have left areas of plant collection unwatered. In the light of this risk to the survival of the human community, agriculture appeared as the stop-gap. It offered initially a strategy of food production which would tide over a settlement until such time as stocks of fish and fowl re-appeared, and the roots of the nut grass could again be collected.

Agriculture must have appeared, on however limited a scale, by 8000 B.P. As was the case in the Natufian of the Levant, sedentary communities were a concomitant of the revolution. Scholarship continues to call them "neolithic (new stone age)," employing a slightly archaic jargon; but the social phenomenon to which the adjective is applied has an integrity of time, place, and character which makes it hard to jettison the term.

The Sedentary Community in Ancient Egypt

As will become abundantly clear as this history progresses, the local town constituted the single most important jurisdictional and cultural unit in the make-up of ancient Egyptian society. At one level the town provided the means to a person's self-identification. In Egypt today everyone knows their town. Everyone, even the dyed-in-the-wool city-dweller, returns there periodically, "on retreat" as it were, to don native costume and commune with that "first place" of their origin.

In spite, however, of the centrality of the town in ancient Egypt, it is difficult to establish a taxonomy of settlement in the Nile Valley and Delta. Just as we noted the uniqueness of Egypt's geographical isolation, so too we should acknowledge the uniqueness of the *polity* this ancient people developed; for theirs was the first territorial or *nation* state in history, in contradistinction to the *metropolitan* or *city* state, a political concept which was to dominate men's minds for millennia to come. In attempting to explain this fact one has to ask the essential question: why did the town *not* suggest itself as the basic unit co-extensive with political jurisdiction? Should the argument fasten upon socio-economic exigency, geography, or demographics; or should we ferret out some underlying ideological factor? And what is to be said of *communication* as a factor? It has been maintained that people could live together in larger areas and greater numbers only when more effective forms of communication became available.

Part of the confusion may lurk in the nomenclature. What exactly is a "town" or "city?" Is it any "central place" beyond a minimal size (but how do we quantify "minimal?"), depending on its position in the central place hierarchy of the society concerned? Or is it a settlement grown (for whatever reason) to a size where it is no longer self-sufficient and cannot feed itself? Or is it a numerous and nucleated community living in close proximity in which social relations of production have mutated into government? And what is the role of trade and peer polity interaction in defining a settlement as a "city?"

These ruminations of modern scholarship run the risk, as always in such cases, of imposing modern concepts and terminology on an antiquity which thought differently. If ancient vocabulary is allowed to speak for itself, a new light is cast on what people were thinking of when they conjured up the notion "city." *Alu* in Akkadian, *'ir* in West Semitic, *polis* in Greek, and *oppidum* in Latin, all go back to roots involving *fortification:* the "city" is a collection of people living in close proximity, but that fact and its economic ramifications count for naught in assigning the term. They need protection from both man and beast: that is the defining aspect.

In ancient Western Asia the "city"[1] contained a large population, highly stratified with an intensity of craft specialization and a relatively high level of production. While the *territorium* of such settlements is of modest dimensions—in fact larger imperial pretensions might prove inimical to the city's prosperity—nevertheless proximal distribution of such self-sufficient communities provides the optimal atmosphere for intensive trade through which wealth accrues. The ruling class of the socially-tiered, metropolitan state is, by the very nature of the community, removed to a significant degree from the subsistence base of agriculture and animal husbandry on which the city relies.

A second, and significantly smaller type of human community may be singled out in a West Asian context. This settlement has limited, "parochial" interests, and a primarily agricultural purview[2]. These show the limited purposes of regional storage of produce, seed-corn, provender, and livestock, transshipment of produce, and protection for landlords, wealthy farmers, and minor officials. While a parochial settlement can exist independent of a larger polity, it is not organized for political control or dominance.

A third type of community hierarchically ranged beneath the parochial settlement is the small farming village[3] for them that work the fields, and the storage of farm equipment and animals. Such a hamlet must be situated close to the parochial settlement, at best within a day's march, in order the better to transfer produce, and thus occupies the position of a satellite. *En tant que tel*, it clearly can never exercise political dominance.

If these three exist naturally within the framework of an agricultural/pastoral population, there are other types of settlement which owe their existence to conscious acts of policy. The *capital city*[4] for example is created solely for the purpose of governance, and its primary population comprises power-wielders. Historically it often originated in a paramilitary encampment or the conqueror's erstwhile domicile, or even a brigand's camp. The fortified enclosure[5] is entirely military- or labor-oriented: it protects military personnel or provides shelter for workers. Such a fort cannot support itself, and exists only so long as the society which created it has need of it. Finally, the cult center[6] enjoys an origin beyond easy explanation. Often it is sited where, in the remote and forgotten past, people sensed the presence or manifestation of the supernatural, and wished to make the experience permanent. The cult center may be an integral part of the metropolitan state or a capital city, but not necessarily: the divine favor implied in the cult center's existence is enough to ensure a degree of independence.

Of the six types of settlements passed in review above, ancient Egypt knows all but the first, the metropolitan state. The *sine qua non* for this category-term, viz. large size and location near resources and transit corridors, has little or no application in the Nile Valley and Delta. In Egypt there is no locational advantage to the siting of settlements: the same access to food-stocks—fish, fowl, and riverine fauna—and to arable land may be had anywhere in the alluvial plain. The physical and spiritual separation of an elite from the community's farming base in, say, a Mesopotamian city, is not mirrored in the ancient Egyptian community. Even in the largest settlements the elite live very close to the means of food production, and essentially constitute a farming gentry. The largest towns in Egypt, Memphis and Pi-Ramesses, are described by the poets as bucolic, rural communities. An examination of the main terms in ancient Egyptian for "settlement" drives home the points made above. *Niwt* designates in origin a group of farm huts surrounded by a curvilinear fence or low wall. *Dmit* denotes a place of "touching" where boats put in, and load up for produce for transshipment, and *mryt* a harbor, either riverine or maritime. '*I3t* refers to one of the most common types of land formation supporting a Valley or Delta settlement, viz. the "mound." *Bḫn,* "fortified façade," can apply to isolated farmsteads in the countryside, while *iḥw* designates a cattle stall in a rural setting. Finally *wḥyt,* "village," derives from the word for patriarchal, extended family.

While definition of Egyptian urbanism may at first glance be better suited to a "spectrum accommodating many variants," the terms set forth above point to three major considerations that were satisfied by living together in ancient Egypt. Protection for farmers was paramount, from predators, the elements, and the Nile. Transshipment of produce by Nile or canal, and concentration of kinship groups and livestock counted as secondary, though clearly identifiable, motives. But the conditions and the necessity for creating an Uruk or a Kish are notably absent.

Belief Systems in Prehistoric Egypt

In approaching ancient Egyptian belief systems, the western researcher is handicapped by a mind-set wholly alien to the ethos of the ancient world. We have been taught to distinguish between sacred and secular; but to the Egyptian no such dichotomy existed. The supernatural was everywhere and impinged on the human community at every moment. We, as heirs to the political history of Europe, come to Egyptian history burdened with an "orientalist" attitude, that patronizing and often contemptuous view of the East which has become almost a hallmark of the West. Our own intellectual baggage of categories has imposed such terms upon us as "pantheon," "religious literature," "scripture," "dogmatics," "eschatology," "faith," etc. None of these properly fit the way in which ancient Egypt attempted to deal intellectually with the supernatural, and if we persist in applying them, the resultant view of Egyptian religion will be hopelessly distorted.

In the main our contempt stems from our failure to accept the ancients on their own terms. We have been mesmerized, then repelled, by what to us seems nightmarish symbolism, and disgusted by an apparent inherent inconsistency and lack of logic. But in fact inconsistency and contradiction may be explained in a number of ways: historically, as the amalgam of two or more independent, parochial systems; hermeneutically, as the tendency of the ancients to reduce incompatible concepts to visible symbols; systematically, as heavy use of extended metaphor which eventually achieves substance in its own right. Nor, it might be added, is modern monotheism free of internal confusion and inconsistency; but most believers are unaware of it, and when it is pointed out retreat to the protective shield of apologetics.

No long history of dogmatic belief lay behind the prehistoric Egyptians' attempt to find a workable relationship with the supernatural. The need was immediate. The ancients were faced by the action of powers beyond their observation and detection which impacted on their community and their world. The powers seemed to show the same motivation of will, the same basic capacity to love or hate, to attract and repel, as humankind. In short, it was the nature and behavior of life itself that they imputed to the supernatural. But it was strange and wonderful ($n\underline{t}r$ = "god"), powerful ($s\underline{h}m$ = a "power"), a particular manifestation ($b3$ = personalized force), a numinous being ($3\underline{h}$ = numinous "glorified spirit"). And there was a plurality of them: the context of each encounter with the supernatural is different. An infinity of experience comes from an infinity of powers; and yet that infinity does not preclude predilection in favor of one deity.

The town and the town-god, the local manifestation of the supernatural, are the basic building-blocks in the life and society of the ancient Egyptian community. At once the inhabitant experiences universal and parochial influences from the environment. The dualism inherent in the geography of north-east Africa—Valley and Delta, the two banks, desert and alluvium—the regularity and prominence of the solar cycle, the approximation of sowing and reaping to death and resurrection, the fertility inherent in the river—all inform the shape of the primordial belief system. Yet the town god *(n\underline{t}r niwty)* also exerts a local influence. His or her sphere of activity encompasses the whole range of the community's interests and activities: he created the community and the environment at the dawn of time, he guarantees its fertility and prosperity, he leads his people in war, and he will look after them in death. For their part the people honor him to the exclusion of other deities in neighboring districts, they house him on sacred space **(fig. 1)** and serve him; and since he is a life-form, provide him with food. When they identify themselves it is often by using his name in a compound form.

Figure 1 Early representations and renderings of prehistoric shrines. (Upper—Upper Egyptian shrine, plaited with reeds and mud. Lower—shrine of Neith, goddess of Sais.)

Contemporary evidence on beliefs and cult practices in prehistoric Egypt is difficult to find. When the cravings of an aesthetic sense and the need for individual self-assertion caused a human being to mark his artifacts or available space within his environment, the result does not yield an insight into specific thought. The repetition of geometric shapes gives the comfort of familiarity and predictability, but only confirms a truism of human psychology. Even when the "artist" graduates to representation of life-forms, either in the round in the shape of figurines, or in two dimensional art on pots, ivories, or palettes, we are often at a loss to put name or purpose to the image before us. Under such circumstances it is tempting to assume that reminiscences of prehistoric beliefs and rites may be had in early writings, in particular the Pyramid Texts. But how can we tell that such-and-such a belief encapsulated in a Pyramid Text dates from prehistoric times, since this is never stated in so many words. Genuinely archaic reference and the absence of anachronisms may help to some degree; but one must remember (see chapter four below) that the earliest exemplar of the Pyramid Text corpus, dating c. 2390 B.C., is separated by more than a millennium from the late Predynastic. Myths based on the ecology of the Valley and Delta may with caution be accepted as ancient; while conversely any later ideological symbolism, based on the Pharaonic monarchy, may be excluded with confidence.

Predynastic art suggests the presence already of several entities which will take their place centrally in the belief system of historic times. They may look different from their historic representations—that fact must be explained—but an evolutionary link would seem to be called for. Most important perhaps is the woman and the bull, attested already in Natufian times. The former, with clear maternal and fertility overtones, puts in an appearance in figurines (c) and two dimensional art, and is associated with the cow as queen of heaven or as the heavens themselves. The bull is understood as the mother-goddess's son and, as *k3-mwt.f,* "bull of his mother," turns up as an ithyphallic deity (D) in historic times. Other deities may be attested, including the Seth (Ash) deity, and the crocodile.

With the advent of the second half of the fourth millennium the picture grows clearer as the evidence becomes more plentiful. The sign for "god" *(ntr),* the gonfalon raised aloft above the place where the numen resides, begins to appear, and by early historic times is firmly ensconced. Similarly, the god's servants are in evidence by the First Dynasty, bearing the title which will ever after designate a "priest."

A pattern has begun to emerge which is virtually the same as that which obtains in historic times. Each town deity is connected—this lexical choice is left vague intentionally—with one or more life forms (less often an inanimate object) which appear to be "emblems" in a sense. Most common are animals: cow, bull, lion, crocodile, ram, serpent, hare. Birds are a close second: falcon, ibis, vulture. Insects are less common—beetle and centipede are attested, as are plants and other objects: sycamore, oleander, *ished* **(fig. 2),** *yema,* a pillar, a bundle of stalks, a fossil. The precise relationship between life form and the power in question varies from occasion to occasion. In many cases the deity is conceived in theriomorphic or hybrid form; elsewhere the animal is only an occasional manifestation. The link becomes even looser in those cases where the emblem is only a sort of symbol of the god, imbued with mystic power in its own right, and sometimes worshiped independently.

In examining this roster of town gods from the dawn of Egyptian history, certain caveats must be kept in mind. First, it runs counter to the evidence at hand to postulate a simple evolutionary scheme which would take an emblem through time from "simpler" to "higher" modes of representation. If anthropomorphic or aniconic reference reflects a "higher" plane,

Figure 2 The sacred *ished*-tree. The writing by the god of the ruler's name on a leaf of the tree indicates divine acceptance of the ruler, and inaugurates his rule.

it must be admitted that this occurs in the earliest art. On the other hand, if reverence for whole species represents crass "simplicity," it must be admitted that this occurs in the final stages of Egyptian religion. Second, some of the icons, for example those which appear in early lists of townships, bull, hare, woman, and even the falcon, may betray the intentional imposition of royal symbols in early historic times. Third, the numina themselves are not designated by proper nouns, but by generic terms or epithets, thus *Khnum* and *Ba* mean "ram," Horus "falcon" (lit. the far-off one), *Montu* the "wild one," *Anubis* the "whelp," *Andjety* the "shepherd," *Edjo* the "green one" (i.e. the cobra) and so forth.

A Selection of Egyptian Towns and Deities

Upper Egypt

Elephantine	Ram (Khnum), two anthropomorphic women
Kom Ombo	Crocodile (Sobek) and falcon (Horus) (DD)
Edfu	Falcon (Horus)
Hierakonpolis	Falcon (Horus)
Nekheb	Vulture (Nekhbit) (E)
Esna	Ram (Khnum)
Pi-Hfo	Falcon (Hemen), female serpent (F)
Su-menu	Crocodile (Sobek)
Ermant	Falcon (Montu)
Cos	Falcon
Ombos	Wild pig (? Ash) (FF)
Coptos	Ithyphallic man (Min) (G)
Dendera	Cow
Abydos	Jackal (Khentiamentiu)
Akhmim	Ithyphallic man (Min)
Hut-ka	Ibis (Thoth)
Tjebu	Falcon (Nemty), female serpent (F)
Shashotpe	Wild pig (? Shaw)
Dju-fy	Falcon (Nemty)
Asyut	Wolf (? Wepwawet)
Khayet	Lioness (Ipuyet) (H)
Kusae	Pillar (Wekh)
Hermopolis	Ibis (Djehuty) (I), hare
Beni Hassan	Frog, falcon
Speos Artemidos	Lioness (Pakhet) (H)
Hi-boinu	Falcon (Horus)
Tehne	Lion (?)
Cynopolis	Dog (Anubis)
Saka	Bull (Bata)
Herakleopolis	Ram (Arsaphes; originally Heneb)
Crocodilopolis	Crocodile (Sobek)
Atfih	Cow

A Selection of Egyptian Towns and Deities

Lower Egypt

Memphis	Swathed human male (Ptah), lioness (Sakhmet)
Mendes	Ram (Ba), female fish
Busiris	Shepherd (Andjety)
Imet	Child, female cobra
Xois	Bull
Buto	Cobra, falcon, wild pig
Sais	Woman (Neith)
Djebat	Falcon (Horus)
Bubastis	Cat (Bast)
Leontopolis	Lion (Miusis)
Psiopdu	Falcon (Sopdu)
Letopolis	Falcon (Horus)
Hermopolis Parva	Ibis (Djehuty)

The range of animals reflects the early ecology of the Valley and Delta. Predators are in the ascendant, domesticates rare. Apart from Min, who may in any case be an introduction of Dynasty "Zero," anthropomorphic forms are confined to the Delta.

An historical tendency towards assimilation can be detected in the evolution of the Egyptian belief system. Sometimes the renown or political dominance or quality incapable of present assessment of a particular cult has resulted in other gods of similar ilk being assimilated into the dominant form. This has happened in the case of the falcon. In historic times Horus of Hierakonpolis and Horus Lord of Heaven have so overshadowed other falcon cults that earlier names are mentioned but rarely. Similarly the lioness, the "Powerful One" *(sḥmt)*, especially in her aspect of mother-with-cubs, has exerted a strong influence over the mother-goddess type, so that other goddesses such as Isis, Hathor, Mut, Edjo, Tefnut, and the sun's eye can all appear in feline form and partake of a similar character (**fig. 3**).

The influence of the family as a social unit exerts itself on the supernatural world at an early date. The common historical grouping of the "Triad" (male-female-offspring) appears already at the end of the Fourth Millennium B.C. Historical "jockeying" of one cult with another to produce such groupings is of very little importance: the requirement of progeniture and fertility within a divine context, and the use of the family as grand archetype far outweigh all other considerations.

Figure 3 Forms of the feline mother-goddess.
(Left—Edjo, cobra-goddess of Buto, with Ramesses II. Right—the "Sun's Eye," personification of the sun's destructive heat.)

Understanding the World: Mythic Narrative

Ancient man did not "compartmentalize" his god. The latter was a "Power" which could act anywhere and in any capacity. The notion of a "pantheon," in which the gods are assigned different tasks and are arranged hierarchically, lay far in the future, and would only take shape under the influence of the structure of terrestrial empire.

But, as time passes, and by the very nature of the *how* and *where* the god originally showed himself, it often transpires that one aspect of power tends to predominate. Fertility, of soil, animals, and man, is one such aspect. Wherever it manifests itself it called forth a hermeneutic, couched within a narrative plot pattern.

The annual inundation could be seen in the context of salvation and defeat, or invasion and resistance. The waters contained a great spirit of "Life," unalterably opposed to malevolent "Anti-life," the desert. The battle is joined and the forces ebb and flow; the desert at first retreats but then comes on again. Neither Life nor Anti-life can ever win: the struggle is cyclical and eternal. The simple story which gradually crystallizes pits the falcon, as lord of the alluvium, against the wild pig(?). The plot is open-ended: the fight issues in a series of individual combats which could be augmented *ad infinitum.* Principal among them was the hand-to-hand struggle in which the falcon lost his eye, and the pig suffered his testicles to be ripped off. Under the guise of Horus and Seth (originally *Ash*), these two most ancient protagonists were to provide the *dramatis personae* for a most significant part of ancient Egyptian mythology.

The struggle of Horus and Seth, recounted briefly above, suits the contours of the valley; but like a contest of cosmic proportions takes the Delta as its locale. Again it is the rampaging wild pig that embodies Anti-life; but his quarry this time is the *fledgling* falcon. Mother has given birth to the falcon in a thicket on the floating island of Khemmis in the marshes, whither she has fled to escape the pig-monster. During both her confinement and her weaning of the baby, the mother is afforded the protection of the denizens of the marsh: the friendly cobra (Edjo), the heron of Djebat, and the cow *(Sḫзt-Ḥr)* who suckles the child. Although this form of the story centers upon the helplessness of mother and child, a triumph motif is not omitted: when grown to adulthood, the falcon emerges in glory from his hiding place (cf. PT 1373–75) and destroys the monster. This story, as it has come down to us, is intimately associated with Buto in the north-western Delta (in late Prehistoric times almost a coastal town); but it clearly derives from a type of narrative well known along the eastern Mediterranean coast as far north as the Aegean, in which Monster Sea pursues the Goddess and her Child.

As we have seen, animal husbandry in the form of cattle- and sheep-herding loomed large in the economy of the Delta. The great buck of Mendes, Banebdjed, was renowned for his sexual prowess, as his epithet asserts, "the fornicating ram that mounts the beauties." In neighbouring Busiris the shepherd Andjety preserved the fertility of the flocks and earned the enmity of the hateful Seth.

It is to the prehistoric past also that one must retroject those exercises in cognitive explanation of origin and present state that we are wont to call "creation myths." A large number of these accounts are derived from phenomena frequently seen in the Nile Valley, viz. the annual flood, the re-emerging dry land in the form of hillocks, the alluvium teeming with insect life. In almost all the variant versions the eternal substance, which is said to have existed from the beginning of eternity, was water in the form of *Nun,* the primeval ocean. Out of this dark mass, on the day known as the "First Occasion," there emerges something solid which becomes the podium, as it were, on which the act of creation takes place. Usually the podium is conceived of as a "mound of creation" on which a "creator" is already ensconced. Because in historic times the dominant version of this myth was that of the sun-cult at Heliopolis, the best known life-form as creator is the great golden falcon; but in earlier times one may suppose that, in any given locale, the local *numen* could adopt the creator's role: a snake, frog, beetle, crocodile, or the like. The act itself could be crass, at least in modern estimation: expectoration, self-fertilization, masturbation are all attested means of projecting the cosmos which is considered to be embryonically contained already within the body of the creator. In the version in which the creator is a winged creature, his creative act is effected from above, as he flies up over the Nun.

Variants whose sometime presence in remote antiquity is betrayed by their use in high-flown, poetic imagery of historic times, substitute another solid substance for the mound. It becomes an egg, appropriate if the creator is the winged sun-god "who is in his egg." The egg floats on the Nun, cracks and produces the falcon-chick which grows and flies skyward. The two halves of the shell become heaven and earth. In place of an egg, the life-giving lotus may be the receptacle of creation. The act involves the opening of the lotus to reveal the egg guarded by vulture and frog. From the egg emerges the winged beetle, an avatar of the sun, which rises in the sky and dries the earth with its rays. Alternatively, the petals draw back to reveal the human child with knees drawn up, ready to begin creation **(fig. 4)**. The idea of something *floating* on water even leads to the substitution of a human head!

Whereas the creation account described above takes self-generation as its focus, a second motif which dates from time immemorial is built upon human reproduction, blown up to cosmic proportions. In the beginning Nun enclosed within itself earth (male) and heaven (female). Creation is an act of strength, in which the two are pried apart by the insertion of air (Shu). In anthropomorphic depictions Shu is represented as a male elevating the sky (Nut) above his head, while standing on a prostrate earth (Geb) **(fig. 5)**. His exertions, aided by a "Multitude" of auxiliary powers, came to be known as the "Upliftings of Shu." But Nut had been impregnated by her mate before separation, and now gave birth to living things, including the sun and stars. Variants of the account transform Nut into a cow, the "cow of heaven" with a starry underbelly, or a goose; and the transformation is followed by Geb who changes species accordingly.

A third myth-pattern involves the combat between hero and monster. Although this had wide currency in western Asia, both in the defeat of Chaos and creation, and in the myth of the Sea and the Goddess, the plot is known from Egypt by fragmentary allusions only, and then usually in a context divorced from creation *per se*. One town in which the combat may have provided the pattern is Hermopolis where the ibis Thoth was the principal deity; but the shape of the story is unknown. The agent of creation is also uncertain, but it may have been a primordial serpent, *Neheb-kau,* and his murder at the hands of the hero. A brief allusion appears in the Instruction for Merikare, where the sun-god fills the role of hero.

In most contexts, however, in which we encounter the motif in Egypt, it has been translated into a cosmic, solar myth of cult inauguration. The hero is the sun, or one of his fierce, female

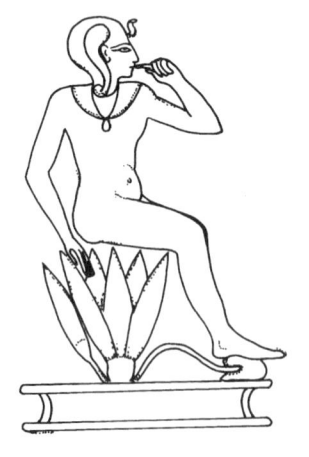

Figure 4   The royal child impersonating the creator emerging from the lotus.

minions in feline form. The reptilian opponent is the dragon of chaos who lurks in the sky or on earth, preventing the assignment of sacred space or passage.

The creation of humankind and animals and the introduction of the benefits of civilization do not seem to have been of moment to the most ancient Egyptians. Some concepts clearly date no earlier than the invention of the potter's wheel or loom, both of which appear in later accounts of man's creation. A popular, and undoubtedly ancient belief had it that human beings were the product of the sun-god's tears which he shed on the first morning of creation. The basis of this notion lies in the value the ancients placed on *homophony:* if two words sound similar it is because they share a common essence. In the present case the *rimi* (tears) of the god become *rome* (men). Also ancient and probably prehistoric is the concept of the creation of man and animals by god the "artisan": god shapes them of mud with his own hands, in his own image, and breathes life into them.

If the community's god had looked after his people from creation until now, he would also prepare for them a place in the future after death. As was the case in the shaping of a cosmogony, so too in the concept of the afterlife: the terrestrial and celestial environment closely informed the notion of the world to come.

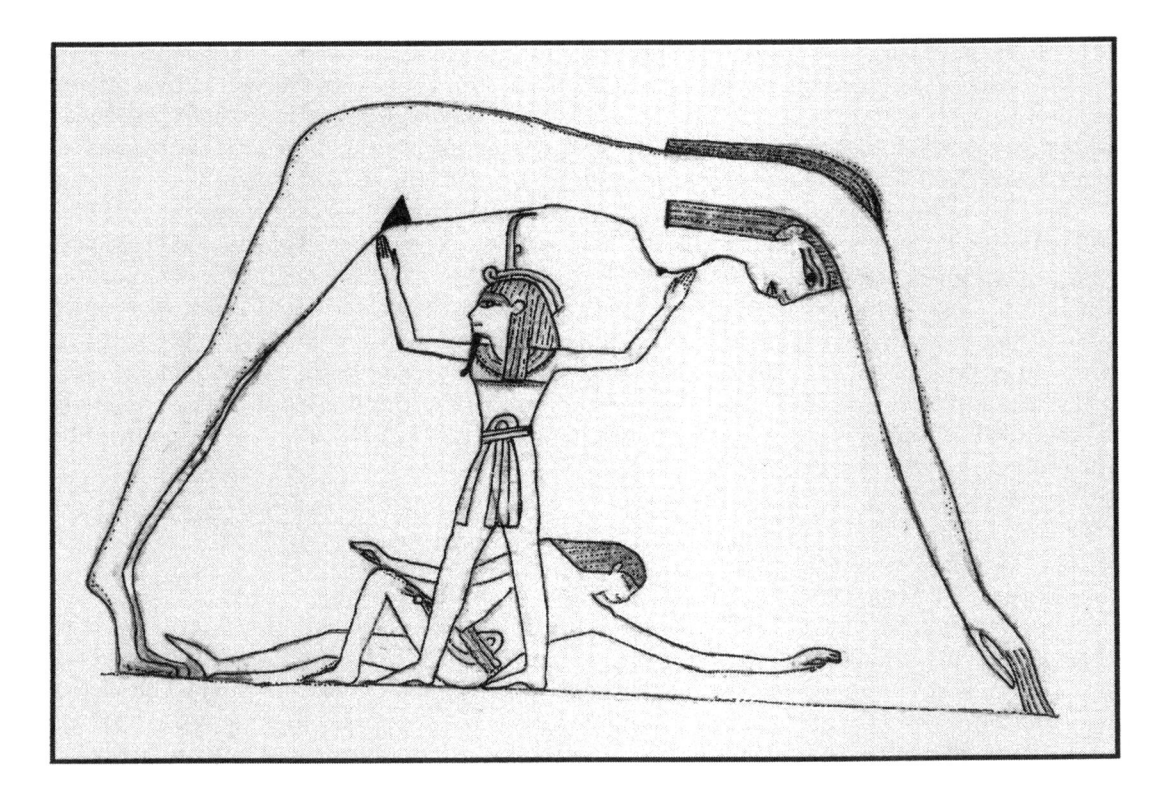

Figure 5 The "Upliftings of Shu": the air god (Shu) raises the sky (Nut) above his head, separating her from her consort earth (Geb).

A very early belief, probably current no later than the Fifth Millennium B.C., can be deduced from the position of burials at Merimde in which the cadavers face north. Egyptians showed a fascination with the circumpolar stars which never set, and longed at death to join those "indestructible ones." Transfigured into glorified beings, birds in fact, carrying lamps, they would unite in an eternal round: "mayest thou become one of the stars!" was a heartfelt benediction.

But a daytime prospect earned an even greater stimulus on the soul and the imagination. The great western desert, that repository of all that was anti-life, held a curious attraction for the ancients. Here the sun and all the stars experienced death on a daily cycle. The realm of the dead came naturally to be thought of as in the west, and its inhabitants, the dead, as "westerners." Cemeteries were most often set at the desert edge at some distance from the settlements of the living; so that the rationalization of death involved, in part, a *journey* to the west. Here the trackless desert posed a problem for the soul: there were indeed "cleared roads of the west" on which the deceased was to journey, but how to find and navigate them? Out there the instincts of a jackal would best avail the traveller, that animal which unerringly finds his way through the wilderness. The dead placed their hopes in the "leader of the westerners," the jackal Khentiamentiu, or the "trail-blazer," the jackal Wepwawet, as their guides to the Beyond. Later both to be taken over into the new ideology of kingship in the early historic period, these gods from the start were intimately associated with the cemetery as the one "that is upon his hill," and "lord of the high ground."

If the foregoing description suits the Valley, where the eye cannot escape the sight of the western desert, the Delta landscape could not offer the same prospect. In place of the desert was the ever-present, treacherous marsh, strewn with inaccessible islands, or levees with isolated settlements. Far out in the misty swamps must be that mysterious and gargantuan "Field of Rushes" where the dead continued to live, and everything was larger than it had been in life. While this would have involved a journey as fraught with uncertainty as travelling on the "roads of the west," the constrictions on living in a Delta environment removed the luxury of burial on the desert edge. Archaeological investigations over the past two decades suggest that burial practices in Lower Egypt were less elaborate than in the Valley, and varied from place to place. Sometimes the burying ground was hundreds of meters distant from the settlement, as at Minshat Abu Omar; elsewhere tombs were found in an extramural position, but immediately adjacent to the homes of the living. At some sites, such as Mendes, burials are found beneath the walls of the houses themselves.

Close proximity of dead to living, its necessity notwithstanding, is paralleled by the concept of a close bond between family and deceased patriarch. The dead remains in the house in the settlement, and in a very special way continues to exist under the aegis of the town god. The context of the family is all important: as head of the house he cannot absent himself. The role of the eldest son is also enhanced by this arrangement: the son summons his father from his sleep in the grave to partake of the offering meal, and supports the widow as "pillar-of-his-mother." Thus life on earth and life in the grave represent a two-tiered rationalization of existence: the offspring champions the father and ensures that life goes on; but the deceased ancestor is still there, and you can still see the place where he lies!

An enormous amount of archaeological work has been done over the past forty years in the area of Egyptian prehistory, which has rendered obsolete any work dated before the 1960s. In general see S. Hendrickx, *Analytical Bibliography of the Prehistory and the Early Dynastic Period of Egypt and Northern Sudan,* Louvain, 1995.

In particular see B. Adams, *Predynastic Egypt,* Aylesbury, 1988; L. R. Binford, *In Pursuit of the Past: Decoding the Archaeological Record,* London, 1983; E. C. M. van den Brink (ed.), *The Nile Delta in Transition, 4th–3rd Millennium B.C.,* Jerusalem, 1992; *idem* (ed.), *Egypt and the Levant: Interrelations from the 4th through Early 3rd Millennium B.C.E.,* London, 2002; J. J. Castillos, *The Predynastic Period in Egypt,* Montevideo, 2002; D. V. Flores, *The Funerary Sacrifice of Animals During the Predynastic Period,* University of Toronto doctoral dissertation, 1999; R. Friedman, B. Adams (eds.), *The Followers of Horus: Studies Dedicated to Michael Allen Hoffman,* Oxford, 1992; J. Gledhill and others (eds.), *State and Society: The Emergence and Development of Social Hierarchy and Political Centralization,* London, 1995; M. A. Hoffman, *Egypt Before the Pharaohs: The Prehistoric Foundations of Egyptian Civilizations,* New York, 1979; C. K. Maisels, *The Emergence of Civilization,* London, 1993; *idem, Early Civilizations of the World,* London, 1999; J. Mellaart, *The Neolithic of the Near East,* London, 1975; B. Midant-Reynes, *The Prehistory of Egypt: From the First Egyptians to the First Pharaohs,* Oxford, 2000; P. R. S. Moorey, *From Gulf to Delta and Beyond,* Beersheva, 1995; M. Rice, *Egypt's Making: The Origins of Ancient Egypt 5000–2000 B.C.,* London, 1991; A. J. Spencer, *Early Egypt: The Rise of Civilization in the Nile Valley,* London, 1993; F. Wendorf, R. Schild (eds.), *Prehistory of the Nile Valley,* New York, 1976.

On the town gods and fundamental mythology, see J. P. Allen, *Genesis in Egypt: The Philosophy of Ancient Egyptian Creation Accounts,* New Haven, 1988; J. Assmann, *The Search for God in Ancient Egypt,* Ithaca, 2001; E. Hornung, *Conceptions of God in Ancient Egypt,* Ithaca, 1982; S. Morenz, *Egyptian Religion,* Ithaca, 1973; D. B. Redford (ed.), *The Ancient Gods Speak: A Guide to Egyptian Religion,* New York, 2002; C. Traunecker, *The Gods of Egypt,* Ithaca, 2001.

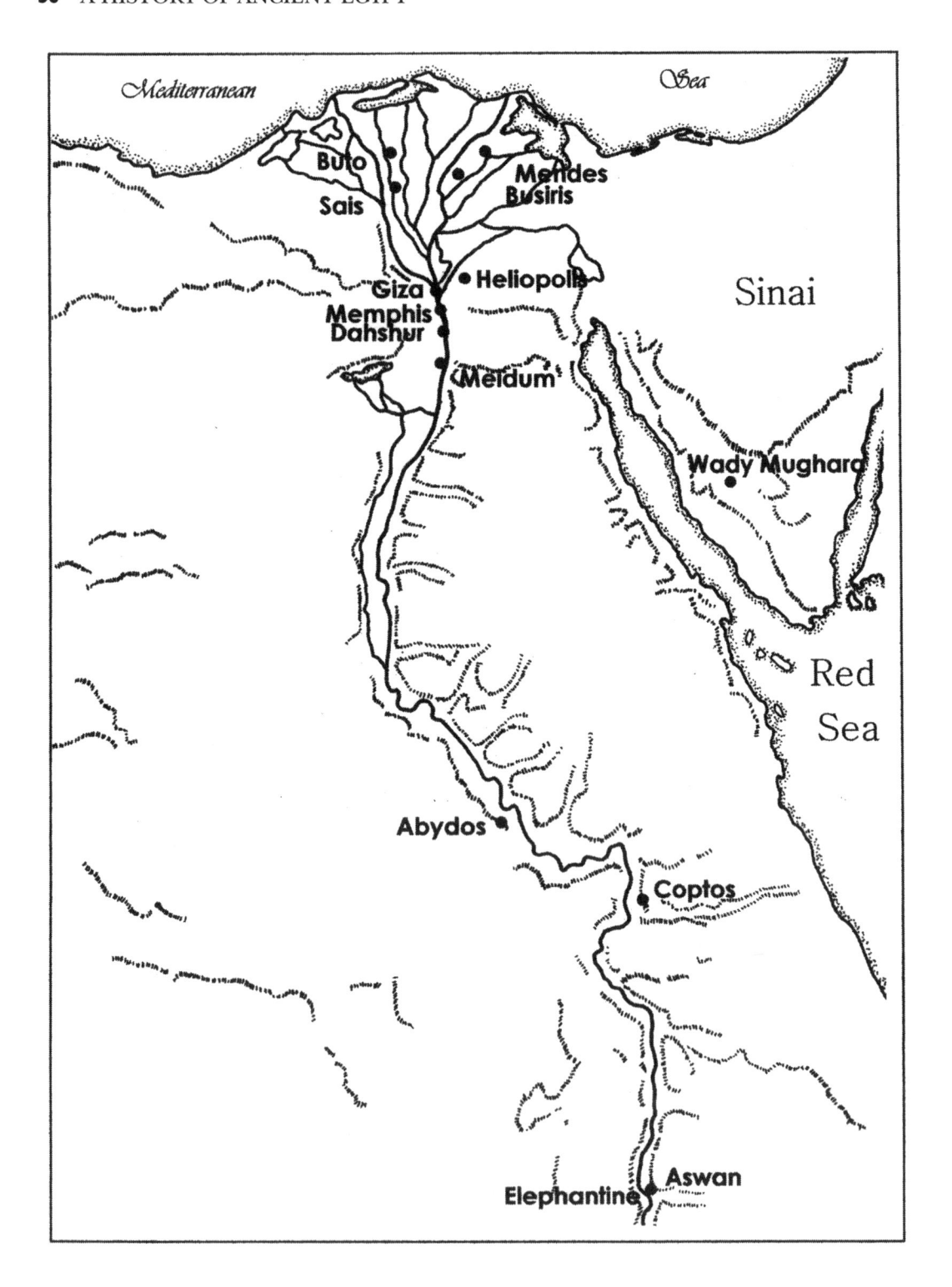

CHAPTER THREE

The Advent of Complex Society and the Rise of the Pharaonic State

ψ

The neolithic communities described in the last chapter were small, self-sufficient villages, numbering no more than a few score inhabitants. Houses were little more than curvilinear huts made of reed and plaited with mud in a type of construction known in England as "wattle and daub." Domiciles and graves alike showed little differentiation in size or appointment: social stratification was virtually unknown. The subsistence base was agricultural with a strong and continued admixture of hunting, fishing and fowling. Though the farmers, as would be expected, show only a parochial interest in their world, nonetheless the presence of objects such as shells from Red Sea and Mediterranean prove that they were not entirely cut off from the outside world. Culture periods, distinguished largely on the basis of pottery shapes and decoration, can be identified, extending from the early fifth millennium into the middle of the fourth: Badarian followed by Naqada I in the south of Upper Egypt, Fayum B and A, Merimdean and Buto-Ma'adi in the Fayum and Delta. The flood plain in Middle Egypt was too wide and the landscape too lacking in inducements to settlement for human capabilities at this stage of social evolution.

The Naqada II Period and the End of the Neolithic

Beginning around the middle of the Fourth Millennium B.C. momentous changes began to overtake the scattered neolithic communities which, up until that time, had shown little inclination to advance technologically, socially, or politically. First, expanded settlements and growing cemeteries give evidence of a significant increase in population, perhaps made possible by a more reliable food supply. A south-north demographic thrust can be detected which brought settlement to middle Egypt, and turned the entire valley from Nubia to the apex of the Delta into habitable territory. Excavations of sites in the Delta prove that Naqada II did not stop at the southern confines of the Delta, but spread through to the shores of the Mediterranean, displacing the older Buto-Ma'adi culture in the process. Second, means of transportation improved. Donkeys become common for porterage, and graceful river boats of lashed reeds make an appearance (AA). Third, technological advancement is in evidence in a wide spectrum of crafts. Stone cutting tools are now manufactured by careful ripple-flaking to produce beautiful, thin knives (A), and axe heads by grinding and polishing. Though metallurgy will continue to evolve, the smith is now capable of using the techniques of beating and casting to provide a range of tools (saws, knives, projectile points) and containers of copper; while at the same time he is beginning to familiarize himself with the properties of gold and silver. Fourth, in the realm of domestic architecture new materials have been adopted. Although the old curvilinear shapes were to remain popular, light materials are giving place to construction in a medium developed earlier, but now spreading far and wide, viz. sun-dried mud-brick **(fig. 1)**. The alluvium of the valley and Delta provided an almost inexhaustible supply of the thick mud required, and the heat of the ever-present sun made brick kilns unnecessary. Finally, and a distinctive criterion for identifying Naqada II, new shapes, styles, and decorative techniques appear in the ceramic record. For the first time decoration includes representations of animals, humans, and artefacts, rather than geometric designs, in contexts which suggest that the potter is engaging in a discourse.

The tangible evidence we have passed in review suggests far more than the mastery of new techniques of manufacture; one cannot help but feel that in the background there lurk great changes in society and ideology. Towards the close of Naqada II certain areas within cemeteries began to be reserved for larger tombs, and valid inference from graphic representations indicates that the same differentiation in size and appointment was to be seen in the towns of the living. In short, a power-wielding "elite" has put in an appearance.

Theories advanced by scholars to account for the relatively sudden leap forward during Naqada II broadly speaking divide themselves under two heads, viz. those which postulate a self-contained, spontaneous process, owing nothing to external interference, and those which attempt to make an external catalyst the defining cause. The theory which fastens upon the refinement of irrigation techniques is a typical and long-standing example of the former. The argument begins with some slight population pressure on a community which is therefore constrained to find a larger supply of food than had so far been available. More food would be provided by increasing arable land. But reclaiming the necessary land from the marsh or the desert involves improving irrigation techniques, and, while this will ultimately result in an increase in the food supply, it will also make possible a further increase in population. That increase can only be sustained by more food, produced on a larger parcel of land, reclaimed again by improved irrigation, and so on. Moreover, once the community recognizes the advantage to con-

Figure 1 Archaic, curvilinear architecture in mud-brick from Mendes; early First Dynasty.

trolling water, it will naturally pursue that advantage, and eventually an elite will arise to provide the required control and organization. In every way this theory runs counter to the evidence. The population in prehistoric Egypt was never of such a size that land naturally available could not satisfy its needs. Fishing and hunting strategies in the food-rich Nile Valley were so easy to apply that the conditions required by the theory would never be experienced. In addition, no community pursues "recognized advantage": it will only budge if forced to, but then it is not "advantage" but dire "necessity." Theories employing external catalysts have unfortunately discredited themselves by being formulated with racist trappings. The 30s and 40s of the 20th century witnessed the introduction of the "Dynastic Race" hypothesis, which credited *all* the advances (a prejudiced locution) to the ideas brought in by a new race from the north. This new race ultimately provided historic Egypt with its ruling class, superimposed on an original "African" substratum.

Egypt and the "Uruk Phenomenon"

Archaeological work coupled with new models derived from sociology and economics has, over the past generation, forced us to look at the revolutionary changes of Naqada II in a wholly new light. No autochthonous process nor dynastic race is a necessary postulate. The increasing evidence speaks for itself and points increasingly to the competition in local society for the control of resources.

For nearly a century scholars have been aware of a number of significant features in the material culture of late Naqada II which have no prior history in the Egyptian cultural assemblage. The mud-brick architecture briefly alluded to above frequently shows a unique decoration on external surfaces, of vertical niching from top to bottom, sometimes to the extent of niches within niches to double or triple degree (B). The monumental, niched façade of a large public building, later the palace of the king, was called a *s(h)arakhu*. Neither the niching nor the name are Egyptian. In the field of decorative art a number of motifs appear in Naqada II which have neither an origin nor a future development in Egypt: they appear with relative suddenness. Wild beasts tear at passive prey, fantastic felines with serpent necks face each other in balance, a bearded hero with turban holds apart two lunging lions (C), bound captives are clubbed to death. In some aquatic scenes strange new boats with upturned prows and sterns jostle with the graceful Nile craft. Toward the close of the period a new device is found in use for purposes of identification, the cylinder seal usually of stone, carved with a design which can be transferred to wet clay by rolling (D). Again: the form and purpose are alien to Egypt.

All these innovations can be found in contemporary Mesopotamia where they are widespread and characteristic of the *Uruk* period, c. 3600–3100 B.C. The conclusion seems inescapable that, during the later Naqada II period, contact had been set up between the Tigris-Euphrates and the Nile. Moreover the initiative must have come from Mesopotamia: there are no Egyptian traits discernible in Uruk culture (**fig. 2**).

The reasons for this "probe" towards the west are complex, but in the main have to do with the nature and needs of Uruk society. The period is one in which a movement towards *urbanism* had at last come to fruition, and true cities of substantial size—40–50,000 inhabitants seems to have been the norm—dotted the plains of Sumer and Akkad. Unlike their Egyptian counterparts which, as we have seen, never attained the status of true metropoleis, the Uruk communities were highly stratified societally, with craft specialization creating complex levels of professional

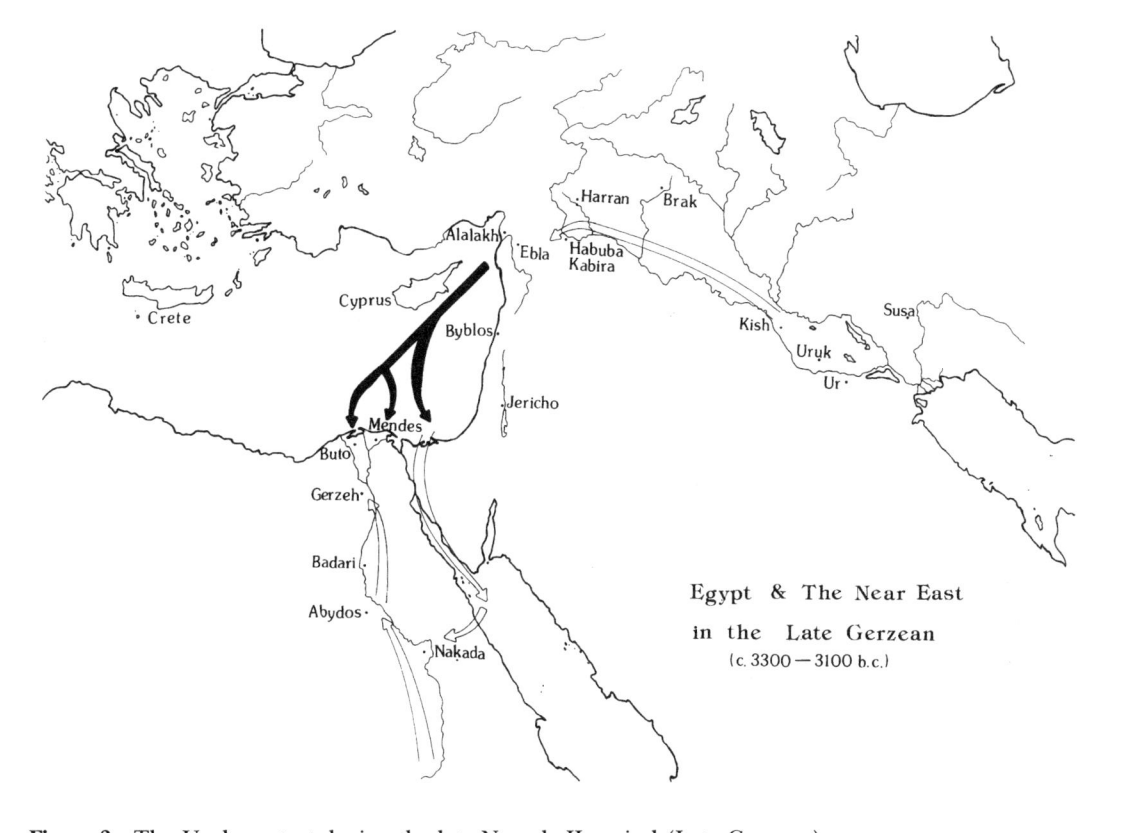

Figure 2   The Uruk contact during the late Naqada II period (Late Gerzean).

activity, and a power-wielding elite at the summit. Such a large city could scarcely support itself from the relatively small territorium to which the presence of adjacent cities limited its holdings; and food, goods, raw products, manufactures, and services of necessity had to be acquired abroad. This led to the creation and constant use of an ever-extending series of transit corridors linking the cities of the Tigris-Euphrates plain with far flung regions where prospectors and traders secured the material the home city required. The routes led east into the Iranian uplands, north into the foothills of Armenia, Assyria, and Anatolia, and west into Syria and the Mediterranean coast. In a few places "colonies" or work camps seem to have been established in order to facilitate the flow of goods back to the mother cities; but, whether colonized or not, the cities and areas into which the southerners penetrated showed rapid signs of acculturation, and soon donned the full garb of Uruk civilization.

Egypt was only the farthest and latest destination reached by Uruk traders. Since, to judge by the representation of Mesopotamian ships (with the upturned prows mentioned earlier) on Egyptian objects, contact must have been set up by sea, traders probably used the route around the Arabian peninsula and up the Red Sea to make landfall at the mouth of the Wady Hammamat. Recently the appearance of architectural features—clay "nails" reminiscent of Uruk techniques of decoration—in the excavations at Buto has suggested that a second maritime route may have led from the mouth of the Orontes in Syria across the Mediterranean to the coast of the Delta. Although in this preliterate period, just before the appearance of writing, we lack textual evidence regarding motivation, it seems fairly clear what attracted these foreign Asiatics to north-east Africa. Egypt had large quantities of gold and exotic sub-Saharan products, the latter transiting regularly down the Nile.

Traits of Uruk culture adopted by the Egyptians were far fewer and more ephemeral than those which impacted the cities of northern Mesopotamia and Syria; but in a few key areas a decisive influence was felt. Some of the most ancient toponyms in the eastern and central Delta are not Egyptian, but derive from West Semitic, or Akkadian roots, suggesting an early presence of people from Western Asia. The later accoutrements of the king of Egypt, white crown, sceptres, carrying chair, are arguably of West Asian origin (E); and the name of his palace, referred to above, viz. *s(h)arakhu*, derives from an Akkadian root meaning "to be lordly, glorious, uplifted." The Egyptian script, which was just about to be brought to birth, contains several signs the phonetic value of which are derived from West Semitic or Sumerian, not Egyptian.

The Rise of the First Dynasty

One further phenomenon of the Naqada II period can probably, though indirectly, be put down to the effects of contact with the Tigris-Euphrates region. Three settlements in southern Upper Egypt, all on the west bank of the river, and at least one in Lower Egypt, began to expand in size and complexity. Hierakonpolis, 115 km north of the First Cataract and located at the mouth of a wady leading west into the desert (F), shows an uninterrupted archaeological sequence from the remote stone age into historic times. The town deity was the falcon Horus, "the far-off one," the patron of the "Great One," the leader of the community. Directly across the river was situated the town of Elkab, whose vulture deity Nekhbit shared in the patronage of the neighboring headman, and whose shrine was appropriately enough called the "House of the Great One" (G - right middle). One hundred kilometers north of Hierakonpolis almost directly opposite the opening of the Wady Hammamat lay the town of Naqada (from which the period takes its name), where Seth, Horus's opponent, was revered. The settlement's ancient name, *Ombos,* means "Gold-town," and clearly indicates a strategic location favorable to the control of the gold-mining region of the eastern desert, accessible through the wady. About 85 km, as the crow flies, northward still, the town of Abydos nestled close to a point in the western cliffs where a route led west into the oasis chain (H). The town god of Abydos was a canine, Khentiamentiu, "the First of Westerners," associated with the wolf(?)-god of Asyut, Wepwawet, "the Opener of the Ways," both intimately connected with the Afterlife. And it was here at a very early date that the family of leaders from Hierakonpolis staked out a burying ground which for all time lent a peculiar sanctity to the city. In the northwest Delta the town of Buto (I) sprang to prominence at the same time. In the Fourth Millennium B.C. it was virtually a coastal port, enjoying contact with Syria. The local deity was the cobra-goddess Edjo, "the Green One," and local mythology made her a protagonist in a myth patterned on the plot monster vs. mother and child.

Whether the event was fraught with violence and coercion is unknown, but well before the end of the Naqada II period the three towns of Upper Egypt had amalgamated under the leadership of the headman, the "Great One" of Hierakonpolis. Nearly two hundred kilometers (125 miles) of Nile Valley passed under the suzerainty of one man: at a mythological level

First Dynasty	
Menes	c. 3095–3060 B.C.
Aha	c. 3060–3025 B.C.
Djer	c. 3025–2994 B.C.
Edjo	c. 2994–2974 B.C.
Den	c. 2974–2942 B.C.
Andj-ib	c. 2942–2922 B.C.
"Semsem" (?)	c. 2922–2912 B.C.
Qa-a	c. 2912–2880 B.C.

Horus and Seth enjoyed uneasy reconciliation, embodied in the person of the leader, while the two canines, the falcon, and (sometimes) the pig mounted standards held aloft when the Great One marched in procession or went to war. The new enclave had eliminated all competition in its quest for ownership rights over all the products and minerals the Mesopotamian merchants wanted. It was strategically located to control one of the access routes used by Uruk traders, the Wady Hammamat, and to exercise a monopoly over goods passing out of the desert or down the Nile, as well as the gold coming from the eastern desert.

Northward expansion followed naturally toward that other sector of north-east Africa where traders from West Asia were penetrating, viz. the Delta. If, as we have pointed out above, no particular location in the Nile Valley offers particular advantage, there is no reason to view the valley and its inhabitants as naturally segmented. The Nile is a single, indivisible transit corridor which can be negotiated with ease and speed; if the Great One at Hierakonpolis sits over the southern end, there is no reason why he should not naturally consider sitting over the northern end! Moreover, it must have early dawned on the leader that expansion of hegemony over several communities brings immediate advantage. Rivals are eliminated and disjunctive elements in the population neutralized; food stocks increase dramatically and fugitives and others from other communities flock to Great One's banner. In all, the leader creates a web of personal and reciprocal alliances and obligations of which he is the center: he does not inherit this from his father, nor pass it on to a successor. He is the sole dispenser of power while he lives.

The extension of the authority of the Great One of Herakleopolis did not take place without violence. Not all were prepared to cede possessions and freedom to the new man from the south. The violent motifs in the art of Naqada II-III deal in pejoratives: the defeated enemy are depicted naked, with unkempt beards and hair, either already slain or about to be executed. A specific identification may be appended, but this is not really necessary; whoever they are, the artist is determined to make them out to be the "bad guys." It is quite likely that, when the people from Hierakonpolis failed to stop at the apex of the Delta, the settlements of Lower Egypt resisted too. A decorated palette from the close of the fourth millennium depicts a series of fortified towns (**fig. 3**) identified by primitive hieroglyphs as being apparently located in the environs of Buto, under attack by symbols closely associated elsewhere with the numinous power of the Great One.

Figure 3   The so-called "City Palette," showing on the left seven fortified enclosures under attack by symbols of the incipient monarchy: falcon, scorpion, lion.

It is difficult to establish the identity of the first chief of Hierakonpolis who could claim to lord it over the entire country. Early leaders preferred to project their power by several graphic symbols—bull, falcon, crocodile, scorpion, jackal, even hare are attested—and to mask their birth or given names. By the time of one who favors the scorpion as a symbol and has therefore come to be called "King Scorpion," and his successor Nar-mer (possibly "the dangerous *nar*-fish"), a realistic claim could be made to rule of both valley and Delta. Narmer is depicted on his famous palette wearing both white and red crowns, historically indicative of rule over both halves of the country **(fig. 4)**.

It is important to realize that the feat accomplished by Narmer and his kin was absolutely unique; no one knew what was to come, as there was no precedent on which one could pattern oneself. The victor faced hard choices. On the one hand, having acquired a good deal of booty of all kinds, Narmer could retrace his steps back to Hierakonpolis, disband his men and enjoy the spoils. But, over and above the prizes of war, the extension of personal hegemony over the entire country brought unexpected possibilities which had to be acted upon lest advantage be forfeited. For one thing the unrelenting advance of the leader from the south had been crowned at every step by success, and people always are attracted by a winner. The number of men surrounding this protégé of the falcon god now exceeded anything seen before; and with such a force great things could be accomplished of which a neolithic village could never have dreamed. For another thing, with the whole land at his feet, the acquisition of its wealth need not be a one time occurrence: with his men he could go back time and time again, and ask people everywhere to make contributions. If this rosy picture were to be realized, however, the leader had to refrain from disbanding his men, and had to locate them (and himself, of course) at a strategic point from which oversight of his domain would be facilitated. Neither his home town, nor Ombos, Abydos or Buto offered the right location.

Werner Forman/Art Resource, NY

Figure 4   The obverse of the Narmer Palette, showing the king dealing the *coup de grace* to an enemy chief.

The Creation of a Civil Service
and the Mechanisms of Government

One signal accomplishment of the First Dynasty, for that is what in the final version of the King-list Narmer and his successors are called, was the creation of a new settlement just south of the apex of the Delta. Here, on land which may in part have been reclaimed from the Nile, Narmer established his residence centered upon a fortified keep called, after the white plaster applied to the bricks, the "White Fort." About seven centuries later the by then expanded city took a name associated with the pyramid city of Pepy I, "Pepy-is-Firm-and-Perfect" *(Pepy-men-nofre)* or *Memphis* as it was to be known for ever after. We should imagine the original town as a growing agglomeration of rough huts, shrines, and storage areas clustering around the niched and buttressed walls of the fort. Rectangular or oval fortifications were the order of the day, and several such enclosures were located within the region of greater Memphis, some to house the leader and his closest followers, others the rank and file; still others serve cultic and mortuary needs. The names, which have been preserved on early wood and ivory labels, as well as on sealings, betray a mind set pre-occupied with security and projection of power: "(the enclosure called) Protection-Surrounds-the Lord," "(the enclosure called) Horus-is-the-Rising-Star," "(the enclosure called) Seat-of-Horus-the Harpooner" (perhaps at Buto), "(the enclosure called) Terror-of-the-Two-Lands."

The density of population in the environs of the White Fort enabled the ruler to call up reserves of manpower that no one else could match in north-east Africa or the Levant, but certain practical problems demanded immediate solutions; and it was those solutions that created the earliest organization that we would call a "civil service." The logistics of housing, equipping, and feeding such a population called forth, not only craft specialization, but also a commissariat devoted exclusively to collecting weapons and implements, acquiring food stocks from the countryside, prognosticating the availability of future food stocks, providing and maintaining storage facilities. In short this cadre of organizers and controllers was concerned with laying hold on the gross domestic product of the land of Egypt and redistributing it to fill the needs of this new phenomenon, viz. a capital city and district.

Since it would be difficult to collect and redistribute produce without quantifying it, a system of measurement was imperative, and all the evidence points to the early First Dynasty as the period when a system of weights and measures was introduced. Recent research suggests that in origin the system depended on the appreciation of the relationship of weight to volume in the case of the two basic cereals in the Egyptian storehouse, viz. emmer wheat and barley. The inventors made it a "closed system," that is to say a system in which linear measures and area can be deduced from weight and volume.

But it is not only commodities that demand measurement: a civil service must be able to measure *time* in order to reckon precisely phases within the agricultural year, and prognosticate accurately lengths of time remaining until planting and harvesting. Presumably the neolithic Egyptians paid attention to the phases of the moon, and indeed the very ancient names for individual days of the lunar month suggests that they did. But lunar time spans were ill fitted to measure the most important phenomenon of the peasant's year, viz. the annual inundation; for individual floods may be separated from each other by as few as eleven or as many as fourteen lunar cycles. What was needed was an occurrence which repeated itself with precise regularity. For this the Egyptians looked heavenward. One celestial event which always seemed to coincide with the height of the flood was the heliacal rising of the star *Sothis* (our Sirius) on the eastern horizon just before dawn on July 18–19. Although successive risings may vary by a few hours, averaging the number of days through observation over a generation would have been sufficient to hit upon 365 days. After some experimentation, the Memphite savants produced, by the close of the 29th century B.C., a civil calendar of twelve months of thirty days, each beginning on the dark of the moon, to which were added five "epagomenal" days to produce the required total. Three seasons of four months each were identified, corresponding to the farm calendar: *akhet,* "inundation," *proyet,* "cultivation," and *shomu,* "harvest." Since the calendar represents a measurement the value of which for government and business community alike depends on its precision, once started it cannot be allowed to suffer subtraction or addition of days. At the inception of the calendar its inventors clearly had been unaware of the five hours and forty-eight minutes over and above the 365-day span; and by the time someone realized the error, the rising of Sothis which should have occurred on the first day of the civil calendar was falling several days early. There is no evidence an adjustment was ever made, and the day of the star's rising continued to move forward until, after 1,460 years, it would once again fall on the first day of the civil calendar.

Pre-occupation with a *sexagesimal* system, naturally fostered by the rough equivalence of twelve months to the length of the year, is to be detected in mechanisms used by the Egyptians for reckoning the length of night and day. Each was divided into twelve hours, the daylight hours being marked on shadow clocks or water clocks, those of the night identified by the rising of certain stars. Since the heavens moved throughout the year, every ten days a new set of stars had to be used as markers.

Scales of measurement, important though they are for collecting, assessing, and redistributing produce, are useless in identifying the item and quantity of collection, from whom it has been collected, and where it is destined. Moreover, in an economy of scale, such as Egypt was being transformed into, information about identity and quantity which must be passed at long range between people who had never seen each other before was multiplying beyond human ability to commit to memory. Some *aid to memory* was desperately required, more permanent and reliable than human faculties of recall and enunciation. And the aid ought to appeal to one of the senses other than auditory, sight being distinctly preferable; and therefore the medium must take *graphic* form. Now from as early as Naqada I the minor "arts" of decoration on pot, palette, or rock had uninterruptedly evolved into a figurative discourse **(fig. 5)**. Iconic composition served the purposes of statements of ownership ("this pot belongs to . . . [sign]"), destination ("this pot is donated to . . . [sign]"), practical messages ("gazelles are here"), or projection of personal power ("I [in my sign] am here"). The civil service could use such discourse, but the parameters of the signifiers had to be narrowed and an enumeration system added. A drawing or scratching of the image of a wine jar on a surface accompanied by

Figure 5   Naqada II pot decoration, showing what presumably is a goddess (with arms raised) on the left, observed by two males in what may be an early representation of a triad. The ship is typical of Egyptian Nile craft of the period.

eight vertical strokes could, by common consent, signify nothing other than "eight jars of wine." The representation of a dead body along with two lotus plants meant precisely "2,000 dead." Although a single language, that of the inventors of the script, lay behind the signs, once the icons and numerals had been agreed upon, the text could be "read" in any language. But in the present case those sending messages and those receiving them spoke only Egyptian, and the signs would have to accommodate that language only. Conveying concrete items and numbers by icons was a relatively straightforward advance; but the savants were challenged when they had to *identify* those involved in producing, transporting, or receiving the commodities. How was one to represent graphically an individual name, or a common noun? If the name denotes a visible attribute—"shorty," "big-nosed," "blackie," "fat-head"—an appropriate icon can be used as a metonym of the individual in question. If a concrete homonym, a like-sounding word, exists, then the name or noun may be so represented; thus a fox-skin apron *(mst)* may be used to "write" the word "offspring" *(ms)*, a beetle *(ḫpr)* for nouns derived from the root "to become" *(ḫpr)*, the lungs-cum-windpipe *(nfr)* for names derived from *nfr*, "beauty, beautiful," the "basket" *(nb)* for "lord" *(nb)*. This use of homonyms demands latitude of application, as vocalization is not always exactly similar; but at the same time it awakens the imagination. For the icon is now wholly separated from what it signified, and the imagination is forced to link picture solely with sound. For any speaker of Afro-Asiatic, to which family ancient Egyptian belongs, sound means plosive, fricative, palatal, laryngial, and glottal articulation, in short *consonantal* sounds. In contemplating an icon it was not the *vocalized* pronunciation, nor the syllabic composition that impressed the Egyptian, but the consonants of which the word represented by the object were composed. In cases of words composed of two consonants only, of which the second was weak (like *alif* or *yod*), the graphic icon in some two dozen cases came to stand for the strong consonant alone by the acrophonic principle, thus producing a set of alphabetic characters.

Government Archives

We can trace the earliest development of this script, misnamed by the later Greeks *hieroglyphic*, "sacred characters," for at least two centuries, perhaps slightly longer. By the beginning of the First Dynasty (reign of Narmer) for all intents and purposes, the principles and lines of evolution outlined above were complete, although experimentation was to continue for another two to three centuries. While some of the early examples of writing (Dyn. 0 to Den) are frequently beyond our understanding at present, all genres ostensibly served the needs of the government bureaucracy: seals for identification of officials and their authority, tags for noting contents of bales and storerooms, pot inscriptions to identify contents and donors, name-markers for tombs, standing stone markers *(stelae)* at the doors of public buildings for identification and protection, messages, inventories, or accounts written on papyrus (an early form of paper made from the papyrus plant of Lower Egypt) **(fig. 6)**.

Although the time "yard-stick" of the *year* served an immediate purpose, it was useless in long range planning based on the estimate of height of inundation and size of harvest over an extended period. Measuring the Nile height and quantifying harvest yield were easy enough, but records of them had to be maintained over a sequence of years. It was imperative, therefore, not only to identify individual years, but to keep them in their proper sequence. Curiously, from the point of view of us moderns, identification of a year suggested to the

Figure 6 (a) Grave stone of a woman named Nofret, Abydos. (b) Label, recording 164 beads in a necklace, Naqada. (c) Jar docket of the draftsman (?) Nofer, Saqqara. (d) Apotropaic "serpent stone."

ancients a *name*, not a *number*, and years came to be "tagged" by, not one, but several salient events of that twelve-month period. Those events deemed important enough to be used included the carving of divine statues, the erection of enclosures, temples, and royal buildings, and the suppression of uprisings or foreign campaigns. A copy of the whole, accompanied by a record of the height of the inundation for that year, would be carved on a square or rectangular "ticket" of wood or ivory, and deposited in the archives. For purposes of dating when commodities were received or stored, a copy of the master could be made and attached to cord, door-handle, or basket. While the masters of the individual annals have been lost, the secondary copies have turned up in excavations in appreciable numbers **(fig. 7a–c)**.

As time passed, however, the civil servants became aware of a problem inherent in this system. It was difficult enough to remember, with the passing of time, four or five separate events datable to a single year; it was well nigh impossible as the generations rolled on correctly to maintain the *sequence* of these "event clusters." A handier and self-evident mechanism was required if the collection of annals were not to degenerate into a mass of disconnected and dimly-remembered facts. Before the reign of Qa'a, last king of the First Dynasty, someone had hit upon the idea of using for mnemonic purposes, not individual and unique events, but events which recurred on a regular basis. Thus, if it were known that festival X occurred once every three years, the mention of the "seventh occurrence" of that festival would indicate the twenty-first year of the reign in question. Two events which occurred in alternate years in regular sequence were the "Appearance of the King of Upper and Lower Egypt," apparently a public manifestation of the leader, and "The Following of Horus," a royal progress for inspection purposes throughout the entire country **(fig. 7d)**. Although continuing to be performed into the

Figure 7a Ivory year rectangle of Hor-aha recording, *inter alia,* a voyage to the shrine of Neith of Sais, the festival of the running of the Apis-bull(?), offerings at Hierakonpolis(?), and a voyage to Buto.

Figure 7b Ivory year rectangle of Hor-edjo, recording the carving of a statue of Thoth, the founding of a rectangular enclosure of <Horus> the Harpooner(?), the building of a shrine to the patron goddesses. Note the inclusion on the upper right of the frond, indicating "the year of . . . ."

Figure 7c Ivory year rectangle of Hor-den, recording the celebration of the jubilee, a military expedition to the south with the demolition of fortresses. To the right are the name and responsibilities of the king's seal-bearer Hemaka.

Figure 7d   Ivory year rectangle of Hor-Qa'a, recording the year of the sixth royal progress. To the right are the name and title of the king's (chief) sculptor and carpenter, Nofer.

Third Dynasty, Following and Appearance were replaced during the Second Dynasty as dating tools by a much more convenient sequence, viz. the biennial cattle census in which all livestock in the country were tallied. Thus the "Third Occurrence of the Cattle Count" would indicate the sixth year of the reign, "the year after the Third Occurrence" the seventh year and so on.

If still extant, the annals would have proven a remarkable source for the history of the Old Kingdom, but unfortunately preservation is spotty. As a pious act Neferirkare I of the Fifth Dynasty (early 24th century B.C.) "published" all the annals up to his time on stone, presumably in the temple of Ptah at Memphis. A fragment of this monument, only about 10% of the whole, is at present housed in the museum of Palermo in Sicily, while several small fragments have been recovered from the site of Memphis itself. They demonstrate that the physical size of the annals expanded markedly in the Fourth Dynasty, and that from the reign of Khufu this medium was used increasingly to broadcast the monarch's pious donations to the gods, denoted by the formula "he made it as his memorial for god X, making for him a . . ." followed by the specific bequest.

While arguably the most important document in the archives, the "House of the God's (i.e. the king's) Book(s)," the specific name for the state library, once contained a wealth of documentation, now mostly known to us by name only. There were cattle census figures and draft lists of able-bodied men, work-orders, royal charters of immunity, tax documents, and royal rescripts, all under the general oversight of an "archivist," assisted by "document-handlers" charged with delivery of rescripts and letters. These documents and their keepers fulfil needs that are intensely practical; but as time passed genres were added to the collection that were less prosaic. These included medical texts and the pharmacopoeia of which the earliest kings are said by tradition to have been authors, as well as religious books containing orders of service, hymns, and beatification spells (see below).

Second Dynasty	
Hotep-sekhemwy	c. 2880–2860 B.C.
Ra-nebi	c. 2860–2840 B.C.
Ny-neter	c. 2840–2803 B.C.
Wadj-nes	c. 2803–2797 B.C.
Senedy	c. 2797–2793 B.C.
Peribsen	c. 2793–2752 B.C.
Khasekhemwy	c. 2752–2733 B.C.

"The Hermeneutic of Horus": the Creation of a Royal Mythology

The complex state and the society upon which it rested took two centuries to evolve, but already at the beginning it was evident to all that the evolution was not spontaneous, but was brought about by the genius of the leader and his men. To no lesser degree than a calendar and a writing system, Egyptians had to have an explanation of who this leader was and why he exuded such obvious power. The theology of kingship will dominate our enquiry as we proceed with the political history of Egypt over three millennia; but two fundamental explanations which are rooted in the phenomenon of unification of the land must be examined now.

The "Big Man" who had extended his fiat over all Egypt was known to be the protégé of the falcon god Horus. As such he shared with the deity the role of guarantor of the peace and fertility of the river Valley and Delta, the "Black Land," and the opponent of the "Red Land," the sterile desert of Seth. But, as neither could enjoy ultimate triumph, a kind of equilibrium had of necessity to be achieved; and the king of Egypt came early to embody both divine figures, two opposites in controlled tension. Still, his origin was ineffable. Where had he come from? While living, he dominated the life of the community to the exclusion of all else, and his siblings and even his progenitor remain in the shadows, so to speak. Yet he was destined for death, and a new "Big Man" would again dominate the scene, and again overshadow all others.

It was that passage from life to death, a major exigency in the story of the communal leader, that called forth one of the fundamental myths of Egyptian kingship. Horus did not suffer a natural death, but was *done* to death at the hands of Seth. The narrative, adjusted over time in many slight permutations, paints a backdrop of jealousy, malice, and deceit. The embodiment of order and fertility was murdered, drowned in the waters of the Nile and because of this those waters ever after exuded an essence of fertility. But the concept of Horus was that of the *living* falcon: the deceased king could not return in that guise. Now his seat belonged to his son, the new Horus, while he was translated in death to the western horizon. There, by virtue of his erstwhile kingship, he continued to enjoy rule over "those that are there," the "Westerners," euphemisms both for the dead. His was a parallel universe, cloned from Egyptian society: he had a throne, crown, regalia, and a court, and exercised an otherworldly judgement similar to what he had meted out on earth. The dead king's future existence, however, was not wholly ethereal, for his place of final rest continued to be visible to the living, on the cliffs to the west of the Nile where a mock-up of his palace in life housed his remains. This was his final *seat,* and since in life he had performed the quintessential role of *doer, maker, cult-master, progenitor,* this great mortuary establishment took the name "Seat-of-the-Maker," or *st-ir.* Extended as a metonym for its occupant, *st-ir* became an appellation for the king-in-death, vocalized in later times as *Osiris.*

It is characteristic of Big Man societies that the present holder of the position by definition cannot legitimize himself as leader by reference to ancestry. He must do it himself, forge his own alliances, create his own prestige, empower himself. But his situation remains tenuous in spite of what he does, and the subconscious desire to see one's power continue beyond the grave provides a powerful incentive to use heredity as empowerment. Legitimation through inheritance informs a second great myth which the early Old Kingdom devised to render the new phenomenon of the living Horus permanent. The urge to know and identify the living Horus led to the delineation of the hypostasis, or underlying reality, of the generation which had given him birth: his father Osiris in the guise of his eternal seat, his mother the Throne (Egyptian *Isis*), his female guardians, his mansions (Egyptian *Hathor,* "the Mansion of Horus," and *Nephthys,* "Mistress of the Mansion,") and even his sometime opponent Seth. Throne, palace, Nile, and desert answered the question in part only, for Horus claimed to be a god of the highest potency, ruling the universe. Where had his parental generation come from? And now, in answer, the savants pressed into service those autochthonous stories of primordial time: Osiris and his wife, along with Seth and Nephthys, were offspring of earth and sky, Geb and Nut; and through Geb specifically flowed the right of inheritance. This pair were made the children of air and moisture, Shu and Tefnut, the very essence of life itself, and they in turn became the progeny of the creator himself, Re the sun god. The resultant cycle of nine gods, the ennead (Egyptian *psḏt,* "the Nine") developed into a concept of seminal importance for the Egyptian belief system; but in origin, for the king, it established his mythological pedigree of descent from the creator god himself. Moreover, through the male line of four genera-tions—the number "four" in Egyptian thinking conveys the notion of totality—the Horus-king could lay claim to being the encorporation of water, earth, air, and the fiery heat of the sun, the four elements of the cosmos **(fig. 8).**

The perfection of these mythological concepts took several centuries to realize, but once in place they endured largely unchanged until the end of Egyptian history. The result was a royal image, a mythological mask, which more or less concealed individual identity. Even the official names of the king (five in number by the close of the Old Kingdom) **(fig. 8)** present him in the cloak of divine leadership: he was Horus-so-and-so written in a *s(h)arakhu-*simulacrum **(fig. 9),** the favorite of the Two Ladies (Edjo and Nekhbit, patron goddesses of Lower and Upper Egypt), Horus-triumphant-over-the-Ombite (Seth), king of Upper and Lower Egypt, son of the sun-god. Then followed his birth-name, in a sense the only concession to his earthly birth.

THE MYTHOLOGICAL PEDIGREE OF THE KING

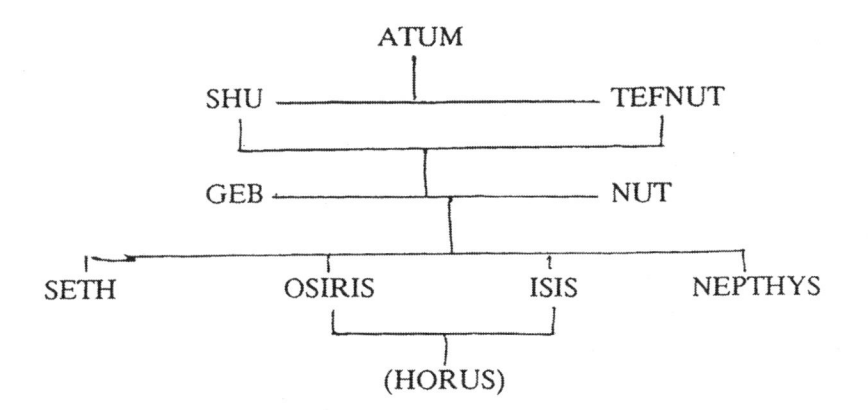

THE FIVE-FOLD TITULARY

1.   Horus-Mighty-Bull

2.   The Two-Ladies (man/favorite)

3.   "Golden"-Horus

4.   King-of-Upper-and-Lower-Egypt ("He-of-the-swt-plant", "He-of-the-bee")

5.   (Birth name)

6.   Epithets: the Perfect God, the Great God, the Lord, Horus-and-Seth
                    Sovereign, Person of....(often translated "Majesty")

Figure 8   The Mythological Pedigree of the King and the Five-Fold Titulary.

Figure 9 Mortuary stela of Hor-edjo, showing the falcon perched on the roof of the *s(h)araku* building, with its niched façade.

Strangely, though the Horus-king had by main force united the Valley and Delta, no designation emerged from those who thought up titulary to denote him as king of a united country. "He-of-the-*sut*-plant-and-the-bee," i.e. King of Upper and Lower Egypt, no matter how each element came later to be used—artificial confinement of usage and false back interpretation is widely attested—continued to define the king of Egypt well into Roman times. Consonant with his dual nature, he was at first assigned dual burial: the old burying ground at Abydos was retained, apparently for the true burial, while a mock-up or cenotaph was constructed at the cemetery at Saqqara opposite Memphis (J).

The Nascent State: Expansion and Reaction

Although the fragmentary condition of the annals and the lack of monumental inscriptions makes it very difficult to try to write a history of Egypt during the early third millennium, nevertheless certain trends show through the murky state of our knowledge. First, the violence which had attended the union of Upper and Lower Egypt did not stop with the creation of a Memphite residence. The Horus-names of the First Dynasty kings consistently reflect the desire for intimidation by threat of violence: Horus-is-a-fighter *(Hor-aha)*, Horus-is-a-seizer-of top-knots *(Hor-djer)*, Horus-is-a-decapitator *(Hor-den)*, Horus-is-a-ripper-out-of-heart(s)" *(Hor-andj-ib)*, Horus-has-his-arm-raised *(Hor-Qa'a)*. Year names in the annals refer to the "smiting" of foreigners **(fig. 10)**, or the "hacking up" of fortress so-and-so. Rock art in areas beyond Egypt's frontiers feature the chastening message of the head-smiting scene, in which the king with arm

Figure 10 Ivory rectangle of Hor-den, shown smiting an inhabitant of Palestine. To the right the Standard of Wepwawet precedes the king, while behind him is written the name "Inka" (an official?). The whole is glossed on the extreme right by the text, "first occasion of smiting the East."

raised is about to crush the head of a grovelling enemy with a mace or axe; or the heraldic falcon brings the dishevelled "Bad Guys" for execution. Second, the First Dynasty showed a distinct tendency to expand. Controlling Mesopotamian thrusts to tap Egyptian resources—such penetration ceased about the middle of the Dynasty—or raising the frontiers at the First Cataract and Mediterranean did not quench a desire to control resources further afield. The rock art of Nubia bears witness to military excursions into the northern Sudan, albeit of no immediate consequence; and the archaeology of the Negeb and greater Gaza region has yielded such caches of pottery and Egyptian sealings that some have postulated Egyptian attempts at colonization. At the very least this, admittedly, sparse evidence from the First Dynasty reflects the desire to create a sphere of influence beyond Egypt's boundaries, an expectation which was to be realized during the Third through Fifth Dynasties.

Third, during the first two dynasties there is unmistakable evidence of dissent within Egypt, leading to sporadic uprisings. Year dates sometimes refer to the destruction of settlements with obvious Lower Egyptian names, and it has been suggested (though with scant evidence) that the First Dynasty tombs at Abydos and Saqqara were fired in such a rebellion. More suggestive, though maddeningly difficult to interpret, is the evidence of the so-called "Seth Rebellion" of the Second Dynasty. After the eighth king of the First Dynasty, Horus Qa'a, the later King-list tradition makes a break, and begins a Second Dynasty. Although the Turin Canon, reflecting the King-list tradition of the 13ᵗʰ century B.C., does not countenance such a break, the name of the first king of the Second Dynasty, Hotep-sekhemwy which means "the Two Powers (i.e. Horus and Seth) are at Rest," might be taken to refer to the restoration of calm after a period of unrest. This king and his two successors, Ra-nebi and Ny-neter, span the best part of a century, and their large tombs (though rifled) and the fragmentary annals and sealings give proof of peace and prosperity. Towards the middle of the Dynasty, however, the King-list tradition and the later ancestral offering lists alike betray a confusion of names which plausibly arose through rival claims for legitimacy and internal strife. Of particular importance is a king Peribsen whose name does not appear in that form in any list, although he continued to be honored by an offering cult during the Fourth Dynasty. Peribsen replaced the ubiquitous Horus-falcon which, from a time well before Narmer, had always perched a-top the *s(h)arakhu* simulacrum to denote the Horus-name, with the wild pig emblem of Seth, or Ash as Peribsen calls him **(fig. 11)**. In addition to this the king is referred to in one sealing as Ash's son. Given the antipathy between Horus and Seth, such a blatant dismissal of the god uniquely associated with Egyptian kingship must have a profound ideological reason. But how is it to be interpreted? Was someone, for whatever reason, superficially rethinking the theological foundations of kingship, or does the change betoken a deeper social malaise, or a geopolitical fissure in the state? The plot thickens when the epigraphic and textual evidence of the next (or next but one?) reign is passed in review: a king who displays both falcon and wild pig a-top his *s(h)arakhu,* takes the significant Horus-name *Kha-sekhemwy,* "the Two Powers have Arisen," with the addition *Neb.wy-hotep-imef,* "The Two Lords are at Peace in him." A number of pots dated to the reign of Khasekhemwy and unearthed at Hierakonpolis bear the inscribed commemoration of a year date entitled "year of smiting the inhabitants of the Delta"; while a basalt statue of the king from the same site bears on its base the scratched representation of scattered cadavers, glossed by the text "northern enemies 47,209." A rather striking confirmation that the close of the Second Dynasty witnessed a

Figure 11 The "Horus"-name of Peribsen, showing the Seth (or Ash) animal replacing the falcon.

violent repression of northern dissent comes from the excavations at Mendes in the east central Delta. Here two major building phases of the Archaic Period, the lower dated by sealings of Hor-aha and of officials datable to the reign of Hor-den, is capped by a destruction phase 35 cm thick, above which the city of the Third and Fourth Dynasty was built.

No matter what one may think of the sparseness of the evidence, it is difficult to escape the conclusion that the reign of Peribsen represents a reaction on the part of some segment of the population against the Horus kings from Hierakonpolis. That the center of the reaction may have been located in Lower Egypt is strongly suggested by the objects of Khasekhemwy's reprisal, as well as a curious trio of kings represented in the Turin Canon, though not in the Abydos ancestral offering list, who sound from their names like northerners. Do they represent an erstwhile northern state, broken away from the south?

Further Readings

The advent of a complex society has over the past two decades become a focus of research on the Egyptian state. For a comprehensive bibliography see S. Hendrickx, *Analytical Bibliography of the Prehistory and the Early Dynastic Period of Egypt and Northern Sudan,* Louvain, 1995. In particular, and apart from works cited at the end of the preceding chapter, see the following: C. K. Maisels, *Early Civilizations of the Old World,* London & New York, 1999; M. Rice, *Egypt's Making: The Origins of Ancient Egypt,* 5000–2000 B.C., London & New York, 1990; A. J. Spencer, *Early Egypt: The Rise of Civilization in the Nile Valley,* London, 1993; *idem* (ed.), *Aspects of Early Egypt,* London, 1996; B. G. Trigger, *Early Civilizations: Ancient Egypt in Context,* Cairo, 1993; T. Wilkinson, *State Formation in Egypt: Chronology and Society,* Oxford, 1996; *idem, Genesis of the Pharaohs,* London, 2003.

On the "Uruk Phenomenon" as a factor in the rise of the Pharaonic state, see G. Algaze, *The Uruk World System*, Chicago, 1993; S. Mark, *From Egypt to Mesopotamia*, College Station, 1997; P. R. S. Moorey, *From Gulf to Delta and Beyond*, Beer Sheva, 1995; M. S. Rothman (ed.), *Uruk Mesopotamia and its Neighbors*, Santa Fe, 2001; H. Weiss (ed.), *The Origins of Cities in Dry-Farming Syria and Mesopotamia in the Third Millennium B.C.*, Guilford, 1986.

On writing and the calendar, see O. Goldwasser, *From Icon to Metaphor: Studies in the Semiotics of the Hieroglyphs*, Fribourg, 1995; R. A. Parker, *The Calendars of Ancient Egypt*, Chicago, 1950; R. Parkinson, *Cracking Codes: The Rosetta Stone and Decipherment*, London, 1999; A. Robinson, *The Story of Writing*, London, 1995; A. J. Spalinger (ed.), *Revolutions in Time: Studies in Ancient Egyptian Calendrics*, San Antonio, 1994.

On annals and archives, see D. B. Redford, *Pharaonic King-lists, Annals, and Daybooks*, Mississauga, 1986; T. A. H. Wilkinson, *Royal Annals of Ancient Egypt*, London, 2000.

There are many works devoted to an analysis and explication of ancient Egyptian kingship. Among the more profitable are H. Frankfort, *Kingship and the Gods*, Chicago, 1948; D. O'Connor, D. P. Silverman (eds.), *Ancient Egyptian Kingship*, Leiden, 1995; J. G. Griffiths, *The Origins of Osiris and His Cult*, Leiden, 1980.

On the early development of the state, see B. Adams, K. M. Cialowicz, *Protodynastic Egypt*, Princes Riseborough, 1988; T. A. H. Wilkinson, *Early Dynastic Egypt*, London, 1999.

CHAPTER FOUR
The Third and Fourth Dynasties
The High Old Kingdom

———————— ψ ————————

Third Dynasty

Djoser	c. 2733–2703 B.C.
Sekhem-khet	c. 2703–2700 B.C.
Kha-ba	c. 2700–2699 B.C.
Neb-ka	c. 2699–2697 B.C.
"Huny" (?)	c. 2697–2687 B.C.

Fourth Dynasty

Snofru	c. 2687–2639 B.C.
Khufu	c. 2639–2591 B.C.
Ra-djedef	c. 2591–2583 B.C.
Khafre	c. 2583–2537 B.C.
Menkaure	c. 2537–2519 B.C.
Shepseskaf	c. 2519–2516 B.C.
[ ]	c. 2515 B.C.

Khasekhemwy's "solution" to the tendency on the part of some Egyptians to dissent from the union of the Two Lands, although attested by meagre evidence, cannot be misinterpreted. If for no other reason, the Egypt which Khasekhemwy left behind is so different from what precedes, that one can only characterize his reign as a watershed in the history of the country. Egypt would in the future suffer dissention among the population, and the secession of certain parts; but the lines would be drawn on a wholly different trajectory than in the Archaic Period.

The Worship of the Ancestors and Mortuary Economics

Throughout Egyptian history two views of authority existed in tension: authority derived from the competence of the individual, and authority derived from ancestry. We have seen how the Pharaonic monarchy evolved as a Big Man system out of the former; but it could not ignore the legitimacy conferred by a pedigree. In short, the ancestors continued to exercise a strong influence on the living from beyond the grave.

From the earliest times the Egyptians entertained specific views as to what constituted the ethereal, non-corporeal part of a human being. Two things impressed them greatly, viz. the individual personality and the life force. The personality, imbued with imagination and power, was conceived in the form of a human-headed bird called a *bai* **(fig. 1),** who at death was liberated from the individual, and was free to roam all over the universe (A). That its connexion with the personality of its owner should not be sundered, the *bai* was obliged to return periodically to its former home, and on a particular night of the year households would light lamps and put bowls of water before the door as an enticement. At the same time the *bai* would flutter down into the tomb to rest on the breast of the corpse, duly recognize him as its owner, and enter into momentary communion. Since recognition was all important, efforts were directed towards preserving the appearance of the cadaver from the earliest antiquity. The skins and matting placed over the body in prehistoric times were replaced with careful wrapping of the corpse in linen during the First Dynasty, while the softer parts of the body, liable to decay, were "fleshed out" in the Second Dynasty by the use of carefully placed linen padding under the

Figure 1 Bronze *bai*-bird.

bandages. The natural dryness of the desert helped considerably in the preservation of the body, but nonetheless artificial means suggested themselves. During the Third Dynasty the bodies of royalty and the upper classes were treated with aromatic substances, such as natron and resin, in order to arrest decay, an embalming process which at the outset took the best part of a year to complete.

Of equal fascination to the ancient Egyptians was the life force which they sensed resided in living things. They called it the *ku,* a word cognate with a root from which were derived such words as "work," "bull," "food," and the like, all suggesting energy and action. The *ku* was conceived as a double of its owner, born at the same time and occupying the same space during life, a notion that lives in the folklore of rural Egypt to the present day. *Ku* and owner enjoyed a reciprocal support during life, but at death the *ku* fled away, leaving the body without life. In a sense the elaborate preparation for death which we associate with Egyptian mortuary beliefs was concerned with re-uniting *ku* with body, an act described as "going to (join) one's *ku.*" As life could be supported this side of the grave only by the ingestion of food, so in the Beyond the availability of sustenance was all important. Meals implied a family setting: the tomb became the "House of the *Ku,*" and food for a sort of last supper always accompanied the funeral rites. But as the body lay inert under the earth, it was difficult to imagine how it could take advantage of any foodstuffs; consequently it would need some mechanism whereby food and drink were mediated to it. Such a mechanism was found in a "receiver for (the purpose of) life," (Egyptian *shespe-ankh*), in the form of a representation of the deceased either in two dimensions or in the round (B). Such *ku*-images, or *ku*-statues, could be placed at or in the tomb and, when properly activated by a magical ceremony known as "Opening-the-Mouth," could transfer food and drink to the *ku* and its owner. The family of the dead was expected to provide and offer the edibles upon a special offering table laid before the *ku*-statue. A formula, "the jubilant summons," called the deceased to the meal, and there it was believed the family could commune with their departed relative.

It became obvious at an early date that mortuary offerings, intended to be presented in perpetuity, frequently were discontinued if the family died out or moved away. Moreover there was always the problem of where the offerings would come from, and who would pay. The risks involved were addressed in several ways. It became customary for the family to strike a bargain with "*ku*-priests", many of whom belonged to local shrines, to provide the offerings and service the tomb. The food would come from landed endowments, farms and plantations owned by the family or, in the cases of the highest officials, donated by the king. The specific farms were sometimes depicted in art on the walls of the tomb as female personifications bearing offerings, glossed by caption texts identifying the parcel of land and its location. The food and drink to be presented by the priests, carefully specified as to nature and amount as well as the day of the calendar, would "revert" to the priests in the form of a salary, after the *ku* had satisfied itself. The size of the remuneration varied depending on the wealth of the family, and whether the priests had other employment and were simply "moonlighting." The whole agreement was drawn up in the form of a contract between the family, or the individual (before he died), and the priests identified by name, and papyrus copies distributed to the contracting parties as well as the state archives. Some of the earliest extended inscriptions we possess consist of such contracts, carved on the walls of a tomb for all to see. By the Third and early Fourth Dynasty "reversion" of offerings in the form of wages had become the norm, and a special department of government created to oversee and regulate this form of redistributive economy.

This overriding preoccupation with preparation for death is reflected, beyond the realm of practical "mortuary economics," in a sort of far-sighted risk management. What if the family died out, priests reneged on their contract or the tomb was pillaged? The cessation of food offerings would be absolutely fatal to the *ku* and its owner, and so a "fall-back" position was devised to surmount this worst-case scenario. The solution was sought in the power of magic. From as early as the First Dynasty a scene had been devised showing the deceased seated before an offering table laden and flanked with food and drink, and fronted by a grid containing the names of specific meats, vegetables, beer, wine, and confections, a veritable "mortuary menu." Above the head of the figure were written his or her name and titles, a trusted means of fixing identity and ownership (c). This scene of the "funerary meal" was the most important element in the appointments of an Egyptian tomb, ensuring, as it was expected to do, a magical means of making food available for the dead for all time. Originally carved as a tableaux on a slab stela, by the end of the Third Dynasty it had been transferred to the lintel over what is known as the "false door," a mock-up of a formal aperture next to the offering table which represented the interface between the realm of the living and the dead. If magic was as powerful as the Egyptians believed it to be, it could be used to solve other problems related to life in the Beyond. The need for servants over there, satisfied in the earliest royal burials by the ritual killing and interment of factors at the time of burial, issued shortly in the inclusion of servant statues in the tomb which could be activated if work needed to be done.

Survival after death, however, ultimately depended upon the actions and approbation of the living; and one need not be a family member to intercede. Piety demanded that any visitor to a tomb make an offering, but often food and drink were not to hand. Under these conditions an offering formula would magically ensure the availability of the foods named to the dead, and mention of king and gods would tie the formula to their munificence, thus: "an offering which the king and god X gives, that invocation offerings may proceed, consisting of bread, beer, beef and fowl . . . [other foods may be inserted] . . . for the *ku* of" followed by the name of the deceased; or "a thousand of bread, beer, beef, and fowl for the *ku* of . . . (name)." So important were these formulae that the tomb owner would do anything to entice visitors to come into his tomb; and the wall reliefs and paintings which, by the close of the Fourth Dynasty, became standard in large tombs, are in part designed to attract visitors "who may enter my tomb see what I have done in life." Once inside the guests are confronted, not only by the scene of the mortuary meal and the *ku*-statue, but also by an inscription in which the tomb owner makes a formal address to "all ye living upon earth, who may pass by this my tomb."

Now the deceased can reason with the living: "ye shall offer me of that which is in your hands. But if there is nothing in your hands, then ye shall say orally, 'A thousand of bread, beer, beef, and fowl . . . for the *ku* of (name)." If the visitor is disinclined to comply perhaps through laziness, an argument is in order: "(the offering formula) is indeed no outlay of your own wealth, (but simply) breath of the mouth, advantageous to the blessed dead; for a good deed is more advantageous for him that does it than to him for whom it is done." Even if visitors are illiterate, as must have been frequently the case, the message will still get through: "O all ye scribes who may read, and all ye people who may listen!" A visitor may feel more inclined to co-operate with the dead if the tomb owner had been of exalted social status; and so from the Fourth Dynasty on the speaker includes a statement of who he is and what he did in life.

The result is a new genre, a biographical statement, which will become increasingly common over the centuries, and graduate to the status of a quasi-historical document.

The Evolution of the Tomb and the Monument of Djoser

The practical considerations of the Afterlife we have outlined above are mirrored in the technology and ideology of tomb development. The mounded graves of the prehistoric period, associated in form with the mound of creation and promising new life, had developed in the outgoing Naqada II period into a formal mock-up of the house of the living or the palace of the king. A brick-lined pit below ground contained the body of the owner with a supply of food, while the rectangular superstructure (D) or *mastaba* (Arabic "bench") was compartmentalized in a series of rooms for storage. Until the reign of Den the lack of an independent entrance to the pit meant that the mastaba could only be erected after the funeral; thereafter a descending staircase from outside permitted the construction of the entire installation before the death of the owner. Early experimentation threw up forms which proved ephemeral: an internal stepped core encased within the massif of the rectangle, or a row of modelled bull's heads on a projecting platform running round the mastaba. The use of niching on the external walls survived longer (E), but by the beginning of the Second Dynasty niches were obsolescent, save for two which marked offering places on the east face. Sometimes a small edicule might be placed on top of the mastaba **(fig. 2)**. Typical of the rectangular enclosures of the Archaic Period, attested by sealings, are a series of so-called "desert palaces," large mud-brick enclosures in the desert at Abydos (F). Each of the First Dynasty kings seems to have erected one but, beyond an educated guess that they fulfilled some sort of mortuary function, we have no idea of their purpose.

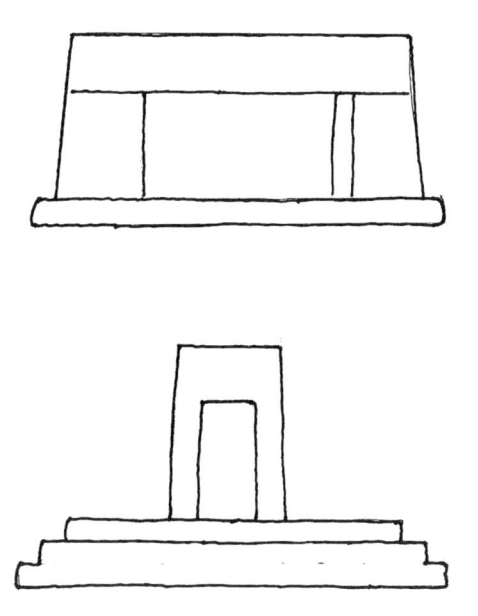

Figure 2 Schematized renderings of mastabas from hieroglyphic determinatives.

From the beginning security seems to have been an issue. The extensive use of mud brick during the First Dynasty ensured a degree of permanence a mound of earth could not provide; by the close of the dynasty stone had been introduced in the form of a portcullis-slab let down to block the descending staircase after the burial (G). Archaeology has revealed little of the development of mortuary architecture during the Second Dynasty. The tombs of Peribsen and Khasekhemwy at Abydos continue to use mud brick for a complex of subterranean chambers, but the superstructures have been destroyed. At Saqqara two large rock-cut hypogea of over seventy rooms and over 125 meters long, were cut south of the Step Pyramid, and to judge from sealings these mark the tombs of Ra-nebi and Ny-neter of the early Second Dynasty. Their superstructures, however, have not survived.

The true impact of Khasekhemwy's violent solution to the tendency to dissent among certain elements in the Egyptian state, and thus to harm the union of the Two Lands, can best be seen in the monumental accomplishment of his successor Djoser, whom Manetho assigns as head of a new Dynasty, the Third. Until Djoser the ideology of the royal tomb had interpreted the structure as the simulacrum of the palace, reproduced in the most durable materials available. The attraction of the idea of an Afterlife with the sun had superimposed on the palace notion the concept of the mastaba as a "place of ascent." The unresolved union of two lands, however, insisted that there be two "places of ascent," one at Abydos, the other at Memphis.

Djoser brought completion to the half measures of the Archaic Period by a revolutionary advance, both on ideological and technological fronts. Undoubtedly he was aided by his general factotum, "the seal-bearer . . . hereditary prince and high-priest of the sun-god" Imhotpe, who may well have been responsible for the major innovations of the reign. On the plateau of the western desert at Saqqara, overlooking Memphis, he constructed a vast enclosure 544 by 277 meters, reproducing the contemporary mud-brick enclosure of the White Fort itself (H). In the process of construction it seems Djoser's builders had to remove some earlier tombs, but they piously secreted their contents in subterranean galleries on site. Within the enclosure were two sets of underground, rock-cut passages (I) and two burial shafts and chambers, and two buildings encorporating heraldic designs of Upper and Lower Egypt. The new "union" of the Two Lands was now reflected in concrete fashion in the physical union of south and north within the confines of the complex: the Abydene and Saqqara tombs were now brought together. The tomb superstructure was planned to cover the northern of the two shafts, and was originally designed as an enormous mastaba which, in the course of construction, was twice expanded slightly. The planners were clearly groping after something, but it was not until this stage that they made a break with the past and a quantum leap into the future. Rejecting the old palace simulacrum as the basis for the royal tomb design, Imhotpe placed four mastabas, each diminishing in dimensions from the one beneath, upon the original tomb; and not content therewith, expanded the base and added two new tiers to create a six-staged *step pyramid* (J). For increased stability the core of the structure was built in stacks of blocks sloping inwards. The superstructure now resembled a giant staircase mounting to the heavens, and, when cased in polished limestone reflecting the sunlight, became a veritable "staircase of light" upon which the deceased king could mount up to his father the sun. The entry to the subterranean apartments of the Step Pyramid comprised a sloping shaft entering on the north side, and pointing upwards to the circumpolar stars, "those who know not destruction."

From the standpoint of technology the Step Pyramid complex also represents a break with the past. Stone had been used sparingly in construction during the Archaic Period—the erection of a small temple entirely of stone by Khasekhemwy was considered a red-letter event—but Imhotep and his architects handled limestone with a limited degree of confidence. Everything within the complex, buildings, surrounding walls, and the pyramid itself, was built of limestone, albeit with block units of manageable size. Pillars in stone occur with relative frequency, though each is attached to a support wall by a "tongue"-wall, as though the architect doubted how much weight a free-standing column could bear (K). Two curious features of the architecture are bound to impress the viewer. First, the inspiration for architectural form derives from the type of construction in light materials with which the builders are familiar. Columns reproduce plant forms, picket fences (L), door-posts (M), and log ceilings (N) are done in stone, even the enclosure wall shows seep-holes of practical use only in mud-brick construction. Second, only the temple on the north side of the pyramid is a functional structure, designed for the worship of Djoser by his priesthood. The vast majority of the remaining buildings have solid cores of rubble: they are "dummy" buildings of use to the spirit world, not that of the living.

The step pyramid form provides a bridge to what was to come in the Fourth Dynasty; but it also inspired Djoser's immediate successors, four or five in number, of the Third Dynasty. Each attempted to emulate their great forefather by planning their own step pyramid with enclosure, but none lived long enough to complete their work. They maintained Memphis as a residence, and their chosen burial sites continued to be Saqqara or its immediate environs. Only the last of their number, "Huny" as he was later known—the original name is still debated—decided to move far afield.

Advances in Pyramid Construction

Huny's choice for both residence and pyramid site fell on a spot some fifty kilometers south of Saqqara known today as Meidum (after a palace Thutmose I constructed there one thousand years later). The monument he began remains today a most enigmatic structure (O). It seems to have been planned as a seven-staged (later eight) step pyramid, but subsequently, so the conventional theory runs, suffered transformation to a true pyramid by having the steps filled in. The problem, however, is that the Meidum structure does not resemble a pyramid, either step or true, an embarrassment which necessitates a corollary to the theory, viz. that an enormous amount of masonry must somehow be missing. Today the "pyramid" looks like a truncated obelisk set on a podium with sloping sides, and such it may have been intended to look like from the beginning. Since the obelisk is a cultic form intimately associated with sun worship, the preoccupation with solar worship and theology once again would rear its head.

Huny was succeeded not by his legitimate son and heir, but by a son by a lesser wife, named Snofru. Although he contributed minimally to the completion of his father's monument, Snofru's name came to be associated with the Meidum pyramid to the extent that visiting dignitaries throughout the New Kingdom mistakenly identified it as his burial place. But in reality Snofru had plans of his own and to carry them out he moved his court back to a spot on the southern fringes of Saqqara called Dahshur.

At Dahshur Snofru erected not one, but two massive pyramids on a north-south axis, separated from each other by two kilometers. In terms of sheer volume of masonry the Dahshur pyramids place Snofru first of all Old Kingdom kings in size of construction; but the reason why two were required is not entirely clear. The southern of the two, called by moderns the "Bent Pyramid," shows a change in the angle of incline from fifty-four degrees in the lower part to forty-three degrees midway up the side (P). This curious fact has been often explained by assuming that the architects, during the course of construction, realized that such a steep incline would result in collapse if it were carried through, and therefore prudently changed course. But the point of change in the incline is so regular and so skillfully made that there can be no doubt that the bent shape was intended from the beginning. The fact that the Bent Pyramid, with its limestone casing, has a whitish hue, while its northern neighbor glows red, can only be interpreted as the contrast between white for the southern crown and red for the northern. (In fact, preoccupation with the contrast appears in one of the annalistic year rectangles preserved for Snofru on the Palermo Stone).

Snofru's long forty-eight-year reign constituted a turning point in the history of Egypt. The late King-list tradition, mindful of this fact, dutifully begins a new dynasty, the Fourth, at this point. Snofru's family was large, and many of his older children appear to have predeceased him. It was in fact a younger son, perhaps the last surviving offspring, of his chief queen Hetepheres, that finally succeeded him. This son, named Khnum-khuf-w(y), would make his name live forever as *Khufu* (Greek *Cheops*), builder of the largest pyramid ever constructed, the Great Pyramid of Giza.

As his father had done, Khufu uprooted his court and, while some of his cousins continued to reside and be buried at Dahshur, moved thirty kilometers to the north, to a site on the west of the Nile called Giza. His pyramid, called "Khufu-is-a-Horizon-Dweller" (Egyptian *Khufu-akhty*), was planned for the edge of the cliffs, while a residence city was constructed in the alluvial plain below. Today a suburb of Cairo, Giza is located at the point where the Valley debouches into the Delta; and from the north-east corner of Khufu's pyramid the plains of Lower Egypt are visible to the north, and the valley of the Nile to the east. No better location could be conceived to convey the notion of the "Balance of the Two Lands," and to illustrate the role of Pharaoh in uniting all Egypt. Two of Khufu's sons and a grandson occupied the Giza residence for over a century, turning the site into a hub of activity and a rival to Memphis and Saqqara.

The Great Pyramid (Q) is a monument to technological skill and organization of man power. Scarcely eighty years had passed since the architects of Djoser had launched into the unknown realm of stonemasonry, and now their descendants were confident masters of the medium. Quarrymen were adept at extracting, not only sandstone and limestone, but also stones of all types including basalt, diorite, and granite. Copper chisels and saws, hardened by annealing, and dolorite hand hammers were used with great success on even the hardest stone. Transport of stone from quarry to work-site involved sledges dragged by oxen or gangs of men along lubricated slip-ways. Ramps and possibly wooden fixtures were used in raising the stones, averaging two tons in the Great Pyramid, although the exact placement and form remains conjectural. Engineers, cognizant of weight and pressure, could now construct relieving chambers or corbelled vaults, first seen in crude form in the Pyramid of Meidum (R), with breathtaking precision and grandeur. No longer were inclined stacks of core stones deemed to be necessary, as in Step-pyramids: now horizontal courses were used, cased in highly polished fine limestone from the quarries at Turah across the Nile.

The Fourth Dynasty: the Apogee of Royal Power

The king of Egypt had come a long way from his beginnings as a "Big Man" scarcely five centuries earlier. The kings of the early Fourth Dynasty, Khufu, his son Khafre **(fig. 3),** and his grandson Menkaure, had achieved a position of authority and personal wealth rarely if ever duplicated in later times. All power and authority resided in Pharaoh and was only delegated to his officials. A person who secludes himself in his palace and is but rarely seen, yet who can at a mere word cause a giant monument to appear on the western cliffs, must have special attributes different from humankind. His superior intelligence and powers of enunciation were actually deified in the form of the gods *Sia* (intelligence) and *Hu* (authoritative utterance), and he was accorded the title "the Perfect God," or "the Great God." From the Third Dynasty the king's name was written in a horizontal oval symbolizing the world, to indicate that his jurisdiction was not narrowly confined but embraced the whole earth. The central and supreme position occupied by Pharaoh in the political and social structure of ancient Egypt is nicely summed up in the pithy response of a New Kingdom vizier to an imagined question: "Who is the King of Upper and Lower Egypt? He is a god by whose actions people live, the

© Sandro Vannini/CORBIS

Figure 3 Head and shoulders of diorite statue of Khafre.

© Archivo Iconografico, S.A./CORBIS

Figure 4   Statue of Khafre.

father and mother of all men, alone, by himself without equal"; and again ". . . (he is) the good shepherd who enlivens his host, the father and mother of everybody."

Such a god on earth has advanced far beyond the status of a leader on the battlefield, and now sits in holy splendor within his palace **(fig. 4).** His person was so divine that he could be approached only by people of royal blood who, like himself, shared in the divine essence and exuded divine power **(fig. 5).** So his personal servants, valets, butlers, barbers, hair-dressers, stewards of wardrobe, toiletries, and the like came from the extended royal family. Since Pharaoh was a god of the highest potency, everything he came into contact with would receive his divine essence, and thus become a holy thing in its own right, deserving of worship: his clothing and jewelry, his crowns and headdresses, his throne, carrying chair and sunshades, even his razor!

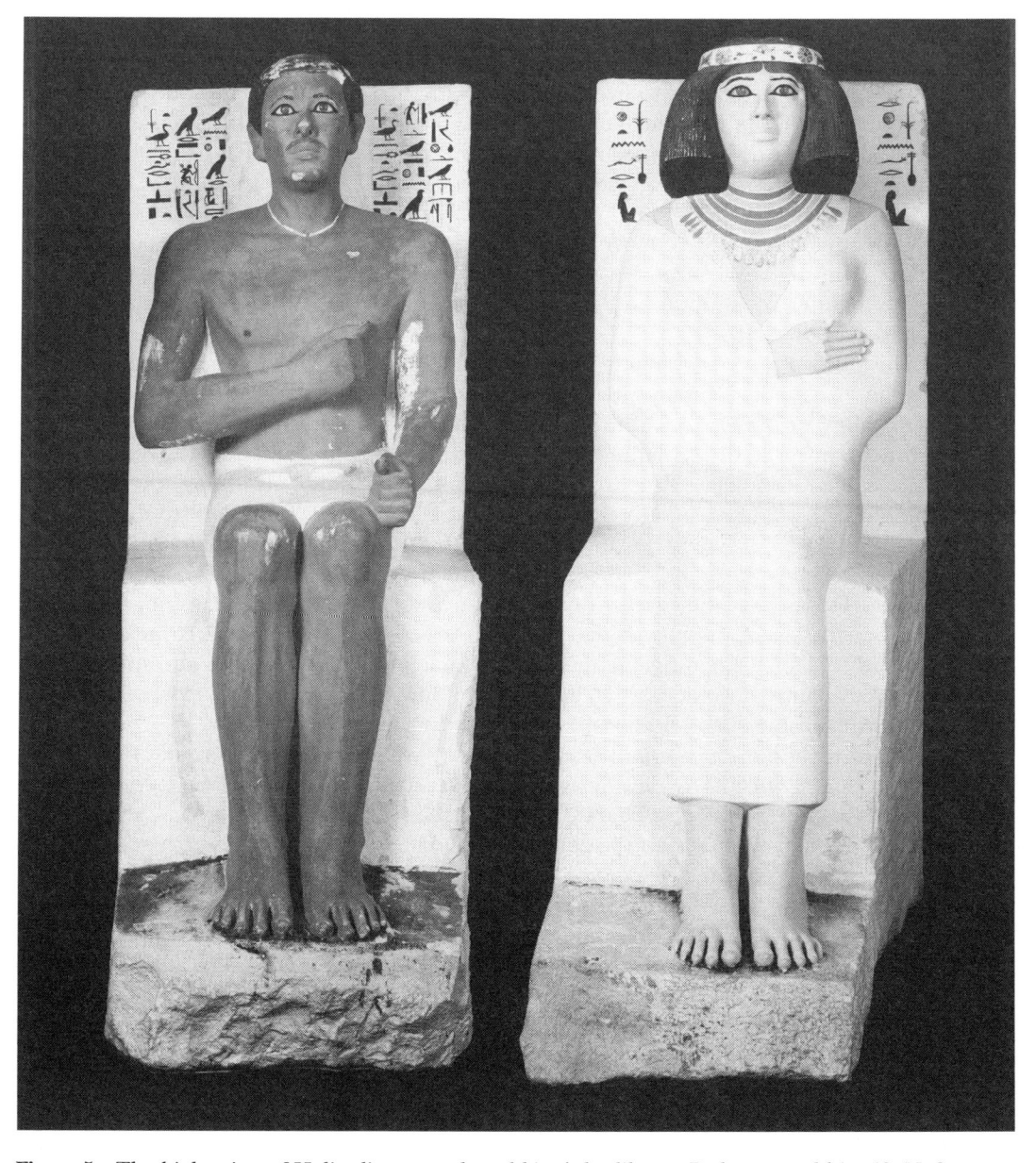

© Sandro Vannini/CORBIS

Figure 5   The high-priest of Heliopolis, general, and king's bodily son Ra-hotpe and his wife Nofret; probably cousins of Khufu.

It would be wrong, however, to view Pharaoh as an unprincipled autocrat. His exalted status had turned him into an ideal figure, masking the individual in the guise of a stereotype which he was obliged at all times to live up to. The king had to suppress his individuality and perhaps his imagination in deference to the ideal. By the end of the Fourth Dynasty traditional procedure and the royal stereotype had caught the Egyptian monarchy in an ever tightening grip from which it was never quite able to free itself. Not that the king wished to liberate himself: the whole system was imbued with a suasion directed towards urging the Pharaoh to don the mask and act exactly as the role demanded. When the Greeks became familiar with Egypt in the 6th through 4th centuries B.C. they found the kings of the time behaving quite innocently in the manner royal tradition demanded, and branded their antics, especially on the battlefield, as "mindless acts."

One constraint placed on the king's actions emanated from the realm of law. From early prehistoric times Egyptian communities had fashioned a customary procedure which in historic time is called variously "laws of the township" or "laws of the land." Complementing this local law for the purpose of regulating the state at large, was the "royal law" (Egyptian "*king's commands*"), edicts promulgated by each Pharaoh and over time constituting a vast body of what we would call "statute law." For the most part the state wisely refrained from overriding local custom, if it did not in any way interfere with the needs of the central authority. But in cases of serious crimes those indicted could be hauled off to Memphis, to stand trial in the "Broad Hall of Horus," i.e. the royal tribunal. As far as we know the Egyptians never drew up a law-code, but they were mightily concerned with precedent; and in legal contexts we find them constantly citing earlier judgements from far back in time, all recorded and stored in the archives. Pharaoh himself would have to be facing an imminent and present threat to the state to justify his overturning such binding precedent.

Closely tied to, and even informing, legal attitudes was the Egyptian concept of *ma'at,* one of the most difficult concepts to identify by a single translation. To the ancient Egyptians *ma'at* meant "truth, reality, justice, right dealing, order, proper management," a range of meanings spanning politics, society, and even the cosmos itself. The gods, guarantors of peace, prosperity, and security, were said to "live" on *ma'at* as though it were part of their very nature; and every morning at dawn, as the god's shrine was opened, a figurine of the goddess *ma'at* with a feather on her head would be presented to the divine image. The king was expected to conform all his actions to the demands of this concept, and he demanded a like adherence from his judicial officials: "[judging] according to *ma'at* before all men" is what is required. The just official was characterized as "one who inspires love of himself (in others), who does what will be useful in the future, one with initiative who carries through what he is told (to do), one in whom there is no moral lack." Nowhere was the word *ma'at* ever succinctly defined by the Egyptians, but this was not necessary. Like such overriding concepts as "democracy" or "liberty" in our culture, *ma'at* and its counterpart *gereg,* "disorder, falsehood," were known intuitively by everyone who had been brought up in the Egyptian way of life.

Pharaoh's Government

The civil service of Egypt was now a smooth-running machine. To a great degree it had "modernized" itself. After the reign of Djoser the organization of the state around great mud-brick enclosures which concentrated manpower was abandoned, and new structures and redistribution of authority signalled a striving for centralization and greater efficiency.

The two highest offices under the king in the Fourth Dynasty were the vizier or prime minister, and the chief of all construction work of the king. Both were royal relatives, accountable directly to Pharaoh. The vizier for his part had the general oversight of all the departments of government, except construction, and supervised the "Six Great Halls" a sort of high court. He was also responsible, as a kind of mayor, for the "Pyramid City" of the reigning monarch, usually located adjacent to the pyramid construction site to house the scribes, engineers, skilled craftsmen, and various support staff working on the tomb. The chief of all construction work of the king, formally independent of the vizier's authority, supervised all activity having to do with the construction of the pyramid and its temples, the training of craftsmen, and the conscription of unskilled labor.

The government departments, known collectively as the "Offices of the Residence," present us with an organization with the complexity of a beehive. Most of our evidence as to how it worked comes from the large number of official titles which office holders display in their tomb reliefs and biographies, especially from the close of the Fourth Dynasty. These can be divided into two types, function-designations indicating what an official actually did in his job, and titles of rank (Egyptian "standing") reflecting his position in the hierarchy. One is impressed by the number of scribes, ranked in a complex pecking order, and constituting a chancery. This "support staff" is present in all departments, recording everything, writing letters and memoranda, doing the accounts, keeping inventory and conscription lists, and filing reports. One set of papyrus documents, which has survived from the mortuary temple of Neferirkare (Fifth Dynasty) shows us the complexity of scribal book-keeping: the cache includes a duty table for the coming month for everyone employed, daily records of income, a one month account table, salary sheets for the month, an account of expenditures, and an inventory of furniture! As one would expect under a dynasty devoted to construction on a gargantuan scale, the Department of Manpower looms large in importance. While skilled professions centered upon ateliers which doubled as schools, and were maintained at royal expense, unskilled labour was provided by the male population of Egypt, who were obliged to work off part of their obligation to the state in manual labour. The work force was drawn from all over the country, and was usually organized in gangs of ten men with a foreman. Service was organized on a tri-monthly, rotating system, each gang being on call for one quarter of the calendar year. While in the quarries or at the construction site, the men were outfitted and given sandals at state expense, and there is good evidence that Pharaoh even provided medical attention. Other departments might be called "production units." The "House of the Plow" was a general term for the department concerned with food production, the "House of the Weavers" produced cloth, the "House of Herdsmen of the Residence" functioned as a Department of livestock. The Department of Revenue and Storage included the Granary, Treasury, and the Repository of Royal Luxury Goods and provided storage for the riches accruing to the state through taxation, rents, and trade.

We know less about the taxation system of the Old Kingdom than that of the period of empire, a thousand years later, but enough evidence remains to draw the following picture. The general term for "tax" in the Old Kingdom, *medjed,* comes from a root meaning to "draw tight, to adhere to," and quite properly conveys the sense of unavoidable obligation. The tax on edibles, especially wheat and barley, was deemed most important by the state, which sent boats to collect it. The managers of the many plantations and farms throughout Egypt were obliged to appear before the vizier once a year at the "Great Reckoning," to have their accounts audited; and if malfeasance were detected, they could be given a beating (s). A good deal of the tax was transmuted into labour for the state. Besides the construction work described above, the population (even the priests!) was liable to transporting goods ("porterage"), agricultural labour in the fields, and service in local temples.

The above description applies mainly to the Residence and the Memphite district, and stresses correctly the high degree of centralization of the Fourth Dynasty: the outlying districts were important only for revenue and recruitment. Already in the First Dynasty attempts had been made to subdivide Upper and Lower Egypt for ease of administration, and by the Third the process was complete. Upper Egypt was divided into twenty-two townships (or nomes), each centering upon a large town within its boundaries; Lower Egypt was similarly divided into fifteen townships, later increased to twenty. Many of the township emblems borrow from animals and symbols of royal power; and while some recall prehistoric signs, the townships themselves are artificial creations, not relics of prehistoric bailiwicks. Each division received a number of officials representing the central authority: a territory-director, a superintendent of commissions, a king's business agent to name but a few. In the Delta the title "overseer" of a township was common.

Social Class and the Reward System

In a pre-industrial economy not created by notions of consumerism and profits, and without the necessary concomitants of increased production and a burgeoning group of workers-*cum*-consumers, it is meaningless to speak of middle class, working class, *bourgeoisie,* and the like. The position one occupied in the hierarchical ordering of human society in the Egyptian "beehive" depended on one's *function* (*iȝt,* "office"), coupled with *hereditary rights.* The Egyptians could distinguish status by other categories, e.g. between urban and rural, those with power and those without, "Egyptianness" and "foreignness," humanity vs. divinity. But none of these distinctions informed the *ranking* system (*ʿḥʿw),* the "pecking order," reflected literally in where one stood before the king.

In such a system functionaries at court accounted for the top ranks. The extended royal family comprised a body from which the highest agents of royal power could be chosen. Surrounding them was a trained hereditary elite who operated as "civil servants" *(srw)* and could be found through the realm and abroad. Courtiers and hangers-on, at the periphery of the society of the "Residence City," received such courtesy titles as "unique friend" or "king's gentleman" *(šps-nsw)* or "king's jewel" *(ḫkrt-nsw*—ladies only).

Outside the immediate circle of the court were the "support staffs" (called *smdt* in later times). Not surprisingly in a country potentially rich in food stocks, those concerned with food production, gardeners, bakers, brewers, should have occupied an essential, though low ranking position. In the provinces plantations and "new towns" were administered by managers who, though they may have enjoyed status locally, counted for little when they made the annual journey to the Residence for the great audit. Although there were some freehold tenants, the vast mass of the population in the countryside bore the lable *mrt,* "unskilled labor," a class of person tied to the land and liable for the draft for construction projects. Of slightly higher status were the "resident aliens" (*ʿw*), mainly from the south, who had either been brought to Egypt as the result of hostilities, or had voluntarily offered their services to Pharaoh *(nḥsyw ḥtpw).* They were employed as military auxiliaries and agricultural or construction workers. Skilled craftsmen, sculptors, painters, carpenters, smiths, masons, were essential to the kind of high culture represented by Pharaoh and his court, but they appear not to have been honored as we might have expected.

Such a tightly-organized society would have suffered break-down in short order if its creators had not seen the need for flexibility and incentive. One cannot maintain such a system by coercion alone. In their biographical inscriptions civil servants of the Old Kingdom time and again state openly that their proudest moment was when the king favored them for a job well done. The favor could take the form of verbal commendation in a court setting—"His Majesty praised me for it more than anything"—coupled with physical rewards of costly jewelry. Throughout most of the periods of Egyptian history the reward system occupied a central position in Pharaoh's dealings with his officials; and the numerous expeditions to the eastern desert and Sinai to fetch gold and turquoise must be seen against the backdrop of this common practice.

Pharaoh's Sphere of Foreign Influence

As it had done within Egypt, Khasekhemwy's victory unleashed in dramatic fashion the energies of Egypt abroad. Expeditions numbering prospectors and miners, each led by a seal-bearer of the king, a royal plenipotentiary, ranged far and wide south and north. The insatiable appetite of the state for minerals led to the opening up of turquoise mines (T) at Wady Mughara in the Sinai, and perhaps copper mines elsewhere in the peninsula. In the south the granite quarries at Elephantine (U) and the diorite quarries of Nubia to the south were extensively worked; and an Egyptian settlement to tap copper deposits was established at Buhen at the Second Cataract. At Byblos on the Phoenician coast (V) a similar entrepot was set up (W), with the agreement of the local population with whom the Egyptians enjoyed friendly relations for centuries. Through Byblos Pharaoh had access to the cedar timber (X) Egypt needed for ship-building, flag-staves, and roofing, as well as oil and resin used in embalming. From Khasekhemwy's reign on until the close of the Old Kingdom it became customary for the king to make donations of fine unguents and aromatics in alabaster jars and other trinkets of jewelry to the shrine of the local Ba'al at Byblos.

It is important to note that Egypt's relations with the Sudan and Western Asia, while carried on from a position of commercial and military superiority, could not be characterized as "imperial." No governors were sent abroad, no garrisons implanted on foreign soil. In fact Egypt operated within a sphere of influence. Egypt knew what it wanted in foreign parts, and so did the locals; if the latter had their own self-interest at heart, they would co-operate with the Egyptians and trade or hand over their goods. Pharaoh would then be inclined to reward them with gifts, and count them as "being on his water," the Egyptian expression for loyalty. From the highlands of Jerusalem in the south to Ebla in north Syria, Pharaoh did not distinguish among the foreign rulers: they were all prostrate at his feet. From time to time it was brought home to these foreign chiefs that it might be expedient to dispatch delegations to Memphis; and boatloads of Asiatics are sometimes depicted in the art of the time, arriving at the jetty with hands raised in adoration of Pharaoh.

Relations were not always amicable of course. A foreign enclave might feel sure of its impregnable location, and defy the Egyptians. Then a punitive expedition would be sent out from Egypt to "hack up town so-and-so," and make an example of them to other would-be dissidents (Y). Such an occasion for punishment might also provide the excuse for uprooting the population in the Egyptian version of a "slave raid"; for Pharaoh craved not only foreign goods but foreign manpower as well. Thus in one raid Snofru's troops brought back from Nubia 7,000 prisoners and 200,000 cattle, and in an un-named reign of the same Fourth Dynasty 17,000 Nubians were forcibly seized and brought north to Memphis. Once inside Egypt the Nubians, now called "pacified southerners," would be put to various tasks including agricultural work and service as auxiliaries in the army.

Artificial Consistency in the Belief System: Syncretism

It would be extremely foolish to insist that the Egyptians were not possessed of the faculty to reason logically. Yet can this thesis be maintained in the face of the much-noised contradictions of Egyptian religion? Yes, if we realize that the contradictions occur only when the various Egyptian cults are forcibly combined. Within the context of a single cult harmony must generally have reigned. One may with justification ask how the travelling Egyptian reacted when, upon visiting his kin in the next nome, he discovered a god, a cult, and a mythology diametrically at odds with his own. In fact it must be pointed out that extensive travelling was not undertaken by the majority of Egyptians. But if and when they did go abroad, we may imagine that they would have reacted in either of two ways. On the one hand they might have taken umbrage, and treated the cult of the neighboring nome as anathema. This is precisely what in many cases must actually have happened! The evidence from classical authors bearing upon inter-nome strife, based on the enmity between cults, is too numerous to be ignored. That it did not plunge the country into a state of perpetual anarchy is the measure of the strong, centralized government which had succeeded more or less in uniting Egyptians.

The second postulated reaction of our travelling Egyptian upon coming face to face with religious views in direct conflict with his own, would be to try to see common ground beneath the two sets of tenets and then to harmonize the contradictory dogma. Again, such harmonization is attested; but it must be admitted that such a sober reaction on the part of the masses must have been relatively rare. There are several examples of harmonization at a very early and fundamental level of understanding. As the king in life was ever present throughout the length and breadth of Egypt as an ineffable Life-force, so the king-in-death enjoyed a universal presence unconfined by time and space. He had drowned in the Nile thus bestowing fertility upon the river, and the passion of the great dying and revivified numen of fertility could be celebrated anywhere: he was the great fundament of the reality of the supernatural. And so at many sites Osiris subtly but firmly established himself and the local shrine could, *mutatis mutandis,* be identified as an Osireion, the site of Osiris' death and burial. The mind of the devotee naturally balked at the enormity of the contradiction inherent if this state of things were accepted at face value, and so an explanation was sought. The myth of the gods provided a means. According to the myth, Seth had murdered Osiris. Now he not only murders him, but chops the body into a number of pieces and scatters them far and wide. Isis, upon finding each piece, erects a shrine on the spot and staffs it with a priesthood; and thus does the plethora of Osireions find a rational explanation. Another example of harmonization is to be found in the well-known proclivity of the Egyptians to identify gods of like character in that they seemed to share a basic essence. There must at one time have been many falcon cults up and down the Nile valley, which later merged with the Horus cult, their gods being identified with Horus and their names surviving as mere epithets. In cases where several deities were obviously of the same type, but whose cults would not suffer their individuality to be impaired, recourse was had to aetiology. The Eye of Re brought back by Shu and Thoth transforms herself as she descends the river into a number of forms: a vulture at El Kab, the vulture Mut at Thebes, the cow Hathor at Dendereh, etc. Thus are explained the many cults of "mother"-goddesses throughout Upper Egypt: they are specific, historical manifestations of a single goddess.

But the tendency towards harmonizing the disparate elements in Egyptian religion was characteristic, in the main, of the intelligentsia. Egyptians, like many peoples, were well aware that attempts to express the essence and attributes of the supernatural were ill served by words. Ineffable qualities could only be approximated in speech. And as long as that meta-language does not promote figures of speech *per se* to the status of doctrine, contradiction among metaphors can be glossed over as illusory in several ways. On the one hand, myth can be degraded to the status of simile and extended metaphor, at best to a kind of literary-mystical image charged with an undefined potency. The various names of the sun-god—Atum, Khepry, Re, Harakhte—are not in conflict, but are merely ways of expressing or of stressing some particular aspect of deity; the variant versions of the creation myth are not contradictory, but are merely alternate means of conveying such abstractions as the primacy of the creator, his concern for mankind, his goodness, his omniscience, etc. Again: given the implicit faith in magic spells, the very sounds themselves of which a statement about the supernatural is made up can take on an undefined mystical potency, regardless of whether one statement is logically consonant with the next. Finally, admission that the power the supernatural by definition disposed of could operate for good or ill led thinkers to positing "worst-case scenarios." Osiris, Horus, Thoth, and others were conceived as beneficent in the context of the cult and myth; but suppose they should turn against us for some reason we do not understand? Thus imprecations are available to be hurled at these very deities in the event that they should appear on the scene "in this their evil coming." The sophistication of such thinking must be insisted upon; this is the rationalization of the intellectual, not the simple faith of the peasant. Moreover it is pursuant to the creation and amalgamation of myth; it is not characteristic of the creative, mythopoeic mind.

Since it is from the ruling class that our religious texts come, they must be viewed in the light of this proclivity to harmonize conflicting traditions. They will, then, contain material which is as old as Egypt herself, concepts shared by both king and commoner; but these beliefs will be modified in the interests of a central, ruling authority, and treated in a way different from their acceptance at a parochial level. They will be harmonized in an effort to make them convey truth which to the writer will be consistent and universal.

The King as Perfect God and Man

The mythology of kingship was an intellectual response to the new phenomenon of a nation state and all the problems of rationale which that entailed. It was inevitable that the Egyptians should respond to these problems, and their answers were for the most part consciously formulated. The rise of Re and his cult, which we are about to discuss, may also smack of the inevitable, but its coming about was more gradual and furtive.

The struggle to unite Egypt had produced a theocracy as absolute as it was imaginative. The king of Egypt emerged from the strife a tested and proven god, towering over his subjects. His words, as soon as they emerged from his mouth, assumed a creative force in a more than metaphorical sense. He could with but a monosyllabic injunctive despatch thousands to war, to the quarry, to the harvest, to the dikes, to the pyramid site. Without ever quitting his palace he could cause the enemy to fall in multitudes, stone to come from the mountains hundreds of miles away, grain to heap up in the granaries, ditches and basins to appear all over the valley, and a primordial pyramidal shape, "the Horizon of the God," to rise on the edge of the desert. Everyone worshipped him and dared not utter his name from Nubia to the distant marshes of the Delta. The sand-crossers, the barbarian bowmen, and the vile Asiatics stood in awe of him too. He was rarely seen by his people outside the precincts of his palace, and when he did venture abroad his appearance in the glory of his regalia was likened to the rising of the sun. What majesty! What divine power! What perfection of design! A god without equal lived on earth to order the affairs of Mankind!

And yet, a lingering memory of the ruler as a *man,* albeit a big one, lingered on in the thinking of the Egyptians and manifested itself in a festival called by the word *sed,* or "tail." While the reference is probably to the bull's tail which kings often wore, the festival took the form of a "jubilee," a re-affirmation of the right to rule. The rites can be traced back to the reign of Hor-Aha, if not before—they predate the introduction of Osiris theology—and may have been devised even earlier, when a public display of supernatural approbation was required to re-confirm the ruler's authority. We can trace the festival down to the latest period of native Egyptian history, and it is even mentioned in Ptolemaic times. The Greeks translated the term as the "Thirty-year Festival," and whenever throughout history evidence is full enough, the jubilee is seen to have coincided with the king's thirtieth year on the throne, with only a few exceptions.

Essentially the festival was an act of rejuvenation whereby the king's powers were restored, and the coronation was re-enacted to acquire the blessing of the gods. To that end a complex of temporary structures (z), including reed-shrines for the gods, a robing room, a podium with two thrones, and a race course, was laid out at Memphis and the gods and their priests summoned from all over Egypt. The ceremonies opened with a procession of the gods and their standards and the entire court in train, the king wearing a special cloak and riding in a palanquin. Over the next several days the king, accompanied by a lector-priest, i.e. a priest responsible for reading the hymns and incantations from a scroll containing the order-of-service, would visit the reed shrines in turn, beginning with those of the Upper Egyptian gods, to obtain the blessing and permission of each to continue his rule. At the conclusion of this section of the liturgy, he would proceed to the podium and be crowned with the white crown. The same procedure would be followed with the gods of Lower Egypt, culminating in a donning of the red crown **(fig. 6)**.

At some point in the ceremony, the king would be obliged to run a race, perhaps only a quick-step, around the four sides of a square court. In his hand he held a small document, the deed in fact to the land of Egypt, called "the Secret of the Two Partners (Horus and Seth)," or the "Testament of my Father." As he ran he chanted: "I have run holding the 'Secret of the Two Partners,' the will which my father has given me before Geb. I have passed through the land and touched its four sides. I run through it as I desire!" The symbolism seems clear: the race course is Egypt, if not the world; the "Testament of my Father" is the king's enabling document, permitting continued rule. By running through the world with the testament in his hand, the king takes formal possession of his inheritance and re-affirms his right to rule.

Figure 6 Jubilee pavillion, showing the king (re)-crowned as King of Upper and Lower Egypt.

The *sed*-festival also gave the king the opportunity to show forth and distribute his largesse, a sure sign that the gods are favoring him. Vast amounts of beef, fowl, vegetables, beer, wine, and confections were brought into the royal pantries and kitchens; and each night after the conclusion of the ceremonies, the royal family would feast the assembled multitude at Pharaoh's expense. No wonder that the popular blessing expressed the wish that the king live long enough to celebrate many jubilees!

The Cult of the Sun-god Re

But the brilliant discovery of theocratic absolutism could not remain earthbound. As the picture of the dead king, embalmed and beatified and resting in his "horizon" had given rise to the mythological figure of Osiris, so the phenomenon of the pharaonic monarchy was translated to the heavens. The Pharaoh had a heavenly counterpart; his court and palace had exact parallels above. As there were earthly courtiers and chamberlains, royal secretaries and messengers, so there were celestial beings who fulfilled these functions in heaven. The etiquette of the terrestrial court was the etiquette of heaven, the administrative procedure of one was that of the other. The logical candidate for the position of king in the court above was obviously the earthly king's predecessor, the king-in-death, the great god "Osiris." And it must be admitted that, for all time, at one register Osiris was to remain "the king of those who are (over) there," i.e. the dead. But by the middle of the third millennium another claimant for the honor of celestial king had emerged, viz. the sun.

When did the *mise en scene* become celestial? The process was a gradual one. By 2750 B.C. the unification of Egypt was complete, and the accession of Djoser marked an important advance in royal power. From the sheer size of his mortuary establishment one can tell that Djoser was a ruler who commanded vast resources; but it is the form his tomb took that tells most about the changes taking place in Egyptian thinking and in Egyptian art. As we have seen, Djoser chose as his chief minister the high-priest of the sun-god Re, a certain Imhotpe, who was undoubtedly responsible for the momentous changes in ideology that were about to take place. In place of the traditional mastaba he chose a stepped design of six diminishing tiers which, as pointed out above, approximated a staircase of light. More to the point: it also faithfully reproduced on a large scale the shape of the *benben*-stone, the most holy fetish in the temple of Re at Heliopolis. Upon this gigantic staircase, two hundred feet on a side, the soul of the deceased king would be able to mount to his eternal home in the sky.

References to Re and his cult and theophoric names encorporating solar terms do occur both before and immediately after Djoser, but by no means in significant numbers. If the use of the sacred fetish of the sun as mortuary prototype be taken as betokening the rising influence of the Re cult, it must be admitted that this first attainment was not followed up for over a century. The "Step Pyramid" form was retained and, as we have seen, soon developed into a true pyramid with smooth sides, but it served only to enhance the status of the absolute monarch. The largest pyramid ever built was completed within one hundred years of Djoser's death by King Khufu at Giza, a few miles north of Memphis. Nearly five hundred feet high, Khufu's monument contained over two million blocks of stone, the average weight of a single stone being between two and three tons. The mortuary temple and causeway which lay to the east of Khufu's pyramid were decorated with fine reliefs depicting mortuary rites and showing the king in the company of the gods. But the right to use such decoration was not extended to Khufu's nobles as it had been under his predecessors. Except for a small slab stela showing the deceased at his funerary meal, a piece of equipment as indispensable as our tombstone, the mastaba tombs of the nobility surrounding Khufu's pyramid were bare (AA–AB). The same restrictions were placed on the use of statuary. In the onomasticon of court and government officials it is rare to find a commoner of non-royal blood during this reign; and no royal plenipotentiary or expedition leader anywhere inside or outside of Egypt would dare to carve anything but Khufu's name, and that alone, in the official inscription that he left as record. This ruthless exclusion of any but royalty from the ranks of the privileged (a policy which continued under Khufu's second successor, Khafre) worked to the detriment of the great king's memory. In later times, some two thousand years after his death, he and his son were remembered as tyrants who had closed all the temples of the gods, and grievously oppressed their people.

The years during which Khufu and Khafre ruled could be viewed as an interlude of reaction when a rising "support staff," a species of aristocracy, was held in check, and when the incipient power of the sun cult was temporarily eclipsed. Difference in tomb design during this period suggest that ideas old and new were contending with one another: Djedef-re, Khufu's son and successor, moved away from Giza to the north and constructed a pyramid which in design is a throw-back to early forms. Curiously, the last king of the dynasty, Shepseskaf, reverted to the mastaba type of tomb! In light of the importance to the Egyptians of form and archetype, such changes are not without significance.

Ultimate victory, however, went to Re. Beginning sporadically in the later Fourth Dynasty, the title "son of the sun-god" was added to the royal titulary. Of the kings who reigned from the death of Khufu to the beginning of the Sixth Dynasty (c. 2350 B.C.), nine out of thirteen bear names compounded with Re. Six of the rulers of the Fifth Dynasty (c. 2500–2350 B.C.), the branch of the family which supplanted Khufu's immediate progeny, erected special shrines to Re adjacent to and often rivalling in size their own modest pyramids. Userkaf, the founder of this dynasty and distant relative of the last king of the Fourth Dynasty, seems even to have made provision for a sun cult within the precincts of his own pyramid temple. Although but legend, a story circulating five centuries after his death made him and his two successors offspring of the wife of a priest of Re, begotten by the sun god himself. What this disparate evidence shows is that for reasons we can today only guess at the king of Egypt was slowly losing his ideological pre-eminence, and had begun openly to defer to the cult and person of Re. With the end of the Fourth Dynasty the absolutism of Khufu's monarchy was broken: the restrictions on men of non-royal birth were eased and over time many were appointed to high office. The position of ultimate sovereign, high god of the universe, gravitated heavenward where it was assumed quite naturally by the sun-god.

The Royal Mortuary Temple

In light of the strong and well defined beliefs regarding the Afterlife and the requirements of the dead, it should be no surprise that from the end of the prehistoric period every tomb included in its physical lay-out provisions for the service of the dead. Initially the east side of the mastabas, featuring the two niches and offering table and facing the valley, dominated the planning of the grave. Both Qa'a and Djoser, however, attached complexes of rooms, undoubtedly for mortuary service, to the north face of their tombs. Down to the end of the Third Dynasty the tomb and associated buildings in a mortuary complex stood in isolation on the western cliffs; but beginning with the reign of Snofru access from the valley was provided by a causeway. At both Meidum and Dahshur a sloping corridor led up from a landing stage on a canal communicating with the Nile, to a small shrine located against the east face of the pyramid. Landing stage, causeway and shrine became from Snofru on elements which could not be omitted in the planning of any royal mortuary complex.

While Khufu's installation at Giza retained all these elements, it was with Khafre, his second successor, that the lay-out of the mortuary temple achieved a standard pattern rarely to be deviated from during the rest of the Old Kingdom. At the base of the cliffs a canal joining the Nile and a turning basin were excavated around which would take shape the Pyramid-city. Derived from the earlier landing-stage, a "Valley Temple" (AC) was constructed on the west side of the basin and provided with docks and cat-walks of stone, sloping down to the east, so that the structure could be used no matter what was the height of the water level. From the rear of the Valley Temple the causeway (AD) sloped up to the west to join an enlarged, formal temple built against the east face of the pyramid (AE). The temple featured a fore-hall open to the sky with surrounding colonnade, store-rooms, and staircases to the roof, as well as an offering place and five niches, apparently intended to receive statues of the king. Statuary was ubiquitous, both seated and standing. All were *ku*-statues of the king, designed to receive offerings. Statue groups, especially in the Giza mortuary temple of Menkaure (AF), Khufu's grandson, showed the king in company with the queen, or goddesses, in particular Hathor and personifications of the townships. Sometimes a pair of large standing stelae with the king's name inscribed on them would be set at the very base of the pyramid on the east side; but access to the burial chamber would almost always be found, via a sloping corridor, on the north face.

The planning of a mortuary complex, the "syntax" of room lay-out, ought to provide a guide to the type of worship and service carried on there. Djoser's mortuary temple is relatively large, with a number of rooms and places for offering and censing; but strangely the small installations of Huny and Snofru reflect only a rudimentary service. Conversely, the rapid expansion of the complex under Khufu and Khafre suggests a like expansion of the rituals to be performed there. Can we in any way reconstruct these rituals?

Fortunately two bodies of evidence are available, and in this section we shall deal with the more modest of the two. The papyri from the Fifth Dynasty mortuary temple of Neferirkare, mentioned earlier, give a very clear perspective of that for which the temple was used. Briefly put, the purpose was to serve the deceased king, whose body lay within the pyramid, and provide him with foodstuffs. Only about a dozen priests and an unknown number of assistants made up the staff, being housed in the local Pyramid-city. Their duties involved morning and evening offerings, and special offerings to the king and his mother on feast days; guarding the doors and supervising work-shops; night duty on the roof to observe the rising of stars and announce the passing of hours; ritual perambulation of the pyramid; transport of foodstuffs; paying salaries; taking inventory and keeping accounts. Thus the temple was a business as well as a place of worship. It disposed of an endowment, like any other mortuary cult, and was supported by the king's house.

The Pyramid Texts

The contention, strongly held in the early 19th century that the burial chambers of pyramids contained no inscriptions, was scotched when in the 1870s the pyramids of Pepy I and Merenre of the Sixth Dynasty were opened. Further investigation of pyramids of the same date proved that, from the reign of Wenis last king of the Fifth Dynasty, down to Aba of the Eighth, the burial chambers and corridors leading into them had been inscribed with hundreds of columns of hieroglyphic texts. Beautifully incised and filled with blue paste, the inscriptions are organized into approximately 750 "spells," each introduced by the rubric "words to be spoken," but the order of the spells does not correspond at first glance to an orderly sequence. The genres which can be identified in the corpus represent hymns, prayers, magical incantations, rituals of worship and daily and mortuary liturgies. But the whole is in a state of flux from reign to reign and, on what basis we know not, a criterion of selection is being applied: thus, some spells present in the Wenis corpus disappear under Tety who adds new material, and the same kind of winnowing and augmenting occurs in subsequent reigns. The Pyramid Texts were clearly not a collection of fossils, but a dynamic body of texts meeting immediate needs. They undoubtedly belong to the broad category of "beatification spells" which in scenes showing elite funerals the lector-priest with white sash is depicted reading from an open scroll. In the original papyrus the incantations would all have been in the first person, but in the Pyramid Texts, to avoid misuse by third parties, the name of the king in the third person has been inserted.

While all our copies date to the end of the Old Kingdom, some of the material is of great age. References to sand covering the corpse and to mud bricks recall modes of interment which had passed out of use centuries earlier. Moreover the dialect of the texts can be viewed as archaic (in some cases archaizing), lending credence to claims of antiquity.

Though debated in detail, the general thesis would be accepted today that the Pyramid Texts reflect the liturgies and rituals used in the preparation for death and on the day of the burial. They also constitute a sort of "missal" for use by the cult in the future worship of the deceased king. With their help we can visualize the ceremony: the arrival in the turning basin of the funeral ships, one transporting the coffin, ships that will be buried with the king around his pyramid; the preparation of the body in the Valley Temple and the first of many purifications; the slow movement of the funeral cortège bearing the royal sarcophagus up the causeway to the temple and pyramid. Before the numerous statues and relief representations, and even the mummy itself, a ceremony is performed, "The Opening of the Mouth" which will free the mouth and limbs of stone or embalmed flesh to enable the *ku* to ingest sustenance. Statues and the mummy are asperged with a solution of water and natron, and hooked implements are magically waved in front of the face. For the first time, in what will become a ritual for eternity, priests advance to the offering tables, one bearing the food and drink, the other intoning the formulae, and lay the edibles on the altars. Then they retire backwards, sweeping the ground clean of their footprints.

But the intent of the Pyramid Texts carries us beyond the grave. An overriding concern of the authors of these incantations is to get the deceased king to heaven and into the company of the sun-god Re, for the entire corpus smacks of the solar theology of Heliopolis. The texts imagine the king ascending on a ladder, being wafted up on the great clouds of incense, or being hoisted or pulled aloft by the gods themselves. What we might call "worst case scenarios" concern the lector priests deeply. What if some of the gods should baulk at helping the king to ascend, or actively bar his way? What if the king should find his path blocked by a body of water, the "Lily Lake," and the local ferryman reluctant to ferry him over? Magic and persuasion are called into play. Reluctant gods are threatened with the termination of their offerings, and the reluctant ferryman is both cajoled and subjected to name-dropping. Eventually the king arrives at the court of Re, but a new problem arises: what job can he do, for he must earn his keep? He will do anything from cleaning up, or bailing out the sun-boat, to entertaining the court with his dances! He hopes to be taken on as a secretary, and has no qualms about asking the sun-god to fire his present secretary!

Throughout the Pyramid Texts there runs that unspoken fear that the king may not be the influential fellow he claims to be, or that in spite of his preparations he may perish utterly in a second death. Many hymns contain the flat denial that he has died; no, he is only asleep and will shortly awaken. Can this be the same mighty Horus, the Perfect God, who united Egypt and by whose actions people live? Within the tomb ideological certainty gives way to a debilitating fear that even downsizes the god on earth. In an effort to ensure his immortality the priests attempt to identify him, limb by limb, with the corresponding limbs of the gods, or as a last resort with the person of the sun-god himself: "the king mounted to his horizon, he ascended to the sky, uniting with the sun-disc, the divine limbs coalescing with him that begat him."

Further Readings

On mortuary beliefs and practices, see W. Grajetzki, *Burial Customs in Ancient Egypt*, London, 2004; S. Ikram, *Death and Burial in Ancient Egypt*, London, 2003; S. Morenz, *Egyptian Religion*, Ithaca, 1973 (ch. 9); N. Kanawati, *The Tomb and its Significance in Ancient Egypt*, Cairo, 1987; S. Quirke, *Ancient Egyptian Religion*, London, 1992; M. Smith, *The Liturgy of Opening the Mouth for Breathing*, Oxford, 1993; A. J. Spencer, *Death in Ancient Egypt*, London, 1982; J. H. Taylor, *Death and the Afterlife in Ancient Egypt*, Chicago, 2001; L. V. Zabkar, *A Study of the BA Concept in Ancient Egyptian Texts*, Chicago, 1968.

Understandably the pyramids have given rise to an extensive literature. Among the better treatments are the following: I. E. S. Edwards, *The Pyramids of Egypt*, Harmondsworth, 1986; A. Fakhry, *The Pyramids*, Chicago, 1969; Z. Hawass, *The Pyramids of Ancient Egypt*, Pittsburgh, 1990; M. Lehner, *The Complete Pyramids: Solving the Ancient Mysteries*, London, 1997; M. Verner, *Forgotten Pharaohs, Lost Pyramids: Abusir*, Prague, 1994; *idem, The Pyramids, their Archaeology and History*, London, 2003; on the Giza sphinx, see C. Zivie-Coche, *Sphinx: History of a Monument*, Ithaca, 1997.

On the technological advances, see the relevant passages in A. Lucas, J. R. Harris, *Ancient Egyptian Materials and Industries,* London, 1989; P. T. Nicholson, I. Shaw (eds.), *Ancient Egyptian Materials and Technologies,* Cambridge, 2000.

Works on government and society include the following: C. Aldred, *Egypt to the End of the Old Kingdom,* London, 1965; G. Andreu, *Egypt in the Age of the Pyramids,* London, 1997; R. David, *The Pyramid Builders of Ancient Egypt,* London, 1986; N. Kanawati, *The Egyptian Administration in the Old Kingdom,* Warminster, 1977; *idem, Governmental Reforms in Old Kingdom Egypt,* Warminster, 1980; D. Jones, *An Index of Ancient Egyptian Titles, Epithets, and Phrases in the Old Kingdom,* Oxford, 2000; N. Strudwick, *The Administration of Egypt in the Old Kingdom,* London, 1985.

On Old Kingdom art, see C. Aldred, *Old Kingdom Art in Ancient Egypt,* London, 1949; *Egyptian Art in the Age of the Pyramids,* New York, 1999; W. S. Smith, *A History of Egyptian Sculpture and Painting in the Old Kingdom,* Boston, 1949.

On the king in death, see R. Anthes, in S. N. Kramer (ed.), *Mythologies of the Ancient World,* New York, 1961; J. H. Breasted, *The Development of Religion and Thought in Ancient Egypt,* New York, 1959; C. J. Eyre, *The Cannibal Hymn, a Cultural and Literary Study,* Liverpool, 2002; R. O. Faulkner, *Ancient Egyptian Pyramid Texts,* Oxford, 1969; on the solar cult, see S. Quirke, *The Cult of Ra: Sun-worship in Ancient Egypt,* London, 2001.

CHAPTER FIVE

The Collapse of the Old Kingdom and the Regime of Herakleopolis

ψ

Fifth Dynasty	
Userkaf	c. 2514–2507 B.C.
Sahure	c. 2507–2495 B.C.
Neferirkare	c. 2495–2475 B.C.
Shepseskare	c. 2475–2468 B.C.
Ra-neferef	c. 2468 B.C.
Ni-userre	c. 2468–2437 B.C.
Menkauhor	c. 2437–2429 B.C.
Djedkare Izezy	c. 2429–2397 B.C.
Unas	c. 2397–2367 B.C.

Sixth Dynasty	
Tety	c. 2367–2337 B.C.
Pepy I	c. 2337–2284 B.C.
Anty-em-saf I	c. 2284–2277 B.C.
Pepy II	c. 2277–2181 B.C.
Anty-em-saf II	c. 2181 B.C.
Nitokerty	c. 2180–2178 B.C.
Neferka "the Child"	c. 2178–2177 B.C.
Nefer	c. 2177–2176 B.C.
Aba	c. 2176–2172 B.C.
[two lost names]	c. 2172–2170 B.C.

The last major monarch of the Fourth Dynasty, Shepseskaf, was succeeded, not by his son, but by a member of a cadet branch of the royal family, Userkaf, who may have had ties to the worship of the sun-god Re of Heliopolis. He and his eight successors constitute Manetho's Fifth Dynasty, a period of downsizing, not only in the dimensions of pyramid which thereafter shrank to from 80 to 120 meters on a side (A), but also in the organization of the administration. Mastabas both at Giza and Saqqara are now larger and better appointed (B, C, D), and offer increasing space for scenes from daily life and texts encorporating biographical statements. The support staff of the Pharaonic administration, the owners of these tombs, has now found a voice.

Township and Manor

In any large state the "Center" and the "Periphery" form two opposing foci upon which two forces are at work: a force towards centralization of political authority, in which the broader interests of the country as a whole are served, and a force towards provincialism, in which the particular interests of regions are considered more important. Under the energetic drive of the Memphite royal family the Egyptians by about 2500 B.C. had achieved the centralized system in which the king and his government retained all power, and provincial interests were at state level subordinated to the larger interests of the whole. While support staffs were recruited from the local populations, townships were administered by officials from Memphis. There were many local tasks within a single province, each calling forth an individual functionary: someone to supervise the canal system, an overseer of work-crews, an overseer of commissions, a royal business-agent, a judge, farm-managers, tax-officers, and the like. Several incumbents were needed, and during his lifetime a functionary may have seen service in several townships. Metjen, for example, in the early Fourth Dynasty, could boast at the end of his life of having served in over ten Delta townships. The provincial officials who were regularly dispatched to the local townships were all Memphite by birth, and when their tour of duty ended they would return to the capital to be assigned another post. Upon retirement, rather than take up residence in one of the provinces in which they had served, they would come home to Memphis, there to be buried eventually in the environs of the pyramid of their king. And it was a signal honor for the king himself to favor the hard-working retiree by underwriting the cost of preparing the tomb.

But a highly centralized system is difficult to maintain, if only because of the expense involved. Within two generations of the death of Khafre the stranglehold which the extended royal family had clamped upon the highest offices in the state was broken, and men of non-royal, though elite origins were allowed into the upper echelons, some like Ptahshepses under Shepseskaf even intermarrying with the royal family. In the townships the royal administration was beginning to allow provincial officials a longer period of duty in a particular jurisdiction; and whereas in earlier times a single official might in his lifetime function in several provinces, now the practice was to confine his efforts to one area. Such civil servants, banished for long periods to distant towns, were not always able to appeal directly to the king or prime minister for instructions. They were, more often than not, obliged to rely on their own initiative, and could not be blamed for feeling progressively independent of the crown. Moreover, men who spend most of their lives in a provincial city, though born perhaps at Memphis, are going to be reluctant to quit their adopted homes at the end of their lives for burial back at the pyramid site. Egyptians more than any other ancient nation wished to be buried near the place where they had spent their lives.

It is not surprising, then, that the three centuries of decentralization at the close of the Old Kingdom (c. 2500–2200 B.C.) witnessed the rise of large cemeteries in the provinces, with tombs decorated and inscribed after the fashion popular at Memphis. With the absence of the wealth and excellent craftsmen of the king's residence, in place of free-standing mastabas the provincials had perforce to carve their tombs out of the cliffs beside the Nile, and adorn them as best they could (E). Inevitably art and spelling(!) suffered and the result would be deemed hideous by a sophisticated Memphite (F); but the inscriptions tell us a good deal about the careers of these provincials and their aides. It transpires that, in the course of the Fifth Dynasty, they were rapidly turning into a landed class of local gentry with hereditary rights. Most held the title *ḥꜣty-ꜥ*, an ancient post for a king's man beholden to the monarch for his house and land of which he enjoyed the usufruct only while he lived. Nevertheless, although formal appeal still had to be made to the king for the installation of a son in his father's position, every local official expected his son to follow him in office.

At the same time, perhaps for reasons of economy, the central government instituted a shake-up in the organization of the provincial administration. The old practice of sending out several officials, each with his own task for which he was directly responsible to Memphis, was clearly burdensome, if only from the standpoint of expense. Throughout the Fifth Dynasty the royal government favored selecting a single general officer (*ḥry-tp*, "chief") for each township, and making him responsible to the crown for the running of his bailiwick in all its aspects. Most bore the titles "hereditary prince and *ḥꜣty-ꜥ*" and with the office went the usual manor house and lands mentioned above. One can read further economizing measures, as well as security concerns, into the inauguration of a special office of "Overseer of Upper Egypt," head-quartered at Abydos, with responsibility for taxation and conscription. Usually recruited from an under class, the Overseer of Upper Egypt was directly responsible to the king, and had the unspecified task of keeping an eye on the more remote governors and keeping them in line. By the Sixth Dynasty some of these "provincial governors" in Upper Egypt had taken the title "Great Chief of the Township," roughly equivalent to our "baron." The autobiographical accounts which the barons have left in their tombs indicate quite clearly a pride in independence combined with a discreet, but genuine, deference to the crown. One Pepynefer, the governor of the third township of Upper Egypt, a far-off province in the south close to the Nubian frontier, tells how the king "commanded me to sail south to the Third Nome in the capacity of . . . Chief of the Nome, as the superintendent of Upper Egyptian grain, and as bishop. . . . I increased the long-horned cattle of this nome. . . . I was privy to all the business that was brought up from the Door of the Foreign lands (i.e. the southern border), from the southern countries. I gave bread to the hungry and clothing to the naked whom I found in this nome; I distributed jugs of milk and measured out Upper Egyptian grain. . . . Now I thoroughly pacified all the foreign lands for the palace . . . I rescued the weak from him who was stronger, and I judged two brothers to the satisfaction of both." In other words, we moderns might say that Pepy-nefer's powers encompassed grain supply, ecclesiastical affairs, cattle production, foreign affairs, welfare, economic affairs, and the judiciary. He was in very truth a "High Commissioner!"

The Downsizing of the State

In a land that relies so heavily on an irrigation system demanding a strong and efficient central authority, decentralization can have only a detrimental effect. For the king of Egypt it meant diminished tax returns, increased difficulty in raising a labor force or an army, and consequently the absence of the wherewithal to enforce his authority. Increasingly the monarch was obliged to rely on the agency of trusted officers, whether home-bred or "March-lords," to solve problems. In the Sixth Dynasty Harkhuf and Sabni, $ḥ3tyw$-$ꜥ$ of Elephantine, were charged with ensuring the free flow of commerce with African lands to the south; Weny, a governor of Upper Egypt, was directed to undertake punitive campaigns into Palestine. The Asiatics and the Sudanese, sensing Egypt's growing weakness, began to harass the frontiers. The destruction of the empires of Mari and Ebla in north Syria in the 24th century at the hands of Sargon of Akkad may have had a ripple-effect on the peoples farther south, causing displacement of communities and polities. Tomb scenes of the late Fifth and Sixth Dynasties showing assaults on Canaanite fortresses may be linked with the widespread destruction and abandonment of Palestinian cities as far south as the Negev which archaeology has revealed. The resultant disorder may have set groups of "bowmen" (as the Egyptians called them) in motion towards the Delta. In the Sudan several powerful tribes, called by archaeologists "C-group" people, had settled as far north as the first cataract, and owing no allegiance to Pharaoh, felt free to impede Egyptian trading ventures into Africa.

What other factors were operative in undermining the monarchy at the close of the Old Kingdom we can only guess. While civil servants do not always distinguish between their government job ($i3t$) and their rank ($ꜥḥꜥw$) at court (quite literally the place in line which they occupy before the king), nonetheless the "pecking order" was of prime concern to them. Under the penultimate king of the Fifth Dynasty the ranking order was suddenly modified, a change which might well have given offence! Whether this had anything to do with the alleged palace conspiracy at the start of the Sixth Dynasty is difficult to say, but scandal seems to have dogged the royal family. Later tradition claims that Tety was assassinated, and contemporary records mention Pepy I's divorce from his first queen, purportedly for adultery.

A civil service burgeoning without restraint and beset by demands made by tradition, status, reward, and nepotism, may well have created impossible tensions in a bureaucracy brittle to the point of hopeless fracture; but this could scarcely issue in the sort of systems collapse which the evidence suggests. Much is often made of the insecure economic basis of the state, tied as it was to the "uneconomic" or "unproductive" temple- or pyramid-estates; though in what sense land tied to a temple ceases to be productive is never explained, and one feels that the view is over-simplified. It is true that royal decrees exempting large estates, especially those belonging to temples, from taxation and government interference seem to increase as the end of the Old Kingdom approaches, suggesting a short-sighted abetment of his own impoverishment by the king himself. But again the evidence is so meagre that we may be misunderstanding completely the true purpose of these curious documents.

One factor, long ignored by scholars, has recently come to the fore. There is now incontrovertible evidence that, around 2200 B.C., the entire Northern Hemisphere, from Asia to the Americas, experienced the sudden onset of changing patterns of climate and prevailing winds. The result for northeast Africa was a marked decrease in the annual discharge of the Nile river, entailing a drastic reduction in inundated land, smaller crops and, inevitably, famine.

Contemporary texts speak of "difficult years," "years of 'health-of-heart' (a euphemism for famine)" during which "the entire Southland was dying of hunger and every man was eating his (own) children." Faced with this kind of problem no ancient state, nor modern for that matter, could long stave off collapse no matter how successfully it functioned.

The Collapse

In the 23rd century B.C. Egypt was moving with increasing momentum towards catastrophe, and the restricted food base was affecting real wealth. Tombs became smaller, constructed often of mud brick, and were more poorly decorated (G). Veiled allusions to wars occur from time to time. While the provincial centers seem to continue to flourish according to their own parochial standards, they clearly lacked the model of a vibrant, sophisticated Memphite capital.

The king who was fated to play the role, though not to suffer the ultimate end, of Louis XVI was Pepy II, the longest lived monarch in history, with a reign of ninety-six years (he had ascended the throne as a child). His mother was a provincial girl from Abydos, and during his minority his uncle Djaw functioned as vizier and regent. During the first three or four decades of his reign nothing suggests that the end was nigh: his pyramid was constructed to the same height and fashion as his immediate predecessors', and the relief art decorating his mortuary temple was exquisite. But after his sixty-seventh year inscriptions cease, and the historian is left without evidence.

Upon Pepy's death the elaborate governmental structure broke down, the network of canals was neglected, and famine followed. Pepy's successors were powerless to alleviate the situation. Palace conspiracies swept ruler after ruler off the throne in such rapid succession that the Egyptian historian Manetho, writing two thousand years later, remembered this sorry time as a "Seventh Dynasty," the period when "seventy kings ruled for seventy days."

The consequences for Egypt were horrendous. Province attacked province, and the whole land was plunged into civil war. Added to the latter were the dimensions of a social revolution. The poor attacked the rich, mansions and palaces were laid waste, and the tombs of royalty and the aristocracy were plundered (H, I). The Admonitions of Ipuwer, a declamation the only copies of which date from a thousand years after the period in question, belongs to a genre of "Lament" over the condition of the land. Though conducive to imitation and expansion for the sake of the shock value of delineating generically what the absence of *ma'at* means, there can be no doubt that the form and the theme the genre took and proclaimed are rooted in the real history of post-Old Kingdom Egypt. Ipuwer, a fictional(?) wiseman of the time, describes in a tattered papyrus something of the condition of the land during the troubles: "Indeed, the Inundation comes (regularly), but no one cultivates it. Everyone says, 'We do not know what has happened throughout the land!' . . . Indeed, the poor have become wealthy, and he who never (even) acquired sandals for himself is now a rich man. . . . Indeed, many dead are buried in the river: the flood has become a tomb, and the embalming chamber is (now) the stream. Indeed, the rich are in mourning, while the poor rejoice; and every town says, 'Let us overthrow those who are rich amongst us!' . . . Indeed, gates, columns, and walls are consumed by fire . . . the cities are destroyed, Upper Egypt has become dry (waste)-land . . .!"

How did the Egyptians react to the collapse of their world? Some experienced rage and frustration, leading to the questioning of authority. In one passage, the only place where speaker and audience are described, Ipuwer is represented as speaking to the "Eternal Lord," the creator-sun-god at one register, at another the king himself, and laying the responsibility for the disaster at the feet of this august personage. Others gave up in despair. In an ancient papyrus which dates from a few generations subsequent to the fall, and now preserved in the Berlin Museum, an un-named sufferer contemplated suicide: "To whom can I speak to-day? There is no one righteous, the land is left to those who do wrong. . . . Death is before me to-day like the longing of a man to see his house again after he has spent many years in captivity!" The speaker's *bai*, or soul-personality, urges him on to take his own life, arguing curiously that the traditional preparations for death that the ancestors followed have all proven worthless: "As for those who built in granite and erected halls in fine pyramids as a good work, when their builders became gods (i.e. died), their offering stelae were destroyed! . . . Listen to me, for listening is good for people! Follow the happy day and forget care!" The same implied agnosticism and *carpe diem* philosophy is present in the "Songs of the Harpers," which describe the "West" (i.e. the Afterlife) as a place of mystery which never gives up its secrets: "Make holiday and never get tired of it! Behold, a man is not allowed to take his property with him (when he dies), and there is no one who departs who comes back again!" Still others looked for a deliverer to come and save them from their misery: "A king will come. . .he will satisfy the Two Lands with what they desire . . . and justice shall come into its place while wrong-doing is driven out."

The Social Phenomenon of the "Common Man"

All this rage, despair and longing mirrors a stark social reality. With the certainty of a stable society gone, men flocked to the only strong man who could offer protection, the local manor-lord, the patron, whose fortified villa symbolized safety. Few of these mafia-lords could trace their ancestry back to the Old Kingdom: they were for the most part "new men," *nedjesu*, or "commoners," a status in which they gloried with the overtones of inverted snobbery. The mortuary texts of such squires, whether on slab stelae or in the rock-cut tombs they have left behind, are often richer in biographical material than the wordy texts of their Old Kingdom predecessors. Whereas the latter had boasted of their rank and relationship to the king, the new breed of provincial is aware and proud of his real independence and self-reliance. Some few Old Kingdom titles might be parroted in the self-presentation of these men, but they boast of deeds not titles, and rarely mention the king: "I am a commoner who is good at fighting. . . . I am one loved of his father, praised by his mother, beloved by his siblings, pleasant to his family and children. I was elevated from the back of my father's house . . . and I ruled Thinis because of my character(?) and for the sake of getting things done properly. (I am) one who speaks with his mouth and acts with his arm. There is no man who speaks against (me)"; "I acquired people, cattle, flocks, asses, grain, clothing, [unguent(?); I placed a] ship on the water, trees in the field(?); what I did(?) was by my own strength;" "I was a capable commoner who lived on his (own) property, ploughed with <his> (own) cattle, and sailed in his (own) boat."

As too often is the case when stable government brings security and justice, Egyptians of the Old Kingdom had been lulled into a sense of well-being. But when the judge in the court is grossly unfair in his decisions, when the ruler is a selfish tyrant rather than a beneficent ruler, and when the literate scribe extorts twice the quota of taxes from his illiterate fellow citizens, the thoughts of men turn longingly to better times in the past. In short, an absence of just dealing among men makes them conscious of its value. The Egyptians who lived between 2180 and

2000 B.C. were keenly aware of what they had lost. They loved to tell the story of the peasant, robbed of his donkeys, whose appeal to the judge was deferred to a later date. The peasant persisted and returned day after day until he had made eight petitions. The judge, however, had delayed merely to enjoy further manifestations of the peasant's eloquence, and at last awarded him the case and punished the robber. The literature of the time is loud in its praise of justice: "Justice is great, its usefulness is lasting. . . . Wrong-doing has never brought its undertaking into port" (i.e. to a successful completion). Rulers were encouraged to act right-eously: ". . . you should speak the truth in your house, that the nobles who are upon earth will fear you. Rectitude of heart is fitting for a ruler. . . . Practice justice that you may endure upon earth; quiet the weeper, oppress not the widow, do not remove a man from his paternal inheritance, do no harm to officials or their(?) property(?), beware of punishing wrongfully. Do not kill: it is of no advantage to you." The religious literature voices a concept which is still with us today, viz. that men are born equal in opportunity and have equal rights before the law. In one passage the sun-god is represented as declaring, "I made the four winds that every man might breathe thereof like his fellow . . . I made the Great Inundation that the poor man might have rights therein like the rich man . . . I made every man like his fellow. . . ."

It must have been obvious to the Egyptians that, no matter how eloquently they praised just dealing in one's personal affairs, it was not always justice that gained riches. This old prob-lem in ethics has puzzled men since the dawn of time: why so often do wrong-doers prosper, while righteous men suffer persecution, and die unwept and penniless? Should not God pun-ish evil? And if, as so often happens, the criminal goes unpunished in this life, should we blame God? No, answered the ancient Egyptians; the wrong-doer will receive his deserts in the next life. Already in the Old Kingdom the doctrine of the "king-in-death" had projected the earthly court of the king with all its trappings and the civil service into the next life, where the Great God (the king) would rule over a parallel universe in death, and mete out justice as he had on earth. Just as in real life during the Old Kingdom plantation managers had had to appear before the Memphite authorities for an annual audit, the "grand reckoning," so in the next life one's "books" would undergo official scrutiny. And dimly, the Egyptians began to con-ceive of a trial to take place after death, at which a man's deeds would be examined, and it would be decided whether he had done right or wrong during his life. King Akhtoy reminded his son, the future king Merikare, "As for the council which judges the (morally) deficient, you know that they are not lenient on that day of judging the wretch, that hour of performing (their) duty. It is difficult when the accuser is discerning! Do not rely on length of years: they look upon a lifetime as but an hour. Man survives after death, and his deeds are placed beside him in heaps. Existence there is indeed for an eternity. . . . As for one who reaches it without having done wrong, he shall exist there like a god, swaggering about like the lords of eterni-ty." Osiris, the king-in-death and ruler of the dead, became the judge, and before his throne stood the scales of justice on which a man's heart would be weighed.

Magic and the Coffin Texts

Much of the information about the Egyptian belief system during the Herakleopolitan period comes from a corpus of written material known as the Coffin Texts. With the collapse of the Old Kingdom and the social revolution the pyramids were broken into and robbed, and the archives of the royal residence ransacked. Not only did the administrative documents, formerly "classified," now become the common property of the people, but the Pyramid Texts and the magical literature of the beatification spells were exposed. Ipuwer complains that the lower classes do not know the value of this literature and either tear up papyri in the streets, or repeat spells endlessly so that they lose their magical effect.

Magic was conceived by the Egyptians almost as an element of the cosmos created at the dawn of time which, if controlled properly, could work the will of mankind. Throughout Egyptian history magic was the "secret art of the lector priest," a figure who in later times was to become the equivalent of our "magician," and since to use an incantation effectively the exact wording and tone of voice must be maintained, the *written* form was deemed all important. Books of magic spells were kept in the "House of the God's-Book," a sacred library attached to every temple; and specially potent magical literature, called collectively the "Manifestations of Re," was copied out, stored and meditated upon in the "House of Life," a secret installation whose members ranked as the highest grade of scribe in the land. Magic was used in all aspects of everyday life—for protection against disease, accident, poisonous snakes and scorpions, the evil eye, evil demons, and human enemies; for cures from all sorts of diseases and mechanical injuries; and for private advantage against personal enemies or enemies of the state. A check-list of the (now destroyed) contents of a temple library in Ptolemaic times reveals that much of the temple service consisted of the recitation of magic spells to ward off evil influence which might harm the god, his priests, or the offerings.

On the lips of a skilled lector-priest a magic incantation would be effective "a million times," in the locution of the ancients themselves. There was no defence against it: even the gods must succumb. Often the spell required the speaker to identify himself with the god, thus enhancing the power of the words; even reciting a myth in which the gods took part would also ensure the effectiveness of the spell. The older the incantation the more certain was the magician that it would work, and collections ascribed to the great wisemen of the past were in constant use.

The recitation of a spell was often intended to be accompanied by certain actions, and these were often added in written copies as rubrics to the end of the words to be spoken. Frequently the magician is advised to perform the recitation over figurines or amulets of specified deities. Equally frequent is the instruction to write the text on the amulet in ink, wash it off with beer and drink the resultant concoction. Figures fashioned of wax could, at the word of the magician, grow to life size and perform his every command like automatons. One practice used by the state during the Old and Middle Kingdoms involved inscribing the names of foreign, and sometimes domestic, enemies on red bowls or clay figurines, then smashing the objects while intoning the appropriate curse.

Magic also extended into the realm of the dead. The reason why the Pyramid Texts were inscribed within the burial chamber, in close proximity to the mummy of the king, was to provide him in death with the magical means to overcome the dangers which awaited him in the next life. But herein lay a danger. As well-drawn and accurate images of things and life forms in the real world, the hieroglyphs had resisted partly for magical reasons their own supersession by a purely cursive script. They were in a sense "gods" with latent power. Like the figurines of wax mentioned above, they could be activated by a skillful magician and literally brought off the wall to do his bidding! The risk is obvious. What if the lion- or the serpent-hieroglyph in inscriptions close to the dead were imbued with life, and began attacking the mummy? What if the signs of the seated man or the man holding the stick should come alive and turn hostile towards the tomb owner? The solution in many cases led to the intentional *mutilation* or *omission* of the hieroglyph in question: a lion might be cut in half, a serpent drawn with a knife in its back, or the man drawn with no feet and legs.

Those who broke into the tombs on the morrow of the demise of the Old Kingdom must have stood in awe, not only of the grave goods, but also of the texts on the walls. They may have sensed the importance of these spells, but few could read them. Even the few who were literate must have been mystified by the contents, as many incantations had been devised for esoteric rituals of the monarchy of old, now obsolete. Nevertheless they copied them out, sometimes committing egregious errors of grammar and syntax, or re-interpreting what they did not understand. The tombs of post-revolutionary Egypt could not compare with the aristocratic mastabas of old. Small and drab, they lacked space for the majestic scenes of life on a plantation or in the salons of the nobility, and the stone sarcophagi of the Fifth and Sixth Dynasties were beyond the wealth and the capabilities of people to produce.

As a substitute long wooden boxes, coffins in fact, came into fashion providing at one and the same time the final resting place for the deceased and the only space available for texts or paintings. In place of the grave goods which perhaps most could not afford, a painted frieze depicting these objects was executed around the rim of the coffin, while on the inside surfaces of the box was an array of beatification spells, written in ink in columns. These *Coffin Texts* in date span the time from the close of the Old Kingdom to the end of the Middle Kingdom and represent, for that period, the same "art of the lector priest" to which we were introduced in the Old Kingdom. Many of the Coffin Texts descend directly from Pyramid Text originals, often re-interpreted or botched and misunderstood; but there is much new material as well and a new "slant" on the Afterlife. Now, for the first time, and in contrast to the Pyramid Texts, *rubrics* at the beginning of a spell indicate its purpose, and sometimes directions as to how the spell is to be used, also in red ink, are given at the end.

While the Pyramid Texts were clearly intended for the royal family and the elite, the Coffin Texts serve a less restricted clientele. The overall purpose of the texts is the same as the Pyramid Texts, viz. to promote the welfare of the deceased and ensure a safe passage to paradise. One notable difference, however, between the two bodies of texts is to be found in the increased reliance in the Coffin Texts on personal identification with the supernatural to ensure existence for eternity. Two-thirds of the corpus is made up of *Transformation Spells,* magical utterances designed to change a person's form into a god, animal, or force of nature. Rubrics indicate the purpose clearly: spells are designed to facilitate "changing into Sobek," "changing into Nepri," "changing into Re-Atum," "changing into a falcon," "changing into any god one wishes," "changing into the Nile," "changing into the wind," and so forth. Titles to the spells also yield clues as to the type of Afterlife envisaged. The same basic landscape with the same names shows through as we encountered in the Pyramid Texts; but now violence and danger lurk everywhere. The deceased had to be protected from snares, decapitation, burning, decay, walking head downward, being devoured by crocodiles, having to drink urine, a second death, and many other terrifying fates. More frequently than in the Pyramid Texts there is an appeal to esoteric knowledge: "I know you, I know your names!" and can therefore exercise power over you. But if one does not know a particular incantation or a myth, he can never function because of his ignorance.

Osiris, the Hypostasis of Fertility and Salvation

It is in the Coffin Texts that we gain an expanded view of Osiris (J). We have earlier identified the name "Osiris" with the eternal seat of the dead king, but it had come to encompass a far broader span of supernatural power. The spirit of fertility in a myriad of permutations manifested itself in the latent power of the Nile waters, the young grain *(Nepri)* **(fig. 1),** the flowering tree *(peqer),* the flocks and their shepherd *(Andjety),* the presence of life in death *(djed).* The purview of the god expanded, and presented to humankind that supreme paradox of latent energy. Diametrically opposed to the dynamic, fiery power of the visible sun in heaven, Osiris represented the opposite pole of the dark, silent power of fertility in the underworld. When the two opposites met, as they did in Mendes, the cosmos experienced new life and revivification.

As the presence of fertility knows no geographical bounds save the extent of arable land, so Osiris worship spread without restraint. Although his principal places of worship were Abydos in the south (where he "absorbed" Khentiamentiu), and Busiris in the Delta (where he assimilated Andjety, "the shepherd"), he was known throughout the length and breadth of the land; each major town hallowed part of his body as a relic. The peasantry carried the god to the fields and to the grave as images of grain in the form of the god himself, "corn-Osirises." The cutting and winnowing of the grain recalled the suffering of Osiris at the hands of Seth.

The myth of Osiris kept pace with the evolving concept of the deity. As in all myths, the demands of narratology and innate aesthetic sense transformed the simple story into a complex drama, an amalgam of several disparate themes: the story achieves an independent status, divorced from that from which it originated, and its characters in their essential humanity stand for the tragedy of life itself. The good king Osiris and his loving wife Isis **(fig. 2)** bring prosperity to the Black Land, and in every way prove themselves to be paragons of virtue. This evokes jealousy in the heart of Osiris's brother Seth, who purposes to murder the good god, and supplant him with his own regime. In the old version Seth deals a mortal blow to his unsuspecting brother, and casts the corpse into the Nile. In a more sophisticated elaboration, Seth

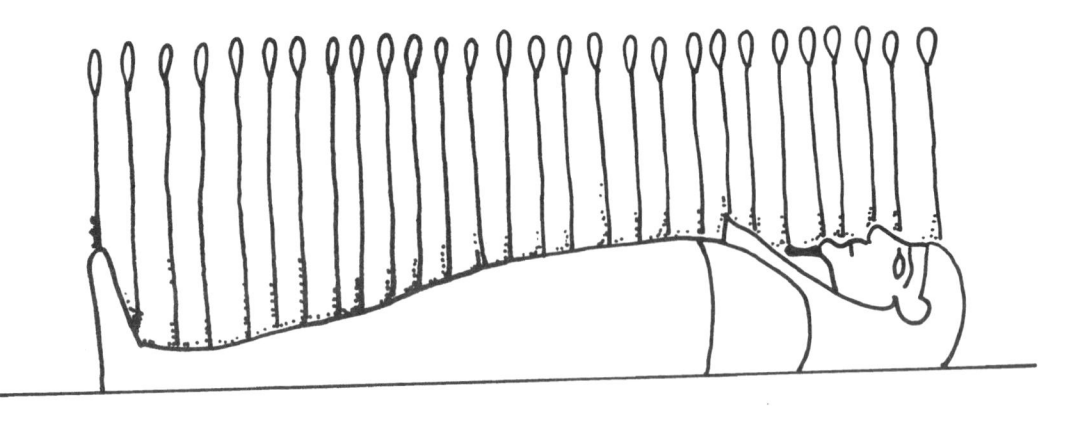

Figure 1 Grain sprouting from the inert body of Osiris.

in company with his accomplices convenes a banquet to which Osiris is invited. Amid the merriment Seth offers as a prize a marvellous coffin to the one who fits it exactly; all try to no avail for it has been made to fit Osiris's specifications, and when he lies down in it, the accomplices nail down the lid and throw the box into the Nile. Thus Osiris floats down the Nile, impregnating the waters with fertility, and comes to rest in the marshes of the Delta. (One version carries his corpse across the sea to Byblos, a reflection of the close contact that city enjoyed with Egypt and the popularity there of a version of the monster-vs.-hero myth type.) At this point the Butic narrative of fledgling hero and distraught mother is grafted into the narrative. Isis finds the corpse of her husband in the Delta, but has only time to hide it before she has to flee into the marshes where she gives birth to the child Horus. Seth, chancing on Osiris's body, in a rage chops it to pieces and scatters the fragments throughout the land. Isis is forced to locate the pieces and bury them individually at the spot of discovery, thus providing an aetiology (the assignment of a cause) for the plethora of Osirian relics.

That part of the narrative which offers opportunity for poignant elaboration is the stay in the Delta marshes. There the papyrus thicket hides mother and child from the marauding Seth, and the friendly animals the cow, the cobra, and the heron assist the young mother in protecting and nurturing the infant. Sometimes Horus is stung by a scorpion and is in danger of dying, until the grief-stricken mother discovers an antidote or devises a potent magic spell.

But at last Horus is grown and emerges from the swamp with his supporters to wreak vengeance upon his uncle Seth. Here again the myth invites expansion: battle after battle takes place but all prove inconclusive. It is at this point that the myth replaces the primitive notion of solution of an issue by force with the more sophisticated concept of a trial before a court. The line between Osiris and Horus, father and son, blurs a little. The bone of contention is the right to rule Egypt and, after reviewing the evidence, the gods who have convened as a jury decide in favor of Osiris-Horus. They acclaim Osiris "justified," literally "true of voice" *(ma'a-khrow)*, or "right by acclamation," and Seth "condemned"; Horus is given the accoutrements of kingship and is duly crowned as successor to his father.

Figure 2   Triad of Osiris with Isis (left) and Nephthys (right).

Osiris, however, could never return to the realm of the living: he was destined for the Afterlife. Anubis, Isis, Thoth, and other gods combined their efforts to provide him the wherewithal to pass over into the next life; he was the first to be embalmed, the first to enjoy the panoply of a funeral, the first to receive protective magic spells, innovations which lent a new meaning to the term "First-of-Westerners."

The immanent power and yet the accompanying pathos of the numen of fertility fostered, nay demanded, the active involvement of the community. Celebration would not only instruct and chasten the devotee; it would actively promote the god's well-being. Throughout the length and breadth of Egypt Osiris's death and resurrection gave rise to festivals at which the god's passion was symbolically re-enacted. The most important took place at Abydos during the inundation season, and involved priests, officials, and laity. The sanctity of Abydos pursuant to its early royal associations had never faded from the collective Egyptian memory, and a prehistoric fetish of a human head with long hair held aloft on a pole **(fig. 3)** was re-interpreted as the head of Osiris, and was encased in a reliquary **(fig. 4)**. The ceremonies involved processions and mock combats in which the laity took part. The priests carried the divine images in the sacred barques upon their shoulders, Wepwawet "the Opener of the Ways," appropriately enough leading the way; followed by the *neshmet* barque of Osiris. On the penultimate day of the festival the procession wended its way from the temple of Osiris out into the desert to a district called *Peqer,* actually the site of the First Dynasty royal cemetery. There in what was in fact the tomb of king Djer, now identified as the tomb of Osiris, the god was taken down into the underground apartments and spent the "Night of the Great Sleep" there. During the night the pieces of Osiris's "body" were magically woven together in silence, and as night ended his call for help was heard above ground. The "Followers of Horus" turned upon the "Followers of Seth" and routed them, and as dawn broke the resurrected Osiris appeared out of the tomb to the adulation of his followers.

For the devotee Osiris had become the great archetype in death. He had led the way, and had in fact triumphed over death. Any believer could emulate the god by living a blameless life and preparing for death and undergoing embalming, just as Osiris had. In fact, by virtue of his

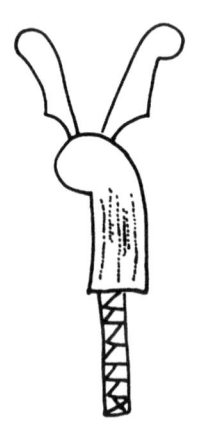

Figure 3   Early representation of the Abydos township standard, showing a head with long hair and two feathers fixed on a pole.

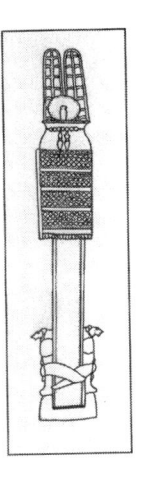

Figure 4   The formal Abydos fetish, the reliquary containing the head of Osiris.

state of preparedness he could *become* Osiris, "a well-equipped, transfigured spirit," and by dying and rising again in him, could lay claim to eternal life. Like Osiris, he could hope to be declared "true of voice" before the judgement seat of the great god, and enter into paradise. "Whether I live or die," sang the saved soul, "I am (one with) Osiris! I go out and in through you, I thrive in you, I grow in you! I have fallen in you . . . (but) the gods live in me!"

The Civil War

Those Egyptians who had longed for a deliverer to save them from their misery eventually had their wish fulfilled, but not before two centuries of intermittent civil war had passed. The initial state of anarchy which had attended the death of Pepy II threw up an "Eighth Dynasty" of eighteen kings (according to the later royal offering-list tradition) who can have occupied no more than fifteen years in total, and represent the last weak attempts by the Memphite residence to save the situation. We hear of plundered necropoleis and destroyed *ku*-chapels, as determined attempts were made to do away with the monarchic memorials of the Old Kingdom. Desperate measures were taken by these ephemeral kings to create an office of dictator for Upper Egypt in an effort to squelch opposition. But Memphis was doomed and its thousand-year hegemony brought to an end shortly after 2160 B.C. when the most powerful baron of Middle Egypt, Akhtoy I of the city Herakleopolis (K), forced his fellow barons to acknowledge him as king. Akhtoy and the seventeen members of his family who followed him upon the throne—no extant king-list preserves their names—are counted by Manetho as the Ninth and Tenth Dynasties, ruling Egypt in fact for only about one hundred years (c. 2155–2050 B.C.). But their government was never strong, since they had always to rely for support upon the provincial barons who jealously guarded their hereditary rights.

About 2134 B.C. one of these barons, a certain Inyotef from Thebes, rebelled against the king in Herakleopolis, and set himself up as rival ruler. Thebes had been a remote and unimportant town during the Old Kingdom, situated in the fourth nome or township of Upper Egypt. Towards the close of the Memphite monarchy, during the reigns of the ephemeral successors of Pepy II, this township along with the seven southernmost nomes of Upper Egypt, comprising the Nile valley from the first cataract to (modern) Nag Hammadi, had shown a tendency towards independence, and had been administered as a unit by the governor of Upper Egypt. Coptos in the fifth township had dominated the region at that time, notwithstanding the attempts by Ankhtify-nakht, a brigand of the third township, to wrest power for himself; but under the Herakleopolitan kings political control rapidly gravitated to the largest bailiwick in the south, the fourth township, Thebes, called by the Egyptians "Wēse".

Thebes's secession from the Herakleopolitan kingdom was a brave, if foolhardy act, for the Theban district could not muster the resources in manpower that Herakleopolis could. Time, however, was on the side of Thebes, as the king did not take the rebellion seriously, taking solace in official prophecies, and made only half-hearted attempts to quell it. In a fascinating Wisdom Text from the time, in which an old Herakleopolitan king gives fatherly advice to his heir apparent, Merikare, the old monarch counsels the young prince on how to treat with the Southland: "do not act badly towards the southern part; you know the prediction of the Residence concerning it. . . . They do not violate our boundary as they said (they would). . . . Your situation vis-à-vis the southern part is good: the burden-bearers come to you with tribute. (The Theban ruler) has no grain that he might give it. Let it be a source of satisfaction to you that they are weakened."

How short-sighted was this contemporary view emerges from the sequel. Inyotef was able to win over the southern bailiwick of the seven southernmost provinces to his cause; and then suddenly he turned loose his bands of retainers and mercenary freebooters against the heart of the Herakleopolitan state. The eighth nome fell with comparative ease during the reign of his son Inyotef II, but thereafter the advance downriver met stiff opposition. The powerful baron of Asyut had decided to remain loyal to the king in Herakleopolis, and the Thebans had no success against his troops. For about fifty years the war surged back and forth in Middle Egypt until, probably about 2050 B.C., almost a century after the beginning of the Theban rebellion, the exhausted Herakleopolitans collapsed. The Theban soldiers under Montuhotpe I marched clean through the north to the Mediterranean, and their curious gaze may even have fallen on Asiatics in southern Palestine.

Thebes was now the master of all Egypt, but a more unlikely city for that role cannot be imagined. Three or four scattered settlements, albeit sizeable, on a broad plain (L) on the east bank of the Nile, in each a simple temple rising above the roofs of the houses, a small cemetery on the opposite bank nestling at the base of the towering cliffs of the Sahara (M), a jetty or two, perhaps a mud brick fortress—this was Thebes at first, the city which poets were later to call the one-hundred-gated mistress of all the cities in Egypt! Montu, a war-god appropriately enough, was the chief deity of the province; but he was native to Ermant, a town farther upstream from Thebes. The latter worshipped a triad of gods, Amun (N), a mysterious god whose name meant "the Hidden One," his wife Mut, "the mother," and their child Khonsu, the "moon." None of these cults, however, inspired the early Thebans to great creations of spiritual worth. Theban art is provincial, not to say barbaric at times; and beside the sophisticated productions of the north it looks ludicrous. No great literature comes from Thebes at this period. In this area too the southerners were completely overshadowed by the north.

The Theban Eleventh Dynasty

Eleventh Dynasty

Inyotef I	c. 2134–2118 B.C.
Inyotef II	c. 2118–2069 B.C.
Inyotef III	c. 2069–2061 B.C.
Montuhotpe I	c. 2061–2010 B.C.
Montuhotpe II	c. 2010–1998 B.C.
Montuhotpe III	c. 1998–1991 B.C.

Yet it was to this period that we must date the earliest attempts to transform Thebes into a capital and residence. The "barons" of Ermant, lately transformed to the rank of "kings," tried to emulate the monarchic tradition of the north by constructing pyramids. Their attempts, however, were those of provincials: their pyramids were mud-brick dummies of modest size, placed above rock-cut burial installations of the time-honored nomarch fashion. Montuhotpe I, on the morrow of his victory, erected a novel memorial against the western cliffs at Thebes: a stone massif (whether pyramid or mastaba scholars cannot decide) (O) surrounded by a colonnade (P) and fronted by a grove of trees planted in pits in the soil. Behind the complex, cut into the rock cliff, lay the tomb chamber of the king. For 500 years this great mortuary temple remained the focal point of the necropolis, and its relief decoration the inspiration for later artists.

The relations between the new Theban rulers of Egypt and the barons cannot be described, for evidence is lacking. Many probably switched allegiance from Herakleopolis to Thebes, while some more stubborn ones may have been deprived of their estates which were then given to loyal supporters of the conqueror. Certain it is, at any rate, that the royal house of the Montuhotpes and the Inyotefs had no desire to replace the manorial system with another form of administration. Perhaps they could envisage no other. For although the military prowess of the Theban house cannot be gainsaid, they seem to have left something to be desired from an intellectual standpoint. Their union of Egypt had been by force, their settlement of issues *ad hoc* and incomplete. Within two generations of the conquest civil war had broken out afresh, and raged for seven years.

Further Readings

In addition to the works on administration cited at the end of the last chapter, see J. Assmann, *The Mind of Egypt*, New York, 2002 (ch. 3–6); H. G. Fischer, *Inscriptions from the Coptite Nome, Dyn. VI–XI*, Rome, 1964; *idem, Dendera in the Third Millennium B.C. Down to the Theban Domination of Upper Egypt*, Locust Valley, 1968; D. Franke, "The First Intermediate Period," in D. B. Redford (ed.), *The Oxford Encyclopaedia of Ancient Egypt* (New York, 2001), I, 526–32; E. Pardey, "Provincial Administration," *ibid*, I, 16–20; I. Shaw, *The Oxford History of Ancient Egypt*, Oxford, 2000 (ch. 6).

No comprehensive work has as yet been produced on the collapse of the Old Kingdom making use of the newly-acquired ecological evidence; see in general N. Yoffee, G. L. Cowgill (eds.), *The Collapse of Ancient States and Civilizations*, Tucson, 1988.

On literature, see M. Lichtheim, *Ancient Egyptian Literature: A Book of Readings, I. The Old and Middle Kingdoms*, Berkeley, 1973; R. B. Parkinson, "Individual and Society in Middle Kingdom Literature," in A. Loprieno (ed.), *Ancient Egyptian Literature: History and Forms* (Leiden, 1996), 137–55.

Magic and Coffin Texts comprise an enormous topic. See in particular the following: J.F. Borghouts, *Ancient Egyptian Magical Texts*, Leiden, 1978; G. Englund (ed.), *The Religion of the Ancient Egyptians*, Uppsala, 1989; R. O. Faulkner, *The Ancient Egyptian Coffin Texts* (3 volumes), Warminster, 1973; L. H. Lesko, *The Ancient Egyptian Book of Two Ways*, Berkeley, 1972; *idem*, "Coffin Texts," in D. B. Redford (ed.), *The Oxford Encyclopaedia of Ancient Egypt* (New York, 2001), I. 287–88; R. K. Ritner, *The Mechanics of Ancient Egyptian Magical Practice*, Chicago, 1993; H. Willems (ed.), *The World of the Coffin Texts*, Leiden, 1996.

On Osiris in his fertility and underworld aspects, see J. G. Griffiths, *Plutarch's De Iside et Osiride*, Cardiff, 1970; *idem*, *The Origins of Osiris and his Cult*, Leiden, 1980; *idem*, *The Divine Verdict: A Study of Divine Judgment in the Ancient Religions*, Leiden, 1991; *idem*, "Osiris," in D. B. Redford, *The Oxford Encyclopaedia of Ancient Egypt* (New York, 2001), II. 615–19; E. Otto, *Egyptian Art and the Cults of Osiris and Amon*, London, 1968; R. T. Rundle-Clark, *Myth and Symbol in Ancient Egypt*, London, 1959.

CHAPTER SIX
The Middle Kingdom

Ψ

Twelfth Dynasty	
Amenemhet I	c. 1991–1961 B.C.
Senwosret I	c. 1971–1928 B.C.
Amenemhet II	c. 1929–1895 B.C.
Senwosret II	c. 1895–1876 B.C.
Senwosret III	c. 1878–1843 B.C.
Amenemhet III	c. 1843–1798 B.C.
Amenemhet IV	c. 1798–1790 B.C.
Sobek-nofru	c. 1790–1786 B.C.

This time the lucky survivor of the mortal conflict between rival claimants was a man named Amenemhet I ("Amun is at the Head"), son of a Theban priest and a woman from the region of the First Cataract on the Nile (the first township of Upper Egypt). In all probability Amenemhet the king is identical with a like-named individual who had been prime minister under the last king of the Eleventh Dynasty, Montuhotpe III, but as far as is known he was not related by birth to the royal family. In plain terms an usurper, Amenemhet was shrewd enough to realize what was required of him if he wished to keep his crown and his life. His adoption of the epithet "repeating of births," or Renaissance, indicates that he was conscious of his role and ambitious to carry it out. His success can be measured by the Dynasty he founded, the Twelfth of Manetho comprising seven kings and one queen, representing c. 215 years of prosperity. Centuries later the Twelfth Dynasty was to be looked back upon as Egypt's "classical" age.

Amenemhet I: the Beginnings of Reform

At the outset, of course, conditions looked no more promising for the Twelfth Dynasty than they had for any of the numerous other regimes which had risen and fallen during the Civil War. Two centuries of unrest had left land ownership in a sorry state, beset by falsified boundaries, shifted boundary markers, and lost records. How many of the disputes in the preceding two hundred years must have taken their rise from quarrels over property claims! A second obstacle to prosperity lay in the continued presence of a manorial system. Although few, if any, of the parochial gentry, the *nedjesu,* could trace their ancestry back to the Old Kingdom, having been ennobled by the Herakleopolitan or Theban houses or by the seizure of raw power, their hold on the townships made the re-creation of efficient and centralized government very difficult. A third drawback to the successful emplacement of the new regime lurked within its own illegitimacy. It was folly to claim to be the descendent of illustrious, ancient kings, for everyone knew the truth: Amenemhet was a usurper of nondescript if not ignoble ancestry. Moreover he had supplanted a regime which had re-united Egypt, and begun the process of healing. Finally, even if his proposed program of reform were exemplary, how could he possibly bring it about without a support staff? Amenemhet lacked the magnificent bureaucratic structure the Old Kingdom had created, which had been swept away in the turmoil of the time of troubles. There was now a crying need for scribes and literati.

Despite these formidable obstacles, Amenemhet set to work with a will. Deeming the problem of ownership certification the most pressing, the king consulted all surviving documents, then proceeded methodically throughout the land, re-surveying the boundaries of towns, townships, and estates. The result was a new land cadastre which, although the original has perished, is still reflected in an abridged version inscribed by his son, Senwosret I, on a chapel at Karnak (A). Amenemhet did not live long enough successfully to address the other problems we have outlined above, but he made a beginning. Although for the first few years of his reign he imitated the Eleventh Dynasty in treating Thebes as the capital, he must soon have realized that remaining in this city meant competing with the favorable memory of Montuhotpe I, in which he was bound to suffer by comparison. And so, around the fifth year of his reign, the new king decided to create his own city free of ancient memories and traditions, wherein he would not be held up to invidious comparison. To this end Amenemhet chose a site a few miles south of Dahshur, within the greater Memphite area (B), and built a capital which he named *'Imn-m-ḥȝt-it-tȝwy,* "Amenemhet-is-the-Seizer-of-the-Two-Lands," after his death reduced to "Itj-towy." The king continued to show a discreet reverence for the memory of his immediate predecessors, but now within the confines of his own city he could cleverly publicize himself as the real deliverer of Egypt from disunity and disorder.

The Dynasty never forgot, however, their southern origins, and Thebes continued to be honored. At a spot on the east bank, opposite the great monument of Montuhotpe I, there had long been a shrine to the township god, the falcon Montu; but now a new god had appeared, the very deity signalized in the dynastic name, *Amun,* or the "hidden one." The name is not entirely unheralded in the roster of Egyptian gods, yet the geographical origins of the Theban Amun remain unknown. Senwosret I, in his ninth year, publicly announced (BB) his plans to expand the worship of this deity, and to that end founded a temple (C) adjacent to Montu's, called "(Senwosret III)-is-Most-Select-of-Places." (A shrine to the god had existed here in the Eleventh Dynasty, but Senwosret's was a new foundation.) While Amun, or Amun-re in his manifestation as a solar avatar, was to be the honored god, the temple became a sort of royal family memorial, added to or refurbished by kings of every family and place of origin for fifteen centuries.

Did Amenemhet I sense that these measures were insufficient? In any regime, ancient or modern, the point of transition from one C.E.O. to another is always fraught with risk and danger. It may have been that Amenemhet judged the risk in his own case to be excessive, for in the late second or early third decade of his reign he seems to have elevated his eldest son and heir apparent, Senwosret, to a co-regency, in which the young man was allowed to assume the panoply of kingship. It was a practice that later kings were also to adopt.

Thirty years into the new dynasty an event occurred which suggested the House of Amenemhet would go the way of all ephemeral regimes of the past two centuries. Rather than liquidate his enemies, Amenemhet had attempted to conciliate them; and for his pains he was assassinated. This tragedy made a deep impression on the six members of his family who, successively, followed him upon the throne of Egypt during the next two centuries. Embittered by the fate of their great progenitor, each of the six seems to have remained more or less aloof from his subjects. A poignant document written up under Senwosret I represents the old king bestowing his wisdom on his son from beyond the grave. After describing the assassination, the author makes Amenemhet say to his son and heir in a posthumous discourse on regal behavior, "Do not fill your heart with a brother, do not make friends, do not become intimate with people: there is no point to it. When you lie down, guard your heart yourself, because a man has no friends when times get bad. I gave to the pauper, I brought up the poor man, I made the nonentity reach (his goal) as though he were somebody. (But) it was he who ate my food that made rebellion, the one to whom I had given support that revolted against me. He who wore my linen looked upon me as already dead, who used my myrrh was already pouring a (funerary) libation for me!"

What king or divine monarch is it that can inspire within the heart of his subjects the will to assassinate him? The pharaonic monarchy had come through the time of troubles largely shorn of the dignity with which it had been surrounded during the Old Kingdom. It was one of the commendable achievements of the House of Amenemhet, the Twelfth Dynasty, that they succeeded in restoring the divine kingship to its former status. This was a conscious achievement, and involved the skilful production of what we might call "propaganda" literature.

The Writing-School

While some evidence suggests the existence of a scribal school during the Ninth and Tenth Dynasties, it is with the founding of Itj-towy that a school of formidable proportions, staffed by creative writers, makes its appearance in the service of the regime. The needs were immediate and practical. Students needed to be, not only schooled from the ground up in writing, but also introduced to the *forms* of writing they would be expected to reproduce. They had to be able to write the highly formulaic forms of decrees, letters, inventories, and reports, in the style the state required. Book-keeping and ledger entries required skills in mathematics and a knowledge of the fiscal apparatus of Pharaoh's government. The technique used in all cases was rote learning, entailing the copying of written models and the memorization of important texts. Already in the Herakleopolitan period the father of king Merikare recalls how, in his school days, he and his companions had to "sing the writings."

In a community that is largely illiterate, oral composition and transmission tend to dominate in the dissemination of knowledge and information; but in a highly centralized state such as ancient Egypt it must be accompanied by the written word, if only as an aid to memory. Throughout Egyptian history one can sense a tension between orator and scribe. One skilled in speech was both admired and hated, for he could stir a multitude; one with precise speech, incisive tongue and good choice of vocabulary earned the indulgence of the crowd and could speak freely. Even the king strove after oratorical skill: "the sword of the king is his tongue," said Merikare's father, "speech is stouter than any weapon!" If, however, one were seeking accurate reporting on any subject of importance one had to turn to the written word. Scribes poured scorn on information passed on "from mouth to mouth"; this was merely the "narratives of the people" or "of those who lived aforetime," and was liable to be grossly exaggerated. But since neither rote learning nor dissemination of information was possible in Egypt without its being transmitted orally, scribes frequently copied out an orally composed speech, or, if they were the authors, composed in writing a sort of *parlando,* a composition to be spoken.

Numerous scribal tricks are in evidence in surviving writings which are intended to facilitate the memorization process. In Ipuwer, for example, couplets the contents of which are similar and difficult to remember in sequence, are linked by like-sounding words or phrases at the end and/or beginning of each segment. A much-used model letter, although it contains words and expressions which would expand the students' vocabulary, makes no sense at all in terms of the order of the topics discussed. In fact that order is meaningless: the sentences and paragraphs hang together only because of homophonic elements providing links that will aid the memory. Students frequently sounded out the piece they were copying in an effort to commit it to memory at the same time.

But students were obliged to learn more than what would be of practical use to a secretary. The sayings of the ancestors retained a reputation for wisdom that could not be ignored but had to be transmitted to future generations. The genre which the Egyptians called *seboyet,* "teaching," encompassed a wide range of knowledge, but in particular a species of practical "wisdom" which an older generation might bequeath to the young. A common format, which in fact is found throughout the ancient world, conjures up the moment when an old man on the point of death takes his son aside, and gives him a set of precepts which will help him make his way in life. This type of "self-help" book is still with us today, in the form of such works as Carnegie's *How to Win Friends and Influence People.* Examples from the Middle Kingdom to enhance their reputation are ascribed to known wisemen of the Old Kingdom, the high-priest Imhotpe, the viziers Ptahhotpe and Ka-gemni, the prince Hordedef. The appeal is universal: the short paragraphs are addressed to all ages and all walks of life.

The Literature of Persuasion

Not only did this school fulfill the need for literate civil servants, it also created a literature and an ideology of great merit and high standards. The magnanimity and good government of the Twelfth Dynasty were celebrated in poetry, story, and prophecy. "Adore the King—may he live forever!—in your innermost being," sang the contemporary poet in advice to his fellow countrymen. "Cleave to His Majesty in your hearts. He is 'Wisdom' who is in (human) hearts. His eyes search out every body, he is Re by whose brightness people see. He brightens the Two Lands more than the sun disc, he fertilizes the land more than a great inundation, he fills the

Two Lands with invigorating strength. . . . He gives sustenance to those in his following, he nourishes him who adheres to his path. The king is sustenance, his mouth is increase. . . . He is Khnum (creator god) of every limb, who begets, who brings people into being. He is Bast who protects Egypt. He who adores him shall escape his arm, he is Sakhmet (the goddess of pestilence) towards him who transgresses his command, but he is gentle towards the weak(?). Fight for his name, be guiltless in respect of an oath (taken) by him, and rid yourselves of deeds of slackness. The one whom the king loves shall achieve a revered state, (but) for him who rebels against His Majesty there is no tomb. . . . Do this and your limbs shall be sound."

It was under Senwosret I, Amenemhet's illustrious son and successor, that the Writing School began to produce pieces that centuries later were to be held up as masterpieces. At the time of composition, however, they were intended in large measure to legitimize the new royal family. The story of a wise lector-priest Neferty, gifted with second sight, who at the request of king Snofru of the Fourth Dynasty casts his vision into the future, forecasts the horrors of the period of civil war. This piece of discourse, specifically said to have been written down by Snofru himself, ends in a prophecy that a saviour-king "Ameny the Triumphant" will one day come to set things right. A popular adventure yarn describes the chequered career of the courtier Sinuhe who, at the time of the assassination, took fright and fled into Western Asia where he remained in exile for many years. His adventures among the bedu of Palestine are told with great relish, and cast a flood of light on nomadism current on Egypt's borders in the 20th century B.C. But, fascinating as these rollicking tales were, they do not constitute the main message of the story of Sinuhe. Believing that the new king Senwosret would kill him if he came back, the homesick fugitive declined to return until eventually the king's own invitation overcame his trepidation. The poignant scene of return and reconciliation stresses a clear message: come home, ye Egyptian exiles! Egypt is your home! The king is compassionate and forgiving! A fairy story about a sailor shipwrecked on an island inhabited by a magic snake makes a similar point: do not wander abroad, for Egypt is your home! Embrace your wife and children and end your days in the comfort of your native surroundings.

The persuasion literature of the Twelfth Dynasty stands in contrast to that which dates to the preceding centuries of Herakleopolitan rule. Unlike the anonymous discourse of protest which admittedly lingers on as a genre to be copied self-consciously, Twelfth Dynasty creations come from identified narrative agents who enjoy a hegemony which eliminates any question of truth value. A named wiseman delivers himself of a critical statement of great importance for the times; or dominant figures of the past become paradigms of the malfeasance the Middle Kingdom is seeking to eliminate. While oral discourse drew the contempt of the scribal class as being unrestrained and unreliable, Twelfth Dynasty literature was created *in writing*, with clear authorial intention, albeit for *parlando* purposes which attempted to elicit a specific hearer-response.

The conscious attempt to lionize the "House of Amenemhet" and bolster its legitimacy took other forms besides didactic injunction and message-narrative. It was probably the scribes of the writing school who were responsible for the creation of a true king-list, listing the kings of Egypt in sequence with the lengths of reign of each duly noted. The ingredients already had been put together in the Old Kingdom in the form of a set of annals recording major events of each year; but the Twelfth Dynasty distilled this material as well as other surviving evidence. Some of the latter was faulty or only partially preserved, and Old Kingdom dating practices were not always clearly understood. Nonetheless the scribes managed to produce a list which, starting with the "reign" of the creator god, traced the kingship of Egypt through the gods and demi-gods to the human occupants of the throne down to the members of the present dynasty. The exercise thus placed Amenemhet and his descendants squarely within the legitimate line of monarchs which could be traced back to the dawn of time. The Twelfth Dynasty kings themselves contributed to their own public relations through recourse to a form of discourse which, while it bespoke their common origin, nonetheless allowed them to promote their own interests. A public speech, although inscribed in a mortuary context, was in very truth an address to the living, to be construed as an oral pronouncement. Non-royalty had indulged in such pronouncements during the Old Kingdom, and in the subsequent time of troubles it had become very popular among the commoners of the period. The Eleventh Dynasty kings, who had emerged from the ranks of the self-made gentry, the *nedjesu,* naturally made use of this type of public promulgation in the form of speeches to army and court; and the Twelfth followed suit with a vengeance. The public pronouncement in the form of a speech from the throne, celebrating victory or peaceful achievement or declaring policy, became vastly popular as a means of directly addressing the mass of the population.

While essentially working for the "Establishment," the scribal teachers of the Writing School showed an enlightened self-interest in producing works that would inculcate in their pupils and society at large an overriding love for their profession. To this end they made use of the Wisdom genre, or *seboyet,* "teaching," which we briefly touched on above. A beloved and much-copied exemplar of this type of didactic teaching tool was the "Satire of the Trades," which imagines a man advising his young son on the advantages of being a scribe. In the course of his disquisition the father describes a wide variety of occupations—the builder, messenger, soldier, weaver, fisherman, etc.—and loses no opportunity to denigrate them by pointing out the excessive labor and scant remuneration involved in each. But ". . . as for the scribe, every place of his is at the Residence City and he will not be poor in it!. . . . I will make you love writing more than your own mother. . . . Behold! There is no profession free of a boss, except for (that of) the scribe, (for) he is the boss!"

The Reorganization of Egypt

In spite of its tentative beginnings, the Twelfth Dynasty was to prove itself perhaps the most competent and enlightened family to rule Egypt in ancient times. Under their rule Egypt enjoyed something of a return to the prosperity of the Old Kingdom at its height. Locating the new capital within the greater Memphite region placed the regime within the penumbra of the Old Kingdom pyramids, a form the Twelfth Dynasty kings gladly espoused. Their pyramids arose, not only adjacent to Itj-towy (modern Lisht), but also at Dahshur close to Snofru's monuments and in the Fayum. Though cased in the usual fine limestone, the new pyramids could not compete in engineering with the mighty structures of the Fourth Dynasty, being built with rubble cores some of which contained fragments of relief from dismantled Old Kingdom tombs (D). Once again, as of old, the mines of Sinai produced copper and turquoise in vast quantities; the quarries were humming with activity as a great building program was begun.

As luck would have it, the beginning of the Second Millennium B.C. coincided with the return of climatic patterns favorable to Egypt, and high inundations came with greater regularity. The gods seemed to be looking with favor on the house of Amenemhet! Arable land began to expand in the valley, and elsewhere land reclamation was practiced. The new land thus acquired was placed under the control of an "overseer of ploughland," divided into state-owned farms and worked by gangs of conscripts numbering about twenty each. The Fayum was especially favored by the kings of the time, who recovered large amounts of land around the lake by the construction of dams, canals, and basins to regularize the water's flow. Senwosret II and Amenemhet III even chose to live and be buried in this area.

The re-organization of government which was to be a lasting contribution of the dynasty must be viewed in light of two important facts: 1) the continued presence of a landed gentry, and 2) the (initial) impoverishment of the new house. The inauguration of the writing school had, as its primary objective, the creation of a cadre of literate civil servants who would provide a support staff to the officers of the king. Their presence helped to strengthen the office of vizier, who was given more power than before, as a general overseer of all the workings of government, whether at the capital or in the provinces. Only the treasury and the office of chief treasurer were beyond his purview: these reported directly to the king. A large record office was established as part of the vizier's bureau, and here were deposited copies of every legal and administrative document, especially those having to do with real estate and bequests. Out of the period of civil war had emerged, curiously, the value inherent in consultation and discussion, which had manifested itself in the phenomenon of a "council of the king's house," a body vested with advisory and juridical powers. The Twelfth Dynasty took over this "privy council," to which was added a "Council of Thirty" associated with the king, about which we know little.

Administrative problems continued to confront the central administration in the provinces. Amenemhet had restored order in Egypt by compromise with the landed aristocracy, and had even added to the ranks of the gentry by rewarding his own faithful followers with township titles. The provincial manor-lords, or nomarchs, were allowed to retain their hereditary estates, and many grew richer than any of their predecessors during the civil strife. Some held their own courts, and mimicked the king in erecting colossal statuary and mortuary complexes (E). The king, however, reserved for himself the privilege of confirming an heir in his patrimony, a mere formality it seemed, but one which could be transformed into an effective lever if the need arose. During the first four reigns of the dynasty relations between the king and these "barons" remained polite and marked with tact and diplomacy. But by the end of the Dynasty the landed gentry had, for the most part, disappeared. We can no longer trace their long family trees as the line of their tombs in the provincial necropoleis (F) comes to an end. What happened? Did the central, royal authority perpetrate a bloodless coup against the provincials, or was there resistance and a bloodbath? Could it be that, exercising both prerogative and force, the king at a given moment obliged the heirs of the provincial aristocracy to relocate their domiciles at Itj-towy, much as Louis XIV was to do in the case of the French nobility?

Whatever happened, and in the present state of the evidence we are allowed only educated guesses, by the reign of the fifth king of the line, Senwosret III **(fig. 1),** a new and more centralized form of provincial government is in place. This depended on the appointment of mayors and town councils in the major cities and towns, and the seeding of "department"-officials—their precise role is unknown—throughout the realm. The title of one important class of official, *whmw,* derives from a root meaning "to repeat, to communicate information," and stresses the desire of the administration to keep abreast of what was going on everywhere, and to make known its decisions. For the *whmw* or "reporter/herald" as the word might be rendered, both carried information to the king, and also announced to the people the king's decisions.

(c) Gianni Dagli Orti/CORBIS

Figure 1 Head of Senwosret III.

The Reign of Amenemhet III

The revitalization which these reforms contributed to the life of the Dynasty is evident in the reign of Senwosret III's successor, Amenemhet III **(fig. 2–3),** who was to become the "Lamares" of later legend. While royal inscriptions from the reign are almost wholly missing, making it impossible to write a political account of goings on, private texts are very numerous, and bespeak forty-four years of unequalled prosperity. Mining expeditions to the Sinai turquoise mines became almost annual events, and new mines were opened up as old ones became exhausted. It was Amenemhet III that brought to fruition the land reclamation project in the Fayum, where 17,000 acres of arable land were recovered. A canal nine miles long and 300 feet wide, according to later classical accounts, was dug from the Nile into the lake, along with a lock(?) to regulate the water flow. To commemorate his work the king erected at the edge of the lake two colossal statues each on a podium over five meters tall, which at inundation time were flooded by the rising waters (G).

© Gianni Dagli CORBIS

Figure 2   Granite statue of Amenemhet III.

Several miles to the east, at a point where a branch from the river enters the Fayum depression, Amenemhet constructed the larger of his two pyramids, the pyramid of Hawara. While the pyramid itself is of modest dimensions (102 meters on a side and 58 meters tall) and mediocre construction (a mud-brick core cased in fine limestone), it incorporates several ingenious devices, including dummy doors, false passageways, and trap doors, all designed to thwart grave-robbers. (It appears not to have been successful). In contrast to the pyramid, the mortuary temple on the south side was gigantic. Twelve centuries after its construction Herodotus visited the site, and was astounded by what he saw: "I have myself seen it, and indeed no words can tell its wonders . . . though the pyramids were greater than words could tell, and each one of them a match for many great monuments built by the Greeks, this maze (the mortuary temple) surpasses even the pyramids. It has twelve roofed courts, with doors over against each other, six face the north and six the south, in two continuous lines, all within one outer wall. There are also double sets of chambers, 3,000 altogether. . . . The outlets of the chambers and the maze

Figure 3 Sphinx of Amenemhet III.

of passages hither and thither through the courts were an unending marvel to us. . . . Over all this is a roof of stone like the walls, and the walls are covered with carved figures" (translation of A.D. Godley, *Loeb Classical Library*). This structure survived more or less intact nearly into the Christian era: and all who saw it were staggered by its size, complexity, and opulence, to the point that they dubbed it the "Labyrinth" after the mythical Minoan building at Knossos. Today, however, the site lies completely bare, having been turned into a quarry probably in late Roman times (H).

The Twelfth Dynasty and the External World

Outside Egypt the Twelfth Dynasty's interests lay upriver to the south and to a lesser extent in Western Asia. The Libyan coasts and the desert oases posed no threats; and remote islands across the seas were mere curiosities, although there is some evidence for trade with the Aegean. Far-off lands to the east, though presumably known to Egypt, offered no interest whatsoever; places in Mesopotamia are conspicuous by their absence.

Egypt's hegemony over the lands south of the First Cataract had been lost during the reign of Pepy II, as a new ethnic element, the cattle-herding C-group people, made its entry into Nubia and the northern Sudan. These people made no pretensions of urban living, moving from camp-site to camp-site, and burying their dead within stone rings lined with bucrania. During the period of weakness under the Herakleopolitan Ninth and Tenth Dynasties, Nubians seeking employment as mercenaries experienced no difficulty in entering Egypt from the south, and they became a common sight in the ranks of the city armies in this time of strife. Kings of the Eleventh Dynasty seem even to have actively recruited south of the First Cataract. Simultaneously a major political entity began to take shape centering upon the city of Kerma, south of the Second Cataract on the Nile. Its rapid growth and ostensible power threatened Egypt's southern frontiers, and as early as the reign of Montuhotpe the Great had occasioned retaliatory measures. Amenemhet I in a series of punitive or pre-emptive strikes hammered the territory between the First and Second cataracts, and Senwosret I emulated his father, carrying his arms clean through to the region of the Third Cataract. By the reign of Senwosret III the formal frontier had been pushed to Semna at the Second Cataract on the Nile, and two fortresses built on either bank to control shipping and the movement of peoples, and to provide a bulwark against Kerma to the south. As Senwosret III states explicitly on his frontier stela, the purpose was to regulate the migration of the Sudanese tribes: they were to be permitted to go north to trade only, not to settle. Within the territory thus delimited the Egyptians planted mud-brick forts at strategic points to protect shipping and provide staging areas for expeditions into the gold-bearing wadys. For while the first and foremost reason for the forts was protection from the south, they also provided centers for gold ore collection and smelting, whence regular shipments could be made back to Egypt. At first the forts were small affairs ranging from 50 by 60 meters (Semna east) to 1,000 × 130 meters (Buhen), though heavily fortified with thick walls, bastions, moats, and glacis. Garrisons were small: at Uronarti there was space for only about twenty-five families. Their mission was clear from the names given the forts: "Repelling the Madjay," "Curbing the Deserts," "Subduing the Barbarians," and the like. Circuit patrols and an efficient system of letter-delivery kept the forts in touch with one another and with the military command back in Egypt. It was these forts, initially tiny islands of Egyptian culture in a sea of "C-group" Nubians, that were to provide the nuclei from which civilizing influences radiated to the barbarians and thus eventually "Egyptianized" the entire region (**fig. 4**).

Western Asia was more difficult to keep under permanent control by implanting garrisons, and the Twelfth Dynasty fell back on the example of the Old Kingdom in trying to establish an amorphous sphere of influence (**fig. 5**). Palestine and southern Syria had suffered from the same drastic changes in climate that Egypt had experienced in the late 23rd century B.C. Cities were destroyed or abandoned to the extent that one can no longer speak of an "urban" life style. The thinning population became transhumant and dependent on flocks and herds, adopting a migratory existence tied in to seasonal movement from camp ground to camp ground. It was this type of society that the hero Sinuhe (see above) fell in with during his exile in Asia, where he found nought but tents and stockades, skin-clad natives, cattle and sheep.

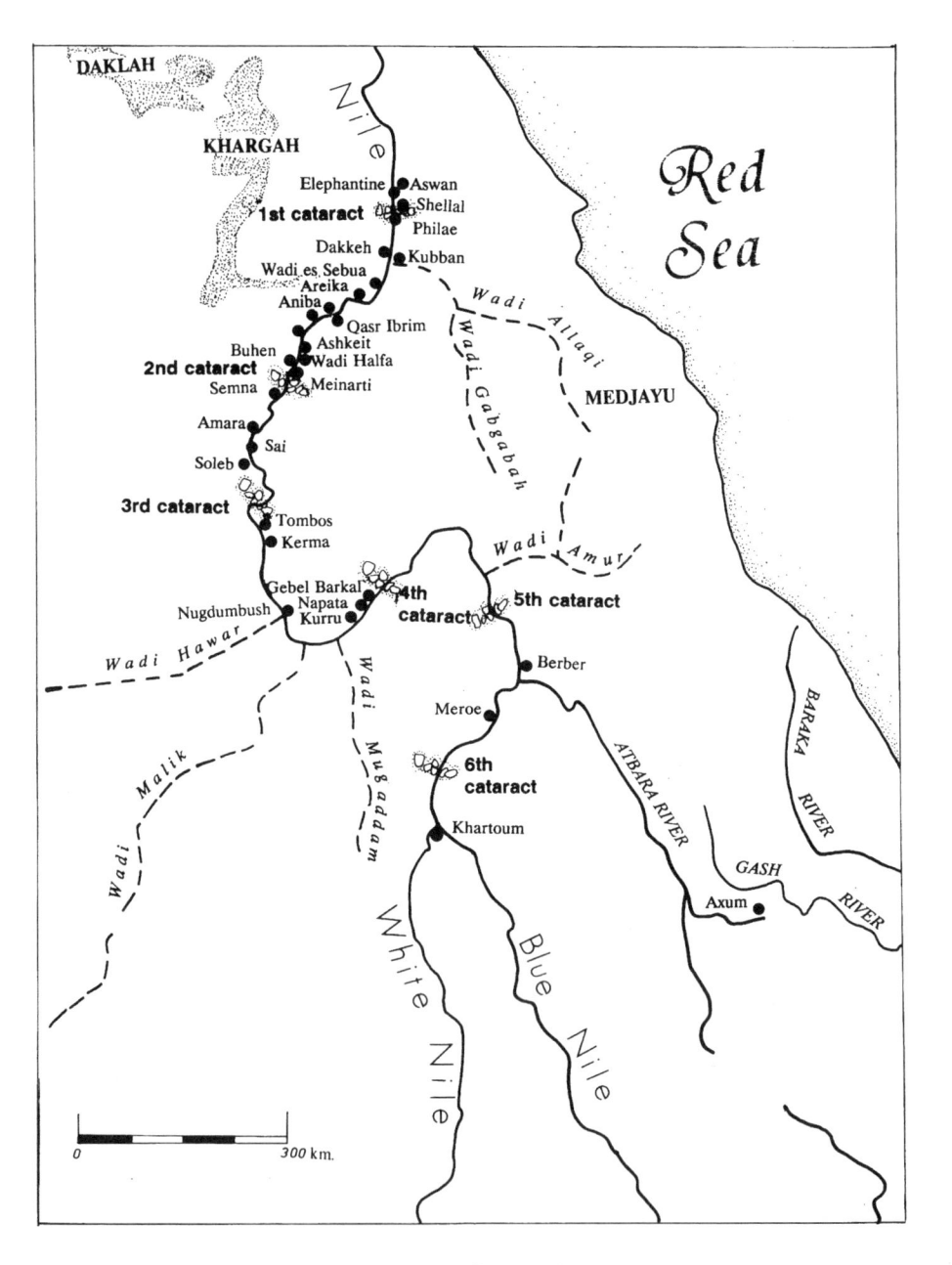

Figure 4 Map of Nubia and the Sudan in the Middle Kingdom.

EGYPT & THE LEVANT IN THE 3RD MILL. B.C.

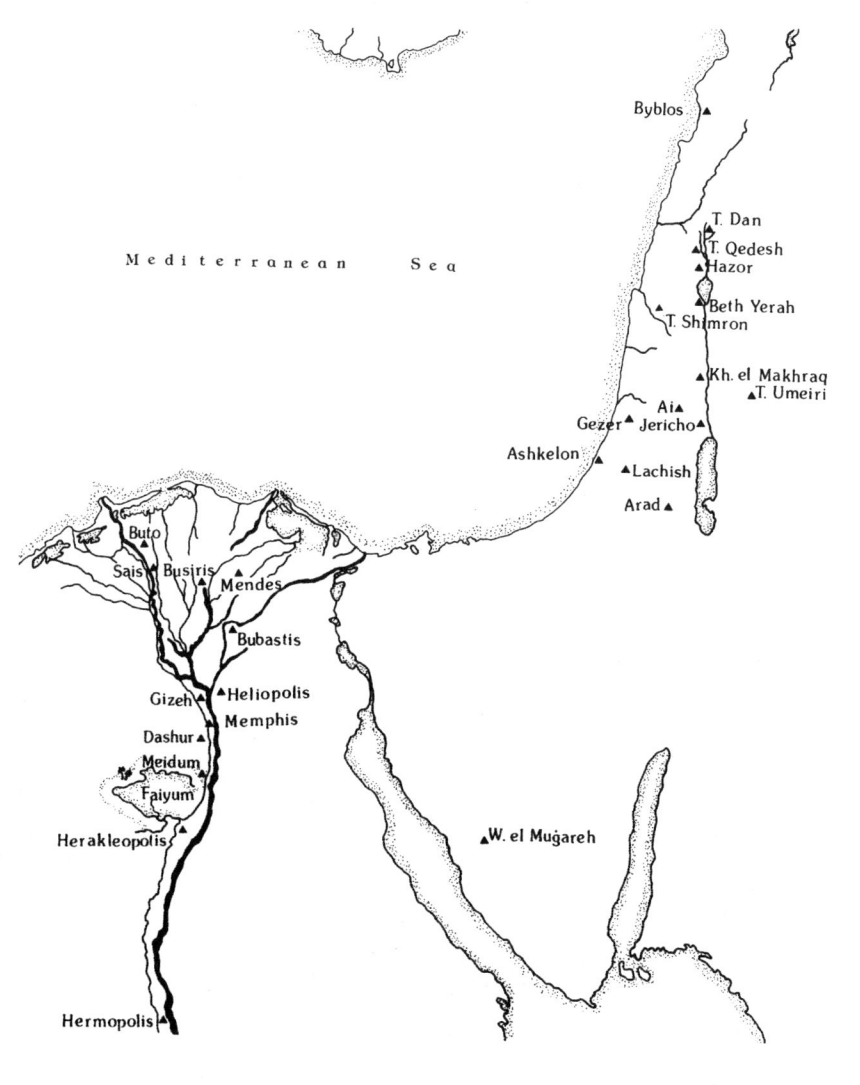

Figure 5 Map of Egypt's northern sphere of influence.

Egypt's relations with Western Asia during the Twelfth Dynasty represents a return to the concept of a "sphere of influence" current during the Old Kingdom. The Levant, its produce, resources, and manpower, belonged to Pharaoh by rights inherent in his divinity, and if he needed anything from the region, his men would go and get it. A surviving inscription from the reign of Amenemhet II (first half of the 19th century B.C.), probably annalistic in nature, shows how the system worked. In a single year expeditionary forces, in one case in ten troop carriers, visited the coast of Lebanon, certain Syrian principalities, and even the island of Cyprus in search of a wide variety of items. Thousands of captives are brought back along with tens of thousands of units of foodstuffs and minerals. The natives of the Levant in the 20th and 19th centuries B.C. were too sparse in number, too uncultured socially and too disunited politically to offer much resistance. But this situation was not to last.

Further Readings

On the political history of the Twelfth Dynasty, see W. C. Hayes, "The Middle Kingdom in Egypt," in I. E. S. Edwards and others (eds.), *The Cambridge Ancient History* (Cambridge, 1961), I, ch. 20; R. Leprohon, *The Reign of Amenemhet III* (PhD dissertation, University of Toronto, 1980); C. Obsomer, *Sesostris Ier*, Brussels, 1995; S. Quirke, *The Administration of Egypt in the Late Middle Kingdom*, Whitstable, 1990; *idem, Middle Kingdom Studies*, Whitstable, 1991; I. Shaw (ed.), *The Oxford History of Ancient Egypt*, Oxford, 2000 (ch. 7); W. K. Simpson, "Twelfth Dynasty," in D. B. Redford (ed.), *The Oxford Encyclopaedia of Ancient Egypt* (New York, 2001), III, 453–57.

On literature and the writing school see J. L. Foster, *Thought Couplets and Clause Sequences in a Literary Text: The Maxims of Ptah-hotep,* Toronto, 1977; *idem, Echoes of Egyptian Voices: An Anthology of Ancient Egyptian Poetry,* London, 1992; M. Lichtheim, *Ancient Egyptian Autobiographies, Chiefly of the Middle Kingdom,* Fribourg, 1988; R. B. Parkinson, *Voices from Ancient Egypt: An Anthology of Middle Kingdom Writings,* London, 1991; *idem,* "Types of Literature in the Middle Kingdom," in A. Loprieno (ed.), *Ancient Egyptian Literature: History and Forms* (Leiden, 1996), 297–312; *idem, The Tale of Sinuhe and Other Ancient Egyptian Poems, 1940–1640 B.C.,* Oxford, 1997; W. K. Simpson, "*Belles Lettres* and Propaganda," *ibid,* 435–46.

On Egypt and the external world, see D. B. Redford, *Egypt, Canaan, and Israel in Ancient Times* (Princeton, 1992), ch. 3–4.

CHAPTER SEVEN

The Decline of the Middle Kingdom and the Hyksos Conquest

—————————————— ψ ——————————————

The Twelfth Dynasty was to cast a long shadow down through the ages. Its kings and wisemen became legendary, its monuments entered the realm of fantasy. The administrative reforms it championed turned out to be lasting, and the dialect it promoted, Middle Egyptian, became the highly regarded literary dialect to the end of Egyptian history.

The Downsizing of the State

Within a generation, however, of the death of Amenemhet III in about 1795 B.C. the monarchy seems to have relinquished a good deal of power. His son, Amenemhet IV, while exhibiting great vigour in his *res gestae*, lasted no more than a decade on the throne and was succeeded by his sister who may have married outside the royal family. Her husband(?) and successor, Sobekhotpe I, was traditionally designated as the founder of the Thirteenth Dynasty. But the latter consisted for the most part of a series of unrelated monarchs who held the throne for very short periods. In fact the duration in years of this curious regime, c. 120 years (to 1665 B.C.) corresponds roughly to the number of kings who (according to the Turin Canon) occupied the throne! No satisfactory explanation has been found for this rapid turnover, although one suspects a combination of disease, palace conspiracies, and perhaps arbitrary selection in defiance of dynastic succession. That some reigns may have been contemporary has been suggested, but the king-lists give no inkling of this, and in cases which can be checked, normal succession appears to have been the rule. That royal ideology was suffering progressive weakness can be inferred from the dilution of titles of royal relationship: king's-son and king's-daughter are frequently used in a metaphorical sense for royal plenipotentiaries. Itj-towy remained the residence, although many of the kings continued to be Theban born, and all Egypt from the Second Cataract to the Mediterranean remained under one crown. Royal burials are few, but those identified are either located within the precincts of a Twelfth Dynasty mortuary complex, or at Saqqara.

For the first half-century the record throws up a few kings of greater resourcefulness, such as Khendjer, Sobek-hotpe III, and Nefer-hotpe, who were clearly trying to put the kingdom in order and recapture the glory of the Twelfth Dynasty; but from 1725 B.C. one can discern a steady and irreversible decline in royal power. If there was any continuum at all during the century following 1790 B.C. it was provided by a family who monopolized the office of vizier (prime minister), and each of whose members spanned during their period of tenure several reigns. About seven generations of these viziers can be traced which, on an acceptable generation count, would cover about 140 years. Their power is indicated by their ability to issue decrees in their own names and to erect imposing statues of themselves. Declining as Egypt was in this century, however, there was no return to the disunity of former times: the centralization of the administration remained a permanent contribution for many generations to come.

Whatever its cause, Egypt's slow decline during the Thirteenth Dynasty left its mark on the record of physical remains. No major pyramids nor mortuary temples can be dated to this period—Khendjer's modest structure at Saqqara is the exception that proves the rule—as no king lived long enough to complete one. Although a later check-list of kings who made donations inscribed on a wall at Karnak mentions many kings of the dynasty, no additions were made to the temple of Amun at Thebes, the royal chapel founded by Senwosret I. Few if any expeditions visited the mines in search of precious metals and gem-stones, a sure sign of the decline of the official reward system. More serious for national security was the abandonment of border fortifications (ostensibly because of budgetary restraints), especially those carefully planned and sited by Senwosret I and III in Nubia. As garrisons were withdrawn, the Kushites of the Kerma kingdom moved in to take possession, or to burn and loot. In the event statues, stelae, and other memorials of the erstwhile Egyptian presence were removed as trophies to Kerma. Worse was to follow. As the 18th century drew to a close, Kushite armed forces met no resistance as they crossed the Elephantine frontier and invaded the towns of Upper Egypt as far as Thebes itself.

Relations with Western Asia

On the north of Egypt's Asiatic sphere of interest major changes had begun to take place already during the second half of the Twelfth Dynasty. The mighty empire of Ur, centered upon the city of that name in southern Mesopotamia, had presided over a century of economic prosperity from Iran to the Phoenician coast beginning around 2050 B.C. But by the middle of the 20th century, contemporary with the high point of Senwosret I's reign, it began to disintegrate. A new ethnic block, generally called (though with no great ethnic or linguistic precision) the Amorites, began to emerge from an original homeland around Mount Bishri in Syria. Unlike Akkadian, their language was West Semitic and ancestral to such later languages and sub-dialects as Ugaritic, Phoenician, Canaanite, and Hebrew. Their hostile movement eastward and northward into Mesopotamia was undertaken at the expense of Ur, whose empire rapidly collapsed. In the aftermath, by 1900 B.C., the map of Western Asia shows a series of warring states ruled by dynasties with Amorite names, scattered from the Iranian foothills to the Lebanon mountains: Isin, Larsa, Eshnunna, and Mari in Mesopotamia; Yamkhad, Qatanum, and Hasor in the Levant.

The arrival in force of the Amorites had repercussions as far south as the Egyptian frontier. The contemporary archaeological record in Palestine during the period called Middle Bronze II b–c attests to the presence of a new ethnic group (presumably Amorite in language) markedly increasing the population. The long period of transhumant occupation by rustic nomadic groups (A) came to an end, as old town sites were re-occupied and new cities constructed. New types of fortification reflect the prevalence of interstate strife and innovative military hardware characteristic of the warring states to the north and north-east. The development of the battering ram (Akkadian *iasibu*) and the siege tower (Akkadian *dimtu*) necessitated thickened walls of field stone (B) or sloping glacis of cobble or plaster (C). New settlements or the extensions of old ones were protected by massive earthen ramparts with sloping outer faces and external fosses; gates had double or triple doors positioned between massive towers (D). Tactics relating to offensive warfare also benefited from invention. Bronze daggers and scimitar-shaped swords came into use, and a strengthened, "composite" bow entered the paraphernalia of the armoury. This was the period when a new animal was domesticated in numbers, for use primarily for transport in a military setting. The horse, the "Ass of the Mountains" as the animal was dubbed by the inhabitants of Mesopotamia, was at first considered *infra dig* by the elites of the Amorite states; but it was not long before its potential in drawing moving platforms (chariots) was realized.

During the Thirteenth Dynasty Egypt remained largely unaffected by this military culture which was taking shape on its northern flank. Enforced or voluntary movement of Asiatic factors into Egypt, which had begun in the Twelfth Dynasty continued into the Thirteenth. A papyrus in the Brooklyn Museum, dated around 1725 B.C., records the unskilled labor apparently on an Egyptian estate. Of seventy-seven legible names forty-eight are "Amorite," and only twenty-nine Egyptian! The Kahun papyri from roughly the same period mention Asiatics occupying such posts as door-keepers, professional entertainers, and personal servants. The Austrian excavations at Tel ed-Dab'a, the ancient *Hwt-wa'ret* (Avaris) in the Delta (E–F), have revealed an increasing assemblage of Asiatic pottery and artefacts of MB II b–c horizon which eventually exceeded in quantity the native Egyptian material. This may indicate the presence of Amorites from the Levant resident at Avaris for commercial purposes.

Clearly during the later Middle Kingdom Egypt was experiencing difficulties in controlling its old spheres of influence, both in south and north. While some merchants and prospectors are known to have operated in the north from their scarab seals or biographies, punitive campaigns were no longer feasible (nor possible!) in the face of the new strength of the Kerma kingdom and the Middle Bronze Age states of the Levant. One recourse, however, remained open to the state, a curious exercise but one which had been practiced from time immemorial, viz. cursing. As we noted in our examination of Egyptian magic, as far back as the Old Kingdom the practice of "smashing the red bowls," or crude images of the enemy had been known and used to commit to destruction and oblivion individual foreigners, usually chiefs, and sometimes recalcitrant Egyptians. The names of the condemned would be written in ink on the bowl or figurine and the latter, to the accompaniment of appropriate magic spells, would be ritually broken. Several major lots of such "execration texts" have come to light, two in particular from the late Twelfth Dynasty (the "Berlin and Mirgissa bowls") and the mid Thirteenth (the "Brussels figurines") being germane to our present quest. The formula usually names a chief of a locality or town, whether in Nubia or Asia, together with "their mighty men, their runners, their confederates, their associates . . . who may rebel, who may conspire, who may fight, who may intend to rebel," and commits them to death. Each collection gives the impression of a comprehensive list—omissions of any potential rebels would be dangerous!—and thus may be used to reconstruct demographic patterns. The two groups illustrate the passage from the transhumance of the world of Sinuhe to the urbanism of MB II a–b. The Berlin-Mirgissa group shows us a sparsely inhabited Palestine, with several chiefs identified by district, and few towns mentioned. The Brussels group on the other hand lists many more chiefs, and each is associated with a specific town rather than a region. The towns listed include those of the coastal plain from Gaza to Haifa, Shechem in the highlands, the Jordan Valley, Transjordan, the region of Damascus, and the Phoenician coast.

One exception to the ubiquitous hostility that seems to underlie the Execration Texts is the case of the city of Byblos. From as early as the Archaic Period of Egyptian history Byblos had enjoyed uninterrupted relations of amity with Egypt, for whom it had provided the conduit for the much-coveted cedar of Lebanon. While during the heyday of Ur it had been drawn within the ambit of that great empire, by the time of Amenemhet III it had returned to the Egyptian fold. Ten generations of rulers from that point until the beginning of the New Kingdom enjoyed friendly relations with the Pharaohs, transporting timber on demand and receiving rich rewards. So close was the connexion that the Byblian headmen began to write their names and to carve inscriptions in Egyptian hieroglyphic script, calling themselves "hereditary prince and $h3ty$-^{c}," and thus adopting the status of an Egyptian mayor. The fourth of the line, Antin (flor. c. 1715 B.C.) had himself depicted worshiping the cartouche of the Egyptian king, with the wish (in hieroglyphs) "may Re-harakhty grant that he adore Re every day!" The title "ruler of rulers," which Antin bore and which was presumably sanctioned by Pharaoh, betokens an expanded horizon for Byblos. One of the Byblian tombs dating two or three generations after Antin contains a jar with the inscription "ruler of foreign lands," and with that appellative we enter a new phase in the history of Egypt and western Asia.

Within a decade of 1670 B.C. a weakened Egypt fell victim to invasion and occupation by an Asiatic group speaking a West Semitic dialect akin to Amorite. No contemporary account of the incursion has yet been discovered, and the only connected description is offered thirteen centuries later by the Egyptian historian Manetho: "Out of parts to the east men of despicable ethnicity marched boldly against (Egypt), and seized it easily with overwhelming force without fighting a battle. And having taken prisoners those who had been leaders here, they

The Hyksos

Salitis (Sheshy)	c. 1666–1663 B.C.
Bnon (?)	c. 1663–1655 B.C.
Ya'qob-el	c. 1655–1644 B.C.
Khiyan	c. 1644–1604 B.C.
Apophis	c. 1604–1569 B.C.
Hammudi	c. 1569–1558 B.C.

thereafter savagely burned the cities and demolished the gods' shrines. They treated all the inhabitants most hatefully, slaughtering some, and leading into slavery the children and wives of others. Then finally they bestowed the kingship on one of their own, Salitis by name, and he resided in Memphis, exacting taxes from the south and north of the land, and implanting garrisons in the best sited positions. . . . He found a city optimally sited lying on the east bank of the Bubastite river called Avaris. . . . And this place he built up and fortified with very strong walls, and settled there . . . an advanced guard."

Manetho's narrative, formerly written off by historians as colored by more recent invasions of Egypt, is confirmed by eye witness accounts dating a century after the onset of the Asiatic occupation, which speak of destruction and hatred. It may well be that the presence of commercial enclaves of Asiatics, such as the one at Avaris, abetted the coming to power of their congeners from across the Sinai; but the take-over of political power has all the hallmarks of an invasion nonetheless. As we shall see there was to be little if any elite emulation on the part of the Egyptians or the Hyksos: the two groups occupied two solitudes.

Manetho gives Phoenicia as the place of origin of the group, but his (Egyptian) source probably used a general term for the Levantine littoral, as opposed to the hinterland. The Egyptians called the newcomers by their age-old term for anyone from across the eastern frontier, viz. *A'amu;* but the new rulers were known by the political designation *heqau-khasut,* "foreign rulers," which over the centuries was garbled into *Hyksos.* Micro-dating of the Hyksos in Egypt cannot be done on the basis of contemporary epigraphic evidence, as it is very sparse indeed; and recourse to archaeological seriation is even less reliable and leads to such preposterous conclusions as that one of the "Hyksos" must be dated before the "Hyksos"! In the Turin Canon, copied out three centuries after the expulsion of the Hyksos, six rulers were named, but because of a hole in the papyrus only the name of the last is preserved. Whether this corresponds to historical reality is unclear; but by the 3rd century B.C. six Hyksos kings continue to constitute Manetho's Fifteenth Dynasty.

While later native Egyptian rulers were to boast that they had wiped all trace of the Hyksos from the land, modern excavation has revealed a number of Hyksos sites. Several burying grounds in the Wady Tumilat and on the eastern fringe of the Delta have been identified and partly excavated. Two Hyksos fortresses have been unearthed, one at Tel ed-Dab'a (Avaris) with mud-brick walls as sturdy as Manetho suggests; the other at Tel el-Yehudiya twenty miles northeast of Heliopolis, where huge ramparts of packed sand, pebbles and gravel can be seen from a great distance (G). In the wake of the Hyksos conquest Asiatic groups began to cross the Sinai and to colonize the eastern fringe of the Delta and the Wady Tumilat. Beyond this, however, they did not go, and it was left to Hyksos garrisons (as Manetho suggests) to hold the rest of the Delta and Middle Egypt. Memphis they pillaged of monuments. Some statues and blocks were taken to Avaris to adorn the new fortress; others were despatched to kings in Western Asia, perhaps as diplomatic gifts.

The archaeological record has made it abundantly clear that the Asiatics in Egypt kept themselves apart from the native population. Examination of human remains at Avaris have suggested that an incoming male population intermarried with local women; but if so a strong patriarchal streak must have prevented the acculturation of the invaders. Cemeteries of the newcomers, such as those in the Wady Tumilat, yield pottery and artefacts of a purely MB IIb type, remarkably similar to the cultural assemblages of northern Palestine and southern Syria. Excavations at Tel ed-Dab'a/Avaris have unearthed a series of mud-brick, tripartite axial temples of a pattern at home in the Levant, with no observable influence from Egyptian architecture or cultic practice. Similarly artistic motifs, found on the few decorated seals and surfaces which have been brought to light, are almost indistinguishable from elements in the repertoire of MB IIb artisans in Syria. Presumably the Hyksos rulers and the elite were not illiterate, but it is not certainly known what script they employed among themselves. One intriguing possibility takes us to the turquoise mines of Sarbut el-Kadim in the western Sinai where, scattered around the site and adjacent to the mine shafts a series of between thirty and forty inscriptions were discovered in the early 20ᵗʰ century; since then an additional group has been uncovered in Upper Egypt. These texts are written in a new script, often dubbed "Sinaitic," which is almost certainly alphabetic, employing the acrophonic principle (*a* is for "apple," *b* is for "bat," *c* is for "cat," and so forth); but in this case the language which provided the sound value was a West Semitic language which we might subsume under the umbrella rubric of "Amorite." While it may be that the idea of representing single, consonantal articulations by picture-signs was inspired by hieroglyphs, the resultant script is wholly different and is based on a West Semitic vocabulary. The date and place where this new alphabetic script was invented have been hotly debated, and from its subsequent history in the Levant a location north of the Sinai is to be preferred. Guesses as to date range from the Middle Kingdom through the early New Kingdom; but the identification in one inscription of the proper name *ʾabob* or "Apoph(is)" strongly militates in favor of the Hyksos era. If, however, the Sinaitic alphabet had been used at this time, in Egypt no Hyksos site to date has revealed any examples.

Local communications with the natives required some concessions to the Egyptian script. Once the Hyksos were ensconced in Egypt Egyptian scribes were employed to render the Amorite names of the kings into hieroglyphic script, but these transcriptions were used mainly on signet rings.

Historical records on the basis of which a history might be written are almost wholly lacking. The first three kings, together ruling for little more than two decades, have left scarcely a trace. It may have been about this time that we must place the short reign of the enigmatic Nehsi, who calls himself on his statue and an obelisk (both undoubtedly from Avaris) "beloved of Seth, lord of Avaris (var. lord of the mouth-of-the-arable-land)." His relationship to the "[heir]s (?) of legitimate rulers" whom he mentions on the obelisk is obscure. Only the fourth and fifth rulers, Khyan and Apophis, began somewhat tentatively to erect monuments in the Egyptian language and script; but if the latter really could, as he claims on a writing kit he bestowed on one of his scribes, read and write in hieroglyphs, he must be the exception that proves the rule.

What sort of government the Hyksos espoused can only be guessed at on the basis of spotty, circumstantial evidence. The Egyptian king-list tradition refused to acknowledge them as true Pharaohs, preferring to label them simply "foreign rulers"; but the tradition did, in fact, preserve a genealogical myth that must go back to the Hyksos themselves. In the Turin Canon of kings, the six Hyksos names are preceded by approximately thirty-two names which are not Egyptian in the main, and probably represent the roster of Amorite "ancestors" which several contemporary regimes in western Asia used in order to enhance the prestige of their dynasties. While the six Hyksos kings in Manetho can be matched up fairly successfully with names found on Hyksos seals and monuments, a sizeable number of seals with Hyksos names finds no match; and one is left to wonder what role these otherwise unattested worthies played in the scheme of things. That the Fifteenth Dynasty promoted a quasi-"feudal" system, in which a body of lesser chiefs and sheiks owed allegiance to the king in Avaris, has much to say for it.

Manetho preserves a curious allegation in his history that the Hyksos dynasty comprised "shepherds and brothers" from Phoenicia. While the understanding of -*sos* in Hyksos as the word for "shepherd" is a late misunderstanding arising from the confusion between two homonyms, the "brothers" harks back to a genuine cultural reminiscence. From the records of Thutmose III and cuneiform archives from Emar on the Euphrates, it is clear that in certain Syrian communities of the Bronze Age power was exercised, not only by a (town)-ruler or headman, but also by an influential council termed "the brothers." It is tempting to discern this phenomenon underlying the political reality of Hyksos governance.

Hyksos relations with the broader world of the eastern Mediterranean are more difficult to delineate. Apophis refers to the god Seth having "placed all lands beneath his feet," and claims "a greater name than any other king" as one "who protects far-off lands who have never (even) seen him." This sounds bombastic, but may arise out of some real event. While the old notion that the Fifteenth Dynasty enjoyed an imperial hegemony over much of the Near East is clearly incorrect, a limited presence and commercial interest beyond the borders of Egypt is very probable. Hyksos scarab seals have been found along the southern coast of Israel, prompting the theory of a Hyksos "barony" centered perhaps on Sharuhen; while inland in the Negeb the large city represented by Tel Haroer and its territorium may have owed something to the monarchs in Avaris. Further afield contact was established with the Minoan civilization on the island of Crete. Cuneiform texts from Mari and (later) Ugarit on the north Syrian coast, speak of Kaphtor, Egyptian *Kftiw*, as a desirable commercial and cultural contact. Now the excavations at Tel ed-Dab'a/Avaris have unearthed fragments of frescoes depicting bull-leaping, remarkably similar to the same type of decoration in the "palace of Minos" at Knossos. This evidence of contact presaged an era of brilliant commercial exchange with the Aegean, which was to flourish between 1500 and 1200 B.C.

The Egyptians were later to claim that they had suffered much under the Hyksos, and that statement pretty much mirrored reality. Upon the conquest of the land, the remnant of the weakened Thirteenth Dynasty disappeared, perhaps executed by the invaders or put to flight; and Itj-towy, although still occupied, ceased to be the capital. The Hyksos experienced difficulty, however, in extending their control further south than Kusae, the fourteenth township of Upper Egypt, and were obliged to suffer a "rump" administration of native Egyptians to set up a government in Thebes (in Manetho the Sixteenth Dynasty). Attempts shortly after 1600 B.C. to subvert Thebes by force were largely unavailing, and on the eve of the Hyksos expulsion the border remained at Kusae. In the territory under direct Hyksos control the native population found itself compromised. The majority perhaps bowed to reality and co-operated with the invaders. These were later castigated as having "obeyed the call of the Asiatics," and were treated as collaborators.

Great offence was given to the Egyptians by the cultic innovations introduced by the conquerors. Seals and scarabs of Fifteenth Dynasty date give prominence to a hero god, in the act of flexing his muscles in mountainous settings, and to a nubile female, presumably his consort. Folklore circulating three centuries after the Hyksos expulsion accused king Apophis of having "made Seth his lord," to the exclusion of all other deities. Since from the outgoing Twelfth Dynasty the Egyptian Seth had been equated with the Canaanite hero god Aleyan Ba'al, "the lord," it is tempting to identify the macho mountain god with Ba'al, and the female with his consort Anat or Astarte. Egyptian gods, however, and their cults within territory dominated by the Hyksos, languished through inattention. To the Egyptians it appeared that Re, the sun-god, has refused to countenance or sanction the rule of the hated foreigners.

The Hyksos in Later Tradition

The Hyksos occupation of Egypt was a watershed in the history of North-east Africa and the Near East, and was decisive in shaping the next 500 years of Egyptian history. The disaster lived on in the collective memory of the Egyptians, and is alluded to in several later texts. It would be surprising if a like memory, but from a totally different vantage point, did not survive in the Levant among the descendants of those "Amorite"-speakers.

One such folk memory, apparently of Phoenician origin, passed into Greek guise and is known to us today as the legend of Io. A priestess in Argos in Greece, Io was beloved by Zeus; but when Hera discovered this example of her husband's philandering, she changed Io into a cow. Stung by a gadfly, the cow migrated around the eastern Mediterranean, and upon the banks of the Nile regained her human shape. In Egypt she gave birth to Epaphos, and her subsequent descendants numbered Belos, Aegyptos, and Danaus. The eventual expulsion of her progeny from Egypt brought the Phoenicians to the east coast of the Mediterranean and, through Danaus, the Argives to Greece.

The specifics of the legend point temptingly to the Hyksos. "Io" reminds one of a possible vocalization of the Egyptian word for "moon," current in personal names at the end of the Hyksos period; while an equation of Epaphos with Apophis and Belos with Ba'al seems beyond reproach. Also significant is the four-generation span during which Io's descendants are supposed to have occupied Egypt, a computation which would admirably fit the 108 years of Hyksos rule. Archaeological indications of close contact between Minoan Crete and Egypt (as well as the Levant in general) now can be elicited from the presence of bull-leaping scenes from the palace at Avaris, strongly reminiscent of similar scenes from Knossos. Although thematically different, the frescoes unearthed in contemporary palaces at Ugarit, Alalakh, and Mari, must be compared to those from the Minoan context.

A second account of early ethnic history must also be passed in review in attempting to fix the Hyksos in later tradition. This account likewise recalls the descent from the Levant to the banks of the Nile of a tribal leader named Jacob with his clan, and their settlement, as was the case with the Hyksos, along the eastern fringes of the Delta. Through one of their number they exercised political control, and for a time stood in good odor with the native inhabitants. Like Io and her descendants, they too occupied the land for four generations, according to one of their traditions. Eventually the native Egyptians turned hostile and, after trying to enslave the group, were obliged through divine intervention to expel them. Led by a prophet, they then retraced their steps across the Sinai desert whence they had come and, after many tribulations, ousted the inhabitants of Canaan and settled in their place. The people in question are the ancestral Hebrews, the *Bene Yisrael,* the Israelites, and the details of the account are given in the books of Genesis and Exodus. Interestingly, one of the early Hyksos rulers, attested by scarabs, was called "Jacob-(*el* less likely -*addu*)."

Further Readings

Over the past thirty years or so the picture of the outgoing Middle Kingdom and the Hyksos period has changed drastically, thanks to excavations in Palestine and the eastern Delta. New inscriptions have likewise contributed to the modified picture. It is important, therefore, in addressing the period, to read the most up-to-date literature. The following meet the criteria:

M. Bietak, *Avaris-Pi-Ramesses,* Oxford, 1979; *idem, Avaris, the Capital of the Hyksos,* London, 1996; W. V. Davies, L. Schofield (eds.), *Egypt, the Aegean, and the Levant,* London, 1995; E.D. Oren, *The Hyksos: New Historical and Archaeological Perspectives,* Philadelphia, 1997; K. Ryholt, *The Political Situation in Egypt During the Second Intermediate Period,* Copenhagen, 1997.

CHAPTER EIGHT
"... With Their Tribute on Their Backs"
The Rise of the Egyptian Empire

Ψ

Eighteenth Dynasty	
Ahmose	c. 1568–1543 B.C.
Amenophis I	c. 1543–1523 B.C.
Thutmose I	c. 1523–1514 B.C.
Thutmose II	c. 1514–1504 B.C.
Thutmose III	c. 1504–1450 B.C.
Amenophis II	c. 1451–1424 B.C.
Thutmose IV	c. 1424–1414 B.C.
Amenophis III	c. 1414–1377 B.C.
Amenophis IV (Akhenaten)	c. 1377–1360 B.C.
Tutankhamun	c. 1360–1351 B.C.
Ay	c. 1352–1349 B.C.
Horemheb	c. 1349–1318 B.C.

During the century of Hyksos domination in the north the tiny state of Thebes continued to exist, virtually unnoticed by the conquerors in Avaris. The Theban ruling elite of this period, the Sixteenth Dynasty, did not constitute a single family, and the rapid turnover of rulers which was endemic in the Thirteenth Dynasty continued to plague the Sixteenth. They managed to survive simply by tendering allegiance to the Asiatics and becoming vassals. But what unworthy descendants of the mighty Pharaohs of the Twelfth Dynasty were those tribute-paying kinglets of the south! Shut off from the Sudan and Asia, and therefore unable easily to get timber, metals, or luxury goods, Thebes eked out a miserable existence of the lowest order, which renders all the more pathetic the grandiose titles her kings persisted in assigning themselves (A). An astute observer in the year 1600 B.C. might well have concluded that as a center of political and economic power Thebes was finished.

The War of Liberation: the Seventeenth Dynasty

By one of those unexpected reversals of history, however, within two generations of the turn of the 16th century Thebes had recaptured its former pre-eminence. Around 1580 B.C. a family of kings of doubtful origin established itself in Thebes, by what means it is impossible to tell. Examination of their human remains which have survived (see below), as well as the testimony of their name *Ta'o,* suggests that they may have been of Nubian stock. Possibly they owed their status to the Hyksos king who had appointed them. In any event, they were made of different stuff from those whom they replaced, and by 1565 they had rebelled openly against Apophis, the contemporary Hyksos ruler.

There is no evidence at present bearing upon the nature of the act of rebellion, nor the initial stages of hostilities. The Theban king may simply have withheld tribute, or overtly attacked Hyksos holdings in Middle Egypt. A later tale that circulated in the 13th century ascribed the outbreak to a Hyksos attempt to impose the worship of Seth (= the Amorite god Ba'al) upon Amun-worshipping Thebes. But this yarn smacks of the fantastic, and, moreover, contains a story-telling motif (the outlandish demand which is impossible to concede) which is quite unhistorical. One piece of evidence, however, which cannot be denied is the mummy of king Seqnenre Ta'o I, the founder of the Seventeenth Dynasty, who presumably began the rebellion. This mummy is the earliest in the great cache of royal mummies discovered at Deir el-Bahri on the west bank at Thebes in the 19th century. The man clearly died in agony: an axe shore away part of his face, and a dagger and spear penetrated his skull **(fig. 1).** It is very tempting to imagine him meeting his fate on the battlefield.

For about a decade the war must have continued, with limited success on either side. Then for some reason hostilities were suspended, and a peace treaty was drawn up. But the Theban ruler who shortly thereafter took the throne, a young sabre-rattler named Kamose, eldest son of Seqnenre, chafed under the conditions of the pact and wished to flex his muscles. "To what purpose am I aware of my strength?" Kamose is reported to have railed at his courtiers. "One ruler is in Avaris, another is in Kush, and I sit (here) associated with an Asiatic and a Nubian. Each man governs his own portion in this Egypt, and I share in the partitioning of the land . . . (the land) is stripped bare because of the taxes of the Asiatics. I will go forth against him, I will crush him! My desire is to save Egypt . . . !" With these words Kamose begins his account of his war with the Hyksos, which was inscribed on two stelae set up in the temple of Amun. The text is a curious mixture of threat and boast, history and propaganda, which belies the claim of complete

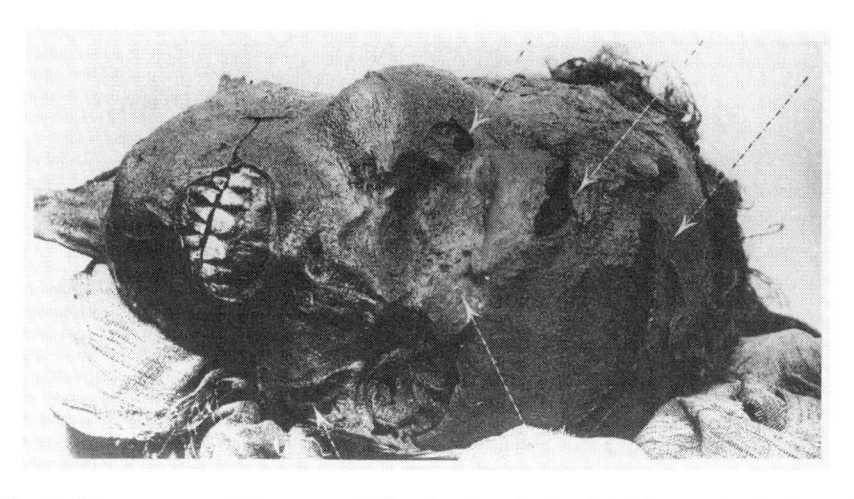

Figure 1 Head of the mummy of Seqenenre Ta'o, showing the battlefield wounds which resulted in his death.

victory. Kamose broke the peace by attacking the Hyksos suddenly, and was able to drive them north into the Delta. He even laid siege to Avaris for a short time, and hurled his defiance at the enemy on the walls of that impregnable fortress: "I spied his (the Hyksos king's) women upon his roof, peering out through his windows. . . . They saw me as they peeped out of the harim . . . saying, 'He is come!' Behold! I *am* come. . . . As the mighty Amun endures, I shall not leave you, I shall not allow you to set foot on the fields, even when I am not (here) with you! Does your heart fail, O miserable Asiatic? Behold! I am drinking of the wine of your (own) vineyards, that which the Asiatics whom I captured trod out for me!" No matter how much their commander threatened, the game but inexperienced Theban irregulars could not carry Avaris by storm, nor could they starve it out. After some equivocal successes in the north Kamose and his men were forced to retire, and presumably the Hyksos recovered the lost ground.

Kamose was followed on the throne by his younger brother, Ahmose. Profiting by his predecessor's mistakes, Ahmose pressed the Hyksos hard, and by 1560 he had returned to the Delta and was closing in on Avaris. Initially the town resisted capture, as in the reign of Kamose, but the Egyptians returned to the attack time and again; and after the fourth assault Avaris was taken. (A calendrical docket on the Rhind Mathematical papyrus suggests the final advance may have been accompanied by unseasonal bad weather). Some part of the Hyksos court and army fled eastward into southern Palestine, along with those few Asiatics who had eluded death or enslavement after Ahmose occupied the Delta. A lengthy campaign was needed to mop up this remnant in the Negeb, but by 1553 B.C. the task was accomplished and Egypt was at long last free of the hated foreign dynasty.

The Early Eighteenth Dynasty:
Spiritual Heirs to the Middle Kingdom

It is difficult to cast one's mind back to the first two reigns of what Manetho calls the Eighteenth Dynasty, of which he makes Ahmose the founder (although in fact he was a full member of the Seventeenth), for the empire period with its physical remains and imperial ideology has overshadowed and obliterated them. Essentially the new Egypt was a timid kingdom unaware of its own strength. The new regime had, however, restored dynastic succession as an informing principle and, of necessity, had acquired a military character: the king was commander-in-chief who led his army in battle, and his sons accompanied him.

Lacking any prototype closer in time, the early Eighteenth Dynasty looked back to the Middle Kingdom for inspiration in art, architecture, and religion; and considered itself the legitimate descendants of the Senwosrets and Amenemhets. A key link was provided by the temple of Amun at Thebes where worship had continued uninterrupted since the days of Senwosret I. Published inscriptions of the Twelfth Dynasty in the temple were copied both for content and style, and festival calendars were slavishly reproduced to the extent that the date of the rising of Sothis was left as it had been around 1800 B.C. In cases where temple renovations demanded the removal of Twelfth Dynasty relief or painted scenes, kings were careful to have the scene recopied on an adjacent wall. Moreover kings resuscitated the practice, which had largely fallen into abeyance, of revealing their successes and intentions in speeches to their court.

In many ways the new dynasty bears a striking resemblance to the Eleventh. Both Ahmose and Montuhotpe were of southern origin, both had come to power through rebellion, and both ruled from Thebes. Both were provincial in taste, and espoused the same bold style of sculpture and relief. Both were keenly interested in Egypt's traditional sphere of influence in the Sudan, where a danger lurked in the continued existence of the Kingdom of Kush, centered at Kerma.

But a new region of potential concern demanded Ahmose's attention, as it had made no demands upon his illustrious forbear Montuhotpe; and that was Palestine and Syria. The Egyptians were very much aware that Amorite kingdoms, of the same ethnic and political pattern whence the Hyksos had sprung, still thrived in the Levant and were ready to renew the Hyksos hegemony over the Nile land. In 1525 B.C. or thereabouts, when the second successor to Ahmose, Thutmose I, acceded to the throne, Egypt was prepared and determined once and for all to remove that threat.

The Coming of the Indo-Europeans

In c. 1520 B.C., with one successful campaign in Kush behind him, Thutmose I moved his capital from Thebes to Memphis and prepared to lead his army across the eastern frontier into Palestine. What sort of map can we envisage the king and his generals poring over on the eve of the attack?

The languages of the peoples we have passed in review in the preceding chapters have, with the exception of the Sumerians, all belonged to what is called the Afro-Asiatic family of languages. That is to say, most of the languages geographically distributed from central and east Africa to the upper Tigris and Euphrates show such marked similarity to one another in grammar and vocabulary that it seems certain they are descended from one "parent" language spoken in distant pre-historic times somewhere in the zone described above. About 1700 B.C. three peoples belonging to a different linguistic family made their appearance in the Near East. That family is the "Indo-European," (so called from its eastern and western geographical limits) and today speakers of Indo-European languages have become dominant not only in Europe but in North America as well. For English, French, Spanish, German, and Italian all belong to this family, not to mention Russian, Persian, Sanskrit, and a host of others.

As in the case of the prehistoric speakers of Proto-Afro-Asiatic, the aboriginal peoples who spoke Proto-Indo-European presumably formed a more or less homogenous group living in a single area. The problem, however, is to isolate that area. Certainly it was north of the Mediterranean, but whether in the trans-Alpine region of central Europe, or in the grassy plains of southern Russia is still a debated point. In any case, an examination of the vocabulary of Proto-Indo-European, as far as it can be reconstructed, and the archaeological remains from the two regions in question, reveals that the speakers of the parent tongue were a war-like group of semi-nomadic herdsmen, possessed of the horse drawn chariot and a fair knowledge of metallurgy. During the closing centuries of the Third Millennium, coincidentally at the same time as the Amorites were bestirring themselves south of the Fertile Crescent, the Indo-European tribesmen began to emigrate from their homeland. Radiating in several directions, bands of wanderers in search of homes ranged as far north as the shores of the Baltic and North Seas, and as far west as the coasts of the Atlantic. Simultaneously two spearheads of migrants were penetrating in the opposite direction, one to the south, the other to the south-east. The evidence for the former is mainly archaeological. One route of immigration can be traced by the beautiful black and red pottery the invaders used. The trail leads out of the Caucasus, through Syria, and into Palestine where it stops, disappears, and the unknown people is heard of no more (c. 2400 B.C.). A second route may be traced westward, via Armenia, into central Anatolia. Here the traces are not so faint, for the invaders settled down and supplanted the earlier culture. Five centuries later they are spoken of as *Khatte* (the Hittites). The south-easterly movement, emanating from the Caucasus after 2000 B.C., deposited two groups of Indo-European speaking people in the Zagros Mountains and the Armenian highland, and eventually brought the Aryans to India (c. 1500 B.C.).

The Indo-Europeans who entered the Near East did not excite animosity in the lands they invaded. Far from wiping out the autochthonous inhabitants, the new-comers imposed themselves as a ruling class upon the original peoples. Both in Anatolia and the plains of Mesopotamia the Indo-Europeans exploited their prowess in horsemanship to set up feudal aristocracies of chariot-owning "knights," or *Maryannu* as they were known in the Indo-European dialect.

In the Armenian highlands and the northern plains of Mesopotamia the aboriginal stock was known as the Hurrians. They had long been known in Babylonia and Assyria, but it was not until the weakening of Babylonian power around 1650 B.C. that they were able to dominate the great plains of central Mesopotamia. Following the death of Hammurabi of Babylon his weak successors found themselves largely unable to supervise their western provinces effectively. A few minor Amorite states sprang up along the Middle Euphrates, and an incursion of Kassites from the Zagros established an enclave north of Babylon. By the close of the 17th century B.C. the Hurrians together with their Indo-European overlords were present in considerable numbers not only in central Mesopotamia but in Syria as well.

The Hittites for their part did not become active in Near Eastern affairs until the first half of the sixteenth century. At first their activity was wholly bellicose. Orienting themselves southwards and eastwards, they repeatedly attacked the erstwhile major Amorite power of Yamkhad in north Syria, and the shrinking territory ruled by Babylon beyond the Euphrates. Around 1531 B.C. one Hittite king, Mursilis I, even succeeded in reaching the capital of that kingdom, and the great city was sacked. In Syria and Mesopotamia a political vacuum followed the destructive attacks of the Anatolian barbarians, as most of the Amorite states of the Middle Bronze Age had passed out of existence.

The first beneficiaries of the carnage were the Hurrians and their Indo-European overlords. By the last decade of the sixteenth century Egyptian texts begin to mention a distant country beyond the Euphrates "which the people call Mitanni." Close to the Tigris another state called Khanigalbat was soon to come into existence. Both were ruled by dynasties of Indo-Europeans, and within a short time ruling houses showing Indo-European personal names began to appear in Syria and Palestine. There was, in fact, a major thrust of a political rather than an ethnic nature, westward from Mesopotamia into northern and central Syria. Here the ambitions of Mitanni were to clash with those of the Hittites, and with the addition of Egyptian armies bent on imperialism, the territory watered by the Orontes was to be transformed into a battlefield for over three centuries.

Empire or Retrenchment?

The Egyptians had begun the war with the Hyksos in an honest attempt to liberate their land. For the immediate successor of Ahmose the fact of the expulsion of the foreigners sufficed, in part, to allay the Egyptians' fears of a new invasion from the north. Although we do not know that contemporaries phrased it this way, the question could have been posed: do we return to the precedent set by the ancestors and try to create, if at all, a sphere of commercial interest in adjacent lands, or do we emulate the Hyksos and establish a permanent presence? The former might have had the appeal of a familiar, tried and true technique, but was it realistic in light of the new geopolitical forces taking shape in the north? The contrary argument might have maintained that to return to conditions of the Old or Middle Kingdoms, when Bedouin could roam right up to the walls of the border fortresses along the Bitter Lakes, was wholly unacceptable in the light of the Hyksos experience. Never again could the dwellers by the Nile rid themselves of the suspicion that such seemingly innocuous nomads were the harbingers of foreign occupation.

While phrasing the problem in this way and postulating a debate might be a modern conceit, the first century of Eighteenth Dynasty rule seems to present these two views in tension. That the more belligerent and novel policy triumphed is clear. Not a few of the Eighteenth Dynasty kings took the epithet "he who smites the foreign rulers who have attacked him". Wars of aggression were at first promoted as nothing but pre-emptive strikes! By this type of casuistry it was simple to extend the argument to justify imperialism *per se:* land *must* be won in order to set the frontiers at such a distance from the Nile that the homeland can never be threatened. This way of thinking is implicit in the expression which came to sum up the act of imperial aggression, viz. "broadening the boundaries of Egypt." Pre-emption had given way to *prevention.*

Although Ahmose and his son Amenophis I (B) had led military campaigns into hither Asia, the king who must be considered the creator of the Egyptian empire in Asia was

Thutmose I. Probably a member of a collateral branch of the royal family, Thutmose achieved the kingship through his marriage to princess Ahmose, daughter of Amenophis I. The single expedition he led reached the Euphrates where the Mitannian forces were routed and a triumphal stela set up. At home reliefs depicted the "East" proffering offerings (D). Though this campaign was never followed up because of his untimely death, Thutmose set a pattern for his more illustrious grandson, who not only copied his forebear's feats, but sometimes his inscriptions as well.

The Matriarchal Regency of Hatshepsut

That grandson was Thutmose III, a lesser offspring of Thutmose I's son, Thutmose II (C). We shall probably never know to what extent the energy, patience, and perseverance, which were the hallmarks of his character, were the result of his early upbringing. Placed on the throne while yet a child, Thutmose III suffered a *coup d'etat* in his second year, when an oracle was delivered by the god Amun himself to the effect that Hatshepsut, only surviving daughter of Thutmose I and chief queen of Thutmose II, was to sit upon the throne and rule Egypt. While Thutmose was permitted to appear in royal regalia with her (E), he was thereafter relegated to the status of titular king during the first twenty-one years of his reign. All Egypt knew this. The correct state of affairs is stated by the old architect of Thutmose I who lived on into the joint reign: Thutmose II's "son sat on his throne as king of the Two Lands, he ruled upon the throne of him that begat him; but it was his sister, the god's-wife Hatshepsut that dominated the country and the Two Lands conformed to her policy, and people labored for her."

Hatshepsut was the fifth in a line of queens who had each dominated her husband and sons. Her great-great-grandmother had once taken command of an army on the battlefield, and at her death she was buried with her weapons like a soldier! Her great-grandmother, Ahmes-Nofretari, had set something of a precedent in ruling for her underage son, the future Amenophis I, during his minority; but while the dyad of mother and son caught the Theban imagination for centuries into the future, Ahmes-Nofretari had never usurped power. But that is what Hatshepsut did. Although ostensibly ruling on behalf of her under-aged nephew, and depicted in female form **(fig. 2)**, Hatshepsut had actually usurped the throne. Other princesses had occasionally taken the throne as *queen*—Nitokerty of Dynasty 6, and Neferu-Sobek-re of Dynasty 12 are examples—but Hatshepsut proclaimed herself *king* (not queen!), and instructed her painters and sculptors to portray her as a man. (For any power-wielder in Egypt the only role pattern was male.) This may not qualify precisely as "matriarchy"; but it betrays a confidence and willingness in replacing patriarchal forms in favor of those of women.

Almost certainly this striking break with tradition has deeper roots than the superficial whim of an individual. In light of the fact that Hatshepsut, in her conservative and archaizing approach to the problems of her time, embodies the more traditional of the two points of view adumbrated above, it is tempting to see her as the leader of a faction resistant to foreign adventures. The ministers she appointed, who obviously supported her, are a curious group. Most came of lowly families. Her vizier and high-priest Hapusonb was son of a lector priest, Puyemre, the deputy high-priest was son of a "gentleman," while her chief stewards and chief herald were of similar low estate; her chamberlain and chief engineer both came of foreign stock. Her closest associate and general factotum (with whom she may have had an affair), Senenmut, likewise could not point to a noble pedigree. Curiously, business documents which

Figure 2 Hatshepsut shown as queen, being offered life and dominion by Seth.

are rigidly faithful to hierarchical order, when listing holders of high office during her reign, rank the chief treasurer, the chief steward, the secretary, and Senenmut *before* Hatshepsut and Thutmose III! What does this say about the distribution of real power?

While Hatshepsut's place in Egyptian history continues to be debated, her reign of two decades was by no means a disaster for Egypt. Moreover her own characterization of her floruit as "years of peace" indicates a conscious attempt to re-establish a traditional and non-belligerent role for Egypt within a mere sphere of influence. One of her speeches "from the throne," the Speos Artemidos inscription, clearly outlines her policy to rebuild, refurbish, and re-equip the country and to engage in far-flung trade. All over the country temples began to rise and a trading fleet of five vessels was despatched down the Red Sea to the East African land of Pwenet (probably Eritrea or Somalia). The queen's mortuary temple at Thebes, begun in the seventh year of the joint reign, and inspired in part by the adjacent temple of Montuhotpe I, proved to be a unique monument to the genius of her steward and architect Senenmut (F). A series of terraces (G) and colonnades (H) which used the natural contours of the cliffs on the west of the Nile led up to a court (I) and sanctuary constructed partly in the living rock, the whole reproducing schematically the coastal "terraces" her merchants had seen in far-off Pwenet. Reliefs and inscriptions in the colonnades along the terraces constituted records of the events the queen considered the most important of her reign: her birth and upbringing, the voyage to Pwenet, the erection of the obelisks. Although some minor wars marred the peace of the queen's reign, it cannot be gainsaid that her national policy concentrated on commerce and rebuilding. In a blatant rewriting of recent history Hatshepsut even took the credit for being the first ruler to reconstruct the devastated temples and the shattered economy after the Hyksos wars.

Hatshepsut's inscriptions are ever at pains to justify her seizure of the throne. She stresses incessantly that Amun had chosen her to be king, and that she had undergone a coronation at the hands of her father, Thutmose I. Before he had died, the great monarch had actually designated her as his rightful heir: "this daughter of mine . . . I have appointed as my successor; lo, she is the one that shall sit upon my throne. It is she, indeed, that shall sit upon this dais. Her words shall direct the commons in every sphere of the palace, it is she, in fact, who shall lead you. Obey her words, unite yourselves at her command." Drawing on the folklore of the "husband-double" in a myth of divine birth (probably of Twelfth Dynasty origin), she even went so far as to claim that it was not really Thutmose I that had begotten her, but the god Amun himself who had come to earth on the night of her conception in her father's form! Throughout her inscriptions, many in the first person, her insistence on her love for her father and his for her betrays a clear father fixation.

The Conquests of Thutmose III

While Hatshepsut had associated the young Thutmose with her on the throne as a sort of "joint" king and allowed him to wear all the crowns except one, there is good indication that by the second decade she was considering perpetuating her "matriarchate" by appointing her daughter as queen. This could not help but create a certain animosity between her coregent and herself; but the matter was resolved by the untimely death of the daughter. It was not until Hatshepsut died (early spring, 1482 B.C.) that the supplanted king could assume his rightful place as ruler of Egypt. During his minority he had probably been placed for training in the army, and it is significant that most of his officials in later life were drawn from the military.

Our sources for the momentous events of Thutmose III's reign are relatively numerous. The king himself, especially later in his reign, delivered a series of speeches to his court in which he reminisces, sometimes in detail, about events on the battlefield. In his fortieth and again in his forty-second year, he authorized the excerpting of the journal known as the "day-book of the king's house," along with certain treasury documents, to create an extended inscription within the Temple of Amun giving an account of the wars of the preceding twenty years in some detail. Soldiers, too, who had accompanied the king on campaign, sometimes included references to their battlefield experiences in their tomb biographies.

The situation in western Asia which Thutmose had to confront amounted to a sort of political vacuum. The erstwhile Amorite states of the Levant had been swept away or reduced, Yamkhad by the incessant pounding she had received from the Hittites, Qatanum and Hazor through pressure from Mitanni or economic attrition. All that remained after the removal of these metropolitan states, viz. the towns and villages with their headmen, invited the imposition of the rule of new masters. By their geopolitical interest in *Kharu* (Palestine), *Takhsy* (the upper Orontes), *Fenkhu* (the Phoenician coast), and *Nukhashshe* (north-eastern Syria), both Egypt and Mitanni were destined to clash on a grand scale and in a manner decisive for the future of the region **(fig. 3)**.

Within months of Hatshepsut's death a confrontation occurred between Egypt and the remnants of the erstwhile Hyksos sphere of influence in Syria. Under the leadership of the king of Kadesh on the Orontes river, a cat's-paw perhaps of the Mitannians, the city-states of Palestine and the Lebanon joined together in a coalition which, Thutmose claimed in his day-book and speeches, was bent on invading Egypt and re-establishing Asiatic hegemony over the

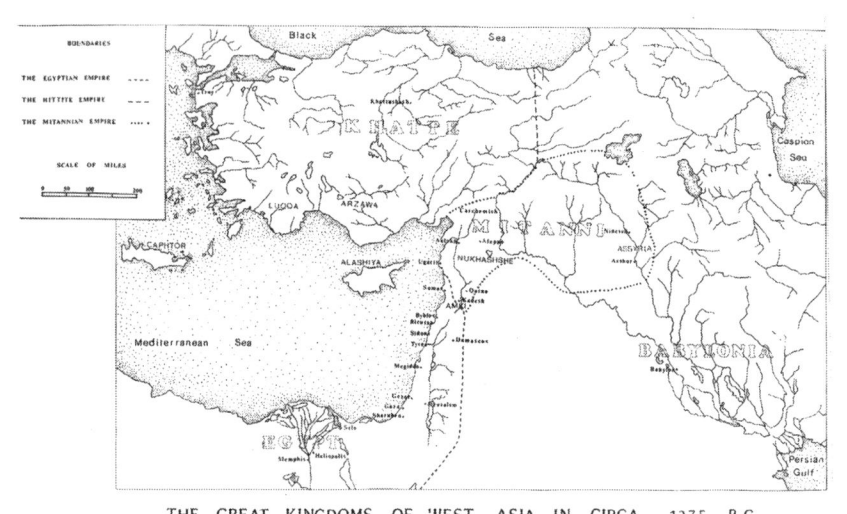

THE GREAT KINGDOMS OF WEST ASIA IN CIRCA 1375 B.C.

Figure 3 North Africa and Western Asia in the 15th–14th centuries B.C.

Nile Valley. The combined armies of the coalition had begun to assemble at Megiddo in the Esdraelon plain (J) when Thutmose decided to act. With an army which we may estimate at roughly 10,000 he hastened north across the Sinai, through the coastal plain, and halted on the seaward side of the Carmel range (mid-May, 1482 B.C.). A daring march through the narrow pass at Megiddo (K) brought the Egyptians within striking distance of the city **(fig. 4),** and on the following day, auspiciously the dark of the moon, the onslaught of the Egyptian chariotry put the Asiatics to flight. Twenty years after the event Thutmose claimed that a seven-month siege had ensued, although there is reason to doubt this. In any event, Megiddo capitulated before the end of the year.

Each spring for the next twenty years the stubborn conqueror crossed the Sinai desert with the same army, and hammered the inhabitants of Palestine and Syria into submission. The overall strategy betrays a far-sighted and dogged approach which combined set-piece battles with march-abouts. The sources for the second through fourth campaigns are missing, but they must have been devoted to the consolidation of claims to Palestine. The next three campaigns (years 29 to 31) were directed up the coast toward the Eleutheros Valley in the Lebanons. In the process of extending the frontiers, a number of coastal towns were transformed into harbors and supply-depots for the Egyptian army's thrust inland across the mountains of Lebanon. By 1475 B.C. all Palestine and the Phoenician coast had been secured, and Kadesh had been captured. In 1472 B.C., in a campaign which shows Thutmose III's military genius to best advantage, the Egyptians finally reached the Euphrates. Knowing that the Mitannians would probably destroy river craft to prevent the Egyptian troops from making a crossing, Thutmose had had

BATTLE OF MEGIDDO

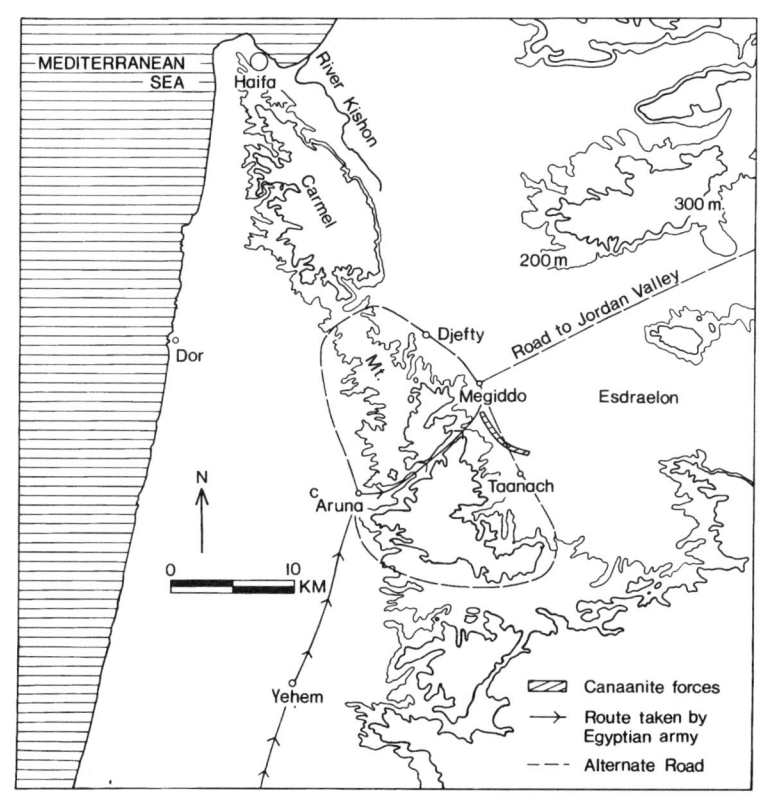

Figure 4   The environs of Megiddo, showing the three routes available to the Egyptian expeditionary force.

the forethought to construct prefabricated landing craft in the mountains of Lebanon, and to have them dragged on carts in the van of the army. Now to the enemies' consternation, they were suddenly launched on the Euphrates, and carried the Egyptian assault troops across. The Mitannians suffered a crushing defeat, and their king fled ignominiously to Babylon, leaving his nobles to hide in the mountains. The Mitannians fell back in awe, their southward movement temporarily halted; but two years later they returned to the attack, and were again worsted by the seemingly invincible Egyptian army. By his death in 1450 B.C. the little conqueror (Thutmose **[fig. 5]** was scarcely 5'3" in height!) had completed the task he had set himself to perform: from Khartoum in the Sudan to the banks of the Euphrates there was no state that did not acknowledge the king of Egypt as lord. Diplomatic presents flowed in from Babylon and Assyria, from the Hittites and Azi(ya) on the Ionian coast, and from Keftiu (Crete).

Erich Lessing/Art Resources, NY

Figure 5 Head of statue of Thutmose III.

The Annihilation of Kush and the Creation of an African Empire

The situation the Egyptians perceived on their southern frontiers seemed equally as threatening as a new Hyksos attack. On the eve of the war of liberation the northern border of the Kerma kingdom extended to the First Cataract, and, as we have seen, the Kushites were willing and able to raid Egyptian towns further north. An intercepted letter from the Hyksos king Apophis, according to Kamose, apprised him of a potential alliance between Avaris and Kerma, whereby the latter would invade upper Egypt to divert the Thebans from their siege of the Hyksos capital. Kamose during his short reign tried, as he was able, to resist the Kushites, and his successor Ahmose had to expel an attempted invasion from the south.

Slowly, however, the tide turned. Ahmose was able to hold his ground at the cataract frontier, and his son Amenophis I, while yet a young man, carried his arms far into Kushite territory. It was left to Amenophis's son-in-law and successor, Thutmose I, to deal the death blow. In his second year on the throne, and before the war with Mitanni in the north, Thutmose invaded the Kerma kingdom in force, penetrating south of the Second Cataract in search of a decisive battle. The Kushites were worsted in a river fight, and Thutmose claims personally to have killed the king of Kerma. With victory complete the triumphant Egyptians proceeded southward still, and Thutmose erected his southern boundary at Karoy, some 300 miles north of Khartoum. While some of the Kushite king's sons escaped to set up short-lived successor states, to all intents and purposes the decisive blow had been struck. Thutmose II in his first year devastated the successor states, and Hatshepsut two decades later led a mop-up operation which finally brought an end to Kushite resistance.

The Provinces of Asia and Kush: A Contrast in Administration

The empire Thutmose had founded in Asia existed principally for the purpose of enriching the coffers of the state treasury. The Pharaoh demanded of the subject peoples **(fig. 6),** as he did of his own native Egyptians, taxes in the form of native products, raw and manufactured, which were to be despatched yearly to Egypt. If the subject states met their yearly assessment, all was well; if they did not, they ran the risk of suffering a punitive raid by Egyptian troops. The headmen of the towns of Palestine and Syria—to eliminate doubt they were called "the towns of Pharaoh"—could quarrel and even war among themselves as much as they pleased; the king of Egypt would interfere only if Egyptian interests were threatened. To ensure loyalty he demanded that his vassals take an oath in his name, a practice which meant that they were temporarily released from their obligation by his death. Pharaoh would also require, however, that a vassal's children be brought to Egypt (L), ostensibly for their education. These would be brought up in Thebes under the aegis and at the expense of the king, and would later return to their Asiatic patrimonies thoroughly indoctrinated with the Egyptian way of life. The ultimate result of this practice was the alienation of the Syrian rulers, all of whom came home speaking Egyptian and with Egyptian names, from their native people, who treated them with suspicion. Few direct controls were imposed on the subject towns. An Egyptian commissioner with a garrison might be installed in the more important cities such as Gaza, Ullaza, and (later) Kumidi; but such garrison cities were few and the number of soldiers would rarely exceed a mere handful. If Pharaoh went on campaign, he might also demand that the vassals in the territory through which he passed provide his troops with food and lodging.

But Egyptian control of their Asiatic province was based on practical considerations, and evolved with the times. While under Thutmose III and his son Amenophis II (c. 1450–1425 B.C.) demands of provincial administration were solved on an ad hoc basis, by the first half of the 14th century a pattern had begun to emerge. Responsibility for the oversight of the towns of Palestine was organized under a group of army captains, each of whom went on annual circuit to the towns he had been assigned. His task was to convey to the local headmen the amount of their tax, to declare any special demands Pharaoh might have, to solve local disputes if necessary, and from time to time to shepherd back to Egypt "the children of the chiefs." On special occasions they would accompany the headmen themselves back to Egypt to provide an audience for a jubilee or a "durbar" (M). (For further developments under the Ramessides, see below.)

The problem of providing Kush (N) with a workable administration evoked a wholly different response from the Egyptian empire builders. A native state had long existed in the south,

Figure 6   Northerners encountered by the Egyptians during the New Kingdom (from top left):
(1) Canaanite of the Middle Bronze Age, in winter costume; (2, 3) Canaanites in costume typical of the
lower Orontes valley; (4) Canaanite of Palestine; (5) Canaanite woman with child; (6) Philistine in
plumed headdress and body armor; (7) Desert beduin (Shasu).

but for some reason the way it was structured did not invite emulation. Egyptian freebooters during the Hyksos era had hired themselves out to the rulers of Kush as soldiers and officials; but they had been too few in number and had enjoyed too limited an experience to be asked to step in. Even before the final victory was won, however, a particular office had been called into existence which was to shape the administration on the African province. The title "king's son" during the Thirteenth Dynasty had been extended in use to designate royal plenipotentiaries, especially fortress commandants; and when applied under Kamose to the commandant of the fortress of Buhen in Nubia, it was a governorship in embryo. By the early Eighteenth Dynasty the qualification "of the southern lands" (later ". . . of Kush") had been added, and the officer in question transformed into a true viceroy responsible for the entire southland from Hierakonpolis to Karoy. Unlike the northern lands where native forms of rule, subservient to Pharaoh of course, were allowed to remain, in the south the administration of Egypt itself provided a model. As the homeland was divided into two halves, each under a vizier, so the thousand mile stretch of valley south of Elephantine was divided into two sub-districts, Wawat and Kush, each with its own deputy governor; as the Egyptian government disposed of departments of fields, livestock, granaries, storehouses etc., so similar bureaus took shape around the viceroy; as Egypt had its own garrison forces, so the south could boast of the "garrison of Kush."

Differences can also be detected in the relative value Egypt attached to her new territorial acquisitions. The lands to the north provided Egypt with a buffer to future invasions, should they materialize. Holding this territory also made it easier for Pharaoh to tap into trade passing along Asiatic transit corridors, as well as to extract at will indigenous products and resources. Among the latter one may mention the volcanic glass of the Negeb, the wheat of Esdraelon, the cedar of Lebanon, boxwood from Amurru, oil from Ugarit, metalware from Syria. Manpower came cheap, and Pharaoh thought nothing of demanding thousands of unskilled laborers to be despatched to his court. But a reverse demographic flow cannot be detected: Egypt sent no colonists into its northern empire. Kush, on the other hand, could scarcely offer itself as a buffer against invasion: the distribution of Nile cataracts had already secured Egypt on the south, and no great power further afield existed in north-east Africa. The south was valued for its minerals and produce, for the sub-Saharan products which came north in trade along the Nile, and for its land as living space. In particular the gold mines in the eastern desert began to be worked as never before during the New Kingdom, and so much gold entered circulation in Egypt that prices were for a time depressed. Colonists were settled along the Nile, either in new towns built for their accommodation, or in settlements centered upon the old Twelfth Dynasty fortresses, now refurbished as town centers. As we shall see, the acculturation of the native population followed quickly.

Cultural Exchange during the Empire of the Eighteenth Dynasty

"Extending the boundaries of Egypt" resulted eventually in some little interchange of ideas between the imperialist power and its new dependencies. The Phoenician coastal towns, some of which supported an Egyptian garrison in constant touch with Egypt by sea, benefited most noticeably. Their rulers spoke Egyptian, wore Egyptian clothing, aped Egyptian manners, and surrounded themselves with furniture of Egyptian inspiration if not manufacture. Some were even able to translate Egyptian hymns and Wisdom Texts into their own West Semitic dialects, and such pieces, "filtering" inland over the centuries, have left traces in Hebrew literature (Psalm 1 and 104, Proverbs 22–23). Three centuries after Thutmose III, Zakar-baal, the king of Byblos, acknowledged his country's cultural debt to Egypt when he said, ". . . technical skill spread out of (Egypt) to the place where I am, and learning (as well). . . ." Greece and the Aegean islands too were becoming familiar with the slow-moving, single-masted merchantmen from Egypt which regularly came to trade at their shores (00). A periplus of ports of call in the Aegean, for the use of mariners, is preserved in a hieroglyphic text of around 1400 B.C. The Egyptian artists were fascinated by the strangely dressed emissaries from Crete who came on embassies of goodwill to Pharaoh, and duly and faithfully recorded the event in tomb paintings. And the Egyptians for their part found within their borders an increasing foreign population from the provinces, both servile and free. A major settlement of Asiatics grew up in the suburbs of Memphis which, centuries later, retained the name "the camp of the people from Tyre." With these immigrant Canaanites, Syrians, and Nubians came their manners and customs, and for the first time we find alien gods in Egyptian guise, their barbaric names transcribed into Egyptian hieroglyphs. The Egyptians were fairly tolerant of the newcomers, and intermarriage was not unknown. The barber of Thutmose III, who had accompanied his master on a campaign into Syria, was assigned a captive he had taken as a personal servant: "I captured him myself when I was following the Ruler. . . . He will not be beaten, nor will he be turned away from any royal portal. I have given the daughter of my sister Nebetto, whose name is Takement, to him as a wife. She shall have a share in (my) inheritance just like my wife and my sister. . . ." But some frowned upon fraternization between the races. A father scolds his wayward son for mixing with Asiatics and submitting to a ceremony designed to make him a sort of "blood brother": "You are wandering like a swallow with its young. You have reached the Delta after a great journey, where you mingle with Asiatics, and have eaten bread (mixed) with your blood."

At an official level the Egyptians continued to perpetuate the topos of Egypt's invincibility and the rottenness of all the "lesser breeds without the law." The chastening themes of official propaganda broadcast on a grander scale than ever the scene of bound captives from the ends of the empire (o), the head-bashing scene, in which Pharaoh punishes the recalcitrant, criminal foreign chief; or the message of universal dominion reflected in the rows of scores of foreign place-names done into hieroglyphs (p), ostensibly commemorating Pharaoh's far-flung victories. Foreign emissaries before Pharaoh's throne routinely abase themselves, kissing the earth, grovelling on their bellies and even on their backs; and those who are slow may even be punched by an attendant.

The topos of state supremacy, a patriotic stereotype no different from that of most peoples, ancient and modern, in fact worked its way into the consciousness of at least one king, Amenophis II, who took it quite seriously. On the twenty-third anniversary of his accession to the throne (about 1428 B.C.) Amenophis was drinking wine in his harim, presumably in company of his ladies. In his cups, he launched into a disquisition on foreigners and thought he would have it transcribed in a letter and sent to his viceroy of Kush. The latter thought so highly of it that he had it carved on a stela which fortunately has survived: "Copy of the despatch made by His Majesty with his own hands to the king's-son <of the southern lands> Usersatet. Lo, His Majesty was in(?) the harim of Pharaoh (Life, Prosperity, Health), drinking and making merry: [. . . I am] one who seized upon [the northerners(?), overthrowing the Asiatics(?)] in all their places! I have no dissident in any land [. . .] Amenophis, [the mighty king who destroyed] the Naharin and laid waste the Kheta! The be[ermaid] Sangar (Babylonia), the servant-girl Byblos, the little girl of Alalakh, the old woman of Arrapkha, and the Taksians—they all have nothing! Really, what are they good for?" (But) "do not be at all lenient with Nubia! Beware of their people and their magicians. See to the labor-taxes of the peasants which you shall bring in order to give it to the (appropriate) officer; if there is no officer of yours, let it be reported to His Majesty. Otherwise one will have to listen to (the following excuses): 'an axe of electrum with fixtures of bronze is missing, and the stout quarter-staff is in a water-hole, and the other one is in the marsh(?)!' Don't listen to their words and don't meddle in their affairs!" And that, in a nut-shell, is the Egyptian attitude towards empire!

Further Readings

For the Seventeenth Dynasty and the expulsion of the Hyksos, see J. E. Harris, K. R. Weeks, *X-Raying the Pharaohs,* New York, 1973; L. Habachi, *The Second Stela of Kamose and His Struggle Against the Hyksos Ruler,* Glückstadt, 1972.

On the Indo-Europeans see A. Harrak, *Assyria and Hanigalbat,* Hildesheim, 1987; R. Drewes, *The Coming of the Greeks: Indo-European Conquests in the Aegean and the Near East,* Princeton, 1988; J. P. Mallory, *In Search of the Indo-Europeans,* London, 1989; T. Bryce, *The Kingdom of the Hittites,* Oxford, 1999.

On the Levant in the early Late Bronze Age, see H. Klengel, *Syria 3000 to 300 B.C.: A Handbook of Political History,* Berlin, 1992; N. P. Lemche, *The Canaanites and Their Land,* Sheffield, 1991; *idem, Prelude to Israel's Past,* Peabody, MA, 1998; J. Tubb, *The Canaanites: Peoples of the Past,* Oklahoma, 1998.

For Hatshepsut, see P. Dorman, *The Monuments of Senenmut,* London, 1988; D. B. Redford, *History and Chronology of the Eighteenth Dynasty of Egypt: Seven Studies,* Toronto, 1967; J. Tyldesley, *Hatchepsut: The Female Pharaoh,* Harmondsworth, 1998.

For the kings who created the empire, see G. I. Davies, *Cities of the Biblical World: Megiddo,* Cambridge, 1986; D. B. Redford, *The Wars in Syria and Palestine of Thutmose III,* Leiden, 2003; P. Der Manuelian, *Studies in the Reign of Amenophis II,* Hildesheim, 1987; B. Bryan, *The Reign of Thutmose IV,* Baltimore, 1990; P. H. Newby, *The Warrior Pharaohs,* London, 1981; G. Steindorf, K. C. Steele, *When Egypt Ruled the East,* Chicago, 1957; P. Lundh, *Actor and Event: Military Activity in Ancient Egyptian Narrative Texts from Thutmosis II to Merenptah,* Uppsala, 2002.

CHAPTER NINE
Monarchy in Crisis

———————— ψ ————————

The contretemps between Mitanni and Egypt was not to last. A flamboyant but ill-conceived campaign down the Orontes undertaken by Amenophis II in about 1445 B.C. met with indifferent success, and thereafter the Egyptians confined military operations to Palestine. Both sides must have realized at an early stage that the war in which they were engaged was proving counterproductive. Moreover, the real enemy of Mitanni, the empire of Khatte, lay due west and was bent, as Egypt was not, on occupying northern Syria up to the Euphrates and even beyond. Perhaps it was time to "bury the hatchet."

The initial move was made by Mitanni. A delegation was sent to Egypt to try to work out an agreement with Amenophis II, who proved surprisingly willing to negotiate. The result was a peace treaty and an agreement on spheres of influence. Egypt was to retain Palestine and southern Syria to a point on the upper Orontes, as well as the coast as far north as the Eleutheros valley; to Mitanni went inland Syria and the coast from the Eleutheros north. This border **(fig. 1)** was to prove remarkably durable over nearly three centuries: violation of the line became, in fact, tantamount to a declaration of war. The alliance was drawn even closer by the marriage of Thutmose IV, Amenophis II's son, to a Mitannian princess, the first in a sequence of diplomatic unions which was to characterize the period of Egypt's empire.

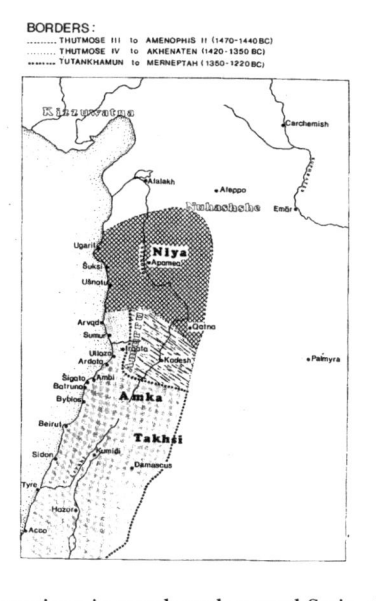

Figure 1 Map of the Egyptian possessions in north and central Syria, showing the progressive withdrawal of the border.

The Reign of Amenophis III

The three generations which followed the death of the mighty Thutmose III had sufficed to fulfill the policy of the Thutmosid House. The Hittite kingdom had entered a period of decline, Babylon was ineffectual under the Kassites, and Mitanni had entered into close alliance with the Pharaohs. Egypt had become the cultural and economic hub of the known world, and Amenophis III **(fig. 2),** Thutmose's great-grandson (1412–1374 B.C.), reaped the benefits of his enterprising predecessors. Amenophis took full advantage of the status and wealth of the country to fashion a court, a society, and a style of art which became proverbial for elegance. Amenophis was Egypt's "sun-king," and so in fact he called himself, "the Dazzling Sun-disc," in whose land "gold is as plentiful as dust"!

This king was not averse to breaking with the norm, and he did so shortly after his accession by marrying a commoner named Tiy (A). This name and those of her father and mother, Yuya and Tuya, are not Egyptian but strongly resemble the onomasticon of Nubia; and the likelihood has to be considered that the family's roots lay among P.O.W.s brought back from Kush by one of the early kings of the Eighteenth Dynasty. By Amenophis III's time Yuya had risen in society to become a lieutenant general and a priest. His daughter became the king's chief queen, surviving his death by at least a decade, and, in the style of the distaff side of the royal house, wielded considerable power in the kingdom (B). His undoubted love for her, however, did not deter Amenophis from other amours (all with diplomatic overtones), and during the course of his lifetime he is known to have also married two Syrian girls, two Babylonian princesses, two Mitannian princesses, and one princess from Arzawa (south-west Asia Minor).

Figure 2 Amenophis III censing and libating before Amun; Luxor temple.

But no Egyptian princess was ever given to a foreign king in marriage. When the king of Babylon requested the daughter of Amenophis III, he received the curt reply, "From of old no daughter of the king of Egypt has been given to anyone." In vain he protested, "Why do you speak so? You are a king, you may do as you wish. . . . If there is any woman who is beautiful in your opinion, send her. Who shall say, 'she is not a king's daughter'?" Nevertheless, no princess was sent.

Many, perhaps most, of Amenophis's marriages were entered into as gambles in the game of political maneuvering. The formal designation of states as super- or second-rate powers is of ancient standing. The Amorites who, as we have seen, appeared in the Near East c. 2000 B.C., conscious as they were of tribal relationships and sensitive to the nuances of political supremacy and subordination, championed a system of international diplomacy in which all rulers were graded as "great kings" or "lesser kings." Great kings were the rulers of super-powers, and were *ipso facto* few in number. Equal in rank, they could if they chose enter into close, friendly relationships with each other, and an unwritten etiquette thereafter obliged them to correspond regularly, exchange gifts, and give their sisters and daughters to each other in marriage. Two great kings who enjoyed such relations were termed "brothers," and a state of "brotherhood" was said to exist between them. No treaty, however, formalized the friendship; it was a mutual, and unofficial, agreement. Lesser kings were usually vassals of great kings. In Amenophis III's day three other kings in the Near East lay claim to the appellative "great king," viz. the Hittite, Mitannian, and Babylonian monarchs.

Already in his second year Amenophis had "commanded the opening of new quarry chambers to extract fine limestone . . . to build castles (which shall last) for millions of years, after he had found buildings . . . fallen into disrepair since the days of old." Thus was inaugurated a building boom of four decades in length the like of which had rarely been experienced before in the Nile Valley (C). Enormous mortuary temples for the cult of the deceased king were erected at Memphis and Thebes (CC) in Egypt, and at Soleb in Nubia, the last-named being the only one which survives, albeit in woeful dilapidation. Nearly every important city of Egypt was graced with a temple constructed at the king's behest. Those of which Thebes could boast included the temple of the war-god Montu, the temple of Mut, the temple of Amun in Luxor (D), and the substantial additions to the main Amun-temple at Karnak.

For the long reign of Amenophis III we have records of only one war, a minor skirmish in Nubia against some local malcontents. There was no need for the great king to lead an army; Egypt could now negotiate on the international level from a position of strength. While the army suffered no diminution in strength and preparedness, the elegant reliefs and painting executed during this reign concentrate on religious rites and the good life, rather than on military subjects.

As would befit someone calling himself a "Dazzling Sun-disc," the king chose his officials from among the noblest families in the land, to create a cabinet of sparkling "blue-bloods." To the god on one occasion Amenophis intones: "[I made] festive your temple, its prophets and common priests being from the upper class, the choicest of the entire land. I put no one there who had not a most esteemed ancestry, stretching back from generation to generation." And the king certainly seems to have been a good judge of character, for his choices became legendary for their excellence and competence. There were the viziers Ramose (E), Aper-el (of Canaanite extraction), and Ptahmose who combined with the vizierate the high-priesthood of Amun and the mayoralty of Thebes; Kha-em-hat, overseer of granaries (F), who brought in a bumper harvest in year 30; the chief steward Amenemhet called Surer who amassed a fortune for Pharaoh; Merimose, viceroy of Kush; Sobek-mosi, chief treasurer; and (not least), Amenophis son of Hapu (G), secretary of labor and recruits, a savant who centuries later would be deified as a god of healing.

Amenophis III's view of himself and his relationship to the gods is a trifle puzzling. Later in his reign his heavily made-up appearance and youthful profile might suggest an attempt to promote a new status within the realm of the supernatural, bordering perhaps on a special deification. Out of the chaos of the Thirteenth through Sixteenth Dynasties had come the concept of the king on earth as the "living replica" *(twt onkh)* of the god in heaven; and Amun-re and Amenophis are indistinguishable apart from the accoutrements. Yet his epithets, though full of allusions to his relationship to his brother deities, are not substantially different from those of his predecessors. One thing seems certain: towards the close of his reign Amenophis was a sick man; this might explain why in his twenty-ninth year he moved his entire court from Memphis to the warmer climate of Thebes, where he built a palace on the west bank (H).

The fourth and last decade of Amenophis III's floruit was occupied with the celebration of three *sed*-festivals, in years 30, 34, and 37. The *sed*-festival, as we have seen in chapter 4 above, was one of the most ancient of Egyptian rituals, its origins dating back to the Pre-dynastic period. Intended originally perhaps to ritualize the replacing of a chieftain grown too old to rule, by historic times the *sed*-festival had become a ceremony of rejuvenation whereby the king's right to the throne was renewed after a reign of thirty years. A reign prolonged beyond the thirtieth year necessitated repetitions of the rite at more frequent intervals. Year 30 of Amenophis III began auspiciously with the announcement of a bumper crop. In the tomb of Amenophis III's superintendent of granaries the king is shown upon a dais in all his regalia, at the "rewarding of the stewards of the departments of Pharaoh—may he live, be prosperous and healthy!—and the governors of south and north, after the superintendent of granaries had reported concerning them that they had handed in an exceptional harvest in year 30." Performed at Thebes, the ceremonies attracted dignitaries from all over Egypt and the empire. To judge by the number of paintings and reliefs devoted to the *sed*-festivals in contemporary tombs, they were regarded as the most important events of the reign.

Amenophis III was ailing towards the close of his life. Curiously, it was at this time that he had carved over one hundred life-size schist statues of the plague-bearing goddess Sakhmet, which he distributed among the Theban temples. In his thirty-fifth year he sent to his brother-in-law, Tushratta the king of Mitanni, to see whether he could suggest any remedies. Tushratta replied that Ishtar, the goddess of Nineveh, had just made an oracular pronouncement: "I will go to Egypt, the land that I love!" So Tushratta despatched Ishtar's cult-image to Egypt with the request, "May my brother honor her, in joy send her back, and may she return. May Ishtar, mistress of heaven, protect my brother and me. . . . Ishtar is my deity, she is not my brother's deity!" Ishtar's therapeutic powers proved ineffectual, however, and within three years the great king of Egypt had passed away, probably before the sixtieth year of his life.

The God Amun and His Cult

The township god of the Theban principality had been the falcon Montu as far back as the dawn of Egyptian history, and it was only with the coming to power of the Eleventh Dynasty that another deity, Amun, began to supplant this original divine patron. Senwosret I **(fig. 3)** of the Twelfth Dynasty established a family shrine at Thebes, dedicated to Amun, and called "(Senwosret)-is-Most-Select-of-Places"; and the god was to serve the family and their successors as protector and guarantor. Amun's origins are obscure. His name means "the hidden one," and is also borne by a Hermopolitan demiurge, but, although a ram was his animal, he is almost always depicted in anthropomorphic form. Hymns and theological texts play upon the meaning of his name, and declare that his true essence is unknown and unknowable. Amun became closely associated with the fortunes of Thebes during the Hyksos period and, as the city assumed national leadership against the intruders, he rose to the status of promoter of national freedom and unity.

Thanks to the Theban victory Amun's stock rose dramatically. Not only did he receive the lion's share of the booty and spoils from foreign conquests which the grateful kings of the time bestowed upon him (I–J), but under the early empire he rapidly assumed the characteristics of a universal ruler. On the pattern of Pharaoh who ruled men, Amun received the title "King of the Gods." Moreover, after the fashion of Ptah of Memphis, the Theban deity was viewed as the

Erich Lessing/Art Resources, NY

Figure 3 Amun introducing Senwosret I to the temple; Karnak, 20th century B.C.

fons et origo of the pantheon, a "sole god who multiplied himself a millionfold, in whom every god has his being." Amun's theological identification with the Sun-god, a union which as early as the Middle Kingdom had produced the compound designation "Amun-re," endowed him with the aspects of a creator-god revered, not only by Egyptians, but by all peoples: "(thou) who didst create all . . . at whose rising every land exults every day in order to praise thee." Such a god, "sovereign and god of all," who can command the respect willy-nilly of all mankind, stands upon a firmer footing than does the earthly Pharaoh who might well experience difficulty, divine though he be, in eliciting a like respect from the same peoples. In light of what was about to break over Egypt, it may be significant that, during the earlier Eighteenth Dynasty hymns to the sun "at his rising and setting" begin to proliferate as never before.

The cult and administration of the temple of Amun at Thebes were overseen by four ranked "prophets," or senior priests, of whom the first would be called by us moderns the "High-priest." From the beginning of the Eighteenth Dynasty the high-priest and his deputy, the "second prophet of Amun," were constrained by a special relationship with the royal family: the king reserved the right to choose the high-priest, and the chief queen exercised a similar control of the office of deputy. While incumbents might look forward to regular advancement through the four highest grades, the king never, until the later Twentieth Dynasty, made his selection of high-priest from the son of the previous First Prophet. Until Hatshepsut the occupants of the high-priesthood of Amun were of little renown; but with the *coup d'etat* of the great queen there took shape a coterie of supporters of whom the First Prophet was the head. Hatshepsut's "father-fixation," with Amun subliminally confused with her own physical progenitor, promoted the political as well as theological status of the god as never before.

Those who served Amun, his priesthood, could not help but share in the exalted status of their divine master. Amun's community had long shown the characteristics of a burgeoning, though closely-knit, fraternity, wherein whole families had found employment, and priestly sinecures were, for generations, to be passed on from father to son in uninterrupted succession. By the death of Amenophis III the priesthood of Amun was well on its way to becoming a virtual state within a state. Moreover, as early as the reign of Hatshepsut the high-priest had received *de jure* primacy over all other priests in Egypt through the bestowal upon him by the monarch of the title "Overseer of All the Priests and Temples of Upper and Lower Egypt," which made of him a kind of archbishop. In spite of the fact that the office of First Prophet was not hereditary, it nevertheless clearly possessed awesome power, for not only did it control Egyptian temples in general, but it also conferred upon the incumbent practical authority over the city of Thebes, and made him landlord of much of the surrounding territory.

The potential for antipathy between the kingship and the high-priesthood latent in this situation is quite apparent. Seven hundred years earlier at the close of the Old Kingdom, the king had lost his position of centrality in the pantheon as well as the body politic. The kingship came to be viewed as an "office," to which was attached a sort of "imperium" bestowed by the gods from ruler to ruler. In the intervening centuries history had thrown up some competent dynasties, but a disquieting number of nonentities had contributed to a gradual discrediting of the "Horus Throne of the Living". The successful monarchs of the Thutmosid house had no difficulty in ensconcing themselves as leaders: the exhilaration of conquest diverted attention from the problem of the equivocal position of the Pharaoh. But once the empire was won and no further battles needed to be fought, to whom went the laurels? Who was the real author and guarantor of the empire, the mighty King of the Gods who was not on earth to flaunt his weaknesses before men, or an effete "Son of Re" who devoted himself to pleasures in his palace? Which of the two was the Universal God and Ruler to whom both men and gods owed allegiance?

Though essentially a mythological statement of the problem, these questions correctly convey the political and sociological elements which were inherent in it. The Egyptians had a choice, theoretically, between direct governance by a living god on earth, or indirect rule through human agents (the priests) by an unseen god in heaven. Some might choose to see the struggle as a contest between the monarchic and the theocratic forms of government. Besides the inaptness of such a modern interpretation in terms of Ancient Egyptian concepts, the historical process at work here is much more complex. There is something in it of the political confrontation of opposing forms of government; there is also certainly a clash of giant personalities, bent unconsciously on ruling Egypt. There may also be an element of rivalry between geographical regions, for the court had long since displayed a preference for Memphis over Thebes as a place of residence. The present writer believes he can sense a fear on the part of the court of the real and potential power which the traditional celebration of the cultus and the piling up of sacerdotal endowments gave to the priesthood of Amun. It is very doubtful, on the other hand, whether one may speak of factions or parties, even if one refrains from imputing conscious policies to them. The priesthood of Amun, it is true, comprised an easily-distinguished interest group; but a "Monarchy Party" simply cannot be detected. Any group of courtiers whose status and wealth depended upon the king would naturally follow him; the Egyptians, in fact, used this very terminology, viz. "to follow" a ruler, or "to adhere to the path" of the king. But such a group can scarcely be termed a political party. It would be better to view the revolution, for such it was, that we are about to describe, as the work of one man who found himself in possession of enormous power, and whose chief aim was to reinstate Horus, the Son of Re, in his pristine seat as head of the universe (**fig. 4**).

Akhenaten: The Man

Upon Amenophis III's death in 1373 B.C. the throne was occupied by the third child of his union with Tiy, a certain misshapen boy named after his father. His older brother, Thutmose, and possibly his older sister, Sat-Amun, had predeceased their father under circumstances that are obscure, and thus the throne was left to one who had enjoyed no special training for the kingship. It was usual at the time to appoint the heir apparent to the high-priesthood in the temple of Ptah at Memphis (κ) where he would be groomed by the best minds to take over from his father in due course; but Amenophis IV had been assigned a tutor of lowly standing, one Parennefer, and had been brought up in the new court at Thebes. About the time of his father's death, or shortly thereafter, he was married to a beautiful woman called Nefertity whose background is unknown, although she undoubtedly moved in court circles. In the relief decoration of the temples her husband was to build at Thebes she figures nearly twice as often as the king, and indeed one of the four edifices he constructed was devoted entirely to her. This has led some, with justification, to suspect that Nefertity may have had a louder voice in the momentous changes that were about to take place than the evidence suggests.

The curious and fantastic form that the king's figure assumed in the new art style about to be introduced has given rise to a debate about the meaning intended. Some see the form as more or less corresponding to reality, albeit treated in an exaggerated and expressionistic manner. Such an acceptance places an obligation on the scholar to explain why the king looks so misshapen, in short from what *ailment* did he suffer. Others, in reaction to what they construe as a naïve approach, view the new canon as a metaphor for the king's "androgynous" relationship with mankind as their "father-and-mother" combined in a single body. This view may be discounted. Egyptian artists well knew the "hermaphrodite" form, and constantly reproduced it to represent satiety; but it bore very little resemblance to Akhenaten's shape! Moreover, the father-mother metaphor is not common in the royal lexikon, and does not figure prominently during the Amarna Period. We would appear to be on firmer ground if we postulate *some* kind of ailment underlying the Amarna "royal shape."

The new king's ailment, undoubtedly congenital, has not yet been identified with a certainty that would convince everyone; but the accumulating evidence is pointing in one direction only. In the complete absence of textual references, reliefs and statuary comprise the sole evidence upon which medical experts must make a diagnosis. Recent studies have tended to

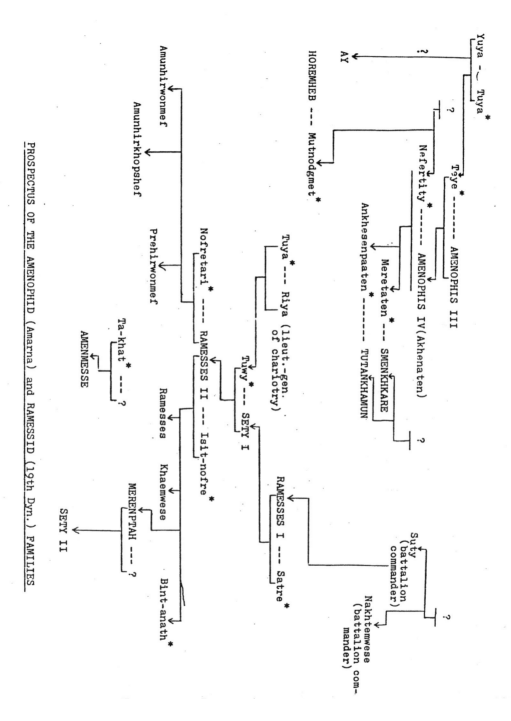

Figure 4 Prospectus of the Amenophid (Amarna) and Ramesside (19th Dyn.) families.

favor a pituitary disorder, "Frölich's Syndrome," or eunuchoidism, diagnoses which, however, do not account for the king's six daughters! The latest research overwhelmingly favors the postulate of the genetic disorder called *Marfan's Syndrome,* or "Abe Lincoln's disease," the checklist for which is consistently matched by what we know of Amenophis IV's appearance and cravings. Marfan's produces skeletal deformities such as elongated skull, sunken eyes, drop jaw, reduced rib cage and distended belly, extended hips, reversed joints, and lengthened fingers, which is exactly what we see in representations of the young monarch (L). Also characteristic of this disorder are deteriorating eyesight and poor circulation, and one is reminded of the king's repeated desire to "see" the sun-god and to stand for hours in his warmth. Marfan's in short had turned Amenophis IV into a pot-bellied, weak-shouldered individual, with enormous thighs, spindly calves, and an elongated head (M–N), precisely opposite to the macho athlete which the kingly model required in the Eighteenth Dynasty to rule an empire (O)!

Paradoxical as it may seem, this misanthropic *bouffa* figure stood over the largest empire the world had known at a time when the struggle of the pharaonic monarchy was reaching a point of culmination. To find a means of epitomizing the royal principle, to eliminate the one great threat to the doctrine of the Perfect God on earth, to focus all attention on the king himself—these were the goals which, perhaps only unconsciously, Amenophis IV set himself to achieve. The means he elected consisted simply of the championing, to the exclusion of all else, the cult and person of one god. Occasionally earlier in the Eighteenth Dynasty the "sun-disc" had been referred to in texts as a metonym for imperial power; and two generations before Amenophis IV, under his grandfather Thutmose IV, the cult of the "sun-disc" (Egyptian *p3 itn*) had received royal patronage, although it remained a relatively unimportant aspect of the solar deity. Under his father Amenophis III, as we have seen, the "Dazzling Sun-disc" had become the king's sobriquet. Although at the outset of his reign the royal sculptors sometimes (perhaps without authorization) depicted the king offering to Amun, Amenophis IV would have none of this. Shortly after his accession the king delivered a speech to his court in which, while acknowledging the gods and their temples, he nonetheless declares that they have all stopped except one, the solar deity whom he identifies generically as the "Sun-disc." At once he elevated this divinity to the highest possible seat, eliminating all other gods from his thinking, as creator and universal monarch. He became "the solitary sole (god) like whom there is no other," an expression of true monotheism. Pharaoh even changed his name from Amenophis ("Amun is at peace") to Akhenaten ("Useful for [the] Sun-disc"), and as such he is known to history. Akhenaten called himself "the beautiful child of the sun-disc," referred to the sun as "my father," to whose inmost thoughts he declared himself privy, and even identified himself physically and spiritually as the god's image upon earth. And so the "Sun-disc," who during life had quite likely passed over, if not dismissed, his second male offspring, now for ever looked down from heaven upon his "beautiful child," and shed his rays over him with an imagined love the little prince had lacked (P).

To grant the Sun-disc anthropomorphic representation in art, however, might have suggested a distinction between the king and his father instead of the unity he intended to convey. Consequently in his third year, and in anticipation of a royal jubilee, Akhenaten decreed that the only iconographic form the Disc was to take was simply a disc from which stylized "arms" could be shown descending. Since the Sun-disc was as much a king as he had been on earth, his name must be written in cartouches (Q), and he must share in the celebration of jubilees as Pharaoh did. He also must have a regal palace, and that must be located in the first

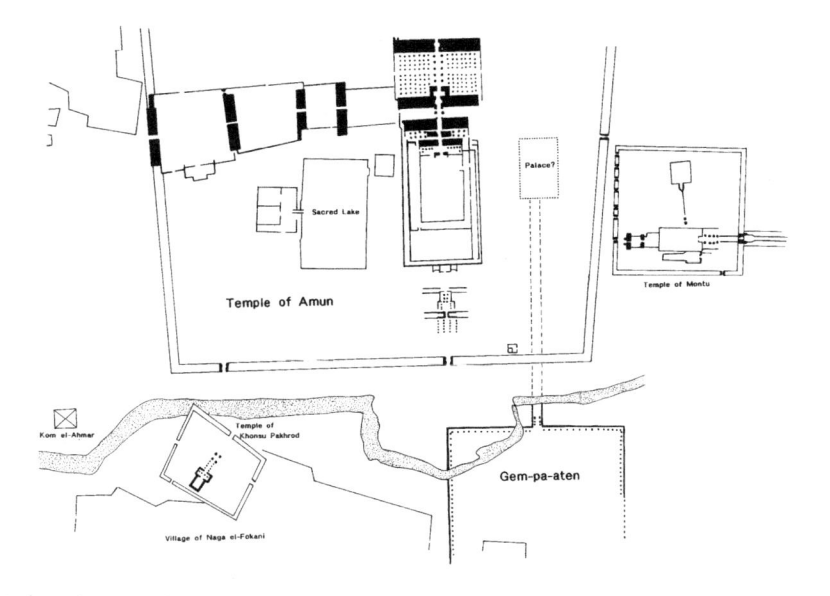

Figure 5   Plan of the Temples of Amun and Montu, Karnak, showing the position of the "House of the Sun-disc" and the Gem-pa-aten.

city of the Empire. In short, the Sun-disc was nothing but the projection into a universal context and in all its purity of the monarchic principle as exemplified by Amenophis III, "light which is (in) the sun-disc."

The Early Years at Thebes

Thebes in 1372 B.C. was the city of Amun, and his large temple there was the focal point of the ancient city (QQ). The visitor to these sacred precincts towards the close of Amenophis III's reign was rowed up a long canal, lined with palms and statuary, to a square turning basin and wharf. Before him, gleaming with its ornaments of gold and electrum, its pennants fluttering in the blue, stood the fortified gateway, or "pylon" (Greek πυλον, "gate"), which Amenophis III had erected as a façade. On either side of the entry stood a tall, slender shaft of stone, bearing an inscription which lauded the king who had erected them. Such shafts are called "obelisks" (Greek οβελισκοσ, "a little spit"), and a good example is the earliest surviving, viz. that of Senwosret I at Heliopolis (R). Passing between the obelisks and through the gate the visitor was confronted by more obelisks and a second pylon which, for one hundred and twenty years before Amenophis III's time, had constituted the front of the temple. The shrine itself containing the image of the god stood at the rear of the temple, with no windows or skylights to relieve a perpetual twilight—a fit setting for the awesome "hidden one." No greater antithesis to the concept of the Sun-disc can be imagined!

But to Akhenaten Thebes was the "first great <seat> of the Sun-disc," and he purposed early to honor the god by a new complex. He chose the unoccupied terrain on the mud-flats due east of the Karnak complex **(fig. 5)** for his "House of the Sun-disc" (*pr-itn*), which centered

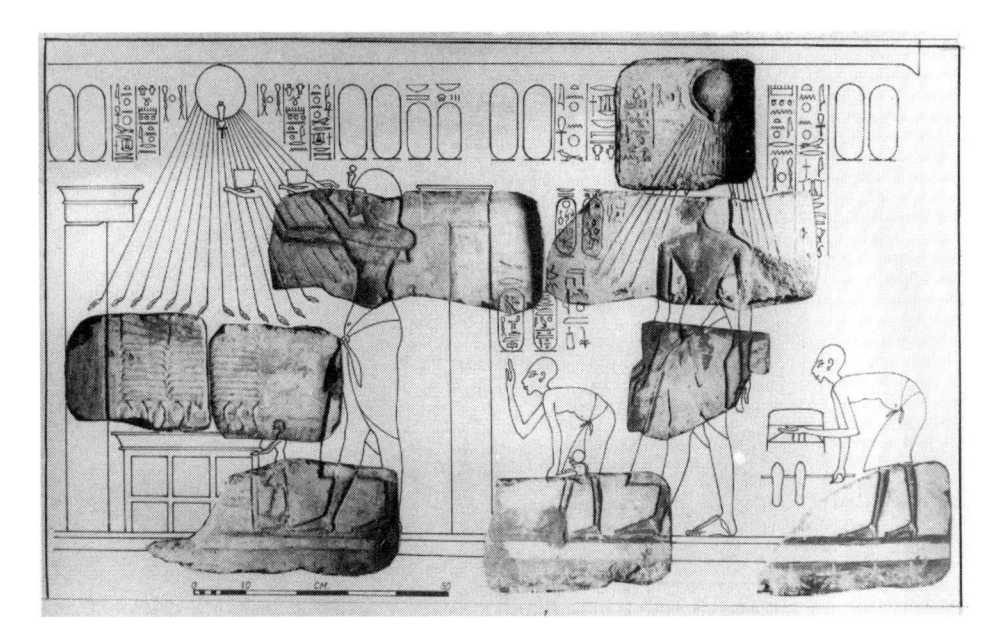

Figure 6 Akhenaten offering to the Sun-disc in a roofless shrine in the temple Rud-menu, accompanied by the high-priest of the sun-god and his personal high-priest.

upon a large podium-altar, facing east towards the rising sun, and approached by a ramp. Shortly after getting the idea, Akhenaten modified the original plan by converting the space just described into a temple open to the sky, comprising two courts fronted by a pylon, and connected by a walled corridor to the royal palace which stood to the west. Three other shrines **(fig. 7)** were built, opening off this axial route, between the Amun temple and the Montu temple to the north. These four, open-roofed structures, were decorated in a new art style whose treatment of form and thematic repertoire is vastly different from what went before. The figure of the king himself **(fig. 6),** exaggerated into virtual caricature in which every detail of the syndrome is accentuated, provided the model for human forms, male and female (s). The occasion for the modifications and also the introduction of a new canon of art was the decision to celebrate a jubilee at the close of the third regnal year. This curious choice of a celebration, which normally would not have been contemplated before a king's thirtieth year, has mystified scholars. Was Akhenaten ailing? Was he counting thirty years from his birth, but if so why? Or did he wish to capitalize on the legitimacy this festival conferred on the ruler, or the goodwill the distribution of royal largesse to the people might engender? Whatever the reason, the walls of the largest of the four shrines, the *Gm-p3-itn,* were covered with vividly painted relief scenes, all hastily done to meet the deadline, depicting in great detail the cultic acts of the jubilee (T, U, V). And Akhenaten was faithful to the order-of-service with one exception: whereas the jubilee was intended to bring all the gods of Egypt together to confer their approbation a second time upon the ruler, Akhenaten had but one god, and it is he, the Sun-disc, who is shown in the relief decoration to the exclusion of all other deities.

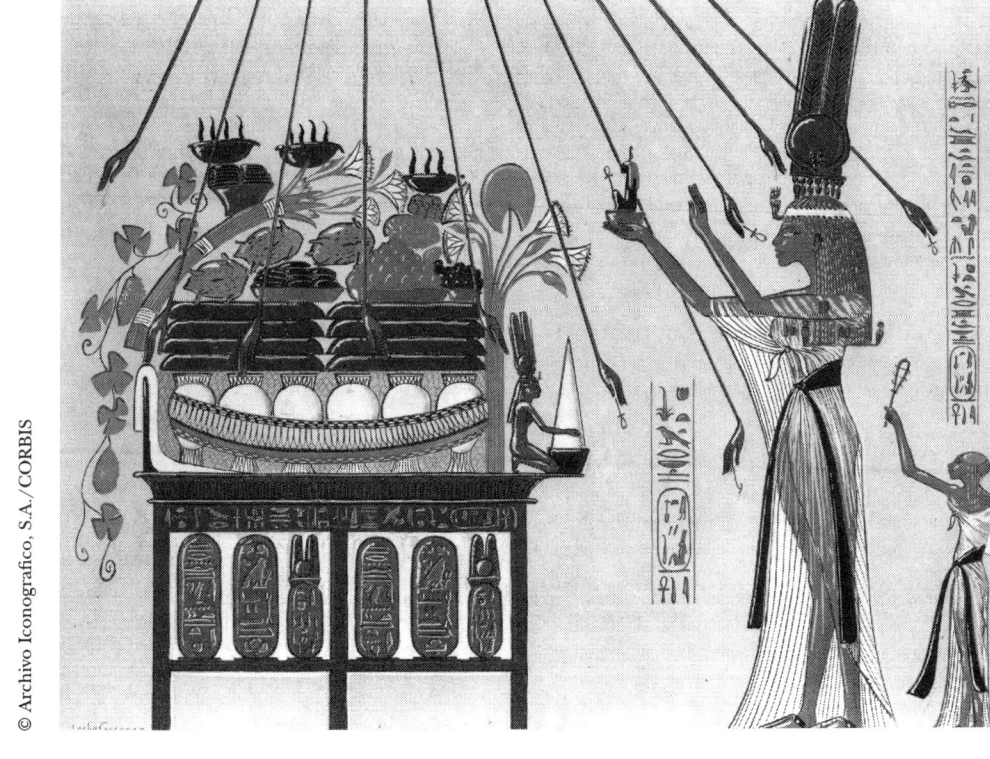

Figure 7 Nefertity with her eldest daughter offering to the Sun-disc, in the "Mansion of the Benben-stone," Karnak.

The New City of Amarna: "The Horizon of the Sun-disc"

Although Akhenaten had organized at great expense a vast programme of quarrying and construction at Thebes and may well have loved the city, by his fourth year he was finding it increasingly difficult to continue his residence. The large complex "the House of the Sun-disc" he had thrown up to his solar god lay within sight of the Amun temple, and while it in no way overshadowed or took spatial precedence over Amun's dwelling, it nonetheless could prove an embarrassment. Moreover, as Parennefer his erstwhile tutor and now food and drink commissar tells us, Akhenaten had begun to divert the incomes of other temples into the coffers of the "House of the Sun-disc," thus shutting them down and putting priests out of work. He may have tried to recruit these indigent ecclesiastics for his new enterprise, but the ideological gulf to be bridged was immense. Amun was the fundament of reality and existence, manifest in and working through a myriad of avatars, the other gods; the Sun-disc was alone, by himself, without equal, working directly on the cosmos. Amun could be immanent, the Sun-disc only transcendent. Amun was mysterious and hidden, known to a few; the Sun-disc was open to view, but known only to his son. Therefore it gradually became clear that Amun and the Sun-disc could never be reconciled on an ideological plane and that Amun would never be unseated from his position of primacy in the southern city. In the fourth year, Akhenaten tells us, "evil words" were being mouthed against him: the Theban interest groups could not tolerate what was going on. If the Sun-disc was to be the king of the universe without rival, it must have a city of its own and Amun had to be denigrated. The former condition was more easily satisfied. Probably late in the fourth year, on a trip down the Nile, Akhenaten had caught a glimpse of a site in Middle Egypt, across the river and upstream from Hermopolis (w), which he convinced himself the Sun-disc had selected as his special "horizon." Construction at once began there on a new capital to be named Akhetaten, "The Horizon of the Sun-disc". By the sixth year Akhenaten and his family were residing in the city, albeit in temporary quarters, as his palace was not yet completed. But from this point on Akhetaten would be his sole residence; he would never live elsewhere. At a string of boundary stelae demarcating the periphery of the new town, Akhenaten swore an oath by his father, the Sun-disc: "As my father lives . . . the beautiful, living Sun-disc, . . . in this place shall I make Akhetaten for my father the Sun-disc; I shall not make Akhetaten for him to the south of it, or to the north of it, or to the west of it, or to the east of it; I shall not go beyond the southern boundary stela of Akhetaten to the south, nor shall I go beyond the northern boundary stela of Akhet[aten to the north]. . . . I shall not make (it) for him on the west side of Akhetaten, but I shall make Akhetaten for the Sun-disc my father on the sunrise side of Akhetaten. . . ."

There can be no doubt that Amarna/Akhetaten was a "dream city" which enjoyed consciously applied town-planning from the start. The whole, located in a plain on the eastern side of the Nile eleven kilometers long by five kilometers wide (x), was laid out along a north-south avenue. To the east lay a series of enormous temples (y), each comprising a series of open courts laid out axially and oriented towards the rising sun; while to the west were docks, warehouses and administrative buildings. The king resided and gave audience in a palace on the north side of the city (z-aa), and his nobles occupied spacious villas built for the most part in the southern sector of the town. To the east, along the low cliffs of the eastern desert (ab), two series of rock-cut tombs were laid out to accommodate the officials of the revolutionary regime (ac). All the departments of government, formerly distributed between Memphis and Thebes, were now centralized in Akhetaten making it a veritable hub of state activity.

The total destruction of Amun and his cult, which was begun just prior to the move from Thebes to Akhetaten, was only the most dramatic manifestation of a hostility towards the pantheon in general. In his fanatical determination to promote the principle of divine kingship, Akhenaten did away with all other gods whose cults, yea whose very existence, diverted attention from his all-consuming purpose. Hatchet-men ran throughout Egypt hacking out the group of three hieroglyphs which stood for "Amun," and also the group to be read "gods," wherever they could find them on existing monuments. People with names compounded with "Amun" or "Osiris" had to find new names, or substitute "Aten" for the anathematized element. What happened to the temple and estate of Amun at Thebes we do not know. We last hear of the high-priest in year 4, when he was despatched to the quarries with the ignominious task of extracting blocks for royal statuary. Most likely the shrine fell into disuse and the priesthood disbanded, as more and more of Amun's property was confiscated for the Sun-disc.

Akhenaten's attack on the cultus and mythology followed logically. We have already noted the predominance of the esoteric in the Egyptian religion. The vast storehouse of myth, with its inherent ambiguity and mystery, lent itself to constant reinterpretation, addition, expansion, and rationalization. Intended originally as a kind of primitive speculation about something that affected man vitally, myth could be transformed in the context of a sophisticated society, such as that of New Kingdom Egypt, into a multitude of forms for purposes far removed from those of their unknown prehistoric authors. The magician could employ a snatch of mythological narrative, spoken verbatim, as a particularly potent spell: the mere utterance of a story about Re's being bitten by a venomous serpent and how he had exorcised the poison, could *ipso facto* be used as an incantation against snake bites. The mystic might recount a mythological episode, accompanying his performance with a sort of mimetic symbolism, in an effort to identify mystically with the leading character in the narrative, and so, in a heightened state of consciousness, to achieve a "transformation" into another being. The ritualist priest in his offering liturgy, while he offered things upon the altar of his god, might liken his acts to the doings of some well-known mythological figure: he was Horus presenting his eye to his father, or (while drawing the bolt from the lock of the god's shrine) he was removing Seth's finger from Horus's eye. The corpus of ever-expanding mythological symbolism constituted a body of potent magic and latent mystical power which was the sole preserve of the lector priests, the most influential members of Egypt's priesthoods. To perpetuate myth in the cult meant to play into the hands of the very people Akhenaten feared most. And so, in a move redolent of iconoclasm, the king purged the canon of art and even the minor, decorative arts of anything which smacked in any way of myth or mythological symbolism, drastically reducing in the process the range of the repertoire on which artists could draw. Nothing was to detract from the centrality and uniqueness of the Sun-disc, or from Akhenaten's right alone to interpret his god to mankind. In consequence the king threw away the old iconography, did away with the myths, and tolerated none but the simplest cultic acts in his temples. The Sun-disc, the heavenly king, was to be worshipped in a sterile purity!

The "teaching" of the new religion, of which Akhenaten's followers speak so much, seems to be epitomized in the great Hymn to the Sun-disc, a copy of which was inscribed on the walls of the tomb of Akhenaten's secretary, and sometime successor, Ay. "How manifold is all that thou hast made!" sang the king in praise of his god, ". . . O sole god, like whom there is no other! Thou didst create the world according to thy desire . . . all men, cattle, and wild beasts, whatever is on earth moving upon its legs, and what is on high flying with its wings. . . . Thou art in my heart, and there is no other who knows thee!" The Sun-disc was not only the god of the Egyptians, but of all lands: "The countries of Syria, Nubia, and the land of Egypt—thou settest every man in his place, thou suppliest their necessities. . . . Their tongues are separate in speech, and their natures as well, and their skins are distinguished. . . . O lord of every land." The hymn thus concentrates on the beneficence and universal dominion of the Sun-disc, but these concepts are not new, and *mutatis mutandis* were also applied to Amun-re during the century before Akhenaten. Certainly they should not lead one to the conclusion that Akhenaten was a humanist—how could one who practiced the impaling of captives be so termed?—much less that his religion foreshadowed Judaism or Christianity! If we must categorize him in modern terms, he should be called a monarchic reactionary with a brilliant imagination; and if he is to be a forerunner of anyone, then, as Toynbee has so aptly pointed out, it must be Aurelian, for the Sun-disc is nothing less than Sol Invictus in a Nilotic form. The present writer, though mindful of the debate on the subject, is convinced he can detect a strong strain of belligerent monotheism in Akhenaten's new cult; but it is the monotheism of sterile intellect sitting atop an empire, rather than the Mosaic or Christian variety.

Of the host of officials who are found at the new capital, only two or three are known to have come from families well known in the officialdom of earlier times. The vast majority were new men in whose tomb bibliographies occurs the tireless refrain, "It was the king that made me great" **(fig. 8)**. Akhenaten apparently did not want the old aristocracy: his father's blue-bloods unsettled him. He was content to surround himself with parvenus, bound to the court by gratitude for the never-ending rewards and largesse which the monarch was always bestowing upon his creatures **(fig. 9)**. The cult of the Sun-disc was not for the common man. Indeed, it is doubtful whether it excited much interest outside the immediate circle of the royal family. In the homes of rich and poor alike there is good evidence that private worship of the anathematized gods continued quietly.

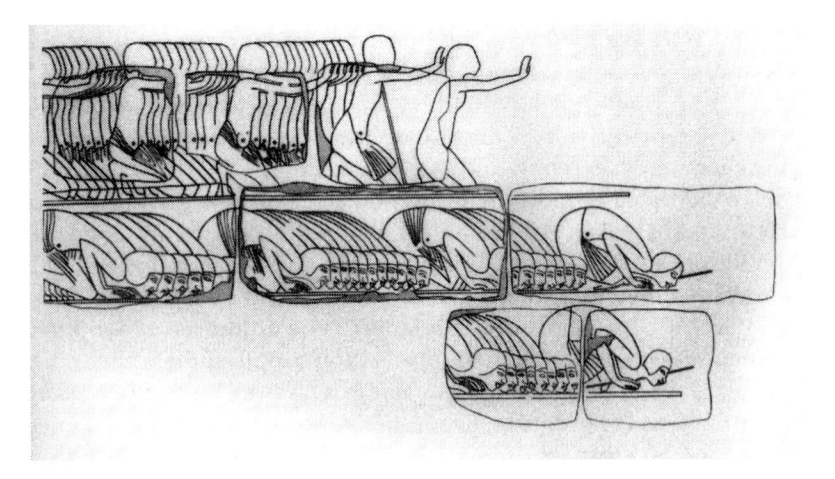

Figure 8   Courtiers and army personnel prostrating themselves before Akhenaten.

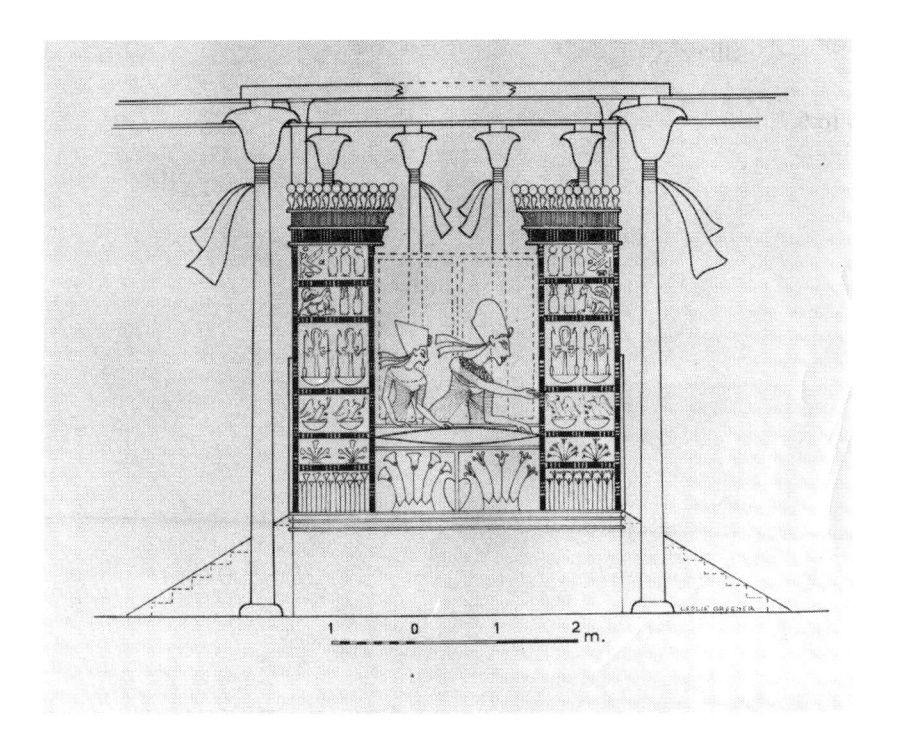

Figure 9 Akhenaten and Nefertit appearing on the balcony, in the "Window of Appearances," to reward a faithful follower.

Further Readings

On the reign of Amenophis III, see L. H. Berman (ed.), *The Art of Amenhotep III: Art Historical Analysis,* Cleveland, 1990; J. Fletcher, *Chronicle of Pharaoh: The Intimate Life of Amenhotep III,* Oxford, 2000; A. Kozloff, B. Bryan, *Egypt's Dazzling Sun-disc: Amenhotep III and His World,* Cleveland, 1992; D. O'Connor, E. Cline (eds.), *Amenhotep III: Perspectives on His Reign,* Ann Arbor, 1998.

The following works have been selected from the ever-growing bibliography on the history of the Amarna Period as the most profitable to read: C. Aldred, *Akhenaten, Pharaoh of Egypt: A New Study,* London, 1968; *idem, Akhenaten and Nefertity,* New York, 1973; C. El-Mahdy, *Tutankhamen: The Life and Death of a Boy King,* London, 1999; R. Freed (ed.), *Pharaohs of the Sun: Akhenaten, Nefertiti, and Tutankhamun,* Boston, 1999; D. Montserrat, *Akhenaten: History, Fantasy, and Ancient Egypt,* London & New York, 2000; W. J. Murnane, *Texts from the Amarna Period in Egypt,* Atlanta, 1995; D. B. Redford, *Akhenaten, the Heretic King,* Princeton, 1984; N. Reeves, *Egypt's False Prophet: Akhenaten,* London, 2001; J. Samson, *Amarna: City of Akhenaten and Nefertity,* Warminster, 1977; *idem, Nefertiti and Cleopatra: Queen-Monarchs of Ancient Egypt,* London, 1985; R. W. Smith, D. B. Redford, *The Akhenaten Temple Project: I. The Initial Discoveries,* Warminster, 1977; J. Tyldesley, *Nefertiti, Egypt's Sun Queen,* London, 1998; B. Watterson, *Amarna: Ancient Egypt's Age of Revolution,* Stroud, 1999.

On monotheism and related matters, see J. Assmann, *Egyptian Solar Religion in the New Kingdom: Re, Amun, and the Crisis of Polytheism,* London, 1995; E. Hornung, *Akhenaten and the Religion of Light,* Ithaca, 1995; B. N. Porter (ed.), *One God or Many?* New York, 2000; H. Shanks, J. Meinhardt (eds.), *Aspects of Monotheism: How God is One,* Washington, 1997.

SINGLE Tu | S

Customer:

Nizar Dajani

A history of ancient Egypt: Egyptian Civilization in Context

Donald B. Redford

E1-N025-F9

W2-CHD-691

No CD

Used - Very Good

9780757522765

Picker Notes:

M _____ 2 _____

WT _____ 2 _____

CC _____

60722892

CHAPTER TEN

The Reaction against Egypt and the Hittite War

Nineteenth Dynasty	
Ramesses I	c. 1318–1316 B.C.
Sety I	c. 1316–1304 B.C.
Ramesses II.	c. 1304–1237 B.C.
Merenptah	c. 1237–1226 B.C.
Amenmesse	c. 1226–1223 B.C.
Sety II	c. 1223–1217 B.C.
Siptah	c. 1217–1211 B.C.
Tawosret	c. 1211–1202 B.C.
Beya	c. 1202–1200 B.C.

In the winter of 1887–88 a peasant woman, while rummaging about in the ruins of Akhetaten, commonly known today as Tell el-Amarna, chanced upon a cache of clay tablets written in Babylonian cuneiform. Friends of hers, only slightly less ignorant, realized that these finds might fetch a price on the antiquities' market. The poor woman, to whom the objects were worthless, was persuaded to surrender her rights to the discovery for something like 50¢. Immediately clandestine digging began with a vengeance, and tablets began to appear in large quantities. All told, perhaps as many as eight hundred were brought to light, of which barely half survived the rough handling of their discoverers. For, unknown to these

19th-century peasants, they had stumbled upon the government offices of Akhetaten, and, as luck would have it, upon that block of offices which contained the "dead files" of diplomatic correspondence from foreign courts. The tablets in fact are simply letters, written by foreign kings and princes to Amenophis III and Akhenaten. There are letters from Babylon, Mitanni, Cyprus, the Hittite capital, Assyria, as well as reports from vassals and governors in Palestine and Syria. In short, the tablets represent a type of correspondence which had been circulating between the capitals of the Ancient World during the century or more of Egyptian domination. But they are more than a typical body of texts: they reflect Egypt's Asiatic empire at a critical point in its history, when to some it might have appeared to be on the verge of collapse. For, at the very moment that Akhenaten was attempting to establish his cult of the Sun Disc, the Hittites were invading north Syria.

The Hittite Threat to Syria

About the time Amenophis II passed away, the Hittite kingdom in central Anatolia entered a period of sharp decline. Autochthonous tribes in the vicinity of the capital, Hattusas, as well as invading Hurrians from the east, may have contributed to the weakening of the state. For several generations the Hittites disappear from view. In one of his letters recovered at Amarna, Amenophis III even opines that the Hittites are finished (as a world power). Then, towards the close of Amenophis III's reign, perhaps somewhere in the vicinity of 1370, the kingdom of Hattusas suddenly reappears in all its strength, led by a king called Suppiluliumas I. From the inception of his reign to the collapse of the Hittite kingdom two centuries later, the history of Khatte is illumined by the thousands of clay tablets, many written in the Hittite language, which have been unearthed at Hattusas.

The life of an empire in the center of the Anatolian plateau (A) was not an unmixed blessing for those who tried to maintain it. True, the Hittite homeland was blessed with copious deposits of silver, as well as iron (which the Hittites did not use much, though they knew how to smelt it). But it was also constantly threatened by wild tribesmen who resented the dominance of the Hittites. And it is therefore not surprising to learn that the Hittite state's energies were largely devoted to the waging of war. Paradoxically, this did not make them brutal. To judge from their laws we should have to pronounce the Hittites the most humane of all ancient peoples. Capital punishment was scarcely known among them; for all crimes including premeditated murder the penalty was a fine, for major crimes a substantial fine, for minor crimes a lesser one. *Lex Talionis,* and deliberate bodily mutilation of the guilty party are conspicuous by their absence from the corpus of Hittite laws. The essential humanity evidenced in the Hittite body social appears also in their dealings with foreign peoples. States conquered by the Hittites and added to their empire were forced to sign treaties with the Hittite king, by which they agreed to pay a yearly tribute, promised not to rebel or assist rebels, and were afforded "protection" by the Hittites in return.

The Mitannian empire in Mesopotamia, the natural enemies of the Hittites in the east, had entered the 14th century B.C. closely allied with Egypt. Amenophis III and his contemporary, Tushratta of Mitanni, had concluded a pact of brotherhood, and Tushratta's sister and daughter duly entered Pharaoh's harim. While Amenophis lived, both states could present a strong, united front against potential enemies anywhere on earth. But, for some reason, upon Akhenaten's accession the young king showed hostility towards his father's friend, and Tushratta had difficulty eliciting responses to his letters.

As Egypt and Mitanni drifted apart, the Hittites saw their opportunity to take political and military advantage. In a sweeping military campaign which took place about 1370 B.C., Suppiluliumas succeeded in destroying the kingdom of Mitanni, between the Tigris and Euphrates, and forcing Tushratta to flee. Akhenaten, deeply committed to his domestic program, was indifferent to Tushratta's assassination which followed shortly, and turned a blind eye upon Syria where the victorious Hittites rolled irresistibly over those minor states which had been vassals of Mitanni, and raised their standard as far south as the southern Lebanons. Suppiluliumas was very careful, however, not to give the Egyptians a pretext for action by trespassing across the boundary separating inland Syria, formerly subservient to Mitanni, from the Egyptian province along the coast and in Palestine. In a word Akhenaten was stymied, even if he had wished to act.

Not all the Canaanite states appreciated being conquered by this new Anatolian imperial power. A number of these Syrian principalities, now bereft of their Mitannian overlord, turned to Egypt for help. "If my lord does not wish to march out," says Addu-nirari, a north-Syrian prince, to Akhenaten, "then let him send one of his councillors with troops and chariots." In another letter Akizzi, the king of Qatna on the Orontes river in central Syria, protests his devotion to Egypt: "O my lord, just as I love the king my lord, so also do the king of Nukhashe, the king of Niya, the king of Zinzar, and the king of Tunanat. All these kings are indeed servants of my lord! . . . O my lord! If with respect to this land a burden is to be removed from my lord's mind, then let my lord despatch the archers and let them come!" For the present Akhenaten paid no attention to such letters. The Hittites seem to have avoided a direct clash with any Phoenician or south Syrian state which had formal ties with Egypt. Perhaps Akhenaten reasoned that until such an indiscretion occurred, he had no choice but to remain inactive.

By 1365 B.C. the Hittites had successfully put down a rebellion, and most of the states of inland Syria had signed treaties with the conquerors from the north. A belated attempt by Akhenaten to drive out the Hittites at the end of his reign failed completely, and the Egyptians were obliged to resign themselves to the reality of a Hittite presence in the Levant. Perhaps before news of the failure of his counterattack reached him, Akhenaten had passed away, in the seventeenth year of his reign.

The End of the Eighteenth Dynasty

While the beginning of Akhenaten's reign is coming into sharper focus with new excavations and discoveries at Thebes, the "Amarna years" suffer from an embarrassing lack of evidence. Over 20% of the inscribed decoration of the sun-temples at Thebes has survived thanks to the recycling of component masonry in later foundations and wall fillings; but Amarna has yielded scarcely 1% of total epigraphic content coupled with a smattering of "informal" inscriptions such as wine-jar dockets. The tombs at Amarna belonging to courtiers contain, it is true, an extensive array of scenes and inscriptions; but their owners are at pains to promote themselves in stereotyped fashion, rather than record historical events. Early in his reign Akhenaten had erected altars to the Sun-disc, as he boasts, in every temple from Elephantine to Sam-behdet (i.e. the Mediterranean coast). But with the abandonment of the temples and the move to Amarna activity at other sites such as Heliopolis, Memphis and Gem-aten in Nubia, in all of which shrines to the Sun-disc had been erected, virtually ceases; and the only light to be had comes from Akhetaten itself.

With the forgoing as a sobering caveat, we may now try to piece together the scattered data to see if a coherent picture may be obtained. In year 9 Akhenaten seems to have refined his religious views somewhat, and changed the official name of his sun god to "Live the Ruler of the Horizon, who rejoices in his name of Re the father who has returned as the Sun-disc." It is unclear what his new revelation entailed, although it may be an elaboration on his view of his filial relationship. Up to year 11 six daughters had been born to him by Nefertity, the second of whom died about that time. In year 12 a great "durbar," or public levee, was held in the new city, to which emissaries from the southern and northern provinces of the empire were obliged to come. Through these years Nefertity's dominance of the courtly scene may have been challenged by a lesser wife, Kiya, who may have been one of the Mitannian princesses sent to the court of Amenophis III; but this threat, if such it was, proved less than that of Nefertity's own eldest daughter, Merit-aten, on whom her father conferred elevated status. Merit-aten may also have married a young nobleman at court called Smenkhkare, but this figure is extremely shadowy. It has even been claimed that "Smenkhkare" was in fact Nefertity in a transmogrified male form; and it is true that some female member of the royal family at the end of Akhenaten's reign adopted the artificial masculine name (in cartouche) of Akh-en-hyes, meaning "Useful-for-her-husband"!

The only other daughter of Akhenaten to attain womanhood—she actually outlived her father by a dozen years—was the third in order of birth, Ankhes-en-aten by name. At about the age of fourteen she was joined in marriage to a young nobleman not much older than herself, whose name was Tut-ankh-aten. An inscription originally from Amarna describes him as "king's bodily son," which may mean that he was a son of Akhenaten by a lesser wife. The events which followed the marriage are unknown and the little evidence we have confuses rather than enlightens us. The untimely death of Akhenaten in his seventeenth year was followed within weeks by the disappearance from the scene of Merit-aten and Smenkhkare (if he existed), and Egypt was left without a leader. A single generation after the passing of the mighty Amenophis III had sufficed to discredit completely the family of the Eighteenth Dynasty. At this point it was probably Nefertity that elevated her fourteen year old son-in-law, Tutankhamun, the husband of her third daughter, to the throne, and prepared to continue the tradition established by her late husband. But her administration had been irreparably weakened, and the economic state of the country was serious. Possibly upon her death the advisors of the young king, in particular Ay, the aging former secretary of Akhenaten, decided no longer to resist the growing animosity of the old interest groups, and to abandon the new city of the Sun-disc. Consequently in the third year of the new reign the court moved away from Akhetaten for ever, and took up residence in Memphis. While the Sun-disc temples throughout the realm were to survive for about fifteen years, restrictions on the old cults were lifted, temples re-opened and confiscated property returned. A generation later no one worshipped any longer in the sun-shrines, and they were torn down. The monotheistic cult of the Sun-disc had survived less than twenty-five years!

Contemporary texts describe the period following the abandonment of Amarna as one of internal chaos and disillusionment. It was, to quote the Egyptian idiom, "a time when the temples of the gods and goddesses from Elephantine as far as the Delta marshes . . . had fallen into ruin, and their shrines had become dilapidated. They had turned into mounds overgrown with weeds, and it seemed that their sanctuaries had never existed. . . . This land had been struck by catastrophe; the gods had turned their backs upon it." The great edict of reform of Horemheb (see below) describes how the army and the tax officials had, during the Amarna residency, been allowed to gouge taxes and extort goods and services from the peasants unchecked. There is no doubt that blame for this lamentable state of affairs must be laid almost exclusively on Akhenaten. Poet and innovator he may have been; but as a civil administrator he proved incompetent.

The unrelieved misery evoked one last effort from the last male scion of the old royal house. The young Tutankhaten changed his name to Tutankhamun, thus expunging the now hated word from his name, as many of his contemporaries were doing, and set about to rectify matters. On the home front he re-opened temples and paid for their refurbishment and staffing from his own pocket. After a hiatus of sixteen years he began once again to build and redecorate within the precincts of the hallowed halls of Amun at Karnak. In foreign affairs he purposed to right a wrong dating back fifteen years. Under Akhenaten a vassal chief governing Amurru, the northernmost principality within Egypt's Asiatic province, had defected to the Hittites, and Suppiluliumas had accepted his obeisance. This was a definite breach of international law, as it meant that the Hittite empire had now ingressed into Egyptian territory. Akhenaten's attempted military response had proven abortive, and for a whole generation the Egyptians had chafed under this humiliation. Sadly Tutankhamun's attempt to carry the city of Kadesh on the Orontes failed also, even though assisted by diversionary tactics on the part of the Assyrians. Shortly after his return Tutankhamun died, and all Egypt was panic-stricken.

Who would now rule Egypt? Tutankhamun's offspring had died in infancy, and there was no one left of the male line, or even of cadet branches of the family! A plague, mentioned in the Amarna Letters and the Hittite annals, which had ravaged the Phoenician coast late in Akhenaten's reign had spread inland to Syria and Anatolia, and (apparently) by sea to Egypt. It is tempting to see its effects in the sudden demise of many members of that glorious court at Amarna, those voluptuaries attending the royal pair, and the members of the royal house itself.

The final act in this tragedy appears as both poignant and outrageous. In the annals of Suppiluliumas drawn up by his son and discovered by the German excavators of Hattusas, the Hittite capital, there survives the copy of letters written by the "queen of Egypt," Ankhesenamun herself. In the first she expresses the dismay and fear she feels at the recent events and the loss of her husband, and pleads that the Hittite king send her one of his sons to be her husband and king of Egypt; in the second she chides Suppiluliumas with being suspicious of her, and repeats her request. The great king relented, and a son was sent; but before he arrived in Egypt Ankhesenamun had disappeared. The last remaining member of the royal house, a brave little queen, was gone, and the Eighteenth Dynasty had petered out.

The Army Assumes Power

The spectacle of Akhesenamun, Tutankhamun's widow, ignominiously begging for a new husband from among the sons of the Hittite Suppiluliumas was too much for some factions in Egypt, in particular the army. Probably shortly after the death of Tutankhamun the military stepped into the vacuum created by his demise, and seized power. The aging Ay, the former secretary of Akhenaten who was also a lieutenant-general, had proclaimed himself king **(fig. 1)** upon Tutankhamun's demise and had arranged for the lavish burial of the king **(fig. 2)**, at which he performed the funeral rites. Some months later the unsuspecting Hittite prince who was *en route* to Egypt for the nuptials was murdered. Though it may not have been Ay's doing—his letters of condolence to Suppiluliumas were found in the Hittite archives—nevertheless the stage was now set for an all-out, and seemingly interminable, war.

Though an old man with but four years to live, Ay managed to set a precedent by proclaiming a fellow officer as his heir apparent. Thus the lieutenant general Horemheb, with no tie of blood binding him to the heretical royal family, ascended the throne surrounded by an aura of legitimacy (B). He had not served at Amarna, and so was not tainted by association with the old, discredited regime; and his military accomplishments in Nubia, falling as they did under Tutankhamun, only enhanced his prestige. His service to the young king did not prevent him from usurping many of Tutankhamun's reliefs (C). Horemheb's long reign of almost thirty years brought Egypt back to a semblance of order and prosperity, albeit at the expense of eschewing for the time being wars of foreign conquest. The anarchy facing Horemheb upon his accession was serious. Yet his methods may seem harsh to us moderns. His great edict of reform, inscribed on a stela at Karnak, lays forth his program in all its details. Government officials and magistrates convicted of corrupt practices were to have their noses and ears cut off, and were to be sent into exile on the fringes of the Sinai desert. New, honest officials had to be sought to replace them. "I trod through it (the land)," says Horemheb in his edict, "both march and interior, seeking men. I sought out princes of sound speech and good character, who know how to judge human nature, who obey the words of the Palace, the laws of the Porte. I promoted them to judge the Two Lands to the satisfaction of Him-who-is-in-the-Palace."

Following Ay's example, Horemheb chose another army officer, the general Paramses who was no relation to himself, to be his successor. Paramses was son of a battalion commander who had seen action in Asia during the Amarna period, and he himself had functioned as a fortress commandant in the eastern Delta. Under the name Ramesses I the new ruler came to the throne in 1318 B.C., already an old man, and immediately associated his mature son Sety (D) with himself as coregent. In keeping with the family tradition, Sety had himself been trained in the army, and held the rank of general at his father's accession. When, scarcely two years later, Ramesses died and Sety became sole monarch, the chain of military appointments to the throne was broken; a new royal dynasty had come to power, and the succession would once again be based on heredity. As if to highlight his positive approach to earthly governance, Sety dubbed his reign "the Renaissance," and "the Beginning of Eternity," apt terms in the light of the beginning of a new Sothic cycle at about this time.

Sety at once set about to settle accounts with Egypt's neighbors. In his first year his armies surged across the Suez frontier and penetrated deep into Syria, thus bringing to an end over thirty years of ineffectual intervention in Asia. In subsequent years campaigns were launched

Figure 1 Cartouches and Horus-name of Ay (later themselves erased) carved over those of Tutankhamun, whose Theban temple is mentioned on the right.

© Gianni Dagli Orti/CORBIS

Figure 2 Gold coffin of Tutankhamun.

against Libyan tribes on the western edge of the Delta, as well as cities like Kadesh, well inside Hittite territory. Sety experienced little effective opposition from either quarter, and was able to represent each expedition as a stunning victory. On the external walls of the great columned hall he erected in the temple of Amun at Thebes Sety proudly displayed reliefs (E) showing "the great chiefs of the Lebanon . . . cutting [timber for] the great barque, 'Foremost of the River' (Amun's ceremonial ship) . . . and likewise for the flagstaves of Amun." Other reliefs pictured block-houses on the route to Gaza (F), booty, and captives, glossed by such captions as, "The booty which His Majesty got from the Shasu (nomadic tribes in the Negeb), which His Majesty himself seized in the first regnal year . . . ," or, "The chiefs of the foreign lands who knew not Egypt whom His Majesty brought as living captives." After approximately six years of intermittent fighting, the Hittites sued for peace. Under their aging king Mursilis, son of Suppiluliumas, they could not hope to withstand the onslaught of the vigorous young Pharaoh. It is quite likely that a formal treaty was drawn up between Sety and Mursilis, for a later text refers to "the treaty of normalcy which existed in the time of Mursilis, the great chief of Khatte." Since, however, such treaties were, in effect, oaths taken by individuals *vis-à-vis* each other, when either or both of the signatories died the treaty became null and void.

But for the interim Egyptians viewed the future with unbridled optimism. Long lines of victorious troops and P.O.W.s once again, as of old, lined the roads approaching the frontier; and welcoming dignitaries waved bouquets and cheered (G). The gods were turning their faces towards Egypt again.

Sety died suddenly and unexpectedly around 1304 B.C aged about forty. His well-preserved mummy, retrieved from the Deir el-Bahari cache in the 1870s, shows a robust individual with a handsome face, some 5′ 8″ tall. His son, named Ramesses after his grandfather, strongly resembles his father. He was already a young man, trained in the military and administrative arts, and with him a special era may be said to begin.

The Accession of Ramesses II, "The Great"

"Wasmuaria Satepnaria Riamasesa Maiamana, the great king, king of Egypt, the valiant of all lands!" The cuneiform transcription of the name with which this string of epithets begins approximates the pronunciation the king would have given his own name more closely than the later Graecized "Ramesses." Impressive as the accompanying epithets are, they pale beside those given the king in other hieroglyphic inscriptions: "Lord of heaven and earth, living sun-god of the entire earth . . . Lord of Fate . . . Khnum (the creator-god) who begets the plebs, who grants life to every nose, who makes all the gods to live, pillar of heaven, joist of the earth . . . whose word creates all sustenance. . . . Rich in years and of great strength, fear of whom has cowed the foreign lands . . . !" Unfortunately, it is just such stereotyped jargon, ubiquitous in Egyptian monuments, that effectually conceals the individuality of the ancients. We are fortunate, then, in Ramesses's case, as in the case of Amenophis III and Akhenaten, to possess some of the king's private correspondence through which it is possible to catch a glimpse, however fleeting, of the "real" Ramesses II.

For a short time before Sety's death Ramesses had been his father's associate upon the throne. In his own words, "I was inducted as eldest son and as heir apparent upon the throne of Geb (the earth-god): I reported on the state of the Two Lands as Chief of the Infantry and the Chariotry. When my father came to the throne in a former generation, I being but a child in his arms, he said of me: 'Crown him as king that I may see his beauty while I live.' He had the chamberlains summoned to fix the crown upon my brow. . . . He provided me with housegirls and royal throne-women(?), after the fashion of the palace beauties; he chose house-maids(?) . . . concubines . . . and nurse-companions(?)."

But Ramesses, upon coming to the throne, did not sit in idle luxury. The first thirty-six months, in fact, were filled with long trips of inspection, and serious decision-making. Shortly after Sety's death Ramesses visited Thebes for the funeral rites, and while there authorized the inception of a vast building program, including temples at Luxor (H), Abu Simbel (I), and Beit el-Wali. On his return trip to Memphis he stayed long enough in Abydos to inspect his father's unfinished mortuary temple (J) and to lay plans for bringing it to completion, an unheard-of act of filial piety. His second year was spent partly on the Mediterranean coast of the Delta, where he corralled some sea-roving pirates, the Shardona, and forced them to enter his employment as mercenaries; and partly on an extended tour of the African province to inspect the administration and to consider sites for possible temples. Upon his return north, in his third year he stopped in Thebes to see the progress on his addition to the Luxor temple. The whirlwind of activity had not ceased, as Ramesses now laid plans for his first campaign into Asia in his fourth year.

The Resumption of Hostilities with the Hittites

The configuration of the border district between the Hittite and Egyptian empires continued to provide occasions for war between the two sides. Although neither has been unearthed by archaeologists, the two treaties in force in Ramesses II's fourth year, one dating from Suppiluliumas, the other from Mursilis II, sanctioned a line of boundary which left Amurru in the Eleutheros valley to the Hittites. Ramesses and presumably his subjects as well chafed at this violation of long-standing rights; but a provocation of some sort was required to justify resorting to military action.

Such an opportunity was not long in coming. As Ramesses and his troops made their way up the Phoenician coast, pausing long enough to carve a stela at the Dog River mouth (K), messengers arrived from Benteshina, the king of Amurru, and erstwhile vassal of the Hittite king. Benteshina was offering nothing less than to switch sides and tender allegiance to Pharaoh! Although by international norms Ramesses should have rejected this offer, it must have seemed like sweet revenge for that earlier defection of Amurru to Suppiluliumas in the reign of Akhenaten. Ramesses accepted the new vassal, and the die was cast: now there *would* be war!

Muwatallis, Ramesses's counterpart on the throne of Khatte, was a man very like himself. The aged and infirm Mursilis II had passed away only a few years before, leaving the kingship to his son, a young man trained and eager for combat. A superior strategist, Muwatallis had moved his command headquarters to a southern city on the border of Syria, from which he proposed to carry out operations.

For what happened next we rely heavily on the copious sources, reliefs and texts, which Ramesses had honestly emblazoned on the walls and the pylons of Egyptian temples. The following have survived: three official copies of the bulletin, six copies of the relief record, five copies of a "poetic" account. During the winter both sides prepared for the coming war. Muwatallis recruited contingents from his vassals in Anatolia (whom Ramesses, always the propagandist, declared had had to be bribed!), and moved a body of 18,000 troops into position in north Syria. Ramesses mustered a force of about 20,000 with accompanying chariotry, and toward the end of April crossed the east Delta frontier at the fortress of Sile, making for Asia **(fig. 3)**. His objective was the key junction city of Kadesh within the territory of Amurru, which he felt he could easily reach, the more so since information gleaned from the locals declared the Hittite forces to be far to north. In fact Ramesses's informants were Hittite "plants":

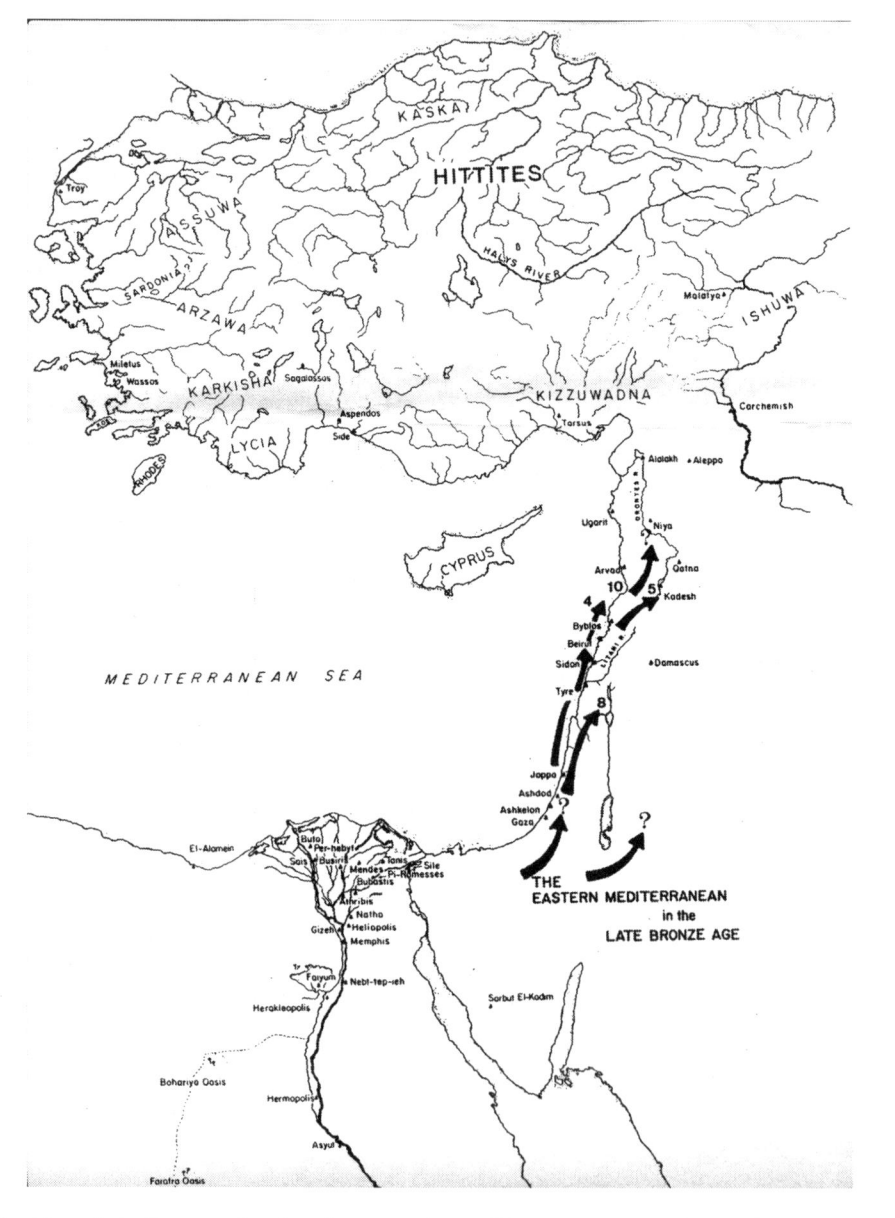

Figure 3 Map of the Levant, showing the campaigns of Ramesses II; numbers refer to regnal years.

Muwatallis and his entire army were lying in wait behind Kadesh, concealed by the sky-line of the city mound (L). Ramesses easily fell into the trap the Hittites had prepared. In his haste to besiege and reduce Kadesh before the arrival of the Hittites the king became negligent of his line of march, and as he approached the city his four divisions were strung out behind him in disorderly fashion over miles of road. At this juncture Muwatallis unleashed 2,500 chariots against the flank of the advancing Egyptian infantry. The Hittite attack came as a complete surprise. The second Egyptian division in line of march was decimated, and Ramesses, who was in process of setting up camp with the first division, found himself surrounded by this vast force of Hittite chariots. In a display of great personal courage Ramesses managed to extricate himself from the trap, and, with the help of his household chariotry, fought off the Hittites until his third and fourth divisions arrived. But it was impossible for the badly-mauled Egyptian forces to continue the fight; and, probably within hours, Ramesses withdrew as quickly as he had come. In the wake of his embarrassing retreat the triumphant Hittites marched as far south as Damascus, and all Palestine simultaneously threw off the Egyptian yoke.

It has become fashionable to write Ramesses off as a buffoon, or at best a foolhardy young man. This adverse judgment usually stems from the disastrous defeat at Kadesh; but ignorance of the Hittite presence reflects badly on the state of the Egyptian army intelligence rather than on the king's generalship. Moreover—and this is sometimes overlooked by historians of the period—Ramesses recouped his losses very quickly. Within three years of the battle of Kadesh Ramesses had subdued the rebellious cities in Galilee on the north of Palestine, and by his tenth year was once again on the banks of the Nahr el-Kelb in Phoenicia. The great military tableaux recording battles in the second decade of his reign place him in Syria proper, engaging his Hittite foe at times almost within sight of the Euphrates. Cities such as Arqata on the Phoenician coast and Satuna, Mutara, and Dapur in north Syria were overwhelmed as the Egyptians advanced.

For the Hittites this did not bode well. Muwatallis had died two years after the battle of Kadesh, and his young son Urhi-teshup had come to the throne. The new ruler was immediately caught up in a feud over control of the state with his uncle, Hattusilis, Muwatallis's younger brother. Neither had time to pursue the war.

The Egypto-Hittite Entente

As Ramesses's twentieth year approached, it must have been clear that a stalemate was developing. Try as they might, the Hittites could not prevent the Egyptian forces from penetrating the Syrian hinterland; on the other hand, Ramesses could never hope to assail his foe inside his Anatolian fastness. A third party was liable to take advantage of the situation if Egypt and Khatte persisted in wearying themselves with pointless conflict, for Assyria under its king Adanirari I was laying claim to the status of a Great Power.

After the annihilation of Tushratta's Mitanni by Suppiluliumas, the strategic plain of Mesopotamia had been occupied by two states, a western (in reality a resuscitation of Mitanni, bordering the Euphrates), and an eastern, Khanigalbat, lying north-west of Assyria. The new Mitanni was nothing more than a puppet of the Hittites, and did not long survive in the power politics of the day. But Khanigalbat was larger and better endowed, and successfully contended with an active Assyria for the rule of Mesopotamia. Twice beaten in battle, Khanigalbat refused to accept defeat, and returned to the fray, much to the chagrin of the Assyrians (who were eventually to administer a third crushing defeat to Khanigalbat and annihilate that state). But the prospect of a new power center on the Tigris, geopolitically oriented towards the west and implacably hostile to the Hittites, forced the Hittite king to reconsider his position *vis-à-vis* the states of the Near East. The Hittite correspondence from Hattusas refers to overtures made by Hattusilis to Babylon, but Kadashman-turgu, the contemporary Kassite king, proved irresolute and his successor unreliable if not hostile.

To compound the problem civil war had broken out inside Khatte between Muwatallis's son and successor Urhi-Teshup, and the latter's uncle Hattusilis. Hattusilis eventually proved victorious, and Urhi-Teshup was dethroned and sent into exile to north Syria. Escaping from his captors, the ex-king fled across the sea to Egypt where he found asylum at Ramesses's court. The prospect of fighting three major states, one of which was egged on by his vengeful nephew, was too much for Hattusilis, and in 1284 B.C., Ramesses's twenty-first year, he sued for peace.

On the twenty-first day of the first winter month in that year, the plenipotentiaries of Hattusilis and of his cousin the king of Carchemish arrived at the new Egyptian capital, Pi-Ramesses ("the House of Ramesses") in the north-east Delta. They came with tablets from their masters, craving peace with Pharaoh, and Ramesses readily accepted. The treaty was drawn up in Hittite, then translated into Akkadian, the diplomatic language of the day, and eventually translated also into Egyptian. Tablets with the Hittite and Akkadian versions have been unearthed at Hattusas, the Hittite capital (modern Boghaz-keui); the Egyptian translation survives upon a wall in the temple of Amun at Karnak. The agreement was essentially a mutual assistance pact. All aggression between Khatte and Egypt was renounced, and the former boundaries between the two empires reaffirmed. Other clauses cover the extradition in the future of political refugees. But Urhi-Teshup, whose case would have called for the most immediate application of this section, was apparently exempted. One paragraph bound Ramesses to act as guarantor for Hattusilis's successor upon the throne, to ensure that his own heir, and not Urhi-Teshup's, enter into possession of the patrimony. Several copies on clay tablets were drafted, two being formally "signed" with the seals of the two great kings, and then exchanged. Ramesses's copy was deposited in a major Hittite temple, and Hattusilis's in the temple of Re at Heliopolis. The gods thus became witnesses to the treaty.

The pact, which as far as we know was not abrogated as long as the Hittite empire existed, opened nearly a century of good relations between the two super-powers of the ancient world (see the next chapter). The Akkadian and Hittite letters which have been recovered by the German excavations from the archives of the Hittite capital help fill in the colorful picture of post-war relations between Khatte and Egypt, and incidentally provide an intimate glimpse of the Egyptian monarch. For a lively correspondence soon sprang up between Ramesses and Hattusilis, as well as the several members of their families.

In the letters Ramesses appears an honest if humorless man, with a tendency to be impatient and to adopt a superior attitude. In replying to a complaint the son and successor of Hattusilis had made, the Egyptian king dictated the following petulant letter: "I have just heard all the words that my brother wrote to me, saying, 'Why as though I were a subject of yours did you, my brother, write me?' And what you wrote, saying, 'As though I were a subject of yours

. . . ,' this word that my brother wrote to me I resent. I am looking at you, and great things you have accomplished in all countries. Surely you are the great king of the countries of the Khatte-land, and the Sun-god and the Storm-god have allowed you to be seated in the Khatte-land in the place of your grandfather. Why should I write to you as though a subject? That I am your brother you must keep in mind. A word that gladdens man you should speak. . . . Instead these meaningless words, not fit to serve for a message, you write. 'I am your father's brother,' thus have I spoken!"

Ramesses regarded the oath of the treaty as permanently binding, and in the correspondence is for ever reminding Hattusilis of it: "I have not broken the oath, I have kept the oath! Behold, the tablet of the oath which I have made for you lies before the Sun-god of Arinna, and before the great gods of the Khatte-land; they are the witnesses to the words of the oath that I have made you. And behold, the tablet of the oath that you made for me lies before the Sun-god of Heliopolis, and before the great gods of the land of Egypt; they are witnesses to the words of the oath that you have made me!"

Letters were also exchanged by the two queens. Nefertiri, the wife of Ramesses, was confident that the peace would be a lasting one: "Re and the Storm-god (of the Hittites) shall uphold the treaty," she wrote to Pudu-hepa, her Hittite counterpart, "and Re shall make it a prosperous peace, and he shall place excellent brotherhood between the great king, the king of Egypt, and the great king, the king of Khatte, his brother, for ever and ever!"

Thirteen years after the treaty was signed, Ramesses married one of Hattusilis's daughters. He had already acquired several foreign princesses in marriage, including a daughter of the king of Babylon, but his union with the Hittite princess was deemed a striking diplomatic success. It is uncertain as to which of the two kings took the initiative in opening negotiations concerning the marriage; but once mooted, the union had the enthusiastic support of Hattusilis. "Behold!" he wrote Ramesses, "As for the daughter that I shall give you, her dowry shall be greater than that of the daughter of the king of Babylon, or the daughter of the king of Barga. . . . Behold, I shall give my daughter attendants, cattle, sheep, and horses, and in this year I shall send them. . . ." After some haggling over the bride-price and the spiteful detention of envoys (a common diplomatic insult in the ancient world), the princess was despatched to Egypt; and her mother, Pudu-hepa, wrote a remonstrative letter to her son-in-law to be. Petulant as was the general tone of this missive, Pudu-hepa could not refrain from wishing her daughter well: "It is my patron deity, as well as the Sun-goddess of Arinna, Teshup, Hepat, and Ishtar that have made me queen, and united me with your brother in marriage; and I have produced both sons and daughters, so that the Hittites speak of my exceptional fertility. . . . As for the daughter whom I am sending to my brother, may she likewise be endowed with an exceptional queenly fertility!"

The daughter in question duly arrived in Egypt, was given an Egyptian name and placed in a harim. A papyrus document which has fortuitously survived gives an inventory of her wardrobe. That is all we know of her, but her arrival signalled the dawn of a new day.

Further Readings

On the Amarna Letters see W.L. Moran, *The Amarna Letters,* Baltimore, 1987; *idem, Amarna Studies: Collected Writings* (J. Huehnergard, S. Izre'el eds.), Winona Lake, 2003; R. Cohen, R. Westbrook (eds.), *Amarna Diplomacy: The Beginnings of International Relations,* Baltimore, 2000; M. Liverani, *Three Amarna Essays,* Malibu, 1979; G. Beckman, *Hittite Diplomatic Texts,* Atlanta, 1999; T. Bryce, *Letters of the Great Kings of the Ancient Near East,* London, 2003; Z. Cochavi-Rainey, *Royal Gifts in the Late Bronze Age, Fourteenth to Thirteenth Centuries B.C.E.,* Beersheva, 1999.

On the Egypto-Hittite war, see T. R. Bryce, *The Kingdom of the Hittites,* Oxford, 1998; H. Gödicke (ed.), *Perspectives on the Battle of Kadesh,* Baltimore, 1985; M. G. Hasel, *Domination and Resistance: Egyptian Military Activity in the Southern Levant, 1300–1185 B.C.,* Leiden, 1998; H. Klengel, *Syria, 3000 to 300 B.C.,* Berlin, 1992; W.J. Murnane, *The Road to Kadesh,* Chicago, 1985.

CHAPTER ELEVEN

The Life and Times of Ramesses the Great

ψ

The late 14th through 13th century B.C. constitutes an historical and economic continuum in the life of the ancient world. It was a time of great prosperity and international commerce; a period when communities exchanged ideas as well as goods. Since it was Ramesses II who in many ways epitomized the spirit of the age, it is fitting to speak of the "Ramesside Era" which, down through the ages, would continue to evoke the memory of the legendary *Sesostris* (derived from Sesy-re, Ramesses' nick-name).

The Royal House of the Nineteenth Dynasty

The Ramesside family had come from the region of Avaris in the eastern Delta, not Thebes and had not been tainted by association with the Amarna heresy. They were a close and loving family, in contrast to the feud-prone scions of the previous Eighteenth Dynasty, and took delight in continuing the work and programs of their immediate predecessors. They patronized the northern cults of Seth, Ptah, and Re, as their birth names clearly indicate, and Ramesses delighted to group himself with these gods (A–B). Within their home town the memory of the Hyksos lived on, and not entirely to the detriment of these foreign invaders. Nonetheless, the tradition established by the Eighteenth Dynasty could not be easily dismissed, and it was wholly impolitic to sever the link between royal family and Amun of Thebes. Consequently the Ramessides continued to lavish booty from foreign wars and endless endowments upon the temple of the King of the Gods, and to embellish the structure with walls, halls, and gates (C). Each year, for the feast of Opet, the king proceeded to Thebes to celebrate the festival, and to reside for several weeks in a royal guest house attached to his mortuary temple (D). Upon his death, the mummified royal corpse would be conveyed to Thebes to be buried in the Valley of the Kings on the west of the city.

But the Nineteenth Dynasty was determined to maintain its northern residence, and to that end one of the suburbs of Avaris was set aside for development. Although plans may have been in the process of preparation under Sety I, it was Ramesses II who, in the dark years immediately following his defeat at Kadesh, began construction of what was to become the vast city of *Pi-Ramesses,* "the House of Ramesses," a rival of both Memphis and Thebes. Poets were fulsome in their praise of the new capital, likening it to the universe itself, and dwelling on its fine appointments and abundant stocks of food. While the site was a little too far north to function as the "balance" or pivot of the two lands, it was nonetheless ideally suited for quick communication by river and sea with the Phoenician coast, Cyprus, and the Aegean. Ramesses moved in as soon as feasible, and set up a third center of administration, complementing Memphis and Thebes. Ancient word descriptions as well as recent excavations by a German mission have helped to sharpen our imaginative vision of what the city looked like: four temples to Amun, Seth, Astarte, and Edjo, a grand palace, barracks, stables, armories, and granaries—an establishment, in fact, on the scale of a Hollywood set, so celebrated that its memory lived on for over 800 years!

Elsewhere in Egypt Ramesses used manpower released from the wars to conduct building operations in almost every city of the land. Typical were the forecourts (E), fronted by tall pylons (F), which he was in the habit of constructing in front of existing temples, thus concealing from the vision of those approaching the work of earlier kings. Many of the buildings erected by Amenophis III were treated in this manner, and one wonders whether Ramesses harbored an unconscious feeling of jealousy for his illustrious predecessor. Quarries were being utilized intensively throughout the reign, and when convenient Ramesses was not averse to ransacking ancient monuments for stone. The Step Pyramid and the Giza plateau were thus pillaged by the great king's men. Existing statuary from earlier reigns were frequently usurped by the simple expedient of carving Ramesses's name over or beside the original cartouche.

But the Ramessides did not simply promote an existential approach to the kingship: they considered themselves the heirs of the primordial ones, the true successors of all the ancestors back to remote antiquity. The king-list and the worship of the ancestors took on a new aura under the Nineteenth Dynasty. The list was modified to encorporate the Hyksos Fifteenth Dynasty and its pedigree, and the whole carried down through the Eighteenth Dynasty to Ramesses himself. Recent history was rewritten. After the demolition of the Sun-disc temples under Horemheb, the names of the three kings who had been at Amarna, viz. Akhenaten, Tutankhamun, and Ay, were excised from the king-list and the heretic himself anathematized as "that enemy of Akhetaten." In festivals, commemorated on temple walls, statues of the fourteen immediate predecessors of the great king (again, omitting Akhenaten, Ay, and Tutankhamun) were paraded before the public; and members of the elite adopted the fad of depicting themselves in a mortuary context making the offering to the royal ancestors, lined up on their thrones, identified by name, often in chronological order. In keeping with the spirit of the historical retrospective, antiquarian interests came to the fore. Ramesses II's fourth son, Khamwese, evinced an interest in examining and restoring ancient tombs and documents; and entered later tradition as a great savant and magician from whom had issued many potent, restored magic spells.

The creation of an empire had given to the kingship a cast which represents the culmination of an evolution set on foot at the dawn of Egyptian history. To the concept of the perfect god on earth, the avatar of Horus, which had its origin in the earliest dynasties, the collapse of the Old Kingdom had added the mantle of the manor-lord, the "commoner"-king who boasted of himself in public and indulged in rhetorical self-promotion. Like a commoner he "spoke (freely) with his mouth, and acted with his arm," and was invincible on the battlefield. He was the very image of the sun-god on earth, and had been chosen by Re. The experience of empire enhanced the physical aspects of the monarch: he was a strong man whose feats of strength could not be matched by anyone else in the kingdom (G). As he was unbeatable on the field of conflict—no one was left standing within the range of his weapons!—so in the hunt no fellow huntsman could equal his bag. Beginning with the reign of Thutmose III it became fashionable for poets to eulogize the king's strength and intelligence by referring specifically to incidents of physical prowess. By the time of Ramesses II this type of rhetorical celebration had developed into a formal genre of hymn in which specifics were sacrificed to generalities, and each stanza ended in the name and titles of the king.

Ramesses conformed admirably to the model of the imperial Pharaoh. An athletic, "macho" specimen of manhood, the ubiquitous war reliefs on the exterior walls and pylons of temples familiarized the Egyptians with the king in a charging chariot, towering over his enemies in menacing fashion **(fig. 1),** or advancing fearlessly on foot while discharging his arrows against a rebellious city. And the eulogies of the court poets poured forth, praising the "good king, one to be boasted of, a sovereign to be proud [of, who has extended] the boundaries of Egypt as far as the supports of heaven. He has renewed the temples of the gods [which] had fallen into ruin: what was (formerly) in brick is (now) in stone, what was in [bronze(?)] is (now) in gold. He has fashioned the great and holy [im]ages in the shrines, he has increased the daily offerings, he has [filled] the granaries and the treasuries . . . the gods are content with *ma'at*, since he appeared on the throne of Atum: every office-(holder) exults, the lands are in festival, there is no orphan or pauper in His Majesty's reign!"

Figure 1   Rameses II charges, alone in his chariot, with his reins wrapped around his waist, against a fleeing, panic-stricken mass of Nubians.

The principal queen, called "the Great King's-wife," (H) did not measure up to the powerful matriarchs of the Eighteenth Dynasty (I); but she nonetheless enjoyed wealth equal to, if not surpassing, that of her forbears. There were, during the long reign of the great king, three Great King's-wives in succession, and each disposed of an extensive household modelled on that of her husband. She dwelled in a palace reserved for herself, and had her own servants, her own food commissariat, her own treasury, and even her own physicians. The queen could also own land in her own right.

Lesser wives and favored ladies were apportioned among harims located in such cities as Pi-Ramesses, Memphis, Thebes and the towns of the Fayum. A "travelling" harim occasionally accompanied Pharaoh on his journeys throughout the realm. It is difficult to say how the inmates of a harim were chosen, although most certainly no woman would show reluctance to join once she had been selected. Better to enjoy the king's largesse in abundance, than to risk starving in the boondocks! Harims were guarded and administered by overseers who seem not to have been eunuchs, and were off limits to most of the population, including the families of the girls themselves. For their own upkeep harim women held landed property in common.

Royal children abounded within the greater palace area (J)—Ramesses sired over one hundred offspring!—and each had his or her own apartments. Wet nurses were much in demand, and when the royal child had emerged from infancy, a tutor would be assigned along with four or five retainers. In keeping with the military origins of the family, most of Ramesses's sons were given training in the army (K); not a few, even while children, accompanied their father on the battlefield. A novel invention of the Eighteenth Dynasty, the "royal nursery," brought together from all over Egypt a group of children of the same age as the heir apparent, and obliged them to live with their mothers in tow in close proximity to the royal family. The "children of the nursery" as they were called were chosen because of their intelligence and physical robustness, and as they grew up with the prince, bonded into a body of true and loyal companions. It should come as no surprise that, when the prince eventually succeeded to the throne, he chose his government officials and military officers from this body of close friends with whom he had grown up.

Government Officials and the Grandees of the Realm (L–M)

In the Ramesside Age socio-economic power depended not, as in the Middle Kingdom, on membership in a landed aristocracy, but on proximity to the person of the king himself. Broadly speaking Ramesside administration is characterized by two types of infrastructure, one military (on which see below) and one civil. High officials and the secretariat belong either to one or the other. A further general bifurcation is to be seen between officers of state (*sr*) who were designated for service wherever the king was pleased to send them, and support staff (*smdt*) who were recruited locally and functioned within a restricted, parochial ambit.

The two highest posts under the king were the vizierate (**fig. 2**) and the office of chief treasurer. The rules of procedure for the office of vizier have survived from an inscription in a vizier's tomb from the reign of Thutmose III, and show us that this function had been divided and reduplicated. The northern vizier, with offices in Memphis, had the oversight of the Delta and Middle Egypt, while his southern colleague in Thebes was responsible for Upper Egypt as far as the First Cataract. Their purview was quite extensive, covering all aspects of daily life in town and country, including the judiciary. All departments of government fell under their con-

Figure 2   The vizier of Upper Egypt, Ramose, shown in his vizier's uniform of a high-cut apron with straps, being asperged by priests.

trol, except one, the treasury: the chief treasurer was directly responsible to Pharaoh, and did not have to go through the vizier's office. In fact the chief treasurer and the vizier did a "mini-audit" of each other's office, files and books each morning, a cross-checking mechanism clearly designed to ensure self-correction.

The royal household was served by two officers, often chosen for ability rather than pedigree. The private holdings of the king, his "privy purse," were administered by the Chief Steward of the king; and since these holdings under the empire had grown to major proportions, the Chief Steward sat over vast amounts of wealth that could easily prove a temptation. To judge from the size of tombs such as those of Kheruef and Amenemhet under Amenophis III, incumbents in this office did not do badly for themselves. A second function, that of Chief Royal Herald, involved the oversight and running of the entire palace complex. The Chief Royal Herald was something of combination of such modern offices as a press secretary, a chief-of-staff of the head of state, and a food commissar. The herald controlled the physical access to the king by officials, ambassadors, or petitioners, and often conveyed information inside to the person of the monarch. He would also be responsible for announcing to the populace decisions made in the privy chamber. Curiously his role sometimes encompassed duties we would associate with a public prosecutor, and to hear one's name on the lips of the herald was a frightening experience indeed! In his responsibility for food supply he was assisted by a staff of cooks and butlers. The latter, often chosen from the ranks of Canaanites, proved to be politically influential as the Ramesside Age progressed.

It was thoroughly in keeping with the ancient Egyptian way of doing things to invest the same committee of officials with both administrative and juridical competence. One such body, the highest in the land in fact, was called the "Council of Thirty." We know too little about this shadowy organization to list its duties, but it certainly functioned as a high court of justice, perhaps a sort of "Court of Star Chamber." Presumably it was made up of the highest officials under the king, the "king's-scribes," who operated as heads of departments. These included the viziers, the Chief Treasurer, the King's steward, the Overseer of the Silver Storehouse, the Overseer of the Granary, the Viceroy of Kush, the Secretary of Manpower and Recruits, the Commander-in-chief of the army, the Chief Lector Priest, the Chief Physician, the Mayors of Thebes and Memphis, and sometimes the Archbishop. A second organ of administration was the *qenbet,* or "court," which sat mainly to hear criminal and civil cases and act as a cross between a board of magistrates and a jury. Each city and town had one, but we do not know on what basis members of the court were chosen. While it certainly was made up of people selected from the local community, the composition changed almost daily.

Municipal administration answered directly to the vizier. While the townships of old were still very much "alive," and their boundaries respected and preserved, their political function had been ceded to the towns. The larger settlements were governed by a mayor, appointed by the central government, and assisted by a deputy, a district scribe, and a town council; smaller towns might dispense with the mayoral position while retaining the district scribe and council.

The Professional Scribes

In our treatment of earlier periods of Egypt's history we have had occasion to remark upon the central position occupied by those able to write; and the New Kingdom more than any other epoch demanded the presence of a scribal class. Scribes were required in every branch of the administration, and therefore enjoyed a relative degree of independence over other middle-ranking bureaucrats. All the upper echelons of the social pyramid, including the royal family, were literate; but in the present case we are addressing the professional secretariat **(fig. 3)**.

The constant need for scribes could only be met by scribal schools, the linear descendants of the "writing school" which we saw come into being in the Middle Kingdom. But now the overriding consideration was the self-perpetuation of the profession itself, not the rhetoric of national persuasion. For some reason the scribes of the treasury took the lead in staffing the schools, and the language of instruction was the current vernacular, the Late Egyptian dialect, the language of the eastern Delta and the Ramesside royal house. But Middle Egyptian was by no means ignored. Students were required to copy out and memorize the great classics of the Middle Kingdom and, in the process, to learn how to compose in the obsolete language. Side by side with the hieroglyphic script, instruction was given in the cursive script of the New Kingdom, an elaborate and florid hand which had an aesthetic appeal of its own.

Figure 3 Scribes writing with their pens on papyrus, additional pens behind their ears, and scribal kits on the ground near them.

The course of instruction reflected the varied demands the outside world would make on the scribal graduate. Several papyri have survived from the Ramesside age, wrongly called "Miscellanies." They are, in fact, the textbooks used in the schools and incorporate *models* to be copied slavishly by the pupils. The intent was to inculcate in the students, by means of such models, the proper way to keep accounts, calculate taxes, draft a variety of letters to superiors and underlings, write official reports, make complaints, tender congratulations, compose adulatory hymns, and, in short, to master the broad range of accounts, epistolography, and *belles lettres*.

Admittedly such a curriculum demanded much of the student. Only those who persevered, or were forced to persevere, could hope for advancement into the profitable echelons of the scribal fraternity. With the prospect of disenchanted "drop-outs" ever before them, the teachers adopted subtle means of admonition. Students were confronted, not only with the classics, but also with new compositions stressing the advantages of the scribal profession. As in the "Satire of the Trades" in the Middle Kingdom, numerous of these new texts described all professions in the most denigrating fashion, except that of the scribe who is depicted as a free individual, his own "boss," not burdened with physical tasks. Diligence and proper deportment will bring a successful graduation. Shun sloth and bad companions: both will result in the stocks or quite possibly jail. And always as an end goal there lurked in the fuzzy future the possibility that the competent student would attain the ultimate in scribal excellence, viz. the status of "Scribe of the House of Life " (see below).

The Professional Priesthood (N–O)

Under the influence of the burgeoning priesthood of Amun, the sacerdotal fraternity had become a professional "closed shop" involving whole families who monopolized priestly posts for generations. More and more of the population was attracted by the prospect of regular income within the fulfillment of the ritual tradition. The temple communities, especially those of Amun, Ptah, and Re, were thus becoming virtual "states within a state." Well might an erstwhile high-priest of Amun address his contemporaries and posterity: "may you bequeath your offices to your descendants, from father to son, in his house for ever!"

The priesthood during the New Kingdom was divided, broadly speaking, into four separate grades. The upper echelons were occupied by "prophets," and "god's-fathers," responsible for the performance of the cult in all its aspects. These were exceedingly wealthy individuals who, by amassing priestly appointments in various temples, could draw on a salary derived from several prebends. They were assisted in the daily operation of the temple by a lower class of priest, called *we'eb,* or "pure ones." They performed the lesser tasks associated with the temple service, involving preparation and carrying of offerings, oversight of cultic paraphernalia, and the performance of general duties relating to support staff. A third grade constituted a sort of "diaconate," concerned with the menial tasks of keeping the temple clean and its equipment at the ready.

Side by side with these functionaries who operated within the temple precincts was a vast secular support staff, for the temple of the New Kingdom was in effect a sizeable landed estate owning property all over Egypt. The running of such an organization required a substantial body of officials, not necessarily priestly in origin. The plantations and fields required overseers, the temple endowments treasurers, the herds of cattle superintendents, the ateliers master craftsmen, the "front offices" scribal accountants. In short, at the height of the empire a typical temple estate resembled, most often on a grander scale, the estate of the highest dignitaries in the land.

A broad perspective on the temples of Egypt during the Ramesside Age is vouchsafed by the Great Harris Papyrus, a comprehensive testimony by king Ramesses III (see below), a sort of inventory of the realm, to be presented at the last judgment to Osiris. This document, now in the British Museum, 133 feet long and comprising 117 columns, lists the holdings of all the temples of Egypt. Not surprisingly the estate of Amun outshines them all. It transpires that, around 1200 b.c., 15–20% of all arable land was owned by the temples, and of this fully three-fourths belonged to the Theban temple of Amun. The latter owned outright 1/2 million head of cattle, 433 orchards, 56 Egyptian and 9 Syrian cities, a merchant fleet of 83 cargo vessels plying the Mediterranean, and over 86,000 laborers (of whom 50,000 were located in the Delta). For the reign of Ramesses III the income of Amun's estate amounted, among other things, to 140 pounds of gold, 1.2 tons of silver, 3,722 garments and 25,000 jars of wine! Amun, in fact, was nine times as wealthy as all the other gods of Egypt combined! The "House of Amun" was well on its way to developing into a "state within a state!"

Commensurate with the wealth and position in society of the New Kingdom temples, a new size and layout had been imposed upon the physical dwelling of a god. Whereas temples of the Middle Kingdom had been enclosed and inward-looking with unprepossessing facade, the *processional* temple of the New Kingdom was organized around a central axis which, projected outwards, provided sight-lines in the form of grand avenues lined with sphinxes (P). Such a format accommodated movement, rather than static presence, and lent itself to dramatic performance. At festival time, when the god appeared to the people, he would be taken from his shrine in the darkened inner apartments (Q) and placed in a portable barque (Q–Q). Then on the shoulders of his priests (R) he would re-enact the moment of creation, passing from darkness to light, through hypostyle halls (S) in which the roof was higher and light filtered through clerestory openings (T), into peristyle courts in which the roof was open to the sky (U), as though the "marsh" with its columnar "reeds" were drawing back; and finally out through a gate flanked by monumental pylon massifs, a simulacrum of sunrise between the mountains of the east (V). Flagstaves of cedar of Lebanon with fluttering pennants would announce to the people the imminent appearance of the deity who would then be carried to the river and rowed on a real boat. The gala nature of the processional was not lost on the Egyptians, who made it a central part of social action as well as ritual, a time when the god was present and blessings could accrue.

The Army

Over the long span of their history the Egyptians in general were not noted for their military ability; but during the Ramesside age, with a royal house steeped in military tradition, the "soldier" *(we'u)* became a highly respected member of society. Gone were the days of a rag-tag army, drawn almost exclusively from local militia. The conquest of empire had produced a well-trained, standing army, with a full-time support staff (w).

In peacetime the standing armed forces were divided into two contingents, located in Upper Egypt and the Delta. Major concentrations are known to have existed around the three main cities, Pi-Ramesses, Memphis, and Thebes, as well as Herakleopolis and certain border forts. Wherever he was located each soldier received a small farm on which to support himself and his family, and if he were unmarried he would be assigned to a barracks (which doubled as a stable for war-horses). Army scribes, distributed among the districts, kept the registers of all military personnel within their bailiwicks, and were responsible for lists of equipment in armories and quartermasters' stores. They also had the oversight of training and discipline, which could be brutal at times, relying heavily on beatings for recruits who were not making the grade.

An important aspect of the army's activity during peacetime was garrison duty. Fortresses to be manned by garrisons were located at Sile on the eastern frontier of the Delta, in the block-houses that dotted the highway between Egypt and Gaza, and along the north-African coast towards Libya. The provinces also received garrisons, in the north at Gaza, Ullaza (later Sumur), Bethshean, and Kumidi, and in the south in the southern province of Kush. Numbers of troops involved were small, rarely exceeding two hundred and sometimes as few as ten. Duration of service was long, five- and six-year time spans being attested, and living conditions very harsh. In fact service in the garrison of Kush bore such an evil reputation, that it was made part of the oath taken in court: if I perjure myself, I shall be sent to the garrison of Kush.

The prospect of a foreign war set the war machine in motion. In most cases the term "marching out" when applied to the king refers to an armed tour of inspection in which Pharaoh and a contingent of troops would march into Western Asia and make the rounds of several cities and districts, planting the standard from time to time in the expectation that locals would appear bearing voluntary gifts. If a district proved in any way recalcitrant, its orchards and farmland would be destroyed; in some cases the main town would be assaulted. If a major opponent appeared with substantial forces, then it was clear that a set-piece battle, such as the battles of Megiddo or Kadesh, was a distinct possibility. Letters would be immediately sent out to the army scribes to muster the standing army, and lists of names would be produced and assembling points assigned.

For especially large engagements the king would requisition 10% of the personnel on landed estates, and elsewhere would authorize impressment to be employed. The army disposed of three basic forces, the infantry (x), the chariotry (y), and the archers. The infantry marched under the aegis of the god from whose city or district they had been recruited in divisions of roughly 5,000 men each, commanded by a general (lit. "overseer of a host") and his adjutant. Each division was further subdivided into battalions under a battalion commander, and companies each under its own captain who carried the company standard. Personal weaponry was rudimentary. An infantry soldier carried an elliptical raw-hide shield and wore a padded cap; his upper body was bare—only officers wore armor—and his offensive weapons consisted of daggers and javelins (z). The Egyptian chariot was of wickerwork and built for speed rather than protection (in contrast to the heavily-armored Hittite vehicle). Drawn by two horses (who were often named), it carried a complement of two, a driver who wore a helmet and sometimes armor, and an archer. Chariots fought in squads of fifty under command of a major, several squads being commanded by a lieutenant general. The archers were the most effective corps in the Egyptian army. They wore long robes and usually stood apart from the melee, peppering the enemy or the defenders on a town wall with deadly volleys of arrows from their composite bows. Modern experiments have demonstrated that these bows had an accurate range of 50–60 meters, and an effective range of 175 meters. An exceptional shot might achieve 500 meters.

The Egyptians had never been good at siege warfare, but under the Ramessides new techniques were being developed. Kamose and Ahmose had taken years to reduce Avaris, and Sharuhen had occupied Ahmose for three years. Even Thutmose III, after his victory at Megiddo, had had to "wait it out," until hunger forced his enemies inside the city to capitulate. Ramesses II, however, knew how to carry a city. Relief scenes from the Theban temples show sappers undermining the foundations of walls and gates, and assault troops climbing siege ladders. All the while the archers keep up a steady barrage of missiles raining down upon the defenders, while flaming arrows attempt to set the houses alight **(fig. 4)**.

Figure 4   The Egyptian assault on a Canaanite city. The scene telescopes sequential acts in the battle: the cutting down of orchards, the volleys of arrows, sappers at the gate, the running up of siege ladders, the hand-to-hand combat within the city.

The Egyptian army of the Ramesside age was never more exhilarated from the standpoint of morale. This can be put down partly to the emphasis Horemheb and Sety I had placed on military training, but perhaps more especially on the rapport between Ramesses II and his army. Not only was he an inspiring and heroic leader on the battlefield, flamboyant in fact in taking a pet lion with him, and sometimes battling without armor, but he also knew how to reward his soldiers. In one scene on a stela now in Hildesheim, the king is shown standing on the knees of a colossal statue of himself, bestowing largesse on his officers standing below him. The prospect of this heroic young father introducing his little sons to the battlefield when they came of age, must have struck the military with a combination of pride and human interest. Small wonder, in view of the figure he cut, that while he yet lived adulation of their commander-in-chief should have crystallized among the troops in the form of a cult of Ramesses the god.

Workers, Peasants, and P.O.W.s: The Demographics of Empire

Estimates of the total population of Egypt under the empire are fraught with uncertainty. Although census figures were kept, the interest of the census-takers lay in the male population fit for service, and so draft lists take precedence over summations of all living souls. The best that the ancient scribes can provide us with is the number of households in different sectors of a city, or the number of farms (and their owners) in a particular tract of the Nile valley. Notwithstanding these *caveats*, an estimate of 5–7 million is probably not too wide of the mark, the vast majority of whom would have lived in a rural setting.

As of yore, skilled workers were confined to their ateliers (ZA–ZB) and labored in the employ of the king, the temple or the upper classes. A few of the best, such as the master-sculptors Men, Bek, and Thutmose under Amenophis III and Akhenaten, might be celebrated for their work, but this was not the rule. Architects and engineers, who mostly came from the elite, might enjoy renown among their contemporaries; but the outline draftsmen, masons, and painters who decorated the products of their work remain for the most part faceless.

Craftsmen served the project to be accomplished, and to that end were settled with strategic ends in view. Mining (ZC) or quarrying (ZD) expeditions required engineers, prospectors, stone-cutters, haulage experts, and the like, as well as unskilled labor, and bodies containing these professions were kept in readiness for the royal command. The shipyard in Memphis needed shipwrights and carpenters to be on call continuously, and so these crafts formed a community in that city. At the festival of New Year it was customary for grandees of the realm to present the king with gifts of fine sculpture and carpentry laid out in the great hall of the palace; and therefore their workshops had to be organized and supervised to provide the goods. Skilled vintners were required for the vineyards on the west and east sides of the Delta, and various agricultural experts plied their trade where they were needed.

The large cemeteries of Memphis and Thebes required a kaleidoscope of professions. Although documents are lacking for the former, the workers' village at Deir el-Medina at the southern end of the Theban necropolis (ZE) has survived along with letters, memoranda, administrative and business documents—the waste-baskets of the village—preserved on ostraca and stone chips. The village, the foundation of which goes back to the early Eighteenth Dynasty, served the varied needs of the undertaking establishment: carving or building tombs (especially those of royalty), decorating their walls in painting and relief, making coffins and mortuary paraphernalia, and performing any other task deemed necessary for a "city of the dead." The town was administered by two foremen and a secretary, and numbered scribes, masons, painters, food-purveyors, porters, and unskilled labor among its population. Like other settlements it had its own *qenbet,* or "court," which sat almost daily to hear cases or make decisions affecting the community at a local level. Workers and their families lived in modest four- or five-room dwellings laid out along streets, the whole surrounded by a low wall. The inhabitants' movement was severely restricted—in view of their importance to the state it was desirable that no one abscond!—and a series of checkpoints monitored their comings and goings.

The three major cities dominated the body politic. Pi-Ramesses housed the king, the royal family and a large segment of the military; Memphis was the bailiwick of the crown-prince in training. Thebes remained connected with the king only through his relationship to Amun and the tradition of Theban burial; yet, in the person of the high-priest of Amun, Thebes possessed a power-wielder in waiting. All three had major courts of law, as well as vizieral offices.

Town and country perforce shared common agricultural interests. City-dwellers were free of the obligation to settle where the majority of their profession lived, and we find in a census list from Memphis the following living side by side: a king's-scribe, a lieutenant-general, a scribe, a guard, a captain, a granary official, a contractor, a chariot officer, a merchant, a ship's captain, a chef, a fowler, a carpenter, and so forth. All, however, while living in town, probably possessed farms in the countryside, and went there periodically to oversee the work on them. The actual tilling and harvesting was performed by menials, farm-hands who were either tied to the soil or rented small plots from the owner.

Since the founding of the empire under Thutmose III the ranks of the mass of Egypt's population had been swollen by the arrival of a large servile population, drawn from both Africa and Asia **(fig. 5)**. At first they came as prisoners-of-war, and were specifically assigned as factors in a temple community. Later deportation was used as an antidote to repeated uprisings: Amenophis II deported close to 90,000 from the Levant, and Akhenaten uprooted a whole tribe in the area of Damascus. Severe measures involved transplanting fractious popula-

(a)

(b)

Figure 5 (a) Canaanite and Nubian prisoners brought before Pharaoh; (b) a Nubian taken into Pharaoh's service as a bodyguard.

tions as far from their place of origin as possible, and thus Asiatics might end up in Nubia or Kush. Canaanites (ZF) and Sudanese (ZG) also arrived in Egypt as part of the taxes levied on the empire, for manpower was as much in demand as produce and manufactures. All foreigners relocated in Egypt were registered by name, family, and ethnic origin in a government office, and were branded on the shoulder with the king's cartouche. Most became field hands on farms and plantations, but those with skills were put to work where their expertise could be of use. Some became engineers or scribes; many entered royal service as elite troops, bodyguards (ZH), or butlers and cooks. A few even succeeded in becoming vizier or chancellor!

The subject of the underclass brings up the question of servitude in ancient Egypt. This is a vexed and complicated problem which cannot be done justice in a work of the present proportions. Suffice to say that in most cases "slavery" is an inappropriate term, as it glosses over a subtle and nuanced set of relationships. In a certain sense everyone in Egypt was a slave to someone else—the vizier calls himself Pharaoh's slave!—the essence of the matter being the relative degree of freedom, discretionary action, and legal rights vouchsafed to a particular individual. Work in quarries and mines might seem on a par with the "Simon Legree" type slavery in the Deep South,; yet many of the miners would not have been reckoned by themselves or the state as "slaves." An ancient Egyptian aphorism put it succinctly: man is born and runs to his master. Almost everyone had a superior to whom he was beholden for protection and help, and to whom he owed an obligation of a certain service or quota of production. For Egypt was a beehive in which everyone had a function: no one could opt out, as it would destroy the hive.

Land-holding and Taxation

It had long been a tenet of the belief system that all the land in Egypt belonged to Pharaoh. And it is true, that through his control of the organs of government he exercised the right of bestowal and confiscation over all farms and plantations. In practice, however, his landed holdings fell within the regulation of the law.

The vast majority of arable land in Egypt was owned, not privately, but by large corporate institutions. First was Pharaoh and his house whose property, "the fields of Pharaoh," were to be seen everywhere. Next, and owning 20–25% of all the land in Egypt, came the temples of which Amun's was by far the biggest and wealthiest. Third in rank, but far down the scale, came such institutions as the queen's house, the harim-ladies who, as we have seen, held their property in common, the state ports, "the landing-places of Pharaoh," and the private estates of the grandees of the realm.

For ease of cultivation and administration the arable land was divided into different sized plots. The basic unit was the "plantation" or farm (*rmnyt*), usually administered by an agent of the land-owner, the equivalent of our bailiff (*rwdw*), who was responsible for planting, tilling and the reaping of the harvest. A category of fields called *khato*-land, the origin of which is not clearly understood, was on the increase during the later Ramesside age. Apparently *khato*-land was land left vacant and in default of an owner (perhaps through death or alienation), which ran the risk of passing out of use if it was not worked. Whoever lived close to a *khato*-plot, usually a priest or a mayor, found himself burdened with working the land at the king's command, even though he had no right to its harvest. Paradoxically the influx of large numbers of foreigners into the agricultural labor force had resulted in a rise in status of junior army personnel, lesser priests, and low-ranking scribes. They could now rent on an hereditary basis small, tenured farms *(posh)* of c. two to seven acres in extent, from a land-owning institution, and sometimes were able to sell them. Such tenant farmers resembled the share-croppers of more modern times: two-thirds of the annual crop was kept by the tenant and the rest went to the landlord as rent (ZI).

The "chief taxing master" controlled the tax system of the Ramesside age, and applied it both in Egypt and throughout the empire. Of the four individual types of impost that will occupy our attention here, the grain tax was by far the most important in the eyes of the Egyptians themselves. Seven or eight papyri, some lengthy, others in fragments, provide a glimpse of how the grain tax was assessed and collected. Papyri now in Brooklyn, Berlin, and Moscow fall under the heading of tax assessor's journals, encorporating surveys of stretches of the Nile valley, with every farm and its current condition carefully noted, and an estimate given on the amount of tax for the current year. Other fragmentary papyri in Amiens, Turin, and elsewhere are tax collectors' receipt books which note who has paid and how much, or whether there are arrears. At the appointed time of year, when the harvest was in and the threshing floors full, the grain barges from the capital would pull up at particular collection points—not necessarily the township capitals—and the peasants would be obliged to appear with their pre-assessed quantity of cereals. The self-serving school texts, composed by the scribes, paint a dismal picture of the condition of the peasant farmer at tax time, never able to meet the amount required, and suffering beatings and collective punishment as a result.

Other forms of tax were scarcely less onerous. In order to provide for the upkeep of institutions dependent upon his support, such as garrisons, workers' villages, and even temples, Pharaoh undertook a budgetary assessment of the needs involved and instituted a "quota"-tax *(ḥtr)* on a segment of the population. A temple, for example, might require 365 bulls a year for sacrifice, and this number would be met by laying a quota tax on the township within which the temple was located. Each grandee, officer, or village-collective would pay a bull, or bulls, according to their means to provide a total of 365, the animals being despatched directly to the temple. Professional and support staffs of institutions, administrative offices, and production units were obliged to pay "dues" *(shayt),* usually in precious metals or manufactures. Two generic terms, *inw* and *bꜣkw,* are often used with vague application to obligations on the part of the tax-payers. The former can be translated literally as "that which is brought," and refers to freewill "gifts," unsought but expected, and therefore tantamount to "benevolences." The latter designates products of labor of a wide variety of activities.

Law during the New Kingdom

The term "law," Egyptian *hpw,* is a common element in the titulary of kings of the empire period. "Establishing good/effective laws" or "laws of *ma'at*" characterized the good sovereign. A constant synonym of *hpw,* however, was *tp-rd,* "instruction," such as one would give to a pupil or novice, and so one senses that inherent in the promulgation of law in Egypt was a didactic purpose. Once stated and learned, law could only be understood as customary procedure or obligation.

While Egypt had no law code as far as we know, the idea of *written* law played a major role in legal thinking. Thoth, the secretary of the gods, was the patron of law, and the hieroglyphic determinative of the word indicates a book-role. What we would call "statute law," in Egyptian parlance the "edicts of the king," although binding because the monarch had spoken them, achieved the status of law only because his words had been inscribed and disseminated abroad in an encyclical. These edicts, called collectively "policy decisions," were copied out and placed in the archives for future generations to consult. In general in court magistrates relied, if not on an inherent sense of what was deemed *ma'at* in a particular case, then on earlier decisions viewed as precedents and arranged calendrically in *law journals.* Numerous examples of cases heard before the court at the workers' village of Deir el-Medina show that the judges were adept at calling up a range of precedents which could be applied *ad hoc.*

The working out of the law in the New Kingdom, as in the Old, involved a judicious amalgam of royal statutory law and local custom. Kings are often associated with "teaching" *(sboyet)* which, because it issued from the king's mouth, had the force of law, and became tantamount to "legal doctrine." Some of this material has come down to us in surviving stelae and papyri, and has to do with the eradication of corruption at a government level—the Horemheb reform decree is an example—or the authorization of social *laissez-faire.* Two examples of the latter are royal statements to the effect that every man is allowed to dispose of his own property in any way he wishes, and that mortuary goods should be "released" for funerals. In all cases kings show themselves to be careful in not intruding on the field of local customary law if it does not contravene an overriding royal edict.

Legal procedure allowed charges, both criminal and civil, to be brought by one individual against another, the whole to be decided before the local *qenbet.* (Cases could be taken to higher courts, and eventually to the vizier's tribunal, but the initiative here lay with the prosecution in consultation with the higher authorities.) In cases, such as property disputes, where written documentation was required by the litigants, the law permitted a stay of two months to allow for the assembling of relevant papers. Trials were often held in the gates of towns or temples and resembled the Latin *quaestio,* a public enquiry or examination *(smtr),* in which torture was often applied. The same term was given to periodic "examinations" of towns and villages in which a high official would grill the locals on anything and everything that had been going on in the settlement. The litigants and their witnesses were required to take an oath in the name of the king "whose power is worse than death." The *qenbet's* decision in a court case was usually a unanimous one—the qenbet "speaks with one voice"—though how that was achieved is never stated. The whole procedure from beginning to end was recorded verbatim by the scribe of the court, and this transcript was then sent on to the archives, eventually to be copied out in the law journals.

Toward the close of the Ramesside age and continuing on well into the First Millennium B.C., a second means of deciding an issue at law was pressed into service. This was the "approach to god," a direct appeal to the supernatural to settle a case or make a selection. Usually at a festal procession of the divine barque anyone, of high or low estate, could step forward and, addressing the god directly, request an oracular response. The latter was probably indicated by movement of the god's barque—"the god nodded"—or by the use of black and white talismans. To a modern mind the priests who bore the barque must come under suspicion, and yet the ancients did not show skepticism at the procedure, and maintained it for centuries.

Punishment in criminal and civil cases varied greatly, but was often harsh. For anything which could be interpreted as treason, such as sedition, overt rebellion against the king, dissidence, larceny (if the king were involved), etc., the sentence was death by fire, impalement, or crocodile. Corruption and malfeasance in government brought mutilation of nose and ears and exile to the north Sinai desert. Theft, breach of contract, and embezzlement entailed double compensation, perhaps loss of property and a beating into the bargain. Perjury, contempt of court, or failure to carry out a court order might be punished by anything from fifty to one hundred lashes and the opening of five wounds, and perhaps consignment to a mine or quarry for "hard labor." For misdemeanors that we would classify as "breaking the peace" or "being drunk and disorderly" stocks were employed as in mediaeval Europe, and collective punishment might be meted out to the family of the malefactor.

Family Life

Our New Kingdom sources, especially those from Deir el-Medina, are full enough to give us a rounded picture of the society of imperial Egypt. To this may be added a magistrate's handbook, the so-called "Law Code of Hermopolis," which, although the present copy dates 1,000 years later, encorporates age-old legal provisions regarding the family. Finally tomb scenes complement the panorama conjured up by word descriptions.

The nuclear family was the building block of New Kingdom society. Although no law made it obligatory, most men at a fairly young age married one wife (zj), albeit entertaining prospects of building liaisons with concubines and girl-friends. Then as now the house of ill repute was a feature of the urban landscape. Rape was frowned upon and could be actionable. We are ill-informed about the marriage ceremony: most likely it involved essentially the drawing up of a marriage contract. Divorce was easy and frequent, and at the will of the husband, but marriage contracts stipulated that in case of divorce bride price and dowry were to be returned. Whether single or married, women could hold property in their own right and could function as their own executors. Before marriage many women sang in temple choirs as "choristers"; after marriage they became "mistress of the house," responsible for the domestic arrangements of the family. It was customary for a dutiful son or friend of the family to care for the widowed mother, and set up an annuity for her.

The production of children was the overriding concern of husband and wife, and people looked askance at the childless couple as misanthropic and irresponsible. Keeping the ancestral inheritance within the family preoccupied all Egyptians, and family law bent every effort to facilitate it. The eldest son, i.e. the oldest male offspring regardless of daughters, inherited the lion's share of the property, while his brothers had to be content with smaller portions, and his sisters only one-third of the inheritance. If there were no sons born to the couple, a daughter might carry the right of inheritance. Childless couples often adopted orphans, or a brother or cousin, and in one case a husband adopted his wife—all in an effort to ensure that family property was not alienated.

Children could look forward to a nurturing atmosphere in the family when they were toddlers and a program of schooling later on. Some scenes show grandparents fondling and playing with the grandchildren, as though they are baby-sitting for working parents. Boys, less frequently girls, could be sent to formal scribal schools when they had reached five or six, but universal education did not apply to the mass of the population, and the "job descriptions" used as school texts show that a bewildering array of professions was open to the children from an early age. The best "graduates" of the schools could anticipate a prescribed *cursus honorum* within a particular sphere of endeavor, government, priesthood, army, technocracy, and rapid advancement as a reward for achievement. And within this social expectation lay the great conundrum of Egyptian society: do we choose the best and brightest man for the job regardless of where he comes from, or do we allow a son to succeed his father in his official function? That the Egyptians solved this conflict between proven skill vs. hereditary right is a credit to their vibrant civilization.

A Day in the Life of . . .

Egyptian society was rooted in the life of the farmer and herdsman, and scheduled its activities accordingly. Day began just before dawn when everyone awoke and prepared to greet the sun with the morning hymn of adoration. Peasants then wended their way to the fields, workers presented themselves at the work site, and in the temples the shrines were opened and the gods were awakened and clothed. After a night of resting moored at a landing stage, ships put out from the shore and continued their journeys. Shadow clocks were set at right angles to the rising sun. Breakfast was taken at dawn by rich and poor alike, and the midday meal, the main meal of the day, six hours later during the noon hour. A light evening repast preceded the setting of the sun and bedding down for the night.

Everyone shared a basic diet of bread and beer. Bread was made from flour produced in stone mortars, and the stone particles in the loaves often caused severe dental attrition. The beer, brewed quickly everywhere, had an alcoholic content of about 2%, and resembled modern Egyptian *bouza*. The tables of the rich would groan with additional foods such as beef and fowl, vegetables, figs, grapes, stews, and confections, and wine would be liberally served. The only time the commons could share in such a sumptuous menu would be at festival time, when king or temple would liberally bestow their largesse upon the people.

Most work was done in the morning and the early afternoon. Manual labor and manufacturing worked to a quota system, and scribes at a worksite kept copious notes on the amount of work accomplished during a day. Roll-call sheets which have survived list the quotas for each man and note whether workers are on the job or are absent, and in the latter case the reason. Reasons given include bereavements, sickness, or "drinking before his god." Months were divided into ten-day "weeks," but workers were paid only on the last day of the month. Wages, or perhaps better "rations," vary widely, and we do not always know why. It may be that the salary scale was graded on the basis of such variables as marital status, number of children the worker had, or possible "moonlighting" at other jobs. At Deir el-Medina the foreman received 5½ *khar* of emmer wheat and 2 *khar* of barley per month—a *khar* is the equivalent of 72 liters—while ordinary workers might earn as little as ½ *khar* of wheat and 2 *khar* of barley. As a loaf of bread cost roughly ⅟₄₀ of a *khar* of barley, and a large jar of beer ⅛, one can appreciate the relative wealth of foreman and worker.

As today, husbands and wives were greatly concerned for the welfare and health of the family. The former could be ensured by diligence, co-operation, and submission to authority; but the latter often posed problems beyond human control. Pathological investigation of mummies has revealed numerous ailments, including tuberculosis, poliomyolitis, arteriosclerosis, guinea-worm, silicosis, dental attrition and abscesses, and problems with the eye. For these diseases there were doctors who knew medicine, and owned or had access to magical spells and medical books; and these written prescriptive texts were sometimes to be found in the private libraries of upper middle class households. Hemerologies were also available which approximated our almanacs. These listed every day of the calendar year and indicated, on the basis of "dated" events in mythology, whether morning, afternoon, and evening were favorable or inimical to certain human activities.

The Egyptians were essentially a happy, optimistic, and gregarious people, and it would be wrong to suggest that disease cast a shadow over their lives. One of the common themes represented in tomb art is the party at which the founder of the feast presides, with his wife, over the revelries. Guests are shown partaking liberally of beer, wine, and even more potent concoctions, while a small band of comely girls sings and plays songs to the accompaniment of harp, pipes, and castanets, or an aged and blind harper extemporizes a *carpe diem* ditty.

The "Literature" of the New Kingdom

While they do not rival in sheer quantity the copies of Middle Kingdom creations, the New Kingdom has bequeathed to us a number of important narrative and didactic pieces, mainly Ramesside in date. (Unfortunately we have no idea how representative are the Late Egyptian stories which were written down and have survived. Many appear to reflect private predilection, and may have been written down "by accident.") Papyrus copies often contain colopha at the end, indicating the copyist and sometimes containing threats against anyone who will criticize the text. Those who wrote the copies include scribes of the treasury, draftsman-scribes, lector priests, and royal envoys, and they often declare that the texts were carefully reproduced "as was found in writing." The papyri belong to a larger, miscellaneous category used for pedagogical purposes, including model letters and reports.

In spite of the assertion that an earlier version lurks behind the present copy, New Kingdom literature owes a great deal to the oral culture of the land. Wisdom texts and related genres may have been composed in written form for oral dissemination, but they draw unconsciously on oral anecdote or aphorism. In the very pieces which pretend to base themselves on an earlier written version, the text is introduced by the words "people say there was once a . . .," the equivalent of the mediaeval dicitur, "it is said that . . . ," with overtones of skepticism. We have already noted such skepticism in scribal allusions to the "converse of the people," a derogatory reference to the folklore of the common people, allegedly given to fantasy and exaggeration. Throughout New Kingdom writings wide use is made of red "verse points" positioned above the line, apparently to control breathing or intonation; and a great deal of these creations can in fact be "scanned," making use of a prosodic meter well known throughout the ancient Near East. The *Sitz im Leben* (real-life setting) of the literature likewise stresses the interweaving of the two traditions, oral and scribal, in a variety of situations. A scene shows the king delivering himself of an extemporized speech, but a bevy of scribes close at hand are depicted copying his every word; a blind harper sings a spontaneous song to the accompaniment of his harp, but the text is already written up in front of him. Written encomia, conforming to a high-flown scribal style, laud the king in a courtly setting; but the meter and the speaker's asides to the audience clearly indicate an oral substratum to the whole.

New Kingdom creations reveal a number of distinct genres. There were tales of the ancestors which arose as aetiologies on known facts or observable monuments, reduced to hermeneutical "readings" at an illiterate level. How had the war between Seqenenre and Apophis really broken out? How had Thutmose really captured the town of Joppa? What had really happened under Amenophis III which led to the disasters which followed? Other tales belong squarely in the category of *Märchen,* stories recounted for their plots alone, with no mention of toponyms or indicators of time, and the unnamed protagonists identified by terms of relationship only. One extremely common type of yarn is derived from the myths about the gods, retold with an eye to narrative techniques, coarse humor, and characterization. Included here are the bawdy stories of Seth (= Ba'al) and his girlfriend the Canaanite Anath or Astarte, the picaresque contendings of Horus and Seth in and out of court, the narrative of the goddess who wandered off and who had to be enticed back with beer, the explanation of how Isis tricked the sun-god into divulging his hidden name, and many others. A whole cycle, of which we have few surviving examples, took shape around the childhood of Horus and the dangers which threatened him. Although much of this was developed to ensure audience reception, their value as potent magic spells continues. Finally: the New Kingdom produced the earliest surviving corpora of love poetry, distinctly similar in format and content to similar bodies of material throughout the Near East.

One characteristic of New Kingdom literature cannot fail to impress the reader, and that is the intertextual dependence of the thematic content on foreign, specifically Asiatic, literatures. The story of the Doomed Prince takes its hero to Mitanni where his fate as a victim of his dog at a water hole distinctly resembles that of Ba'al in certain Ugaritic texts or that of Adonis. The story of the Two Brothers sets one episode against the backdrop of the Lebanons and the Phoenician coast, where the pursuit of the female protagonist by the monster Sea and the emasculation of the hero recalls motifs in the Canaanite mythology of the region. One piece, Astarte and the Sea, is a version of a mythological plot well known at Ugarit, but one in which Seth plays the role of Ba'al. In a sense the culture of conquered Canaan had rebounded to enjoy a conquest of sorts of the imperial power.

Further Readings

On the family of the Ramessides, see P. Brand, *The Monuments of Sety I,* Leiden, 2000; L. Habachi, *Features of the Deification of Ramesses II,* Glückstadt, 1969; K. A. Kitchen, *Pharaoh Triumphant: The Life and Times of Ramesses II,* Warminster, 1982; *idem,* "Ramesses II," in D. B. Redford (ed.), *The Oxford Encyclopaedia of Ancient Egypt* (New York, 2001), III. 116–18.

On the Ramesses-Hattusilis correspondence, see T. R. Bryce, *Letters of the Great Kings of the Ancient Near East,* London, 2003; G. Beckman, *Hittite Diplomatic Texts,* Atlanta 1999.

For studies on the government and administration during the New Kingdom, see G. P. F. van den Boorn, *The Duties of the Vizier: Civil Administration in the Early New Kingdom,* London & New York, 1988; T. G. H. James, *Pharaoh's People: Scenes from Life in Imperial Egypt,* London, 1984.

On priests and temples see D. Meeks, C. F. Meeks, *Daily Life of the Egyptian Gods,* Ithaca, 1996; S. Quirke (ed.), *The Temple in Ancient Egypt,* London, 1997; S. Sauneron, *The Priests of Ancient Egypt,* New York & London, 1960; B. E. Shafer (ed.), *Temples of Ancient Egypt,* Ithaca, 1997; P. Spencer, *The Egyptian Temple: A Lexicographical Study,* London, 1984.

Several excellent works deal with the Egyptian army of the New Kingdom: S. Curto, *The Military Art of the Ancient Egyptians*, Turn (n.d.); A. M. Gnirs, "Military: an Overview," in D. B. Redford (ed.), *Oxford Encyclopaedia of Ancient Egypt* (New York, 2001), II, 400–04; J. K. Hoffmeier, "Materiel," *ibid.*, II, 404–12; E. F. Morris, *The Architecture of Imperialism: Military Bases and the Evolution of Foreign Policy in Egypt's New Kingdom*, Leiden, 2005; T. Savesoderbergh, *The Navy of the Eighteenth Egytpian Dynasty*, Uppsala, 1946; P. Raulwing, *Horses, Chariots, and Indo-Europeans*, Budapest, 2000; A. R. Schulman, *Military Rank, Title, and Organization in the Egyptian New Kingdom*, Berlin, 1964; A. J. Spalinger, *Aspects of the Military Documents of the Ancient Egyptians*, New Haven, 1982; *idem, War in Ancient Egypt*, Oxford, 2005.

On workers and demographics, see A. M. Bakir, *Slavery in Pharaonic Egypt*, Cairo, 1952; M. Bierbrier, *The Tomb Builders of the Pharaohs*, London, 1982; A. K. Bowman, E. Rogan (eds.), *Agriculture in Egypt from Pharaonic to Modern Times*, Oxford, 1999; J. Cerny, *A Community of Workmen at Thebes in the Rameside Period*, Cairo, 1973; R. J. Demaree, A. Egberts (eds.), *Deir el-Medina in the Third Millennium A. D.*, Leiden, 2000; L. H. Lesko (ed.), *Pharaoh's Workers*, Ithaca, 1994; R. Ventura, *Living in a City of the Dead*, Freiburg, 1986.

For land-holding and taxation, see E. J. Bleiberg, *The Official Gift in Ancient Egypt*, Norman, OK, 1997; R. A. Caminos, *Late Egyptian Miscellanies*, Oxford, 1954; S. L. D. Katary, *Land Tenure in the Rameside Period*, London, 1989; D. A. Warburton, *State and Economy in Ancient Egypt*, Fribourg, 1997.

An interest in ancient Egyptian law is beginning to spawn an impressive literature. See in particular the following: J. M. Kruchten, "Law," in D. B. Redford (ed.), *Oxford Encyclopaedia of Ancient Egypt* (New York, 2001), III, 277–82; G. Mattha, *The Demotic Legal Code of Hermopolis West*, Cairo, 1975; A. G. McDowell, *Jurisdiction in the Workmen's Community of Deir el-Medineh*, Leiden, 1990; R. Ver Steeg, *Law in Ancient Egypt*, Durham, 2002; J. Tyldesley, *Judgment of the Pharaoh: Crime and Punishment in Ancient Egypt*, London, 2000.

For the role of women and family life, see S. R. K. Glanville, *Daily Life in Ancient Egypt*, London, 1930; Z. Hawass, *Silent Images: Women in Pharaonic Egypt*, Cairo, 1995; R. M. and J. J. Janssen, *Growing Up in Ancient Egypt*, London, 1990; L. Manniche, *Sexual Life in Ancient Egypt*, London, 1987; *idem, Music and Musicians in Ancient Egypt*, London, 1991; G. Robins, *Women in Ancient Egypt*, London, 1993; E. Strouhal, *Life in Ancient Egypt*, Cambridge, 1992; J. Tyldesley, *Daughters of Isis: Women of Ancient Egypt*, London, 1994; A. Vogelsang-Eastwood, *Pharaonic Egyptian Clothing*, Leiden, 1993.

CHAPTER TWELVE

The Decline of the New Kingdom (Dyn. 20–21)

ψ

Twentieth Dynasty

Seth-nakht	c. 1200–1197 B.C.
Ramesses III	c. 1197–1165 B.C.
Ramesses IV	c. 1165–1159 B.C.
Ramesses V	c. 1159–1155 B.C.
Ramesses VI	c. 1155–1148 B.C.
Ramesses VII	c. 1148–1141 B.C.
Ramesses VIII	c. 1140 B.C.
Ramesses IX	c. 1140–1123 B.C.
Ramesses X	c. 1123–1120 B.C.
Ramesses XI	c. 1120–1090 B.C.

Twenty-first Dynasty

Smendes	c. 1089–1063 B.C.
Psusennes I	c. 1063–1013 B.C.
Neferkare	c. 1013–1009 B.C.
Amenophthis	c. 1009–1000 B.C.
Osochor	c. 1000–992 B.C.
Siamun	c. 992–975 B.C.
Psusennes II	c. 975–940 B.C.

Ramesses II cast a long shadow down the ages. Five centuries after his death kings continued to reproduce his throne-name and epithets, and to copy his profile (AA) in their statuary. His reputation was certainly enhanced by the fact that his reign coincided with high Niles and great prosperity which owed not a little also to his energy and foresight.

Keftiu and the Hau-nebu

Most of the inhabitants of the Near East by the middle of the Second Millennium B.C. knew of the existence of a civilized community inhabiting a group of islands off the north coast of the Mediterranean. Returning merchants told of one large island beyond which lay a sea full of islands and a mainland. The Egyptians from as early as the Old Kingdom had called this far-off region *Hau-nebu* (meaning uncertain); the Canaanites of the Levant referred to it as *Kaptor* (whence Egyptian *Keftiu*); the Hittites spoke of *Akhkhiyawa*. Today we know the large island as Crete, the sea beyond as the Aegean and the mainland as Greece. About 2000 B.C. destruction levels unearthed at Greek sites signal the arrival of a group of people, hailing from the north, who centuries later reveal themselves to be Greek-speakers of the Achaean dialect. The new-comers settled in the ruined countryside, and disappear from view for about three centuries.

Sometime in the 17th century, roughly contemporary with the start of the Hyksos occupation of Egypt, there suddenly blossomed forth on the island of Crete a brilliant civilization centered upon the city of Knossos. To what extent, if at all, this community was stimulated into growth by contemporary societies of the Near East, we shall probably never know. Object(s) bearing Hyksos royal names have been recovered from Middle Minoan tombs on the island; and an Egyptian queen of the 16th century bore the title "Mistress of the Hau-nebu." As demonstrated by the bull-leaping frescoes, mentioned above, recovered from Avaris, and by references to Kaptor from Mari, Crete was clearly in contact with most of the states of the Near East. During the reign of Thutmose III, as we have seen, dignitaries from Crete are shown in Theban tombs bearing diplomatic presents to Pharaoh **(fig. 1)**. In unwalled Knossos—the Cretans

Figure 1   Minoans from Crete in 18th Dynasty tombs.

possessed a navy strong enough to deter invaders—the king or *wanax* of the district erected a vast palace filled with spacious colonnades, halls, and rooms, grouped around a rectangular court fifty meters long. Walls were expertly decorated with frescoes depicting rows of shields, fish, bulls, dancers, and elegant ladies

International Trade and Exchange

From as early as the reign of Amenophis III a prosperous commercial exchange had grown up involving states all over the central and eastern Mediterranean. Called the "Mycenaean Age" by modern scholars because of the key role played in trade by the pottery from that Greek city, this commerce was only intensified and profits increased after the Egypto-Hittite peace treaty had been signed. Now both great empires had access to each other's goods and market places. Trade was largely in the hands of the great kings of the day, and few, certainly in Egypt, could engage in entrepreneurial activity without royal permission. Nonetheless the temples and sometimes high officials were allowed to put ships on the sea to engage in trade, and the "commercial agent" *(shuty)* became a familiar denizen of the market place. In order to open doors, "up front" money was expected to be paid to the ruler from whom one wished to acquire goods and raw materials; and once satisfaction had been assured, the commercial exchange could begin in earnest.

Three of the five great kingships of the 13th century were directly involved in the trade. While Assyria and Babylonia took part only peripherally, Egypt, Khatte, and the state of Ahhiyawa occupied the key points in the trade triangle. There is now little doubt that Ahhiyawa is, in fact, the Greek Achaea, and probably designates the loose, imperial structure headed by Mycenae. Tablets inscribed in a syllabic script called Linear B, and used in the archives of Greek and Cretan cities, bear witness that the language was an early dialect of Greek.

Maritime trade routes (**fig. 2**) connected north Syria and the Phoenician coast with Cyprus and the Aegean islands and mainland; and further afield with Egypt and the north African coast around Cyrenaica. From the latter, specifically Mersa Matruh a little further east, an inland route ran south through the oasis chain and into the Sudan. Curiously this route was extensively used, in spite of the presence of a more negotiable riverine transit corridor along the Nile; perhaps the transit dues levied at Egyptian harbours made the cost prohibitive.

The goods that passed in this exchange are known through a variety of sources: Egyptian hieroglyphic texts, Akkadian business documents from Ugarit in north Syria and Emar on the Euphrates, and Hittite archives. Archaeologically the trade is reflected in the ubiquitous Mycenaean ware found all over the Near East. From Cyprus Egypt sought copper and opium, from Mesopotamia tin, from Greece wool, olive oil, spices, unguent, and table ware. Iron deposits in the Hittite homeland were known, but not yet extensively exploited. Egypt was perhaps more familiar with what the Levant had to offer. Oil ranked high on the list, along with cedar and boxwood, and ornamental metalware of which the Canaanites were master craftsmen. From Egypt's point of view it was a "seller's market," as the entire world craved what the Pharaoh had to offer. It was customary for the kings of the palatine states of the Syrian coast to go together in a consortium, buy a large cargo boat, and send it to the Delta to trade. The goods going north from Egypt featured wheat and barley at the top of the list, followed by sub-Saharan tropical products, and the luxury manufactures of Egyptian workshops.

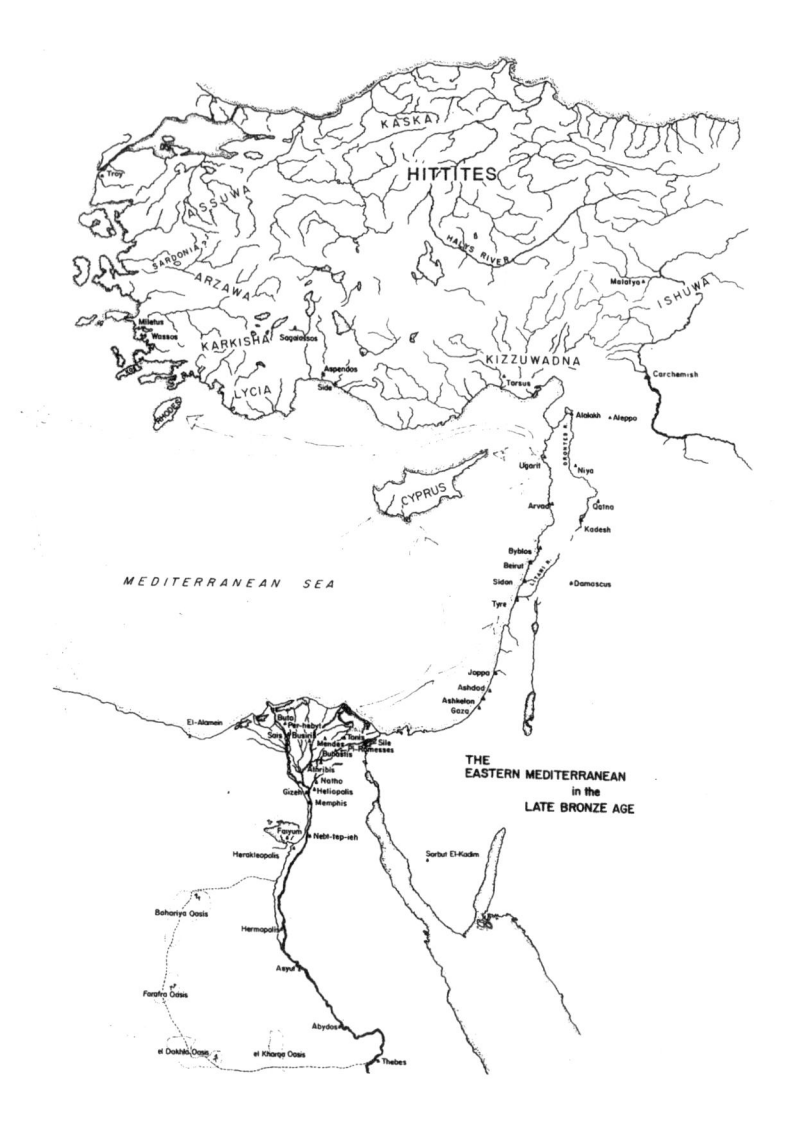

Figure 2 Commercial maritime traffic in the eastern Mediterranean, c. 1400–1200 B.C.

The wreck of a cargo ship dated to the 14th century B.C. recovered by underwater archaeology off cape Ulun Buru on the south coast of Anatolia demonstrates the varied cargo being transported through the sea lanes of the Mediterranean. The ship, about fifteen meters long, was apparently making for the Aegean from Cyprus when it foundered. It was carrying at the time ten tons of copper from Cyprus in the form of 350 ingots, 100 ingots of glass, and substantial quantities of ebony, ivory, Canaanite amphorae, unguents, and spices. Nothing could better illustrate the international nature of Mycenaean trade.

The End of the Nineteenth Dynasty

Ramesses II (A) died in his sixty-seventh year of reign, well over eighty years of age. His mummy shows him to have maintained his robustness to the end, despite the ailments which come with old age. He had sired well over one hundred offspring, whom he loved to have depicted in procession (AB), and had outlived his first twelve sons. *Sed*-festival had followed *sed*-festival with monotonous regularity from his thirtieth year on the throne; and now a veritable clan, "the sons of Ramesses," was in existence throughout the realm.

The thirteenth son, Merenptah (B), who succeeded him on the throne, was already an elderly man when he donned the royal regalia. His mummy reveals a corpulent old man who had suffered the extraction of many teeth, and who was afflicted with degenerative arthritis and arteriosclerosis. The poor fellow had not long to live and scarcely attained ten years on the "Horus-throne of the Living."

Merenptah's death about 1227 B.C. opened the door for a contest for power among members of the extended Ramesside clan. Although the course of events can only be dimly discerned, it seems as though a member of a collateral branch, one Amenmesse, perhaps a grandson of Ramesses II, seized the throne. After a short reign of two or three years Amenmesse disappeared under mysterious circumstances, and the throne was taken by Sety II, grandson (or great-grandson?) of Ramesses the Great. Sety seems to have been considered eminently legitimate by the court, and set about a grand program of construction and decoration. Unfortunately this was cut short in his sixth year when he died suddenly, leaving an embarrassing vacuum. Two prominent figures at court, whose reputations have suffered (perhaps unjustly), viz. the chancellor Beya, who may have been Canaanite in origin, and a princess named Tawosret, immediately filled the gap by promoting their protégé, a young boy named Siptah who was undoubtedly a scion of the Ramesside house. The unfortunate Siptah, as his mummy attests, suffered from birth from polio-myolitis, and was probably only a puppet in the hands of Beya and Tawosret. The former seems to have become the real power behind the throne, writing official state letters to foreign governments. The princess remains a shadowy figure, but when Siptah died she seems to have assumed the royal mantle.

This posturing for power seems to have stirred up revulsion in a certain part of the court. Shortly after 1200 B.C. opposition crystallized in the person of a certain Seth-nakht whose origins are obscure. Was he a member of the extended Ramesside "clan"—all his descendants were named "Ramesses"!—or was the assumption of Ramesside epithets and trappings a necessary affectation? In the one major stela he has left us, a sort of *apologia* for his actions, he describes how he nipped in the bud a plot in which foreigners (Canaanites?) were planning to take over Egypt. Although his tenure of power was scarcely two years, he had the foresight to appoint his son Ramesses to the post of heir apparent; and when, on the morrow of his death "Ramesses III" appeared on the throne, a new dynasty, the Twentieth, had taken over Egypt.

Piracy and the "Sea Peoples"

The rich cargoes carried along the complex of sea lanes we have described above excited the cupidity of those unable, either directly or at a secondary level, to tap into the profits. Those geographically isolated communities along the western (Ionian) and southern coasts of the Anatolian peninsula fall into this category. They were of very ancient origin, many speaking a pre-Indo-European "Luwian" language. Since the creation of the empire of Khatte these coastal enclaves had been inexorably drawn into the Hittite sphere of influence, but because of the mountainous terrain and their familiarity with the sea had been able to maintain a certain degree of autonomy. In fact, in the third quarter of the 13th century, late in Ramesses II's reign, twenty-two communities on the Ionian coast from Lukka (= Lycia) in the south-west to Wilusa (= Ilion) south-east of the Dardanelles, had even formed a coalition to oppose the Hittite king Tudkhaliyas IV.

From as early as the reign of Amenophis III some of these communities had taken to sea-raiding to tap into the sources of the wealth they knew was passing along the trade routes. The king of Cyprus complains to Pharaoh in an Amarna letter that the "Lukka-people" had raided the coasts of his island on a yearly basis, capturing town after town. The Shardana **(fig. 4a–b),** from the Sardinian plain near Sardis in north-west Asia Minor, had been raiding the coasts of the Nile Delta from 1302 B.C. and had fought on the Hittite side at the battle of Kadesh. Ramesses II called them "the unmanageable Shardana, whom nobody could engage in battle," and was so impressed by their prowess that he engaged them as mercenaries in his bodyguard (c). A well-travelled sea lane between the Aegean and the coast of Libya had long been so frequented by people from the Troad that later tradition derived certain local tribes from descendants of "men of Troy."

All this "Viking-like" activity came to a head during the generation following the demise of Ramesses II **(fig. 3).** By chance it coincided with two significant developments in the Aegean, Anatolian, and the Libyan world. For the outgoing 13th century and the inception of the 12th witnessed the demise of Bronze Age Greece with its monumental cities of Mycenae, Tiryns, Pylos, and others, and the creation of the warlike coalitions later immortalized in Greek literature (especially Homer) under the guise of the Trojan War. At the same time western Anatolia was in turmoil. During Merenptah's reign the Hittites had suffered a grievous crop failure, and Egypt had despatched shipments of grain to the stricken country. In Libya during the 13th century two great ethnic blocks had begun to move eastward toward the Nile Valley, although the complexity of tribal organization dictated that half of the group remain sedentary, while the remainder adopt a transhumant life style. Ramesses II had created a series of forts along the coast stretching as far as the present Libyan border, and created the post of Libyarch to keep the locals under surveillance. But, with the great Ramesses dead, two great enclaves, the Labu (after whom "Libya" takes its name) and the Meshwesh (called "Maxies" in Herodotus seven centuries later), began to move upon Egypt. They were accompanied by old friends from the northern shores of the Mediterranean, long familiar with the landing places of the north African coast: the Lukka, the Shardana, the Akwoos (possibly from the island of Koos), the Turesh from the region of Troy, and the Shekelesh, possibly from Sagalassos or Crete. This motley horde bore down on Egypt, by land and sea, in the early years of Merenptah. They occupied the Farafra oasis and began to penetrate the western Delta. News reached the king in Pi-Ramesses in April of his fifth year, and he set the date for a counter-attack four weeks later. At a site near Buto in the north-west Delta the two sides met, and hammered each other for hours. Eventually it was the Libyans who broke, leaving thousands of their dead on the battlefield. Egypt had been saved . . . or had it?

Inscriptions from Thebes and Athribis celebrated the victory in high flown, lyrical form; but the message was far from reality. Although repulsed, the Libyans were not discomfited, and during the twenty years of internal turmoil following Merenptah's death they filtered back into

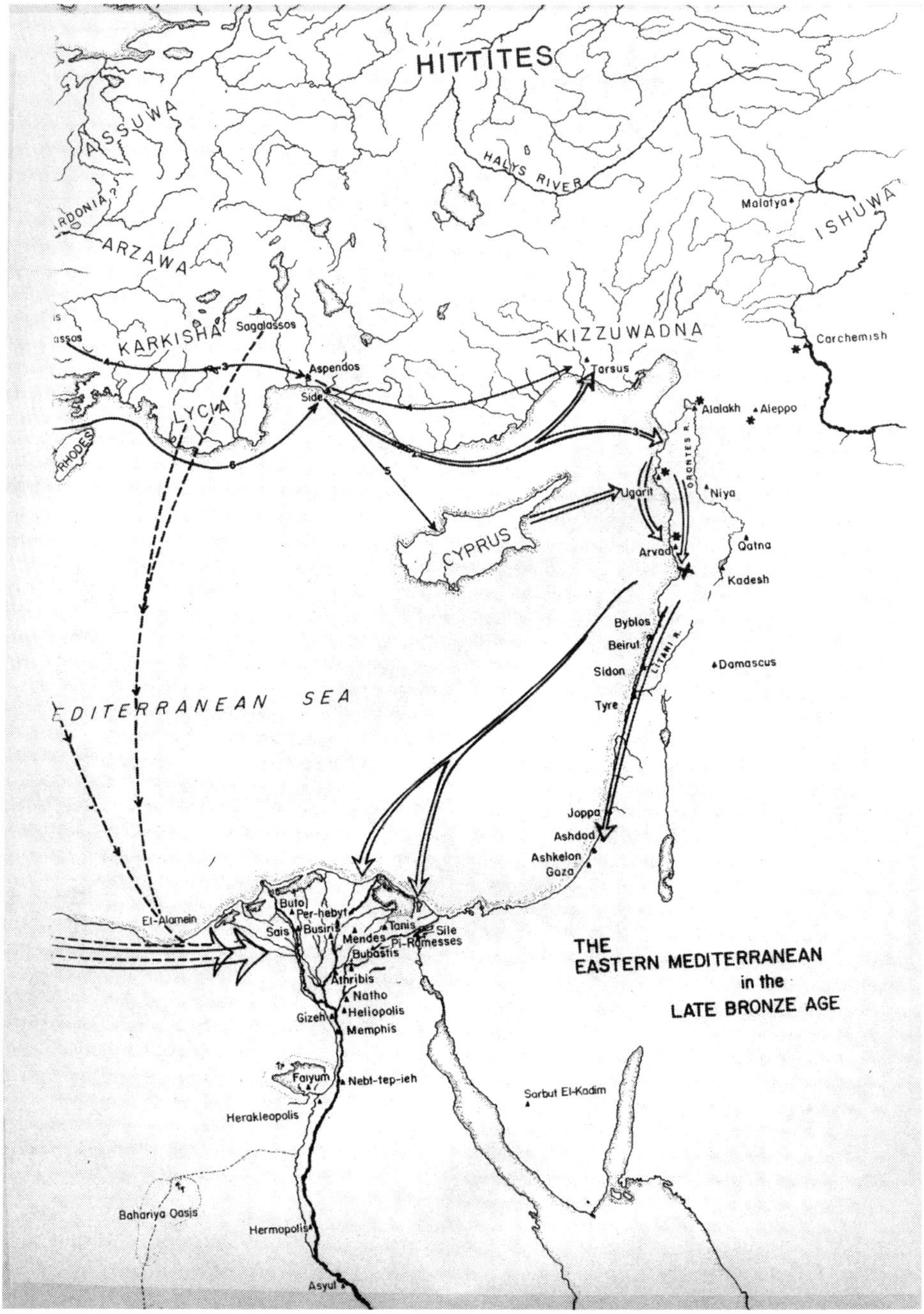

Figure 3   Routes of the Sea People's invasion.

(a)   (b)

Figure 4   Shardana: (a) From Ramesses II's bodyguard (Osiris Temple); (b) from Medinet Habu.

the oases and delta, even reaching the central river. As before, piratical bands from the Ionian coast, including Carians and people from the islands, accompanied the invaders in ships. Two of the pirate chiefs named by the inscriptions bear Greek names, Moschion and Mullos—a harbinger of things to come!

Sources for the momentous international events which transpired in the first decade of Ramesses III's reign are contained in both textual and archaeological records. The largest body of texts, and those which have been known the longest, come from the great mortuary temple (D) of the king at Medinet Habu (E), on the west bank at Thebes. This, the last major mortuary shrine of the New Kingdom, was in process of building during the dozen or so years beginning with year 5, and its external west and north walls and the walls of the first court and one wall in the second contain detailed relief scenes and lengthy inscriptions describing the three invasions of years 5, 8, and 11. While the scenes shed welcome light on costume and battlefield tactics (F), the majority of the texts are written in lyrical form and tend to be highly rhetorical, making it necessary for the historian to "sift" and evaluate carefully. The Hittite annals in cuneiform from Hattusas contain allusions to events related to the period just prior to the invasions, but are of only peripheral value. Of more recent discovery, the archives from Ugarit and to a lesser extent from Emar, shed circumstantial light on the period. Archaeological evidence of destruction, not always easy to sequence and date, comes from excavations on the coast of Israel and north Syria as well as Cyprus, the Aegean islands, and the Greek mainland. Interpretations of the evidence vary widely from traditional acceptance of the general thrust of the data to outright denial that we are dealing with demographic shifts or invasions at all. Unfortunately for its proponents, the denials smack of debunking, and gain no support whatsoever from the plain assessment of the evidence.

A judicious reading of the Medinet Habu evidence yields the following account. Ramesses III found a *casus belli* in his fifth year when, he claims, he was challenged to battle by the Libyan coalition. Beside a border fortress on the western side of the Delta battle was joined and resulted in an Egyptian victory. Egyptian casualty figures list over 12,000 enemy dead, tallied from the count of hands and phalloi in the king's presence (G); Egyptian losses are unrecorded. Whether these figures are to be taken seriously, the aftermath reveals that this repulse witnessed the break-up of the enemy coalition. The Labu (H), who had heretofore taken the lead, now ceded place to the Meshwesh. Though worsted in another attempt to break into the Delta in year 11 (with significantly lower casualties), the Meshwesh were thereafter to take the lead in peacefully infiltrating the land they had attempted to take by force (see below).

Egypt's troubles were by no means over. In an inscription dated to year 8 Ramesses described (in the first person) a new coalition of sea-rovers which took shape "in the northern islands" pursuant to what he calls "the war of the nations." Called by modern scholarship the "Sea Peoples," the alliance numbered the Wassos, either from Caria or Crete, the Danuna, possibly Greeks from the mainland, the Teucrians from the Ionian coast, the Shekelesh from Sagalassos in Pisidia, and the Peleset perhaps from Crete. The Egyptian artists obviously thrilled at the prospect of depicting these strange people (I, J, K) with their helmets, body armour, plumed headdresses, circular shields, long-swords, and ships with goose-head prows. Ramesses indicates that the coalition was on the move with Egypt as its goal, moving east along the south coast of Anatolia, leaving destruction in its wake. Hattusas, far inland, was destroyed and the Hittite empire disappeared. Alalakh, Ugarit, and Emar were overwhelmed, never to be re-occupied. The marauders established a camp in Amurru as their base for a final thrust towards the Nile Delta. Although Ramesses boastfully claims that he established a defensive line in "Djahy," a vague term for the Palestinian coast, the Sea-peoples' land forces with ox-carts carrying their women and children and the combined fleet offshore were not intercepted before they had reached the Pelusiac branch of the Nile! Here the Egyptian army and navy appeared and a major engagement ensued. The Egyptian sources, of course, claim a victory; but one wonders whether it was "Pyrrhic." Admittedly the enemy coalition broke up, but very few appear in Egypt as prisoners. The Peleset (L) settled on the coastal plain from Gaza to Ashdod, where they are better known from their Biblical name the "Philistines," and the Teucrians a little to the north and also on Cyprus. The Shekelesh and some Shardana migrated west to the islands that bear their name, viz. Sicily and Sardinia.

Ramesses III could now boast, "I have caused the woman of Egypt to walk freely wherever she would, unmolested by others of the road. I allowed the soldiers and charioteers to sit idle during my time, and the mercenaries lay at night in their villages without any dread." Peace and prosperity, according to this passage, had been everywhere restored.

Economic Hardship and Social Protest

But no bombastic statement by a king whose mania was to ape his Nineteenth Dynasty namesake could mask the true state of the nation. The fact is that the invasion of the Sea Peoples had done severe harm to Egypt. She found herself cut off now from the lands formerly part of the Hittite empire, to which her merchants had had access for over seventy years. The silver and copper of Anatolia were no longer available; and iron, which other states of the Near East were now about to use on a wider scale, was not identified in Egypt. Moreover exhaustion appears to have afflicted the native mining operations. Within a generation of the death of Ramesses III the Sinai mines shut down, and records of gold mining and quarrying in Nubia cease at about the same time. Gold and copper became much more expensive and hard to obtain.

At the same time the empire was contracting through military weakness and exhaustion. The last reign reflected in objects emanating from the province of Canaan is Ramesses VI, and although two of his successors refer in their inscriptions to military campaigns in the north, it is clear that garrisons were being withdrawn and governors recalled. By 1100 B.C. no territory north of the Suez frontier remained in Egyptian hands. The Sudanese province experienced a similar fate. Low Niles and poor crops forced the population to move north, abandoning the great cities and temples erected by the Thutmosids and the Ramessides. The last Pharaoh to be mentioned at Kawa is Ramesses VII, at Napata Ramesses IX and at Buhen Ramesses XI. In the civil war which marked the end of the Twentieth Dynasty the office of viceroy of Kush virtually disappears, and Egypt's southern frontier withdraws to its original line at the First Cataract.

The Egyptian economy suddenly found itself in straits more serious than any the country had experienced since the period of the Hyksos. Under the successors of Ramesses III prices for grain shot up to five times what they had been during his reign. Granaries were empty and state workers discontented. One of the earliest records of a strike dates from the twenty-ninth year of Ramesses III, but others were to follow under his successors. The official transcript drawn up by the government scribe (now in the Turin museum) describes how the necropolis workmen at Thebes, whose wages were two weeks in arrears, refused to do any further work: " 'We are hungry! Sixteen days have gone by in the month. . . .' " When questioned further by a fact-finding body of officials, they explained, " 'It's because of hunger and thirst that we have been driven to this. There is no clothing, no oil, no fish, no vegetables. Send to Pharaoh our good lord concerning them. . . .' And the provisions of the month were given them on this day."

About two generations after this strike the descendants of these workmen took to graverobbing; and for decades nothing the authorities did could abate the wholesale pillaging of royal tombs. None of the illustrious names of New Kingdom history deterred the thieves. Thutmose III, Amenophis III, Ramesses II, Ramesses III, and a host of others were disturbed in their eternal slumber by profane hands carting off their valuables *en masse*. Many of the grave robbers were apprehended, and the transcripts of their trials have survived on papyrus (some now in the British Museum). Punishment was draconian, involving at times brutal execution, but one senses official corruption and kick-backs. At length the priesthood was driven to trying to outwit the robbers by moving the royal mummies from tomb to tomb. But it was not until the coffins were secreted in a deep shaft at Deir el-Bahari in the 10th century B.C. that the royal corpses finally found rest. There they lay forgotten until accidentally discovered towards the close of the 19th century A.D. They now lie in the Cairo Museum.

The Dynastic Succession of the Twentieth Dynasty

The image Ramesses III presented to the world had two aspects. On the one hand he could legitimately paint himself in the guise of the saviour of Egypt, who had brought peace and prosperity back to his people. But on the other, he could not help going down in history as a greedy king with poor judgment, an image which may have something to do with the great inventory of temple holdings he undertook, and which now constitutes the Great Harris

Papyrus. Whether this adverse reputation was deserved or not, Ramesses's blunders cost his family dearly. At some point late in his reign, and for reasons not known to us, the king set aside his legitimate and designated heir (M) and replaced him with another of his sons. The result was widespread resentment, especially in the harim (N–O), where the mother of the disqualified offspring hatched a plot against the king her husband. The conspiracy spread and eventually took in part of the palace staff and the garrison in Nubia, which was supposed to invade Egypt at the appropriate moment. The assassination was timed to take place during the Theban festival of Opet in his thirty-second year, when the king and his entourage would be in temporary residence in the palace of his Theban mortuary temple (P–Q). We are not sure whether the plot succeeded as planned, although Ramesses did, in fact, die soon after; but the new king, Ramesses IV, acted quickly and rounded up all the conspirators. The papyrus transcripts of the treason trials show that most of the conspirators were condemned to death, although some were permitted to commit suicide. Even though the intended insurrection was quelled, the memory of the suffering divided the royal family for generations to come, and resulted in a feuding which did no credit to the royal line, and may have seriously drained the family's energies.

The troubles of the times find an explanation, at least in part, in a breakdown in authority and administration. The successors of Ramesses III, all named after him, were a worthless lot, and the sweeping generalization of Diodorus is essentially correct: "After Remphis died kings succeeded to the throne . . . who were confirmed sluggards and devoted only to indulgence and luxury. Consequently in the priestly record no costly building of theirs nor any deed worthy of historical record is handed down in connexion with them. . . ." A passing remark about Ramesses XI, the last of the line, in a contemporary private letter gives a good impression of the kings' reputation for utter ineffectiveness: "Of whom indeed is Pharaoh the master? . . . Do not be concerned with what he may do!"

The Priesthood of Amun and the Army

The one "vested interest" that ostensibly stood to benefit by the decline in royal power was the priesthood of Amun-re. By the beginning of the Twentieth Dynasty the estate connected with the temple was fabulously wealthy. Seventy-five per cent of all temple land (itself perhaps one-fifth to one-quarter of the arable land in Egypt) was owned by this god, who could also count on the services of almost 100,000 priests and tenant farmers. The Thebaid was rapidly turning into the "House of Amun," an adjunct to Egypt proper, with a species of sovereignty association.

Over the whole the First Prophet of Amun presided. Since the office was such a potential threat to the monarchy, the kings of the New Kingdom had, as we have already seen, been careful to retain control of appointments, and thus prevent the upper echelons of the priesthood from becoming hereditary. But somehow the incumbent during the early years of the Twentieth Dynasty had managed to coax from the king the honor of passing the function to his son, and when the latter died a second son was allowed to succeed him. It must have looked very much as though this second son, Amenophis by name, was on the verge of laying claim to even higher dignities than priesthood (R).

Curiously enough, however, the real threat came not from the priesthood but from the army. For all his seeming independence, Amenophis was very much a "king's man"; and his identity with Ramesside aspirations may well have accounted for the Theban revolt against him, during the reign of Ramesses XI the last king of the Twentieth Dynasty, probably shortly after 1100 B.C. In a series of moves and countermoves which, unfortunately, remain obscure because they are alluded to only in passing remarks in business and administrative documents, the viceroy of Nubia, Paynehsi, and the army stationed there marched north into the Thebaid and wrought havoc as far north as the Fayum. Perhaps in order to restore order Ramesses XI was persuaded—Amun confirmed it by an oracle—to appoint two "officers," in modern jargon "trouble-shooters," Nesubanebdjed for the north and a military officer, Herihor, for the south. Amenophis survived the incursion of the viceroy, as he states somewhat cryptically in his auto-biography, but disappeared soon after; and in his place Herihor was appointed to the high-priesthood of Amun. This Machiavellian figure, certainly of plebeian origin, lost no time in gaining complete control of the army, priesthood, and civil administration in the Thebaid, and presently the control of the Nubian provinces as well. Within two decades by sheer ruthless-ness he had subverted Thebes, and had taken the cartouche. It fell to Herihor's lot to deco-rate the peristyle hall of the last great building of the New Kingdom still surviving, the temple of Khonsu at Thebes (S). Here we see him in royal regalia, presiding over festivities as if he were Ramesses himself.

Long before this the Ramesside rulers had abandoned Thebes for their favorite northern residence, Pi-Ramesses in the north-eastern Delta; and it is doubtful whether Ramesses XI ever came south, even for festivals. Such a move could scarcely forestall their inevitable doom. When, after about thirty years of rule Ramesses XI died and was succeeded, not by his son—he may not have had one—but by the same "trouble-shooter," Nesubanebdjed, he had appointed a decade earlier, Ramesside rule had come to an ignominious end. The last royal tomb in the Valley of the Kings stands empty and undecorated: the last royal tie between the royal family and Thebes had been broken.

The Tanite Period: The *De Facto* Division of Egypt

An air of legitimacy attached itself to Nesubanebdjed and his descendants. He had come to power under the aegis of the late king and may well have married his daughter; at any rate he had no qualms about calling himself king. Times were hard, and Nile levels had fallen. As a result the harbor at Pi-Ramesses could no longer be used, and the great city was abandoned. Plans were already in place to transfer the capital and royal residence to a site thirty miles to the north-east to a place called "the field of the storm." Using statues (T), obelisks (U), blocks (V), and columns from Pi-Ramesses, which was razed to the ground in the process, a new city, "Tanis" (Storm-town), was erected on the Tanitic branch of the Nile near the shores of Lake Menzaleh. Much of the building was undoubtedly accomplished by Nesubanebdjed himself, who imagined the new city of recycled blocks as a clone of Thebes: Tanis too boasted temples to the Theban triad of Amun, Mut, and Khonsu, and the priestly titles mimicked those of Thebes. But ties between the royal house and the old Thebes had finally been severed. No longer would the kings' mummies be transported south for burial in the Valley of the Kings. Now, innovating under the pressure of reduced circumstances, Nesubanebdjed and his succes-sors set aside part of the great temple *temenos* at Tanis for their own modest burials; and there, under the shadow of the god himself, their interments would enjoy eternal protection. For four centuries this unlikely spot was to be both residence and cemetery of the kings of Egypt.

Nesubanebdjed and his successors comprise Manetho's Twenty-first Dynasty (c. 1075–935 B.C.). They took the full panoply of kingship, and their regnal years were used as a dating frame throughout all Egypt over which they nominally at least laid claim. In fact their control of the south was somewhat curtailed.

Few of Herihor's successors followed their ancestor's example in violating tradition by usurping royal protocol; and those who did show the cartouche, as he had done, did so only in the context of the cult. But all his other powers they closely guarded. In name high-priests of Amun, in fact they were military dictators of the Nile Valley from Asyut to the First Cataract. How they really viewed their nominal suzerains in the northland it is difficult to say; certainly the relations between the two families were often cordial, not to say friendly, for intermarriage was not uncommon. Despite this amity and the peaceful conditions it brought, a sort of twilight had descended upon Thebes. Excavations in the domestic quarter of the city prove that, virtually on the morrow of Ramesses XI's death, villas were abandoned (W) and the populated area shrank drastically. There was no money to build. In place of the boldly cut and grandiose reliefs of imperial times, the Temple of Amun can boast only timid, one-columned texts recording restorations, as its mighty buildings fell into disrepair and squatters moved in to reside within its courts. The city's day was past. No more would a royal house reside within her gates, or claim her as a place of origin. For four centuries the once thriving metropolis would eke out its existence as a provincial town. Thebes' only connection with her illustrious past was the cult and priesthood of the imperial god Amun. That organization continued to thrive. But it had now turned in upon itself, as a small number of large families had monopolized key priestly offices, and had transformed themselves into a social and political elite. In the absence of a royal family, this "family compact" constituted the pinnacle of the social pyramid. Since scions of these families could no longer satisfy their longing for status by insisting upon their close relationship to the king, they had perforce to boast of something else. Long lineage, in fact, now becomes the "status symbol," and beginning in the Twenty-first Dynasty the genealogy becomes an indispensable part of every personal statue inscription.

Although some of the Tanite royal tombs have been excavated, very little is known about the political history of the dynasty. Mention of Nesubanebdjed's merchant fleet in one text might lead us to classify him as a "merchant prince"; but if international commerce was indeed his interest, it involved much more difficult negotiations than his imperial forebears had found necessary. For the Asiatic provinces were now lost, and the descendants of former vassals proved uncooperative. When an emissary of the high-priest of Amun, one Wenamun, with Nesubanebdjed's blessing travelled to Byblos to procure wood for ship-building, he found himself alone in hostile territory. Naïvely, perhaps, he had expected to find a Canaan which was still subservient to Egypt, as under the Eighteenth Dynasty, a sort of "India" in which the "Englishman" was still treated with respect. Instead he found an "India" of the post-1947 era. His demands for cedar were treated with contempt. When robbed in the coastal town of Dor, Wenamun found himself unable to obtain the cooperation of the local prince in locating the thief. At Byblos the king refused to see Wenamun for weeks, and when at last he agreed to grant him an audience, he demanded credentials and payment in full before cutting the trees. Wenamun pointed out that the king's ancestors, vassals of Egypt all, had willingly despatched their tribute of timber. The prince replied, "Of course they did! And if you pay me something, I will do it! . . . Now if the ruler of Egypt were my lord, and if I were his vassal, he would not have to cause gifts of gold and silver to be brought, saying, 'Perform the business of Amun!' . . . But I am not your vassal, nor the vassal of him who sent you! If I cry out to the Lebanons heaven opens, and the timber lies here upon the shore of the sea. . . . What is this silly trip they have had you make?"

Further Readings

On Egypt, the Near East, and the Aegean see P. P. Betancourt, *The History of Minoan Pottery*, Princeton, 1985; M. Bietak (ed.), *The Synchronisation of Civilisations in the Eastern Mediterranean in the Second Millennium B.C.*, Vienna, 2000; S. Bourke, J. P. Descoeudres (eds.), *Trade, Contact, and Movement of Peoples in the Eastern Mediterranean*, Sydney, 1995; E. H. Cline, *Sailing the Wine-dark Sea: International Trade and the Late Bronze Age Aegean*, Oxford, 1994; W. V. Davies (ed.), *Egypt, the Aegean, and the Levant*, London, 1995; O. Dickinson, *the Aegean Bronze Age*, Cambridge, 1994; N. H. Gale (ed.), *Bronze Age Trade in the Mediterranean*, Jonsered, 1991; G. L. Huxley, *Achaeans and Hittites*, Oxford, 1960; C. Lambrou-Phillipson, *Hellenorientalia: the Near Eastern Presence in the Bronze Age Aegean ca. 3000 to 1100 B.C.*, Goteborg, 1990; M. Liverani, *Prestige and Interest: International Relations in the Near East ca. 1600–1100 B.C.*, Padua, 1990; S. Wachsmann, *Aegeans in the Theban Tombs*, Louvain, 1987; D. Warburton, *Egypt and the Near East: Politics in the Bronze Age*, Paris, 2001.

The problems connected with the Sea-Peoples have given rise to seemingly endless debate. The following is a representation of the main points of view: T. and M. Dothan, *Peoples of the Sea: The Search for the Philistines*, New York, 1992; R. Drewes, *The End of the Bronze Age*, Princeton, 1993; A. Leahy (ed.), *Libya and Egypt c. 1300–750*, London, 1990; O. Margalith, *The Sea Peoples in the Bible*, Wiesbaden, 1994; E. Oren (ed.), *The Sea Peoples and Their World: A Reassessment*, Philadelphia, 2000; N. K. Sandars, *The Sea Peoples: Warriors of the Ancient Mediterranean*, London, 1985; S. Wachsmann, *Seagoing Ships and Seamanship in the Bronze Age Levant*, London, 1998; W. A. Ward, M. S. Joukowsky (eds.), *The Crisis Years: From Beyond the Danube to the Tigris*, Dubuque, 1992.

On the decline of Egypt and its empire, see M. G. Hasel, *Domination and Resistance: Egyptian Military Activity in the Souther Levant 1300–1185 B.C.*, Leiden, 1998; C. R. Higginbotham, *Egyptianization and Elite Emulation in Ramesside Palestine*, Leiden, 2000; J. J. Janssen, *Commodity Prices from the Ramessid Period*, Leiden, 1975; C. Manassa, *The Great Karnak Inscription of Merneptah: Grand Strategy in the 13th Century B.C.*, New Haven, 2003; A. J. Peden, *The Reign of Ramesses IV*, Warminster, 1994; *idem, Egyptian Historical Inscriptions of the Twentieth Dynasty*, Jonsered, 1994; T. E. Peet, *The Great Tomb Robberies of the Twentieth Egyptian Dynasty*, Oxford, 1930; D. B. Redford, *Egypt and Canaan in the New Kingdom*, Beersheva, 1990; S. Redford, *The Harim Conspiracy: The Murder of Ramesses III*, Dekalb, 2002; E. F. Wente, *Late Ramesside Letters*, Chicago, 1967.

CHAPTER THIRTEEN

The Libyan Kings (Dyn. 22–24)

—————————— ψ ——————————

While contemporaries may have been slow to realize it, by the last century of the Second Millennium B.C. the Ramesside age was slipping irretrievably away. The land now displayed a new geopolitical configuration, and a new social fabric, thinner and less comfortable, was being woven by strange forces. In violation of Egypt's age-old and haughty tendency towards ethnic isolation, she was now being forced to play host to a new foreign enclave.

The Meshwesh

Although the threat of the Sea Peoples had melted away with the dissolution of their coalition—Egypt's northern frontiers now harbored hostile though relatively powerless remnants of the movement—the pressure of population from the west continued without let-up. From the death of Merenptah until Ramesses III's fifth year the Libyan tribes enjoyed unrestricted access to the western oases and the western Delta, and even two severe defeats at the hands of a revitalized Egyptian army had not altogether stemmed the flood. On the morrow of Ramesses III's victories over them (his fifth and eleventh years), Libyan enclaves are still present in Egypt. Most are now docile and acceptable. A goodly number have been pressed into military service, and, with their wives and children (all branded with Pharaoh's name), are settled in encampments on the outskirts of major towns. The major Libyan tribe, the Meshwesh, are centered upon Herakleopolis and the Fayum, where a military establishment had been in existence since the time of Ramesses II, with another group ensconced in the Delta near Sebennytos. Lesser tribal units are found on the west of the Delta and near Sais (the Labu), and upriver in the Thebaid (the Mahaswen).

By and large the Libyan elements in Egypt kept to themselves. Intermarriage is attested for the upper class, but the Libyan rank and file probably resisted melding with the Egyptian population. Ramesses III had placed Egyptian commanders over the settlements, and tried to make them learn Egyptian; but had also allowed the native chieftains to continue to exercise a certain degree of authority. Rightly or wrongly they initially gained a reputation as marauders who had to be watched closely. To the end of their hegemony over Egypt the Libyans could be recognized as a distinct ethnic component of the population in the Nile Valley, intermarriage being sometimes attested, though not common. Possibly, in spite of Ramesses III's efforts, they retained their own language in certain regions; certainly the Libyan names can be instantly recognized. Their distinctive costume—long gown cut away in front, feathers in the hair—must have made them a colorful sight in the marketplace or temple, at least during the early period of their occupation.

Towards the close of the Twentieth Dynasty the chief of the Meshwesh, one Buyuwawa, had settled in the environs of Herakleopolis in Middle Egypt. Six generations later the descendants of this obscure barbarian had managed to ally themselves with every important center of power in the land. The contemporary chief of the Meshwesh, Sheshonk, was commander-in-chief of Pharaoh's armed forces, his sister had married the high priest of Memphis, and shortly two of his grandsons were to marry into the Tanite royal family and one of the priestly families at Thebes. At Pharaoh's behest a statue and mortuary cult was established at Abydos for Sheshonk's father, Namlot. With connections such as these one may scarcely wonder that the great chief of the Meshwesh, Sheshonk, the great-great-great-great-great-grandson of Buyuwawa, should have secured his own appointment as heir apparent from Psusennes II, the last king of the Tanite Twenty-first Dynasty. And when the latter duly passed away, apparently without male issue, Sheshonk assumed the crown and reigned in Tanis. In the king-list tradition reflected in Manetho, he is founder of Dynasty 22.

Apart from a brief flurry of energetic domestic and foreign activity under Sheshonk I and his son Osorkon I, the two centuries of rule of this family accomplished little and proved devoid of imagination and innovation. Even though all Egyptians realized that they were now ruled by aliens, they continued to ascribe to the Libyan rulers all the titles and epithets due the Horus-king. Curiously, the only peculiarity of character mentioned by contemporaries is the proclivity of Libyan kings to fall into uncontrollable rages.

The practice of New Kingdom monarchs of carving triumphal stelae and relief scenes to promulgate their accomplishments was abandoned after Sheshonk I. Except for the latter's vast court at Karnak (of which the meter-high cornice blocks attest the size) (A–B), a gate in the same temple (C), a lost temple at Memphis, and pedestrian work at Bubastis and Tanis, the nine monarchs of the Twenty-second Dynasty were singularly lethargic in the sphere of construction. Donations, some of substantial size, continued to be bestowed upon the temples, but the kings, the donors, seem otherwise faceless. So seldom were they attested by relief, statue, or building, that in later centuries the oral tradition of the masses, reliant as it was on aetiological interpretation of public monuments, completely forgot about the Libyans, and when Herodotus visited Egypt in the 5th century B.C. his dragoman's account of Egyptian history followed Rhampsinitus (Ramesses III) with the Twenty-fourth Dynasty Pharaohs.

Even today scholars often find themselves lacking in the basic factual evidence necessary to construct something as simple as a king-list for the Twenty-second Dynasty. How many kings named "Sheshonk" were there? Should we introduce into the formal numbering system kings who took the cartouche yet whose years were not used for dating? Did the dynasty live in Tanis? But what of the Twenty-third Dynasty? It undoubtedly overlapped with the Twenty-second, but where was its place of residence, the Delta or Thebes? These and a host of other problems have produced a (sometimes acrimonious) debate through which we shall try to navigate.

Egypt and Asia in the Iron Age

By the mid-10th century B.C., the bleak centuries of the Early Iron Age had drawn to a close, and the Levant was well on its way to recovery economically and politically. The heirs of the destruction wrought by the Sea Peoples were in the main new-comers who had not yet made their mark. They had played no part in the economic and social decline of the palatine states of Late Bronze Canaan, a decline which, as much as the Sea Peoples, accounts for their ignominious end. The place of the defunct Hittite empire was now occupied by new groups from the Russian steppes, the Purukuzzi (= Phrygians) and the Mushki (= Biblical "Meshech"). The vacuum in north Syria on the morrow of the annihilation of Alalakh and Ugarit was gradually filled by the shattered survivors of the once-great Hittite empire; and by the 10th century strong "Neo-Hittite" states were appearing at Carchemish, Arpad, and Samal. Further south, in central and Coele-Syria, the Arameans, a West-Semitic-speaking people, had settled along the Orontes and eastward towards the fringes of the desert. Their incursions into territories adjacent to the Tigris caused great irritation to the kingdom of Assyria. In Damascus in central Syria they founded a powerful kingdom, later to become one of the bulwarks against the advance of the Assyrian empire. In Palestine the sea coast had been occupied, as we have seen, by the Philistines and Tjekel; but the highlands and the Jordan Valley fell to a new tribal group, speaking a West Semitic tongue akin to Amorite, and known to the Egyptians under the loose designation Shasu, "wanderers." One clan of these transhumants, called the *Shasu Yahu,* had inhabited the region of Edom in Transjordan from as early as the 15th century. During the reign of Sety I they had begun to move westward across the Negeb and the Jordan into the highlands of Palestine, where under Merenptah they make their appearance as the *Benē Yisrā'el,* the "Israelites."

The only ethnic element in the Iron Age Levant which had its roots in the older civilization of the Late Bronze Age was located along the Mediterranean coast. Here the old Canaanite enclaves centered in the sea-faring states of Arvad, Byblos, Beyrut, Tyre, and Sidon had managed to weather the onslaught of the Sea Peoples, and in the 10th century were about to embark on a period of daring maritime exploitation, trade, and settlement. The Egyptians had earlier termed the peoples of the Syrian littoral "the Fenkhu," and the Greeks knew of them for their trade in the murex shell-fish, the "phoinix." From one or possibly both of these terms came the name "Phoenician," which the Greeks applied to these strange sea-farers from east over the sea.

Egyptian relations with west Asia under the Libyans were desultory and half-hearted. The traditional links with Byblos and its neighbors were maintained, and statues of Sheshonk I and Osorkon I duly found their way to local shrines. But the Phoenicians could no longer be termed Egyptian subjects. In the south, adjacent to the Egyptian frontier, the Israelites had lately created a polity, thanks to the efforts of an energetic sheikh called David, centered upon a mountain fort named Jerusalem. Solomon his son nurtured monarchic pretensions, but little is known of his reign. Later folklore was to transform him into a legendary figure of wisdom, a sort of Hebrew "Sesostris," who had married Pharaoh's daughter and traded down the Red Sea. If true, this would mean that Solomon had allied himself through marriage with the Tanite court at the close of the Twenty-first Dynasty. The split in the incipient polity of the Hebrews, which followed the death of Solomon, prompted Sheshonk I to intervene militarily; and both the Negeb and hill country of Palestine were devastated by Egyptian forces. Once again, but briefly and without the prospect of repetition, there was seen in the streets of Memphis and Thebes the booty from a foreign campaign in Asia. In the 9th century, however, Egypt became less interested and less effective in dabbling in the affairs of Palestine and Syria. Only Osorkon II, whose expected involvement in Levantine affairs had been prophesied at his birth, exhibited much interest in Asia. Calling himself "the smiter of the Montiu (Asiatics)," Osorkon despatched a token force of one thousand men to the great coalition headed by Damascus which attempted to stem the Assyrian advance at Karkar on the Orontes in 853 B.C. Later, when Damascene fortunes seemed to be on the wane, the wily Pharaoh attempted to ingratiate himself with Shalmaneser III, the Assyrian king, by sending him a present of camels, hippopotamoi, rhinoceros, antelopes, and monkeys.

Such posturings were of little effect, but to their own ultimate chagrin, the states of Palestine and Syria still clung naïvely to the belief in Egypt's legendary might. Both Israel and Judah, the two kingdoms into which the Hebrew community had split after Sheshonk I's attack, looked south to the Nile for support. Thus the history of the 9th and 8th centuries witnesses a continual parade of delegates from the Israelite and Phoenician cities to the royal residence at Tanis, seeking aid against the encroaching Assyrian empire. Trade fared little better. The great days of the New Kingdom, when goods and people from all over Syria flowed into Egypt, and Egyptian manufactures, ideas, and technology spread outward to the north, were forever at an end. Inevitably some luxury items from Egypt, mainly in the form of royal presents, found their way into Samaria and Jerusalem; and the Phoenician cities relayed a trade in rich manufactures of Egyptian origin all over the Mediterranean and as far west as Spain. Moreover strong Egyptian influence begins now to make its appearance in Phoenician art motifs, though slightly transformed and re-interpreted in the process, in work in ivory, metal, and stone. But the presence of these souvenirs of past Egyptian glories in the Levant were the result of Levantine, not Egyptian, initiative.

The Revolt of Thebes

For Egypt was stagnating under dull-witted and repressive leadership. The Libyan rulers had generated a dislike among the native Egyptians that was especially strong in the Thebaid (Thebes had in fact withheld for a time recognition of Sheshonk I's kingship, calling him merely "chief," and for the rest of his reign that king had been at pains to placate the southern city). In order to keep close watch on the south Sheshonk had appointed one of his sons, Auputa, to be high-priest of Amun, and each Libyan king thereafter usually followed suit. But it was a purely military appointment, and the incumbent was not obliged to reside in Thebes; in fact most preferred Tehneh, a fortress-town in Middle Egypt, closer to the Fayum and Tanis. Thus, to the insult of foreign domination, the Thebans found added the ignominy of "absentee directorship"! Under Takelot II, about 834 B.C., the inevitable blow fell: Thebes broke into open rebellion. After an initial reversal, the rebels once again triumphed, and now the uprising began to spread. For a generation the disturbances continued, and a contemporary observer might well have opined that a third Theban "war of liberation" was under way, comparable to the rebellions of Dynasties 11 and 17.

But it was not to be. Towards the end of the 9th century the Libyan forces, under Takelot's son Osorkon, who had been appointed to the high-priesthood, overwhelmed Thebes. Excavation has revealed destruction levels of ash in some of the public buildings dated by carbon-14 to the end of the 9th century (D). Osorkon punished the offenders barbarously (E), committing some to death by burning, and even stormed into Amun's inner shrine and gave the god a dressing down! Order was restored. It proved, however, a Pyrrhic victory. Egypt was exhausted and the Libyan house discredited; never again would an Osorkon or a Takelot lord it over the entire country.

The Decline of Libyan Hegemony

By the end of the 9th century B.C. the Egyptian state was showing unmistakable signs of fragmentation. On the morrow of the rebellions, to save itself, the Tanite House had implanted military governors, often sons or cousins of the king, in the key Delta centers, and by the beginning of the 8th century these had become powerful "barons" with the title "Great Chief of the Me(shwesh)". Although lip service was duly paid the king in Tanis, and his regnal years used by the business community, the Great Chiefs of the Me were virtually independent sovereigns exercising civil and military authority over their city and its environs. Through his sons, who were usually appointed "generals," and the mayors of local towns, the Great Chief effectually controlled the manpower and resources of the district. Since the king had perforce to rely upon the Great Chiefs for the manpower required by any major projects, military or civil, the royal house found itself at the mercy of parochial interests. And since the Great Chiefs often displayed an amazingly narrow self-interest, the Tanite monarch usually found himself without men and without material.

As the Twenty-second Dynasty grew progressively weaker in Tanis, royal prerogatives began to exert an increasing attraction over other power wielders in the realm. In the process the royal ideology of the Horus-king suffered dilution. Piankhy, the Twenty-fifth Dynasty king of Napata (see below), spoke in one of his inscriptions of the type of king made by the gods and a second type made by government leaders. The former was essentially a priest-king, the latter a political junta-leader. Pharaoh had always in theory played the role of celebrant of the cult wherever it was performed, i.e. where any god possessed a cult seat. In the Late Period when the pharaonic monarchy was at a low ebb, this fiction tended to impose on the chief priest at a major cult center the need and the right to masquerade as royalty within the confines of his temple. Herihor and Paynodgem of the Twenty-first Dynasty had already exemplified this development. During the first half of the 8th century B.C. four major cult centers in Middle and Lower Egypt threw up leaders who adopted the cartouche, and who in three cases passed on the prerogative to their offspring. Bubastis, Leontopolis, and Herakleopolis had enjoyed historical connections with the Libyan royal house, the divine denizen of the first, Bast, being considered the progenitress of many a Libyan pharaoh, on a par with Isis. Hermopolis up-river was also ruled by a succession of kings, but the circumstances under which it became a "kingdom" are obscure.

The Bubastite royal house (in Manetho Dynasty 23) founded by a Petubastis who took power shortly before 800 B.C., has posed problems of identification and location. The evidence, scant though it is, suggests that it may have been distantly related to the Twenty-second, Tanite, Dynasty; certainly the royal onomasticon is familiar with the standard Libyan onomasticon, featuring "Osorkon" and "Takelot." Manetho unequivocally locates the Twenty-third Dynasty in the Delta, and assigns it four rulers; yet most of the inscribed material from the dynasty comes from Thebes. One of its members, Osorkon (III), may have even been buried in the Theban necropolis (although it is equally possible that the "Osorton" in question was the first of the name). As to the number of rulers, some modern scholars persist in adding additional names from scattered sources; but none of them can be connected with known members of the dynasty. The fact of its prominence in the Theban inscribed record probably has more to do with the esteem in which the Thebans held the members of the Twenty-third Dynasty, through the person of one of its princesses, Shepenwepet I, whom her father, Osorkon III, had appointed Divine Worshiper of Amun (see below).

Although Egypt around 750 B.C. was partitioned among over a dozen separate principalities, jurisdictions were not territorially protectionist. Movement of goods and individuals between and through the local bailiwicks was permitted by local authorities. All rulers with royal pretensions employed their own regnal years as systems of dating, and the business community in those parts of Egypt which recognized them would date its documents accordingly. If commercial relations existed with several principalities, multiple dating systems would be employed, necessitating equational datings (i.e. "Regnal year x of king A corresponds to regnal year y of king B"). The two great religious centers of Memphis and Thebes helped to confer a legitimacy which the now discredited Libyan dynasts could not. The priests of Ptah in Memphis presided over the rites associated with the sacred Apis bull, a deity rapidly rising to the status of a national god. Cared for like a king during life, a deceased bull was laid away in the subterranean "Serapeum" at Saqqara with great pomp. The ruler whom the priests graciously condescended to allow to conduct the obsequies for a deceased bull, or even simply to be mentioned in the accompanying funerary stela, was duly honored by having his name entered in the king-list. The priests of Amun of Thebes, a city bruised by the rebellion, held out the honor to northern dynasts of having their daughters accepted as chantresses or priestesses within the divine cult.

Egyptian Society in the 8th Century B.C.

The "tribalism" of the Libyans was their own somewhat dubious contribution to the Egyptian body social. Fighting men continued to owe allegiance to their local chief, and in return to receive a small parcel of land for the upkeep of themselves and their families. Although developed by the 8th century into a slightly more sophisticated system approximating a sort of feudalism, the social organization of Libyan Egypt had a decidedly adverse effect on the inhabitants of the country. For it merely abetted a trend towards class rigidity which had been present since Dynasty 21, and was later to impress Greek writers as an illusory caste system.

If you force everyone to follow in father's footsteps, everyone's horizon is going to shrink. To take up father's job will usually mean that one's movements are restricted to one's ancestral environs, i.e. the home town; and more and more in the First Millennium one finds the nome or township looming large in contemporary texts. What was necessity to begin with soon became a virtue: to remain at home is right and good, to wander abroad dangerous and wanton. The Wisdom Books of the last seven centuries of the First Millennium echo the advice: "Do not stay in a district in which you have no people (of your own)," says Onkhsheshonky, ". . . do not let your son marry a wife from another village." "Be on your guard against a woman from abroad," is the advice of Anii; ". . . do not express your whole heart to a stranger." The political uncertainties of the period caused provincial society to turn in upon itself, to unite itself for stability and protection. It is no surprise that the books of wisdom written in the Late Period reflect the atmosphere of a small town, and are intended for members of small, agricultural communities.

There were economic ramifications, too, to the new provincialism. For what we might term the middle and upper classes it became customary to devote all or a substantial portion of their land to the local temple. By the deed the temple would eventually possess the land, but while the erstwhile owner lived he would enjoy the usufruct of it. Whatever the precise origin of this practice, one senses an uncertainty on the part of private land-owners as to their ability to pass on a tract of ancestral land and keep it within the family.

Those who clearly benefited from donations of land were the priests. Classical authors considered them the uppermost class in the state, and thought they had a stranglehold on the monarchy and society. In the sacerdotal phenomenon of the Late Period we are in fact dealing with a hereditary group, avid of the stipends derived from food-offerings in the temples in which they served, who jealously guarded and transmitted to their sons their priestly functions. When the kingship had been the dominant force in Egyptian politics, priests were proud of their relationship to the royal family, and boasted about it on their monuments. It gave them a place in society and a sense of security. But with the withdrawal of kingship to the Delta (Dynasty 21), and the gradual weakening of that institution, the priesthood found the social framework in which they had realized an identity and a security something which no longer existed. Now they fell back on the glories of their illustrious ancestry as a source of support for their position in society. A priest would now include, in the dedicatory inscription on his cube-statue (F), the names of a long line of ancestors with their titles, and his pride would increase if their titles were the same as his. The view was backward; the tone was conservative.

Times were hard and policing ineffective and weak. The typical landscape of the Tanite period focuses upon the walled fortification, manned by a garrison, and providing a haven for local inhabitants from marauders. Letters from one of these forts, el-Hibeh (G–H), dating to the 11th century, reveals how risky it was to travel outside the protection of the fort. The king's writ was virtually non-existent, and robbery and kidnapping would go unpunished.

Further Readings

To some extent the Tanite period, or the "Third Intermediate Period," as it is sometimes called, has suffered through a lack of popular introductions in English. The best works are M. Bierbrier, *The Late New Kingdom in Egypt,* Warminster, 1982; K. A. Kitchen, *The Third Intermediate Period in Egypt,* Warminster, 1985; A. Leahy (ed.), *Libya and Egypt c. 1200–750,* London, 1990; K. Mysiliwiec, *First Millennium B.C.E.: The Twilight of Ancient Egypt,* Ithaca, 2000.

On civil disorder and the Theban rebellion, see R. A. Caminos, *The Chronicle of Prince Osorkon,* Rome, 1958; also *idem, A Tale of Woe,* Oxford, 1977.

On the art of the period, see R. A. Fazzini, *Egypt, Dynasty XXII–XXV (Iconography of Religions),* Leiden, 1988; K. Mysiliwiec, *Royal Portraiture of the Dynasties XXI–XXX,* Mainz, 1988.

On the Wisdom Texts of the First Millennium B.C., see S. R. K. Glanville, *The Instructions of Onchsheshonqy,* London, 1955; M. Lichtheim, *Late Egyptian Wisdom Literature in the International Context,* Göttingen, 1983.

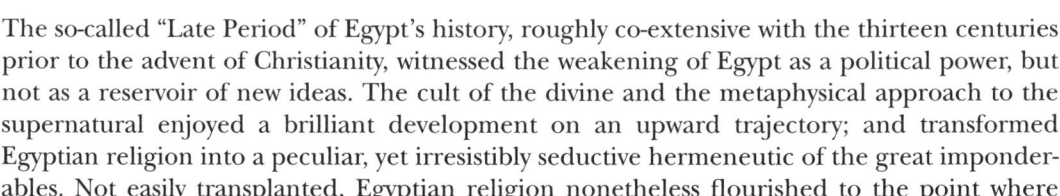

CHAPTER FOURTEEN
The Evolution of the Belief System of Egypt from the End of the New Kingdom to Christian Times

ψ

The so-called "Late Period" of Egypt's history, roughly co-extensive with the thirteen centuries prior to the advent of Christianity, witnessed the weakening of Egypt as a political power, but not as a reservoir of new ideas. The cult of the divine and the metaphysical approach to the supernatural enjoyed a brilliant development on an upward trajectory; and transformed Egyptian religion into a peculiar, yet irresistibly seductive hermeneutic of the great imponderables. Not easily transplanted, Egyptian religion nonetheless flourished to the point where Greeks, Romans, and Asiatics alike succumbed to its mesmeric qualities.

The Syncretism of the Amun Theology

"All gods are three: Amun, Re, and Ptah, and none other. 'Hidden' in his name as Amun, he is Re in face, and his body is Ptah. Their cities on earth abide for ever—Thebes, Heliopolis, Memphis—eternally." The syncretism of the Late Period is explicit. The movement of Akhenaten had been rigorously monotheistic, and had *ipso facto* tried to exclude and annihilate the plurality of deity in its attempt to achieve monotheism. The theology of Amun affirmed the essential unity of the god-head by stressing a triune being, of which all gods were viewed as mere manifestations. Local avatars of the supernatural might be qualified as "Ptah/Amun/Horus (or the like) of . . ." followed by a toponym, much as Mary appears throughout the Christian world; but, while the emanation offered new creation without number, the underlying numinous reality was singular. This way of looking at the cosmos, which had its genesis long ago in the cult of Ptah (see below), provided a sophisticated counter-blast to the simplistic views of Akhenaten, and now dominated the thinking of the upper echelons of the priesthood. In its pre-occupation with mythological symbolism as an outward sign of a spiritual truth, the Amun theology proved to be a harbinger of the intellectual exercises of later Hellenistic Alexandria.

But the cult of Amun was something more than the center for proto-metaphysical specu-lation: it was a rallying point for native Egyptian nationalism in the south. The removal of the royal residence to Tanis and the growing antipathy between the Thebans and the Libyan kings could not have left Amun unaffected. One senses a process of "levelling down" of the Amun phenomenon: gone are the days when conquering pharaohs reg-ularly and without fail deposited vast quantities of booty in the coffers of the king of the gods. True, Amun was to be championed by the Sudanese kings of the 7th century, but to be the patron deity of a foreign group made him considerably less than the great head of the pantheon of the high New Kingdom. The Thebans saw in the cult of Amun their last chance of realizing a dream of re-uniting the country under native leadership. Only the southland was uncontaminated by for-eigners and their strange ways; only the south had remained true to Amun while the rest of the country drifted into apostasy. It is no surprise that the rebellions against the Libyans in the 9th century were led by Thebes. Later, when the role of foreign villain was filled by Assyria, again it was Thebes that provided haven for refugees and a staging area for expeditions to re-take the Delta. Finally, on the eve of the extinction of the ancient Egyptian culture, it was from behind the ramparts of the Theban temenos that the last surviving rebels fought it out with the Greek troops of the Ptolemies.

As Amun's star slowly sank towards the horizon, those of other deities began to rise. At Thebes Montu, the old hawk-headed war-god whose worship antedated Amun's, enjoyed a resurgence from the 7th century on; and at Karnak the plethora of Osiride chapels (A–B) which from the outgoing 9th century begins to enclose the Amun-temple on south, east, and north bespeaks the increasing popularity of the god in question. In the north it was Re that stood to benefit most from the political situation, at least in theory; nevertheless he too was on the wane by Ptolemaic times, and in the 1st century B.C. his temple at Heliopolis was derelict (C). Through her patronage of the Libyan Twenty-second and Twenty-third Dynasties, the cat-god-dess Bast of Bubastis grew wealthy; and a little later during the 7th–6th centuries the promi-nence of Sais brought the mother-goddess Neith to prominence, and for a time her treasury emulated the status that Amun's had enjoyed seven centuries earlier.

When, from the 6th century on, the Greeks came into close contact with Egypt, the gods of the Nilotic land exerted a strong influence over them. The newcomers saw their own deities under different, and admittedly more ancient, guise in the vast Egyptian pantheon. Amun was Zeus, Geb Chronos, Neith Athene, Ptah Hephaestus, and so on. Beyond the assumption of a community of divine relation, however, the Greeks never adopted any cultic practices nor iconographic symbolism, developed within Egypt, for their own gods. Those settled within Egypt became enamored of Osiris and the members of his cycle (especially Isis), and under the Ptolemies their cult not only flourished within Egypt but was exported abroad to the larger Mediterranean world where under the Roman Empire it enjoyed a wide popularity. It was also from an Egyptian, specifically a priest of Neith of Sais, that the Greeks learned through

Solon of the "Atlantis" account, in all probability an euhemerized Egyptian myth of a cosmogonic or mortuary nature (see below).

Animal Worship

The feature of Egyptian religion which bewildered the Greeks and quite repelled the Romans was animal worship. The connection between animal and deity in ancient Egyptian religion is varied and complex, and its origins when sought out retreat into the mists of pre-history. Each temple usually kept one sacred animal within its precincts (D, E, F), a member of the species which the god was believed to have designated and/or inhabited as an avatar. Upon the death of the sacred beast it was given a sumptuous burial in a sarcophagus specially prepared (G). But while there is some indication of reverence shown to entire species in earlier times—the river bank at Mendes during the Twentieth Dynasty was the repository of myriads of pots each containing immature fish—the wholesale infatuation with animal cults is notably absent before the middle of the First Millennium B.C.

One important phenomenon, revealed by archaeology, sets off animal worship in the Late Period from its earlier stages, viz. the enormous animal cemeteries. Whole tracts of the necropoleis or sacred enclosures are now given over to the burial of entire species, whose members were thought to partake somehow of the divine essence of the deity with whom their kind was attached. The texts of the time solemnly prescribe "the procedure for beatifying (i.e. embalming) the limbs of the god (i.e. the animal in question) in the place of embalmment . . ."; and the most pious act a rich priest can perform is the careful interment of the beasts: "On one occasion many falcons were discovered," says one Djed-Hor of the 4th century B.C., "which had not been embalmed in the temple in the Chamber 'Seventy.' They were introduced into the place of embalmment and given (proper) burial . . . with unguent and fine cloth . . . and introduced into the (cemetery). . . ."

We can examine the animal cults in more detail through Greek eyes. Herodotus paints a vivid picture of the reverence for animals he witnessed in the 5th century B.C. "(Egyptians) are forbidden to sacrifice cows on the grounds that they are sacred to Isis . . . the Mendesians hold all goats in veneration, especially males whose keepers enjoy special honors . . . anyone who deliberately kills one of these animals is punished with death; if one is killed accidentally, the penalty is whatever the priests choose to impose; but for killing an ibis or a hawk the penalty is inevitably death. . . . Cats which have died are taken to Bubastis where they are embalmed and buried in sacred receptacles; dogs are buried also in sacred burial places in the towns where they belong. . . . Some Egyptians reverence the crocodile as a sacred beast; others do not, but treat it as an enemy. The strongest belief in its sanctity is to be found in Thebes and (the Fayum); in these places they keep one particular crocodile which they tame, putting rings made of glass or gold into its ears and bracelets around its front feet, and giving it special food and ceremonial offerings."

The Egyptians of the period are not exactly silent about why they display this curious type of reverence. In administrative texts from Saqqara the embalmed animals are specifically termed "gods"; and in a tax return of Roman times fishermen declare that they have avoided catching a certain species because they know such fish are the "images" of the god. The latter thus assumes the form of the supernal archetype, the animals themselves his clones, as it were.

The Personal Piety of the Masses

The deities thus far passed in review have been major, "powers of heaven" as they are called, served by large and influential priesthoods. What role could the masses of the population assume in the cults of such great cosmic forces? Truly the format of worship and cult performance left little room for a laity, and it is not surprising to find them increasingly excluded from the great shrines. The latter often displayed, at the door of an outer court, an inscription which forbade the common people entry any farther into the temple complex. Those so excluded are sometimes specified as those who have recently had intercourse, those with beards, people with uncut fingernails, the unwashed, women, Asiatics, those wearing woollen clothes, mourners, and the insane.

One can imagine, then, this profane mob still avid to witness the processionals in which the great state cults excelled, clustering around the outer gates waiting for the god's barque to appear. Such gates, beyond which the rank and file cannot proceed, are often called "the Gate Where the Plebeians Adore" in the Late Period. It was at these outer gates and pylons that colossal statues were usually set up (H), and monumental reliefs of king and gods carved. And it was often to these images and icons, fully visible from where they customarily stood, that the waiting people addressed their prayers and offered their worship; and in consequence such colossi often received the vernacular epithet "the great god who hears prayer."

But the masses also had a circle of divinities, of lesser standing than the great gods, who seemed closer to the people. These were the "protected images," within their small shrines located in the cities or countryside, and supported possibly by a local rich man. A New Kingdom letter allows a brief glimpse of such beneficent spirits in a roster of Theban gods. In the course of the salutation, after the great Theban triad of Amun, Mut, and Khonsu have been mentioned, the writer includes the spirit of the cedar, Amenophis of the Forecourt, Amenophis the Image, Hathor of the Persea tree, the Eight Apes Who-Are-in-the-Forecourt, and Meret-seger (she who loves silence). A picture is conjured up of the laity directing their attention to the components of the local environment—the solitary tree that stands beside such-and-such a path, the statues of agathadaimones and ancestors which are set up in courtyards, the great serpent reputed to inhabit the desert necropolis.

A touching personal relationship was envisaged between a worshipper and his god, be the latter a major or minor deity. God was "the one that answers the unfortunate," "saving him whom he loves when he is in the Underworld." It was to his own patron god or goddess that the poor man appealed when he had a law-suit pending; and it was the god's barque in procession which the suppliant approached for an oracle when the organs of the law had proven useless. Since it was the priests that bore the barque and by its movement provided the "divine" response, and since the questions (eliciting only "yes" or "no" answers) were designed to produce eventually a specific piece of information, it looks superficially as though the clergy could arbitrarily decide people's fate. In fact, in the insular, relatively closed farming communities comprising urban Egypt at the end of the New Kingdom, the channels and checks of arbitrary power were equally effective and no single individual or group of individuals was able—or willing!—to perpetrate an obviously disjunctive type of activity. Still, decision by public oracle may eventually have proved to be too embarrassing: from the 8th century B.C. it became increasingly common to petition a god by letter, laid in the privacy of his sanctuary. The petitioner sometimes complains of social oppression and pleads that the god be his intercessor; more frequently the document has quasi-legal force, and implores the deity for healing from sickness.

The personal piety of the Late Period borders on self-righteousness. The Wisdom Literature of the time asserts a simple dichotomy in human nature: there are only two types of humanity, the "hot" man and the "silent" man. The former, also referred to as a "follower of Seth," is a hot-headed brawler, a hard drinker, and a lusty lover. The latter is a docile, submissive person, one who does not overstep the mark in any facet of his social life, but who does his work quietly and without complaint. The latter is the model to imitate, the former the person to be shunned. Nonetheless the maudlin piety of the Late Period urges that the hot-head be prayed for, in order that he be saved from his sin.

Sickness and Prophylactic

Personal piety of the sort described above is constantly pre-occupied with a sense of sin. In common with most of mankind, the Egyptians entertained the popular notion that god rewards the righteous and punishes the sinner *in their lifetime.* "When Re shines he regards mankind and what they do(?). He who does good, he does good to him; he who does evil, he does the same to him."

Pursuant to this rough logic, sickness and distress can be construed as a god's punishment for sin. The penitential psalm, a genre which appears in the New Kingdom, comprises an invocation to the gods, a confession by the sufferer of his sin (perjury is frequently mentioned), and an appeal for forgiveness. Carved on stelae with an appropriate vignette showing the sinner in an act of supplication **(fig. 1),** these monuments were presumably set up for all to see in the local shrine. "The servant of the Moon, Huy, says: 'I am the man who swore falsely by the Moon concerning the field(?), and he let me see the greatness of his might in the presence of the entire land. I will relate his power to the fish in the river and to the birds in the sky, and they shall say to their children: "Beware of the Moon, the forgiving one, who is able to relent!" ' " "Giving praise to the Mistress of the Two Lands, the Lady of the House of Amun, the daughter of Re, Meret-seger . . . that she may grant me the forgiveness which she gives; because you are twice just, but I am sinful. Made for the mistress of the house, Tameket." "Giving praise to the Moon, kissing the earth before the merciful one. I give praises to him to the height of heaven; I extol your beauty in order that you may forgive me, that I may see your forgiveness. I have experienced the greatness of your might, you have made me see a darkness of your making! Give me light that one may see, because health and life are in your hand: one lives if you grant him so."

Trial after Death

We have seen how, in the Old Kingdom, the person of Pharaoh provided a kind of bridge between life and death: the king in life presided over the state and the complex society within which humanity found itself; the king in death presided over exactly the same kind of organization beyond the grave. The Beyond was a mirror image of this life: there were settlements, agricultural land, a royal court, courtiers, scribes, a law-court, a judiciary and the highest judge of all—the king-in-death, the "Great God." As on earth Pharaoh and the court travelled by ship

Figure 1 Penitent in supplication before Meret-seger.

on regular progress, so on the celestial Nile the most regular voyage was that of the sun-god in his barque on his daily round. Law would apply over there as it did in life, the same law with the same procedures, sanctions and penalties. Life and death constituted a grand continuum, and debts unpaid and actions unrequited in life would be dealt with by the court in the Beyond. The background and intent was practical: law-suits unresolved on this side would be taken up by the king's court over there.

But the uncertainty to which the lawlessness of the Herakleopolitan Period gave rise did nothing to confirm one's faith in this system. The king in death had proven a weak support on which to rely. Now there were not simply torts, cases of libel and cases of vandalism to be brought to court—humankind had grown impossibly corrupt and evil across the board!—but now acts of brutality and violence abounded, along with cases of robbery, murder, and fratricide. These seemed to dwarf in importance the picayune concerns of a mastaba owner during the Fifth or Sixth Dynasties! How were whole communities of evil-doers to be judged? Was there even a power over Yonder strong enough to try these malefactors? And did it not seem now that *everyone* was a wrong-doer? It was humanity itself that had to be brought to trial! And yet at the same time the stress was on the individual: it was each man or woman who now *individually* perpetrated acts of sin, and thus was responsible directly to god for his or her actions. They could not gain approbation by melding with the social fabric of their congeners, nor by concealing themselves behind the human race viewed collectively.

While some few adopted the spectacular views of agnosticism and hedonism which we have seen exemplified in the Dialogue of a Man with his Soul and the Harpers' Songs, mainstream Egypt insisted on the essential rightness of its belief system. There was a court of law in the Beyond, and, if the Pharaonic monarchy was no longer the adequate model, maybe the gods at large would fill the role. The Herakleopolitan Period throws up the first well-defined court of law on a moral plane in the next life, presided over by divine magistrates. Their purview now is the entire field of morality, the dealings of men with each other, adjudged on the criterion of a social code of ethics. Akhtoy III of Dynasty 10 reminds his son and heir Merikare, "The board of (divine) magistrates that judges the (morally-)deficient—you know that they are not lenient on that day of judging the wretch, that hour of doing their duty! It is difficult when the prosecutor is (all)-knowing! Do not trust in length of years, for they look upon a lifetime as but an hour. A man survives after death and his deeds are placed beside him in heaps. Indeed! Existence over there is for eternity, and only a fool would get angry about that. As for him that reaches it without having done wrong, like a god will he exist over there, striding about freely like the eternal lords!" Borrowed from the concept of state taxation and the annual audit, men came to speak of "the Great Reckoning" in the "Broad Hall of Double-truth, on that day of assessing the blessed dead." Borrowed from the market place, the means whereby deeds were assessed was derived from the metaphor of the weigh-scales: the heart was weighed by Horus against the feather of Truth, while Thoth, the secretary of the court, recorded the outcome in writing (I). The board of magistrates now had a "president," or presiding chief god—the sun-god Re-Harakhte who sees all and knows all, or more commonly the quintessential king of the dead, Osiris (J).

As long as moral rectitude was the chief prerequisite for acquittal and passage into ever-lasting life, the concept could function as intended. But from the beginning another firmly-held tenet in the Egyptians' belief-system exerted a countervailing, if not nullifying effect on the concept of the trial after death, and that was Magic. If the magic spell were at all effective, as Egyptians implicitly believed it was, why could it not be used to hoodwink even the gods themselves?

We have had occasion to examine that vast collection of "beatification literature," the "Pyramid Texts" of the Old Kingdom. These were designed to assist the deceased in a very practical way to maintain physical well-being in this life and the next and secure a place in the entourage of the king-in-death. These spells were not canonical, not static in their composition; but new ones were constantly being fabricated long after the pyramid age was finished. Again we have above passed quickly in review the *Coffin Texts,* the corpus of beatification spells encorporating some of the Pyramid Texts as well as new material, which was current from Dynasties 9 through 13. The collection exudes confidence that the magic will work and that it will provide a person who uses it with an esoteric power. For underlying all Egyptian beatification literature, the collective *Id* exerts an irresistible urge opposed to all morality: the will to survive.

By the New Kingdom the practice was followed of copying beatification spells on papyrus under the new title of "the Book of Going Forth by Day" wrongly called by us moderns "the Book of the Dead." The scroll was intended to be placed within the coffin so that the mummy could take it into the Beyond as a reference guide. Two main editions of the Book of Going forth by Day exist, one from the Eighteenth Dynasty, the other a revision dating to the 7th–6th century B.C.; but both exhibit the same heterogeneous collection of spells, hymns, litanies, declamations, and even short myths all brought together because they were thought to share one thing in common—efficacy as magic.

The power the Egyptians believed resided in the book was awesome. If the gods called you to heaven, if they sent their messenger to take your heart, you could resist: Spell "for preventing a man's heart from being taken away from him. . . . 'Back! You messenger of whatever god! Have you come for my heart? I shall never give you this heart of mine!" Chapter 125 of the Book of Going Forth by Day describes the trial before Osiris and prescribes the appropriate spells. The doors, threshold, and walls of the judgement hall are imagined to have voices, and they intend to bar the way. The deceased is to hail them and call them by name, thus showing that he knew their essence and could magically neutralize them. Then he was to address the magistrates: "What to say upon (your) arriving in this Broad Hall of Double Truth; purging yourself of the sin you have committed, and seeing the faces of the gods. . . . 'Hail to you, you gods who are in the Broad Hall of Double Truth! I know you and I know your names! I shall not fall to your slaughter, you shall not expose my sin to this god whom ye follow! My misdeed shall not come up before you. You shall pronounce me 'Acquitted!' in the presence of the eternal lord, for I have done right'" on earth. Then the deceased was to address Osiris: "Hail to you O great god of Double Truth! I have come to you, O my lord, in order that you might take me and that I might see your beauty! For I know you and I know your name! And I (also) know the name(s) of the forty-two gods who are with you in this Hall of Double Truth who live by keeping watch against evil . . . on that day of assessing character in the presence of Onnophris!"

Then the deceased was supposed to intone a protestation that he had not committed the following sins: "I have come to you bringing *ma'at*. I have not committed crimes against people, I have not made folk wretched, I have not committed sin in the Place of Truth, . . . I have not done wrong, . . . I have not deprived the orphan of his things, I have not done what gods abhor, I have not vilified a servant to his boss, I have not caused pain, I have not caused hunger, I have not caused weeping, I have not killed, I have not ordered killing, I have not inflicted hurt on anyone, I have not diminished the bread-offerings in the temples, I have not defiled the bread of the gods, I have not seized the food offerings of the blessed dead, I have not fornicated . . . , I have not falsified the measure, I have not falsified the *arura* . . . , I have not taken milk from the mouths of babies, I have not deprived cattle of their fodder . . . I have not held back water in its season . . ." and on and on in the same vein.

Yet had the deceased covered all eventualities? Had he plugged every loophole? No! There is one blind spot! Suppose one's most intimate friend should turn traitor and witness for the prosecution? And who is one's most intimate friend, who knows more about the individual than anyone else? One's own heart! And so, slapped on the chest of the mummy, right over the heart is a Heart-scarab with a spell "to prevent (a man's) heart from opposing him in the necropolis. He says: 'O heart of my parents! O heart of my parents! O heart of mine during the time when I was upon earth! Do not take the stand against me as a witness in the presence of the Offering-lords, and say: "he did it in very truth!" so that action will be taken against me. Do not create charges against me in the presence of the great god, lord of the West! Hail my heart, hail my breast! Hail my (very) essence!"

The Afterlife: A Pessimistic View

And so a knowledge of magic had replaced moral uprightness as a prerequisite for future bliss. Even the worst scoundrels could get off in the trial after death! If the gods were just, how could this be? The mind baulked at the enormity of this betrayal of sincere belief.

Two reactions are discernible in ancient Egyptian literature and both, although diametrically opposed to each other, are logical consequences of the degradation of the Osirian judgement. The first is one of pessimism akin to the bleak outlook which prevailed in some quarters during the Herakleopolitan Period, but now it was scarcely relieved by a happy agnosticism or the advice to party on regardless. The belief was widespread in Western Asia, i.e. Mesopotamia, Syria, and Palestine, that the Afterlife, far from being the happy experience the Egyptians imagined, was a miserable existence for eternity in the semi-darkness of an underworld. The dead sat in semi-torpor, without comforts, hungry and thirsty, devoured constantly by rats. In the Epic of Gilgamesh, the hero, Gilgamesh, is once privileged to summon up from the grave the spirit of his old friend Enkidu. At Gilgamesh's prodding, Enkidu proceeds to describe the true situation of the Afterlife: "vermin devour the body as though it were an old garment . . . [it] is filled with dust. . . . Him whose corpse was cast out upon the desert, his spirit finds no rest in the Underworld, and Him whose spirit has no one to minister to it, he eats scrapings from the pot, crumbs of bread, and offal of the streets." In Canaanite/Hebrew belief men go down at death to *She'ol,* the "Pit," to their fathers' eternal abode, where they continue to exist in a twilight zone, half asleep.

Nothing in all this could be more un-Egyptian in terms of traditional belief, and yet it is precisely this kind of Afterlife that is sometimes reflected in Egyptian literature of the New Kingdom and later. A curious folk-story of Nineteenth Dynasty date illustrates the point. A fictitious high-priest of Amun, Khonsu-em-heb, exhibits the type of solemn piety so typical of the later periods of Egyptian history. The story describes how he loves to wander the necropolis, viewing tombs of old, a popular topos in Late Egyptian literature, and during the course of his perambulations one day he chances upon an old, dilapidated tomb. He decides to restore it, and collects workmen to begin the job. While surveying the site before work commenced, he was suddenly confronted by the spirit of the owner who asked what he was doing. When told of the restoration, the spirit answered in effect: why? It's been restored four times in the past already: there's no point in doing it again, for the tomb is still a wreck. And that's not all—the Afterlife is not at all what it is cracked up to be. "There is not eating, no drinking, no [youth, no aged]; no seeing the rays of the sun-disc, no breathing the north-wind. Darkness engulfs the face constantly, no one rises early to go forth." There is here a dramatic and stark counterblast to the traditional Egyptian hope of the Afterlife. Going beyond the harpers, who said that the Afterlife is simply unknowable, the spirit denies point by point the great tenets of faith: that feasting and eternal youth, viewing the rising sun, breathing the cool breeze, and going forth by day are part of future existence. For some Egyptians the Afterlife was synonymous with "that underworld which conceals all its secrets, (where) one enters, but no one comes out! May thy doors open (to) receive {the deceased}, and may it be said to him: 'welcome! You are in your place and your eternal cavern has closed with you!'"

The sweet assurance of heaven in the last scene of Berlioz's *Damnation* or the dogged insistence of Mahler's *Second* on the reality of resurrection are totally alien to this vision of the next life and the prior considerations which gave rise to it. Dwelling on the morbidity of certain gloom became even fashionable: good breeding facing the inevitable with courage. The wife of a high-priest of Memphis just before the time of Christ addresses her husband from the grave: "O my brother, my husband, my friend! Let not your heart grow weary of drinking, eating, drunkenness, and sexual pleasure! Make holiday and follow your desire on earth! Put not worry in your heart, for what are those years upon earth? As for the West, it is a land of sleep and thick darkness, a resting place for those who are there. Slumber is their only occupation—they waken not to see their brethren, they do not behold their fathers and mothers, their hearts long for their wives and children. The water of life which (ought to be) sustaining for all, means only thirst for me, (since) it comes only to those on earth. I thirst although water is beside me. I know not the place where I am, since I came to this valley. O give me running water! Say to me: 'water is not alien(?) To your body!' Turn my face toward the north wind beside the water—maybe my heart will be cooled from sickness. Death, whose name is 'Come!' everyone whom he summons to him, goes to him with a heart terrified through fear of him, though neither gods nor mankind can see him. Great as well as small are in his power, his hand cannot be staid from any he desires . . ."

Resignation in the face of an awful fate might be courageous, but it was the resort of the few. It falls into line with the maverick agnosticism of the Middle Kingdom which continues in one form or another in a jaundiced society right down until Roman times. One could view it, perhaps, as an aristocratic refinement of the release of unmitigated grief which is given in the dirges that the mourning women intone at a funeral.

Reward and Punishment

A much more widespread reaction to the potential of debasement which magic entailed for the tribunal of Osiris involved the institutionalized "carrot and stick," "reward and punishment." It was not right nor acceptable that magic should prevail in a court of law: justice, *ma'at,* must triumph as it had always triumphed ever since the time of the gods. Only the righteous should be allowed to enjoy eternity in the "Elysian Fields," the "Field of Reeds," as the Egyptians called it, where the barley is seven feet high and the wheat twelve, and where the blessed dead will quite literally be giants, fifteen feet tall. Only the well-equipped and righteous souls should be permitted to journey among the crew of the sun-god's barque on a daily basis; only they should experience his nightly death and glorious resurrection at dawn, absorbed mystically into the round of nature throughout eternity. The sinner, on the other hand, deserved severe punishment, and a place where that punishment was meted out. And so we have come to the point of crystallization of the concept of heaven and hell. The intellectual ingredients have been found in Egyptian speculative thought as far back as the Old Kingdom: in the New Kingdom they appear in graphic form.

The Underworld (literally the "Land of Dawn", but certainly subterranean in application) is presided over by Osiris, who appears now more than ever as a sort of Pluto, a king of the dead. In his own words in the Late Egyptian Story *The Contendings of Horus and Seth,* "the land where I am (i.e. the Underworld) is filled with fierce-eyed messengers who fear neither god nor goddess. I send them out and they bring back the hearts of all those who have committed sin, and they (the sinners) remain here with me." Here we have the messengers of death, whom we have met before, and who soon will be transformed into demonic characters much more familiar to us in our Judaeo-Christian heritage. But Osiris has other visitors: again in his own words "When Ptah . . . made the heavens, did he not say to the stars which were in it: 'In the place where Osiris is shall ye set, in the West, each night; and then after the gods also the patricians and the plebs shall come to rest in the place where {Osiris} is.' " And so now no one can escape the clutches of that "Land of Dawn."

The nocturnal journey of the sun through the Underworld had been thought about and given intellectual form by the Egyptians from the dawn of time; but now, in the New Kingdom, it is given graphic form on the walls of royal tombs. In the Old and Middle Kingdoms the burial of the king, although often beneath the surface of the ground, honored the solar religion far more than any concept of what was subterranean, by the inclusion of the pyramid-form as the monumental, visible marker of where the king-in-death lay. For some reason at the outset of the New Kingdom the pyramid as a necessary marker for the royal tomb was largely given up (though it remained in use for private graves), and a new arrangement was devised. Now, while the worship of the king's spirit was carried on in a special mortuary temple on the west bank at Thebes (κ), his body was secreted in a rock-cut tomb in the desert to the west (L). The shaft of the tomb (M) descended into the rock of the desert at a steep angle and terminated far underground in a tomb chamber where the gigantic royal sarcophagus was set. The narrow valley where the tombs are located, the so-called "Valley of the Kings," is only a few hundred yards west of the Nile Valley at Thebes where the mortuary temples are situated, but it was declared off limits to the average Egyptian. No marker was set at the opening to the shaft tomb; they were intentionally concealed from view out of considerations for security.

By their form, location, and decoration the royal tombs in the Valley of the Kings continue to honor the sun-god Re, but now it is through his night-time descent through the Underworld that they hope to assimilate with him. Moreover now Osiris plays a significant role. At sunset the sun passed through a gap in the western cliffs, typified by the opening to the royal tomb, and entered the Underworld which it traversed, traveling in its night-time barque on a subterranean Nile. The Underworld was divided into twelve concentric regions, corresponding to the twelve hours of the night, each surrounded by walls and moats, and pierced by gates. The subterranean Nile passed through these gates, carrying the sun-boat and its solar occupant past watchtowers guarded by dragons and demons. It took one hour to traverse each section. In the deepest part of the Underworld, in that section devoted to the seventh hour, lay the body of Osiris, symbolized in the royal tomb by the royal sarcophagus and the king's mummy inside.

As has been pointed out earlier, the concepts of Re, the sun, and Osiris, the latent power of the Nile, are, in Egyptian thinking, diametrically opposed to one another. The sun is present and open for all to see, dynamic, unapproachable, exuding power, lord of the daytime sky; Osiris by contrast is hidden, concealed, and mysterious, passive rather than active, storing latent power. Already in the Old Kingdom the Egyptians sensed the contrast, and played upon it in religious and secular writings. But neither concept could do without the other. Akhenaten had tried to promote the *physical* sun and its paternal aspect at the expense of action-latency in tension (Re and Osiris), and what had happened to him? Osiris had been great and good while he lived, but what had Seth done to him? Poles apart as they might well be, the two powers, one latent one dynamic, simply had to meet and, for however brief a moment, touch. In the Middle Kingdom the locale had been Mendes, the city of the ram, the Soul of Osiris, in the Delta, where the two forces journeyed to meet each other and embraced. The New Kingdom translated the encounter to the Underworld. Here, in the seventh and darkest hour, the deepest point in the night, when Re languished in weakness, the two touched each other, and the sun revivified was propelled upwards towards the dawn.

The Invention of Heaven and Hell

Imagining the Underworld gave rise to a voluminous literature of "Underworld Books." Originals were undoubtedly kept in the House of Life, and by that very fact labelled as secret mysteries, not to be divulged. Today these are lost. But on the walls of the royal tombs, beginning around 1520 B.C. and extending to 1100 B.C., are inscribed and painted lengthy excerpts of this literature, describing and illustrating what the Underworld was really like and specifying its significance for the deceased. In some cases, especially in early royal tombs, they are drawn in ink in a sketchy manner, suggesting true copies of the papyrus originals. The names of the books themselves suggest the mystery surrounding them. There is the "Book of That-which-is-in-the-Underworld," a comprehensive description of what is down there; "the Litany of Re," with the names and transformations of the sun-god as he traverses the nocturnal region; the "Book of Gates," which deals with the portals of the Underworld; the "Book of Caverns," which has to do with the person of Osiris and the new creation in the seventh hour, and many more. All along the route taken by the night-barque of Re through the Underworld the banks of the subterranean Nile depict the punishments of the damned (N–O)—beheading, mutilation, burning, burying, suspension up-side-down. There is a river of fire and a lake of fire, which the Saved get across easily, but which swallows up the Damned. Hell has graduated from a state of lying in semi-darkness, hungry, thirsty, and bored, to a place of brutal punishment.

We can carry the story much further. A narrative, probably originating in the 3rd century B.C., describes how two people actually went down to the Underworld before death and came back to talk about it. One was the legendary Setna-Khamois, historically a real son of Ramesses the Great in the 13th century B.C., who had become a subject of folklore; the other was a mysterious divine child called Si-Osir. Setna, walking in the necropolis of Memphis one day, saw two funerals. One was that of a wealthy man, who took with him to the grave vast quantities of goods for the next life, and who was followed by an entourage of mourners and friends. The other was that of a poor man who had no large tomb, no grave goods, and no following. Setna naturally concluded that he must have been a sinful man to end up so destitute. Later Setna was given the opportunity to visit the Underworld in the company of Si-Osir. The text describes how they passed from hall to hall (corresponding to the fortified divisions in the older Underworld literature) and what they saw:

"There were some men whose provisions of bread and water were hanging above them and, as they reached out to catch them, others were digging a hole beneath their feet in order not to let them reach them. They (Setna and Si-Osir) entered the fifth hall and Setna saw the blessed spirits. . . . The doorpost of the sixth hall was fixed in the right eye-socket of a man who was pleading and crying aloud. As <they> entered the sixth hall Setna saw the gods and people of the Underworld standing upon their feet, and the servants of the Underworld standing and making report. When they came into the seventh hall Setna saw Osiris the great god, sitting on a throne of fine gold. . . . Anubis the great god being on his left and the great god

Thoth on his right, and the gods of the council and the people of the Underworld were standing on both sides of him, and the weigh-scales were set in their midst. The faults were being weighed against the righteous acts, and as Thoth wrote it down, Anubis would call out (the result) to him. He whose faults were found to outweigh his good deeds . . . his soul was destroyed(?) . . . and was not allowed to breathe the air. He whose good deeds were found to outweigh his faults was led away from the gods of the council of the lord of the Underworld, and his soul flew to heaven along with the blessed spirits. . . . Now near the spot where Osiris was Setna saw a great man clad in fine linen, obviously of exalted rank.

Now Setna marvelled greatly at all that he had seen in the Underworld, and when he came up outside, (Si-Osir) said to him: "Setna! Did you see that great man clad in fine linen near the spot where Osiris was? That is the poor man whom you saw being taken out from Memphis, with no one in his cortège, wrapped (only) in a reed mat. When he got to the Underworld and his faults were weighed against the good deeds he had done on earth, his good deeds were found to outweigh his faults. . . . It was commanded by Osiris to transfer the funeral equipment of the rich man whom you saw being taken out from Memphis (to the grave) with great pomp, to this very poor man; and the latter was placed among the blessed spirits of devout men who are in the train of Sokar-Osiris near the place where Osiris is. The rich man whom you saw was (also) taken down to the Underworld, and when his faults were weighed against his good deeds, they were found to outweigh the good deeds he had done on earth. He was condemned to suffer for them in the Underworld, and he [is the one you] saw with the door-post of the Underworld fixed in his right eye-socket. . . ."

The evolution of the concept, with the clear inclusion of foreign, Greek, motifs, is bringing us to more familiar territory. Heaven and Hell are now clarified and polarized: both reward and punishment are absolute. God is "the vizier of the humble; he does not accept bribes from the guilty . . . he does not countenance 'shalom!' He judges the land with his fingers, he speaks to the heart. He judges the guilty and puts him in the furnace(?), but the righteous in the West!"

We have one stage in the journey yet to take and that is to Christian Egypt. Christianity came to Egypt while the ancient Egyptian religion was still being practiced, and the two overlapped in time. By the end of the 3rd century the new religion was making headway against the ancient Egyptian gods and their temples, and in 391 A.D. succeeded in having all the old places of worship permanently closed. But three centuries of contact had made their mark.

Consider the following statement by an old nun, sometime after the old religion had petered out, a pious and humble old lady who had separated herself from the world. The speaker questions her about "her manner of separation. She sighed and said, 'Friend, I was the daughter of a man, temperate and gentle in his way of life, but feeble and diseased in body. He spent a good deal of time in sleep with the result that many of the townsfolk seldom met him; (otherwise) he kept to his own fields and was engaged in his work there. Whenever he was well enough he would bring in the fruits of the field honestly. Most of his life he spent in bed on account of his illness, but always kept his mouth shut, so that those who did not know him said he was dumb.

'I also had a mother who was the exact opposite. She was more active than all the fellow countrymen and townsfolk. She would talk to everyone, wave her hand at everyone, so that people said that her entire body had grown into one big tongue, and she would be for ever quarrelling. She used to drink wine with uncouth men until she was stoned, and she ran our house like a prostitute with much wickedness; and although we possessed much, we never had enough. For my father on account of his sickness was forced to leave the domestic affairs to her. She defiled her body in every (conceivable) way . . . but no sickness ever afflicted her; her body remained free from disease until the day of her death.

'It happened that my father being sick and often in pain, finally died. And the air was instantly astir with rain, lightning, and thunder—it was neither night nor day! The rain did not let up for eight days and all this while my father['s body] lay on the bed unburied. At last the townsfolk started shaking their heads in amazement, (for on account of his sickness he had been all but forgotten by them all), and they said: "this man was an enemy of god and not even the earth will receive his body for burial and have it decompose within her . . .!" My mother, however, became even more irreverent, and committed all the more bitter, vile deeds with her body. And so she continued to live in defilement and arrogance. But I was young at the time and took no notice of these things. . . .

'After her death I grew up and felt the stirrings of lust in my body. One evening I grew pensive and pondered on what type of life I should choose to live. My father had lived a life of meekness, sobriety, and commendable unselfishness; but I recalled further that nothing good had happened to my father, and that he had spent all his time until the day he passed away in pain and misery. He had died in distress, nor had the earth received his body in peace. If his life had been pleasing before god, why was all this pain his lot? So I asked myself whether my mother's way was good, and whether I should give myself over to wickedness, filth, and bodily defilement. For there was not one evil practice that my mother had neglected to do, and she had always been drunk; yet she had been free from sickness, and had departed this life in health. All right, I decided, I shall live according to my mother's example. So, miserable girl that I was, I gave myself over to a life of evil.

'When evening came, slumber seized me and I slept heavily. Suddenly an enormous man was standing beside me. His face was terrible and his wild appearance terrified me. With a harsh voice he said to me: "you there! What sort of thoughts are in your heart?" But because of his terrifying face and appearance I could not bring myself to look on him. Then he shouted aloud and commanded me to tell him what I had been thinking about. Although I had been perfectly aware of what I had been thinking about, I answered that I had not been thinking of any-thing. Taking this as a refusal, he refreshed my memory, and repeated to me everything I had been meditating upon in my heart. I turned imploring and pleading that he would count me worthy of forgiveness for the intentions I had had. But he said to me: "Have you not seen those two, your father and your mother . . . ?" and he seized my arm and dragged me off. He took me to a great field in which there were many gardens with all sorts of trees whose beauty surpassed description. He led me to a holy place and there my father came to meet me, and greeted me with a kiss. He said to me, "My daughter, live in righteousness." I threw my arms about him and implored him to let me stay with him, but he said: "It is not possible now. If you follow in my ways during your life, you will be brought without delay to this place." I asked him to let me remain together with him, but the one who had brought me there dragged me away, saying, "Come and see your mother burning in the fire. Then you will know what is the good and useful life and you will choose it!"

'He set me beside a house of utter darkness which was filled with clamor and the gnashing of teeth. He showed me a blazing oven, seething with flames, and some terrifying forms standing around it. I looked down into the oven and saw my mother, grinding her teeth as she stood in it up to her shoulders. Around her burned the fire, and her body was being devoured by many worms. When she saw me, she gave a pitiful cry and hailed me: "O my daughter! Woe is me for my own deeds! Woe is me for my own actions! For in life I took no thought for temperance and gave myself over to acts of sin and adultery. I did not think they would punish me, I did not reckon that drunkenness and defilement would mean torment for me. See! For a little pleasure I am penalized and chastised thus, for the little haughtiness I showed, I am wracked in this kind of inquest! See! For the contempt I showed towards god what high wages of pain I receive. All the ceaseless evils have caught up with me! . . . Pity me, your mother, burning and perishing in the fire, pity me whom they torture in this manner . . .!" ' " Guess which way of life the nun chose!

We have come to the heaven and hell of the New Testament, the paradise and inferno of Dante. All the ingredients are there: for paradise, the Elysian Fields, the Field of Reeds, the beautiful gardens; for the inferno, the lake of fire, the flame that is not quenched, the demons, the dragons, the fiery furnace. There is a direct, linear descent here from beliefs formulated, detailed, and fixed in an Egyptian form right through into modern times, with little influence from Western Asia or the classical world. When it comes to concepts of sin, death, and hell, it is Ancient Egypt that we have to thank.

The Island with No Name

It is possible that there is another and slightly more distorted form in which the ancient Egyptian Underworld has come down to us. Consider the following facts:

1. The "Underworld" of ancient Egypt is in the west, and in fact is often called the "West."
2. It is submerged, subterranean.
3. It comprises a series of walled, concentric regions, separated by moats and connected by a single watercourse penetrating the center.
4. It is a seat of power, presided over by "King Osiris."
5. In the center of the complex is an island in which Osiris the king resides.

The actualization of the mound of creation in the form of a stone podium, an "island," surrounded by a channel of water, is known from Egyptian sacred architecture. It occurs in the subterranean arrangements of the Osireion at Abydos, and Herodotus was told that the same arrangement was to be found under the Great Pyramid. (In fact, a recently discovered installation at the same site does, indeed, exhibit this arrangement.) It is a mysterious place whose essence, or "name," is unknown. Now the Egyptian for "island-without-a-name," or "nameless isle," in the contemporary pronunciation of the Late Period would have been *A-at-lans. Is it coincidence that according to Plato the story and description of Atlantis, so similar in detail to the Egyptian underworld, was told to Solon in the early 6th century B.C. by an Egyptian priest in fact?

Further Readings

In general, on the subjects reviewed in this chapter, see W. Clarysse and others (eds.), *Egyptian Religion: The Last Thousand Years* (2 vols.), Louvain, 1998.

On the syncretism of the Late Period, see J. Assmann, *Egyptian Solar Religion in the New Kingdom: Re, Amun, and the Crisis of Polytheism*, London, 1995; J. G. Griffiths, *Triads and Trinity*, Cardiff, 1996.

On animal worship, see S. Ikram (ed.), *Sacred Animal Cemeteries*, Cairo, 2005; J. Malek, *The Cat in Ancient Egypt*, London, 1993; G. T. Martin, *The Sacred Animal Necropolis at North Saqqara*, London, 1981; R. Mittelman, *The Fish-cult at Mendes*, MA dissertation, Pennsylvania State University, 2005; J. D. Ray, *The Archive of Hor*, London, 1976; H. S. Smith, *A Visit to Ancient Egypt*, Warminster, 1974.

A good survey of the popular piety in the Late Period is A. I. Sadek, *Popular Religion in Egypt During the New Kingdom*, Hildesheim, 1987.

On Osiris and the judgment after death, see T. Duquesne, *At the Court of Osiris: Book of the Dead Spell 194: A Rare Egyptian Judgment Text*, London, 1994; J. G. Griffiths, *Plutarch's De Iside et Osiride*, Cardiff, 1970; *idem, The Divine Verdict: A Study of Divine Judgment in the Ancient Religions*, Leiden, 1991.

Beatification spells and Underworld Literature are dealt with in T. G. Allen, *The Book of the Dead or Going Forth by Day*, Chicago, 1974; R. O. Faulkner, *The Ancient Egyptian Coffin Texts* (3 vols.), Warminster, 1973–78; *idem, The Ancient Egyptian Book of the Dead*, London, 1984; E. Hornung, *The Ancient Egyptian Books of the Afterlife*, Ithaca, 1999; see also J. Van Dijk, "Hell," in D. B. Redford (ed.), *The Oxford Encyclopaedia of Ancient Egypt* (New York, 2001), II, 89–91; M. Lichtheim, *Ancient Egyptian Literature III: The Later Period*, Berkeley, 1980.

CHAPTER FIFTEEN
Kush, Assyria, and the Struggle for Egypt

Twenty-fifth Dynasty	
Alara	Early 8th century B.C.
Kashta	?–c. 740 B.C.
Piankhy	c. 740–712 B.C.
Sabaco	712–700 (?) B.C.
Shebitku	705–690 B.C.
Taharqa	690–664 B.C.
Tanwetamani	664–625 B.C.

By the middle of the 8th century B.C. Egypt was effectually dismembered as a centralized state, and had resolved itself into a number of autonomous "baronies." The last scion of the Libyan Twenty-second Dynasty still sat upon his throne in Tanis, but in terms of power he occupied nothing but an honorific position among the great chiefs of the Delta. Someone visiting Egypt from Western Asia or the Aegean around 750 B.C. would have, unless otherwise instructed, come away with the impression that the Egypt of the time was comprised of a host of independent principalities. He would have found in the Delta upwards of seven "fiefdoms" belonging to Great Chiefs of the Me, two townships ruled by self-proclaimed "kings," and two "princedoms";

while, if he penetrated the valley, he would have encountered two "kings" (Herakleopolis and Hermopolis), and a "theocratic" state, the "House of Amun" in the Thebaid. That this weakened and fragmented Egypt was heading for disaster was clear to astute observers in Jerusalem: "The princes of Tanis have become fools," mocked Isaiah, "and the princes of Memphis are deluded . . . and they will fight, every man against his brother, every man against his neighbor, city against city and kingdom against kingdom. . . ." This remarkably accurate assessment and prophecy was not long in being fulfilled.

The Rise of Independent Kush

The 14ᵗʰ century B.C. had found the southern dependencies of Nubia and Kush well on the way to being thoroughly Egyptianized. Scores of settlements along the Nile brought small groups of Egyptian colonists into direct contact with the natives and provided the foci out from which Egyptian culture radiated. While trade and the presence of gold had constituted the initial attraction, the Egyptian administration gradually realized the advantage of developing the region for its own sake. In Egyptian parlance it was a case of "extending the frontiers": the south was now an extension of the homeland. And while it cannot be said that intermarriage of the two juxtaposed races was ever popular or widespread, Egyptian and Nubian got along remarkably amicably.

It was not long before administration by native princes (A) was given up, and the south became the mirror-image of Egypt. In place of Pharaoh stood the "Viceroy of Kush" **(fig. 1)** (Egyptian: "king's son of Kush," earlier ". . . of the southern countries"); where Egypt had often two viziers, one for Upper, the other for Lower Egypt, the south had two deputies, one for Kush, one for Wawat (Lower Nubia). The "overseer of the treasury," "overseer of cattle," "overseer of works," "overseer of all the prophets of all the gods"—all such titles, originally applicable to functions in Egypt, reappear in the microcosm of the south. Kush provided an army, too, "the garrison of Kush," and while assignment to serve in it was to an Egyptian soldier tantamount to exile, it proved an effective fighting force.

Figure 1   "King's-son of Kush, who bears the flabellum on the right hand of the king." The viceroy of Kush adoring the king.

The major settlements had graduated beyond the status of encampments or forts, and were now large towns. Each was administered, as in Egypt, by a "mayor" who was a civil administrator and no longer a para-military commandant. For the finality of the advent of the "Pax Aegyptiaca" in the south is graphically illustrated by the evidence of peaceful conditions of life: the forts built in the Middle Kingdom are no longer used as such, but are often transformed into treasuries or administrative buildings. No more in need of their protection, the unwalled towns of which they were the nuclei have now spread out all around.

The *raison-d'être* of many a settlement is the large temple (B–C) which rises in its midst. The Egyptians did not suppress native cults—the Nubian Dedun and several falcon cults persist beyond the empire period—but the gods they introduced far outshone the local numina. Chief among the newcomers were the hypostases of the Egyptian pharaohs. At new sites such as Sai, Soleb, Abu Simbel, and Gerf Hussein, impressive shrines on the model of processional temples in Egypt were thrown up for the worship of the spirits of Thutmose III, Amenophis III, and Ramesses II, to name but a few. The Nubians were also exposed to the worship of Amun. The divine guarantor of Egypt's empire, Amun was given the rights by the imperial pharaohs to the gold-producing regions of Kush, and cult centers of the "King of the Gods" began to spring up in the distant southland. Chief among these was the Temple of Amun at "the pure mountain," Napata, in the Dongola province. Here Thutmose III had set up a bombastic record of his victories, and Horemheb had refurbished the temple. Under his manifestation as a ram, Amun of Napata exerted a subtle but strong influence over the local Sudanese population, who soon came to accept him as their own.

Around 1100 B.C. a time of trouble set in south of the first cataract on the Nile. Although one minority view, based on little evidence, would minimize the effect of the factors to be passed in review, the three centuries terminating in 800 B.C. were most certainly catastrophic for the south. The civil strife which wracked Egypt during the reign of the last Ramesside king, Ramesses XI, involved the garrison of Kush also, and shortly the southern provinces became the arena for a destructive war between Paynehsi, the viceroy of Kush, and the descendants of Herihor in Thebes. By 1050 B.C. Nubia and Kush were lost to Egypt; inscriptions cease in the south as a dark age begins. A series of low Niles over a protracted period of time brought famine to lower Nubia between the first and second cataracts. The great cities were depopulated as the population retired south or came north, and the magnificent temples were left derelict. The Libyan kings only rarely mention Kush in their inscriptions, and then only as the source of the usual tropical products emanating from central Africa **(fig. 2)**.

The revival of Kush is the story of the kingdom of Napata. Sometime towards the middle of the 9th century B.C. a ruling family of obscure origin, though probably native Sudanese, appeared in the old center Napata. No inscriptional material is known dating from the first five generations of the family, absence of a script probably being the explanation; but around 760 B.C. we find these chieftains beginning to record their names and acts in Egyptian, in the hieroglyphic script. It is quite likely that Egyptian scribes were brought from the north and instructed to record the mighty deeds of the local chief in the Egyptian language. The dialect is rather archaic, drawing its inspiration from the classical Middle Egyptian which had largely passed out of day-to-day use after 1300 B.C., and owing little or nothing to the contemporary dialects of the 8th century. A similar captivation with Egyptian models is shown in burial customs—the chiefs favored the pyramid form of tomb—sculpture and painting and the minor arts. The official cult was that of Amun, and his worship was resuscitated and carried on by the natives with a zeal and

Figure 2 Nubian tribute-bearers from Kush.

a devotion which could not be found in Egypt at that time, not even in Thebes. In fact, what was emerging at Napata was an "Egyptian" kingdom, old-fashioned and puritanical judged by 8th century standards, which was peopled by dark-skinned Sudanese. While the roots of this "Egyptianness" were grounded historically in the elite emulation of the New Kingdom empire, the Sudanese of the 8th century had committed this fact to oblivion, and fervently considered themselves the true heirs to the spiritual inheritance of the gods.

The worship of Amun provided a strong bond between Napata and Thebes. As the Thebans grew increasingly disenchanted with their Libyan masters in the north, they found themselves moving imperceptibly into the orbit of the new kingdom of Kush. In keeping with the common practice of the time, viz. the dedication by a chief of his daughter to the service of Amun in Thebes, one of the early kings in Napata placed one of his own daughters, named Amunirdis (D), in the office of coregent of the "Divine Worshipper" of Amun, who formally adopted her **(fig. 3).** This was a key post, a sort of high-priestess of the god, and, as the adoption of cartouches indicates, it was felt to be a royal function. By 735 B.C. the Kushite king Piankhy had moved garrisons into the Thebaid, possibly at the invitation of and certainly with the acquiescence of the Thebans, and it looked as though the conquest of Egypt, the "manifest destiny" of the Kushites, was about to be realized.

The Assyrian Threat and the Consolidation of the Delta

The pre-occupation of the young Kushite kingdom with Egypt has to be considered in the light of the situation in western Asia. The Delta and southern Palestine were rapidly becoming a power vacuum into which a hostile major power might step. That such a power might be Assyrian must have been alarmingly plain to all astute observers of the period. In 745 B.C. Assyria had emerged from a civil war under the leadership of an able soldier and administrator, Tiglath-pileser III. Although faced by a strong coalition of Armenian and Syrian states, Tiglath-pileser had mustered his forces and launched them fearlessly in a series of decisive encounters with the enemy. Armenia fell in 743, the Syrian state of Arpad in 741, Ullubu in 740, Kullani in 738. In 734 Phoenicia was occupied, and a coalition of Philistine cities routed;

Figure 3   The Divine Worshipper Amunirdis offering milk to the god Amun; temple of Osiris Ruler-of-Eternity, Karnak.

this was followed two years later by the incredible spectacle of a defeated Damascus shortly to be incorporated within the Assyrian empire.

None of the implications of this spectacular spread of Assyrian power could have been lost on the Egyptians. Their position *vis-à-vis* western Asia was equivocal: the states of Israel and Judah inland and the Philistine cities on the coast looked to Egypt for aid, or considered her a safe haven to which to flee in the event of defeat. Decisive aid Egypt of the Twenty-second Dynasty could not give, and in any case the Libyans showed a reluctance to become involved. Providing sanctuary, moreover, would inevitably incur Assyria's wrath. What was required was a strong Delta, and not the political vacuum which now existed there.

About 730 B.C. a certain Libyan chief named Tefnakhte managed by means unknown to ensconce himself in the Delta city of Sais and to extend his direct rule over the entire western half of the Delta. This tract, bordering on the desert, he called the "Kingdom of the West." His apparent strength and incisiveness cowed the rest of the Lower Egyptian principalities—he may also have appeared to them as a saviour—and with their forces in support, he moved upriver, winning over cities one by one to his cause. The strong Namlot of Hermopolis had already tendered allegiance to Piankhy, but now switched sides to become an ally of Tefnakhte, who thus could reckon as his own all of Egypt as far south as Asyut, with one exception. The king of Herakleopolis offered resistance, and his city was promptly besieged by the motley coalition from the north. In desperation he sent out a call for help. This was the only excuse Kush required.

The contemporary king of Kush, Piankhy (or *Piya*, a less probable pronunciation of his name), appears in the "persuasion literature" created for his benefit as a crusty old puritan who loved horses and lived by a strict code of morals. He has left behind the earliest extensive stela inscription from the new kingdom at Napata, and in it he describes in detail his conquest of Egypt. The text was probably written up by an Egyptian amanuensis, and employs a number of novel tropes in delineating the royal character, coupled with older themes reworked in a personal manner. It remains a moot point as to what extent Piankhy himself resembled this word picture of him or continued to lie concealed behind a royal mask; but the portrait is nonetheless spirited, specific, and unusual. In spite of the recency of their appearance in world history, the Kushites are shown by this record to have been remarkably knowledgeable in the modern techniques of warfare developed in the Second Millennium and lately refined by the Assyrians. Siege ladders, battering rams, siege mounds, and slingers were all known to Piankhy, who used them to good effect against Hermopolis which he besieged for a considerable period of time. Realizing what was in store for them, most of the fortified towns of Middle Egypt, the erstwhile allies of Tefnakhte, opened to the Kushites, and the honorable Piankhy refrained from slaying any of the enemy. When Memphis resisted it was assaulted in a single day and given over to plunder. Tefnakhte fled to the north. Piankhy received the homage of the Delta chiefs, and made over the incomes of all the conquered towns to Amun at Thebes. Tefnakhte remained at large; Piankhy was either unable or unwilling to assault the city of Sais. In fact he shortly retired to Napata, without attempting to hold the north by any means other than the ineffectual administering of oaths. For another decade the Delta was left to its own devices, a prey to Assyria, until in 713 matters came to a head. The king of Ashdod, having failed in an attempt to rebel against Assyria, fled to Kush for refuge and was given asylum. Following up on this provocative action, in 712 Piankhy's younger brother Sabaco found a pretext in the alleged illegitimacy, tantamount to treason, of Bocchoris of Sais, Tefnakhte's son, and repeated the great invasion from the south that his older sibling had accomplished. Bocchoris was easily captured, and put to death by fire, the usual penalty for treason. Kushite dominion now extended without opposition all the way to the Mediterranean.

The Kushite Hold on Egypt (712–664 B.C.)

If Assyria had pounced sooner, the Delta would easily have been hers. Israel had been incorporated as an Assyrian province in 722 B.C., Judah and the Philistines were reeling, and Assyrian garrisons and trading posts had been implanted as far south as Wady el-Arish in the north Sinai. But Kush had struck first, and for fifty years Assyrian designs were thwarted by a revitalized Egypt.

Unlike Piankhy, Sabaco did not retire to Napata, but he and his three successors resided at Thebes and Memphis. The succession in the Kushite royal house did not follow a normal progression from father to eldest son, but bestowed royal power on the eldest surviving brother before eldest son. Thus Sabaco, brother of Piankhy, was obliged to regard Piankhy's eldest surviving son, Shebitku, his nephew, as his heir; and in about 705 B.C. Shebitku was duly appointed co-regent with his uncle. Further to solidify his hold on Egypt—was his uncle ailing?—Shebitku made a grand entry into Thebes in 703 B.C. and subsequently summoned princes and princesses from Napata in the south to join him in Egypt in order to create a Kushite court at Memphis.

The basic attitude of the Kushite Twenty-fifth Dynasty might strike us today as self-righteous: only they were truly "Egyptian," worshipping and living according to "true" modes. The rest of Egypt was apostate. The Libyan chiefs were physically unhygienic and neglected sacred dietary laws; moreover they were untrustworthy and parochial in their interests. They had failed to follow the true path in politics. According to Piankhy's assessment of the political picture of his day, kings were being "made" by local noblemen or by priests, in blatant disregard of the "obvious" fact that only Amun had the right and the power to bestow true kingship. The

Libyan chiefs, of course, took a jaundiced view of the Sudanese, whom they considered mere interlopers from the south. There was little point, they would have reasoned, in being loyal to such a dynasty, for the Kushites were wholly wedded to Amun and Thebes, and did not have the interests of the Delta at heart. The Kushite kings well understood the fickleness of the parochial ruling families of Lower Egypt, and soon took steps to neutralize them. In an ironic reversal of the age-old policy of Egyptian conquerors, people from Lower Egypt, among whom were sisters and wives of the local chiefs, were sent south into Nubia, ostensibly as temple servants and priestesses.

Thebes of course willingly accepted the suzerainty of Kush, and the southern monarchs showered her with favors. At last, after four centuries of languishing in the doldrums, Thebes once again began to grow to the proportions she had known under the empire. New colonnaded approaches were thrown up east and west of the temple of Amun (E–F), and the complex was adorned with a number of minor shrines around its periphery. One sector to the northwest of the great temple, called the "Mound of Wēse," was set aside for the worship of Osiris. As population returned, the city expanded its domestic quarter to the north and east, and old enclosure walls of the Twenty-first Dynasty were torn down to be replaced by a new wall and gate to enclose a much larger area, though it probably was never completed. Across the river the mortuary temple of Ramesses III, which had become the center of a town called *Djeme*, was refurbished and provided with new gates.

Nominally the Thebaid, the "House of Amun," was ruled by a princess of the royal house called the "Divine Worshipper of Amun." The incumbent of this office was, as far as we know, sworn to celibacy and therefore had to adopt her successor who was chosen by the king. The Divine Worshipper presided as a sort of queen—her names were in cartouches—over a court modelled on that of her father, the Pharaoh **(fig. 4).** Although the titles of men associated with her court clearly point to power and prestige, the Divine Worshipper herself appears to have been little more than a figurehead through whom the king could dominate the southland

Figure 4   The Divine Worshipper Shepenwepet I officiating at the offering of the hecatomb to Amun, Re-harakhty, and Ptah; the celebrant behind the offering table is her father Osorkon III; temple of Osiris Ruler-of-Eternity, Karnak.

completely. Real power lay in the hands of the queen's major domo, who could look forward to a massive tomb constructed on the west of Thebes in the Assassif district (G, H, I). Nubian grandees were installed in various Theban priestly functions, and the civil administration was placed in the hands of the able Montu-em-hat, Fourth Prophet of Amun and mayor of the city.

In spite of the Delta's skepticism, Kushite rule was a time of prosperity for Egypt. Building programs were established, and temple construction was resumed after the many years of stagnation under the Libyans. Art flourished: the old styles of relief, sculpture, and painting, which were really repetitions of Ramesside models, were now replaced by new, rather harsh norms from the south. The treatment is bold, the craftsmanship excellent. The models consistently hearken back to pre-Ramesside or even Middle Kingdom originals, with the result that the term "archaism" has sometimes, with justification, been applied to the spirit which informs the period.

The gods seemed to be with Egypt, and an exceptionally high Nile in the sixth year of Taharqa's reign (685 B.C.) symbolized the prosperity their favor produced. "(The river) rose greatly day by day and through many days it rose (at the rate of) one cubit per day. It reached the cliffs of Upper Egypt and over-topped the mound(s) of Lower Egypt; the land lay languid in the primaeval sea. . . . His Majesty had the annals of the ancestors brought to him, to see what inundations had occurred in their time; but the like of this was not found therein. For lo! the rain fell in Nubia and made all the mountains glisten; everyone was inundated with possessions, and Egypt was in happy festival. . . ."

The Twenty-fifth Dynasty and Assyrian Expansion

Prosperity at home made possible a united front towards Asia. After their take-over of Egypt the Twenty-fifth Dynasty had come to entertain distant, if amicable relations with Assyria. The leader of the rebellion in the Philistine city of Ashdod in 713–712 B.C., who had fled to Egypt, was extradited to Assyria in 705 B.C. Thereafter for reasons unknown matters deteriorated. In 701 Kushite military assistance was elicited by a coalition of rebels in Palestine, headed by Hezekiah of Judah, and Shebitku responded with a sudden, surprise incursion into Western Asia. With their Judaean and Philistine allies the Kushite army stunned the mighty Assyrian Sennacherib by fighting his forces to a standstill at Eltekeh in southern Palestine. Under Taharqa (690–664 B.C.) the Kushites took advantage of the political and dynastic troubles which marred the end of Sennacherib's reign to take the initiative in Asia. A treaty was concluded with the Phoenician king of Sidon, and Taharqa undertook a limited military offensive in the Levant which extended Egypt's frontiers into the Philistine plain. In 681 B.C., however, a new king, Esarhaddon, came to the Assyrian throne, and began to lay plans for what had been an Assyrian goal for many years, viz. the conquest of Egypt. *Casus belli* were ready to hand: Shebitku's "unprovoked" aggression in 701 and Taharqa's recent incursions in the 680s.

Egypt's chances were equivocal. On the face of it Taharqa seemed in a very good position to resist invasion. His army was well-trained in the arts of "modern" warfare and disposed of weapons and armor the equal of those of the Assyrians. Kushite troops retained a reputation for fierceness, to which was now added fleetness of foot and speed in attack. On the other hand Egypt's eastern frontier had suffered neglect under the Libyan kings. The great border fortress of Sile was still in existence fifteen centuries after its creation, but in need of repair; and the new settlement of Pelusium at the mouth of the easternmost branch of the Nile, thirty kilometers north-east of Sile, was not yet well fortified. The military route into Asia, constructed and much used by the Ramessides, with its dozen way stations between Sile and Gaza, had largely been abandoned. Perhaps Taharqa reasoned that the many lakes and lagoons in the region would prove enough to deter the Assyrians.

The first Assyrian assault in 674 found the Egyptians ready and waiting, and Taharqa defeated the Assyrians at Sile on the north-eastern extremity of the Delta. In 671, however, with the help of the Arabian tribes, Esarhaddon struck farther south across the Sinai desert, and entered Egypt via the Wady Tumilat. Desperately Taharqa fought a rear-guard action as he retired to Memphis, but the Assyrian attack was irresistible, and the great capital fell to the enemy battering rams more easily than it had to Piankhy fifty years earlier (J–K). Taharqa fled south to Thebes, leaving his family to fall into Assyrian hands. The Delta dynasts and their towns were sworn to uphold the "oath of Asshur," and were all given Assyrian names! There began a decade of confused marching and counter-marching in which great destruction was wrought throughout Egypt and Thebes was itself once sacked. No sooner had Esarhaddon retired from Egypt, placing his confidence in a small garrison to hold Memphis as well as the loyalty of the Delta chiefs, than Taharqa returned, occupied the Delta, and threw out the Assyrian forces of occupation. Esarhaddon again marched against Egypt in 669 B.C., but died *en route,* and the campaign was aborted. In 666 B.C. Ashurbanipal, Esarhaddon's son and successor, mounted a second invasion of Egypt in the face of which Taharqa prudently retired, leaving the Delta to be re-occupied by the enemy. The Assyrians again retired. Two years later they were probably lulled into a sense of security by the death of Taharqa; but their confidence was premature. Taharqa's nephew, Tanwetamani, took the throne in Napata, and at once came north with his army in 663 B.C. and occupied Memphis. In all this, like true turncoats, the Libyan chiefs of the Delta towns played one side off against the other, transferring loyalty as the need required. Now they prostrated themselves before Tanwetamani and offered him allegiance; but within months, on hearing of the imminent arrival of an Assyrian expeditionary force, they switched sides again. Tanwetamani fled to Thebes with his troops, but on this occasion Ashurbanipal did not stop in the Delta. He pursued the luckless Kushites who scrambled back to Napata, and occupied and plundered Thebes itself.

To devote more troops of occupation to Egypt proved impossible for Assyria, fighting as she was soon to be in Elam and Babylonia. Consequently it seemed expedient to Ashurbanipal to appoint a viceroy who could have the responsibility for Egypt's loyalty rest upon his shoulders. Ashurbanipal chose, wisely it must have appeared at the time, a native Egyptian, one Necho, the chief of the city of Sais and probably the grandson of Tefnakhte. While Necho did not disappoint his suzerain's trust, Ashurbanipal came shortly to rue the day he had selected this Saïte family; for Necho's son, Psamtek, who stepped into the post of viceroy on his father's death in 664, had a mind and will of his own.

Further Readings

The discipline is blessed by the presence of several up-to-date histories of the period of the origins of the Kushite state and the Twenty-fifth Dynasty. Among these one may profitably peruse the following: J. R. Anderson, *Treasures from Sudan*, London, 2004; A. J. Arkell, *A History of the Sudan from the Earliest Times to 1821*, London, 1961; W. V. Davies (ed.), *Egypt and Africa: Nubia from Prehistory to Islam*, London, 1991; R. G. Morkot, *The Black Pharaohs: Egypt's Nubian Rulers*, London, 2000; D. O'Connor, *Ancient Nubia: Egypt's Rival in Africa*, Philadelphia, 1993; D. B. Redford, *From Slave to Pharaoh: The Black Experience of Ancient Egypt*, Baltimore, 2004; P. L. Shinnie, *Ancient Nubia*, London, 1996; L. Torok, *The Kingdom of Kush: Handbook of the Napatan-Meroitic Civilization*, Leiden, 1997; D. A. Welsby, *The Kingdom of Kush: The Napatan and Meroitic Empires*, London, 1996; *idem* and J. R. Anderson, *Sudan: Ancient Treasures*, London, 2004.

For Kush, Assyria, and the Levant, see J. Boardman and others (eds.), *The Cambridge Ancient History III, Pt. 2: The Assyrian and Babylonian Empires . . .* , Cambridge, 1991; A. K. Grayson, *Assyrian and Babylonian Chronicles*, Winona Lake, 2000; E. Lipinski, *The Aramaeans, Their Ancient History, Culture, Religion*, Louvain, 2000; G. E. Marfoe, *Phoenicians*, Berkeley, 2000; J. M. Miller, J. H. Hayes, *A History of Ancient Israel and Judah*, Philadelphia, 1986; B. Oded, *Mass Deportations and Deportees in the Neo-Assyrian Empire*, Wiesbaden, 1979; W. T. Pitard, *Ancient Damascus: A Historical Study of the Syrian City-state . . .* , Winona Lake, 1987; G. Roux, *Ancient Iraq*, Harmondsworth, 1964; H. Tadmor, *The Inscriptions of Tiglath-Pileser III King of Assyria*, Jerusalem, 1994.

CHAPTER SIXTEEN

The Spirit of Sais
The Twenty-sixth Dynasty

—— Ψ ——

Twenty-sixth Dynasty	
Necho I	671–664 B.C.
Psamtek I	664–610 B.C.
Necho II	610–595 B.C.
Psamtek II	595–589 B.C.
Apries	589–570 B.C.
Amasis (Ahmose II)	570–526 B.C.
Psamtek III	526–525 B.C.

As the dust of the Assyrian expeditionary force dissipated on the horizon of the Sinai desert in 663 B.C., after their last and most destructive invasion, it seemed as though the Delta and Middle Egypt were on the verge of relapsing into the pettiness which had so weakened the region in the 8th century. Kush, having been soundly trounced by Ashurbanipal, was in no mood to try her luck again north of Thebes; in fact Tanwetamani had once again taken up residence in Napata. The chiefs of the Delta principalities had vented their wrath against the person who to them symbolized Assyrian dominion, viz. the collaborator Necho of Sais, and somehow contrived to put him to death once the Assyrians had departed. (It is also possible that Tanwetamani had had Necho executed.) His son, Psamtek, had been forced to flee to the marshes of the Delta for refuge.

A Note on Sources for Saïte History

While the successes the Twenty-sixth Dynasty enjoyed in all fields of human endeavor cannot be denied, the evidence for them is elusive. Archaeologically the Saïte kings, although they engaged in temple building and restoration, have largely been eclipsed by Nektanebo I and II of the Thirtieth Dynasty, and the early Ptolemaic kings, all of whom rigorously promoted construction work. If the fad was revived (which is very doubtful) of committing head-smiting tableaux and chariot scenes to temple façades and pylons, nothing has survived from the much denuded sites of Sais or Memphis. The Saïte period stands largely bereft of textual sources for a number of reasons. First, the New Kingdom practice of a king haranguing his court from the balcony, and having his words recorded and inscribed, had long since become obsolete, and was not favored by Psamtek and his successors. The few stelae that have come down to us are somewhat stilted compositions divorced from an everyday context, and drawn up in an archaic mode using stylized diction. We have reason to believe that day-books or journals continued to be used by the organs of government, but almost nothing of this genre has survived and no excerpts were committed verbatim to stone. Second, private biographical inscriptions are more numerous, but concentrate on the accomplishments of the individual, albeit in the service of the king. Third, while business documents are fairly plentiful, official government transcripts and private letters are not, leaving a substantial gap in our source material. The archives at Sais and Memphis, which must once have contained this material, have long since fallen prey to marauders.

In the light of this dearth of sources, we are perforce thrown back on to the following: 1. the account of Herodotus (Book II) who preserves a good deal of the folklore about Saïte kings which was told him on his trip to Egypt barely seventy years after the fall of the dynasty; 2. cuneiform sources of Assyrian and Neo-Babylonian origin, which, however, mention Egypt infrequently; 3. scattered and infrequent references to Saïte kings occurring in later classical authors; 4. a smattering of Biblical asides; 5. the family history of the Pediese clan, drawn up in preparation for a court case, which spans the period from Psamtek I year 4 to Darius I year 10 (c. 660–515 B.C.); 6. a small number of biographical inscriptions from dignitaries of the time, intent on commemorating their own beneficent acts. None of this provides a firm foundation for political, or even social, history.

The Triumph of Psamtek

A folk-tale circulating two hundred years later told how, having temporarily come to terms with eleven of his fellow Delta dynasts, Psamtek and the eleven took a solemn oath in the temple of Ptah and poured a libation to the god. In his haste, the presiding priest had put out only eleven earthenware cups for the libation, and Psamtek being at the end of the line was obliged to use his metal helmet as a container. An oracle having independently prophesied that supreme power would go to the one of them that poured from a metal jar, the dynasts drove Psamtek from their midst and he fled to the Mediterranean coast. A second oracle declared that the fugitive would receive help from bronze men who would come from the sea. The oracle was fulfilled, Psamtek realized, when a Greek ship full of hoplites lost its way and came to shore near the place he was staying. Having befriended them, the exiled Saïte used them to help him regain his city and eventually to extend his rule over his Delta rivals. There may well be a modicum of truth in this tale, for, as we shall see, Greek mercenaries shortly appear in the Egyptian army. Certain it is that by 660 B.C. Psamtek, backdating his reign to his father's death three years earlier, had won the day, declared himself king in Sais, and had begun to re-organize the country.

His efforts were assisted by a series of fortuitous events elsewhere in the ancient world. In the late 8th century B.C. a group of peoples from the steppes of southern Russia called the Cimmerians had begun to move southward through the Caucasus, apparently uprooted by the more distant Scythians. The Cimmerians attempted to cross the Euphrates, but were prevented from doing so by Sargon II of Assyria, and thereafter were deflected westwards into Anatolia, where they invaded Phrygia. In 680 Phrygia was annihilated, and its king Mita (= Midas) was killed. Pressed eastwards again by the resistance of Gyges of Lydia, by 657 the Cimmerians posed a threat to the Assyrian heartland. Assyria could ill afford this distraction, as she was faced by an Elamite revolt shortly after 663 and a Babylonian uprising ten years later. There was no possibility, under these adverse conditions, of Ashurbanipal fighting on all fronts, and Psamtek realized the time had come to declare independence. By 656 B.C. he had signalized his stance by signing a mutual assistance treaty with Gyges of Lydia, piqued perhaps at Ashurbanipal for not helping Lydia against the Cimmerians. It may well have been that the first Greek troops to arrive in Egypt, presumably from the Ionian coast under Lydian control, did so pursuant to this treaty with Gyges.

Thus was inaugurated the Twenty-sixth, or Saïte, Dynasty, the last period of political and cultural revival of native inspiration that Egypt was to experience. The process of restoration and reform was in fact a family accomplishment which, arguably, had been begun by Tefnakhte and Bocchoris seventy-five years earlier, and was just now being brought to fruition. These enlightened and able monarchs were to hold Egypt together for about 140 years, though not always with the approbation of their subjects.

The Re-unification of the Two Lands

Upon the accession to power of the new Saïte regime Egypt was beset by the same political and economic problems which had confounded earlier power-wielders, and had now grown serious through their long defiance of a permanent solution. The north continued to be plagued by the purblind parochialism of local chiefs, while the south still owed allegiance to Amun and Kush. This split required healing. In 655 Psamtek took the appropriate steps, but with great circumspection. Thebes continued to be ruled by the mayor Montu-em-hat, protégé of the Twenty-fifth Dynasty, and by the Divine Worshipper Shepenwepet II, princess of the royal house of Napata. The queen was prevailed upon to adopt Psamtek's little daughter Nitokris (A), and (perhaps in return) Montu-em-hat and other Kushite officials were allowed to keep their posts. Nitokris went south in splendor, accompanied by a great flotilla carrying dignitaries from all over Egypt; and the progress symbolically stressed the extension of Psamtek's power. Personnel, both civil and priestly, who had owed their appointments to Kush were gradually and peacefully eased out of office; and Psamtek appointed men loyal to himself: Aba-sonbu the chief steward, Nespakashuty governor of Upper Egypt, and Padi-amenemope the king's own friend and confidant. The new dynasty had, in fact, re-united all Egypt.

A second problem grew out of the first, viz. the continued confrontation with the Twenty-fifth Dynasty, still surviving at Napata. It could be argued, and in fact the Delta dynasts did so contend, that Psamtek was illegitimate. The last "legitimate" Pharaoh was none other than Tan-wetamani who had at least been accepted in Memphis in 663 and countenanced by Ptah.

Whether Tanwetamani ever seriously contemplated a second return to Egypt we do not know; and Napata remained strangely silent at Psamtek's take-over of the Thebaid. Nevertheless Psamtek strengthened the southern frontier at the First Cataract, and placed a garrison of for-eign troops there. Sporadic razzias on both sides issued, fifty years later, under Psamtek's son Necho II, in a full scale invasion by Egyptian forces. Within the decade the next king, Psamtek II, despatched a second, and much larger expeditionary force into Nubia (593 B.C.). While the king, who was a sickly individual, waited at Elephantine, his troops smashed their way into Kush, defeated the Twenty-fifth Dynasty army, and laid Napata waste. On the return a garrison was left at the Second Cataract to keep watch on the south. But it was not really necessary. Though per-haps it was not realized at the time, this major campaign in which Greeks, Judaeans, and Syri-ans participated as mercenaries, finally put an end to the threat from the south. The surviving Kushite royal family withdrew from Napata and resettled at Meroe, about 190 miles to the south-east, where a "Meroitic" kingdom survived into the fourth century after Christ.

The Central Government and the Saïte Court

Though of Saïte origin, the kings of the dynasty realized the folly of trying to rule from a city so far to the north and soon located the offices of the central government in Memphis. The office of vizier experienced something of a revival, although many viziers also bear religious titles, sug-gesting a new cultic side to their responsibilities. Another resuscitation from the past was the function of "king's-herald," which in the New Kingdom had been the designation of a sort of press secretary and chief of staff. Saïte incumbents sometimes combine a paramilitary and juridical function with their other duties. Government departments mirror what has come to be expected in state organization: a department of granaries, a department of arable land, a treas-ury and gold and silver store-houses, whose officers often show such archaic titles as "seal-bearer of the King of Lower Egypt." The judiciary is little known during the period; but it too throws up the archaic title "the six great courts (of justice)." What might today be called a "Department of Health" is well attested under the authority of the "chief physician" of the realm.

The chancery needed to run such an increasingly complex administration kept pace in size and efficiency; but these were attained only through a rigid concentration on scribal train-ing. Already during the revival of the Twenty-fifth Dynasty, if not before, the old cursive script of the New Kingdom called "hieratic" had begun to fall into disuse, having been considered too florid for practical use. During the Kushite period hieratic became increasingly cursive ("abnormal hieratic"), but under the Saïtes the script was even more drastically abbreviated. The result, "Demotic," has the appearance of a short-hand, easy to use by professionals, but requiring time to master. Nonetheless it admirably served the demands of the new state.

Sais had impressed Piankhy and the Assyrian kings as the only Delta city (B–C) which could reasonably be considered a power center from which Lower Egypt could be controlled; but we have no idea what courtly tradition had grown up in the city during the 8th century to make it so attractive. The city could trace its history from prehistoric times when, along with Buto, it had formed a sort of political nucleus in the north-west Delta. Now as then the great temple of the mother goddess Neith, along with ancillary shrines of Osiris and Atum, dominated the city. Similarly in the fiscal sphere her treasury dominated the Saïte economy. Perhaps already in the 26th Dynasty the later practice was in vogue, of donating a percentage of customs dues to Neith's treasury. In any event the city became the premier city in Egypt, overshadowing Tanis and perhaps even Memphis for the duration of the regime. The penultimate king of the dynasty, Amasis, contributed a gate, obelisks, and a sphinx-lined (D) dromos to the approach to the temple, as well as colossal statues of himself. Probably all the kings of the dynasty arranged their burials within Neith's temenos, in conformity with the practice inaugurated by the Twenty-first Dynasty, but the tombs of Apries and Amasis towered over the others, flanking the temple to the right and the left **(fig. 1).** The nature of Neith's complex, being a venue both for her worship and that of the deceased kings, called forth a very large priesthood, some of whom gained an international reputation for wisdom. Whether daily or mortuary, the services were provided with a variety of functionaries denoted by archaic titles and assisted by large choirs of singers, troupes of dancers, and orchestras.

For the first time since the days of Pi-Ramesses Egypt produced a sophisticated and well-appointed court. The Saïte kings surrounded themselves with a body of high-ranking courtiers drawn mainly from the Delta. In contrast to their functions, which may be passed off briefly in

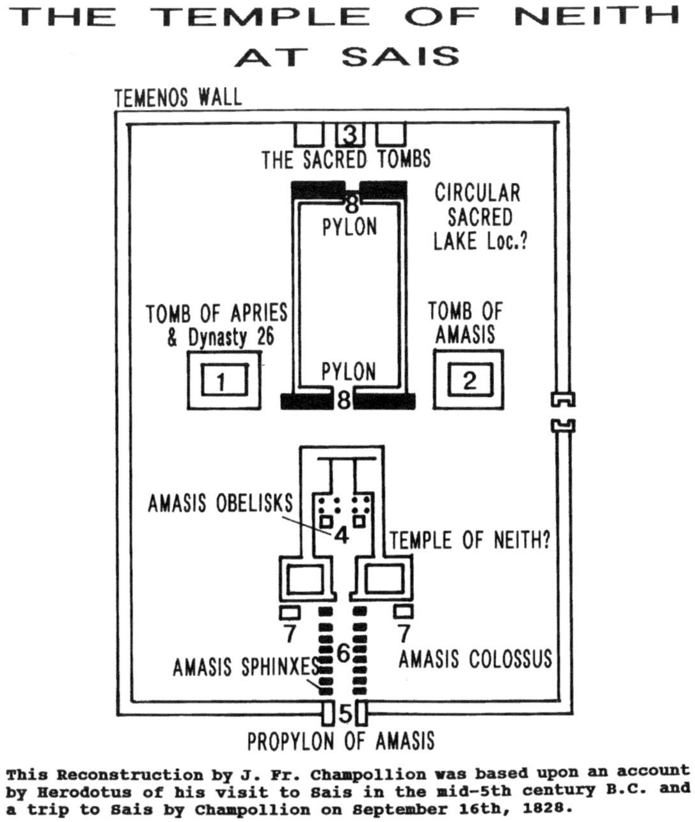

THE TEMPLE OF NEITH
AT SAIS

This Reconstruction by J. Fr. Champollion was based upon an account by Herodotus of his visit to Sais in the mid-5th century B.C. and a trip to Sais by Champollion on September 16th, 1828.

Figure 1   Temenos of the goddess Neith, Sais (after Champollion).

extended titularies, these grandees take obvious pride in courtly and priestly titles. The former are often so archaic or archaizing that they conceal meaning; the latter link the bearer with gods all over Egypt. Titles denoting priesthoods in a single nobleman's titulary betray the upper class practice of holding prebends in a temple, often inherited over several generations, which provided an income requiring little if any service in that temple. While little can be gleaned from the biographies of the nobility regarding the doings of the king, they nonetheless acknowledge the king's authorization of the work they carried out. This almost always consisted of deputized work on behalf of the state, such as refurbishing or constructing a temple, quarrying and setting up a stela, digging a sacred lake, restoring a cult, or performing a mission. While the state undoubtedly underwrote the work, we are on occasion left to wonder whether the grandee himself shouldered some of the cost. Most noblemen, in spite of a seeming independence, deferred to the king by taking a special "surname," compounded with the royal prenomen, to be modified if a new king came to the throne.

The Restoration of Provincial Administration

We have already discussed the state of the land under the later Libyan domination of the second half of the 8th century. Whatever its origins and sometime merits, the Libyan society and administration had proven dysfunctional by the time of the Kushite conquest; and if the Twenty-fifth Dynasty refused to remove the Libyan chiefs it was only because they felt they could more easily work through an existing structure. But the heyday of the Great Chiefs of the Me was now far in the past.

Psamtek I felt no compunction to honor any self-asserted right to rule on the part of the landed Libyan families whose parochial attitudes had so contributed to Egypt's weakness. Their essential conservatism bedevilled any attempt to modernize, just at a time when, in terms of military reform, it was essential that Egypt come up to the standards set by Assyria. Psamtek had erected his new state in opposition to these Libyan clansmen, and he could scarcely look to them for support. In 654 B.C. he decided to act. He took up residence in the old capital of the Twelfth Dynasty at Lisht, and there authorized a review of all the townships in which Libyan clans were resident, from Oxyrrynchos to the Mediterranean. Branding them "trouble-makers for the king's-house," he forthwith had them expelled from office and some from the country as well; and thereafter proceeded to break up the large baronies in the Delta, bestowing large tracts of confiscated land on the temples. Those Libyans who did survive did so only through subordinating themselves to the new regime.

Psamtek's organization drew on older norms, going back in some cases to the Old Kingdom, and was a thorough "clean up." A governor, responsible directly to the king, was appointed for Lower Egypt and another for Upper Egypt. A master of riverine shipping with extensive control over internal commerce was headquartered at Herakleopolis. The re-distribution of power under these officers at the provincial level laid stress, as of old, on the primacy of the local township and its metropolis, whose mayor functioned as local governor, or *nomarch*, as the Greeks called him. The nomarch's duties entailed land distribution and the allotment of seed grain, collection and despatch of taxes in kind, and juridical presidency of a sort of local, "leet-court." In some cases, depending upon the location of his township, priestly duties occupied him as well. Temples within a township were exempt from taxation, as they had not been under Assyrian occupation, and traditional sources of temple income were returned. Township controllers monitored the taxation of individuals, and Amasis in the middle of the 6th century even instituted an annual registry of personal income clearly with an eye on taxing it. The nomarch was assisted, if not monitored(!), by a secretary, a bailiff, a commissioner, a chief-of-police, and a head of the local militia, the *kalasiris*. The nomarch-system was established in theory throughout the length and breadth of the land, including the western oases which had now been taken over formally by the state; but in the extreme south the bailiwick of the Divine Worshipper of Amun naturally took jurisdictional and administrative precedence.

But Thebes was now far away, and the king was content with leaving its affairs in the hands of trusted men and his daughter (or sister). The city continued to thrive, and the *faubourgs* created by the Kushites became more prosperous than ever. Excavation has revealed multi-storied villas belonging to temple personnel lying east and north-east of the great temenos. Priestly statuary of excellent manufacture continued to adorn the ambulatories of the Theban temples, reflecting the apparent wealth of their owners. In Rylands IX the priests of Thebes appear from time to time, but their influence in northern courts is minimal. They were southern provincials with a country dialect, and the northerners tended to treat them with either condescension or a downright dismissive attitude.

The Reorganization of the Armed Forces

Even the moves adumbrated above—the expulsion of Libyans, the revamping of the administration—had not instilled complete confidence among contemporaries that Egypt was now free of danger. Psamtek I took pains to cultivate his remaining, native soldiery: "His Majesty enjoyed himself in viewing his army performing . . . after the land had been quietened and his enemies defeated. . . ." The king erected something "upon the western highland to strengthen the morale of his troops and to lift (the spirits of) his infantry. . . ." An opportune sequence of full inundations from 655 to 648 B.C. presaged prosperity: the king was "beloved of the Nun, Amun, and Hapy (personification of a high Nile), the father of the gods. . . . His father Amun has brought it about in order to make his reign a time of prosperity!"

The army and its officer corps required re-organization as much as any other branch of the government; but, as was typical of Egyptian behavior, no officer commanding troops was solely a soldier, and often combined civilian duties with the military. The armed forces were placed under the control of a supreme commander-in-chief, assisted by a multitude of generals and lieutenant-generals to oversee the various branches of the services. A corps of infantry shock-troops was organized, and the chariotry increased. An elite regiment, "the premier thousand of the military" (*hermotybies* in Herodotus's transcription, but hopelessly misinterpreted by him) was created, under the authority of a commander-in-chief, to serve partly as a royal bodyguard. The army organized a recruitment service under the direction of a "colonel of raw recruits"; but the commanders of the township militias (*kalasires*) were expected to supply contingents for expeditionary forces. Drawing on the precedent of Ramesside times, the Saïte kings revived the scribal commissariat to draw up draft lists, inventories, pay sheets, and records, and to oversee the military archives. Necessary though this flurry of activity in re-adjusting the hierarchy may have been, the army and navy still required re-fitting to bring it up to date. The armed forces of the world had long since adopted iron as the preferred metal for the manufacture of weapons and armor, but in Egypt no iron was available in antiquity. Moreover the lack of good timber for ship-building in the Nile Valley reinforced the same old dependence on the Phoenician coast that the

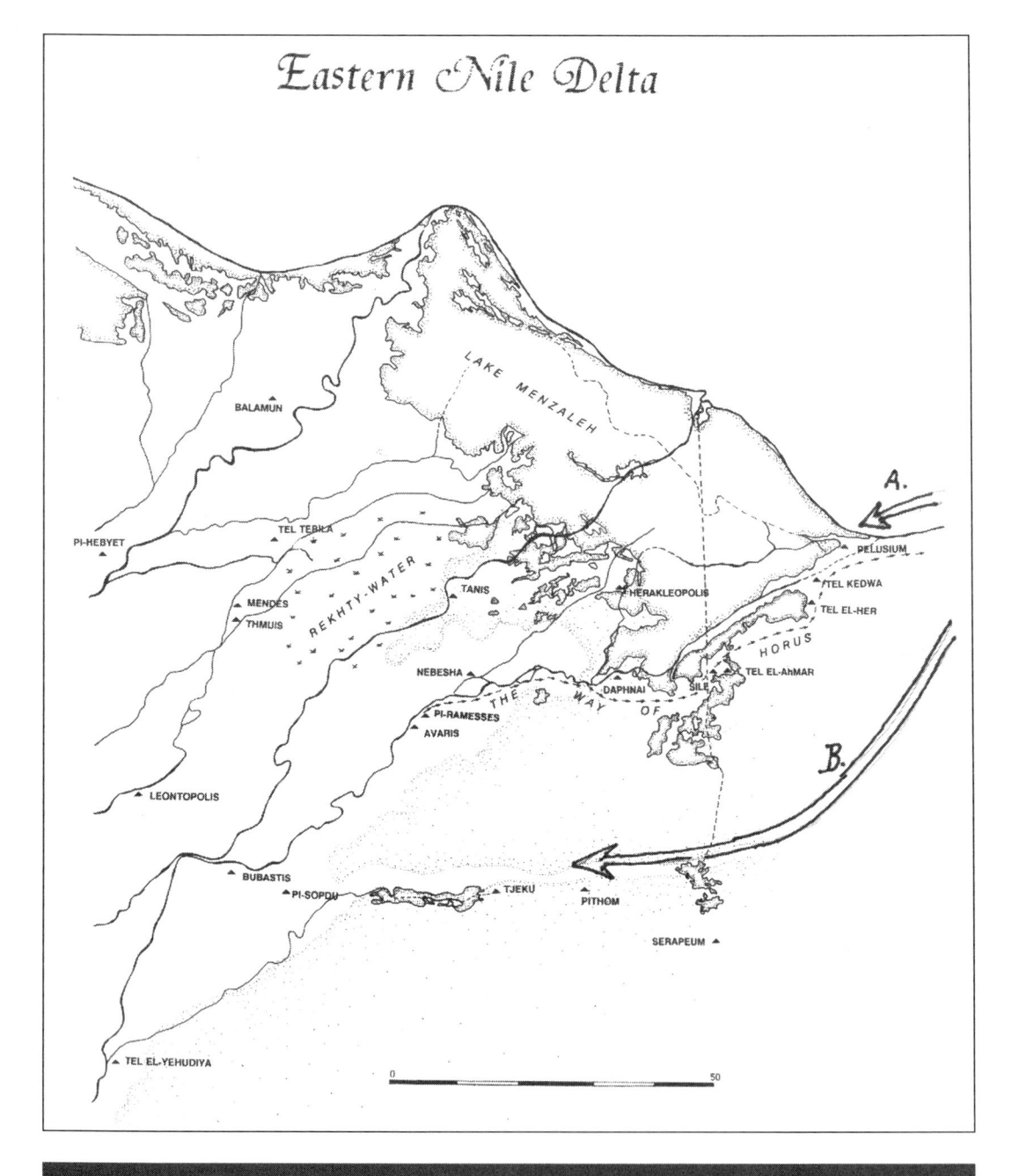

Map Key

A) Assyrians (674 B.C.), Persians (525 B.C.);

B) Assyrians (671 B.C.)

pharaohs of old had experienced. In the 9ᵗʰ century the Phoenicians had devised a sleek type of multi-purpose, sea-going vessel, and by the closing years of the 8ᵗʰ century (traditionally 704 in Corinth) the Greeks had introduced their own version, called a "trireme." The Saïtes adopted the form, though lacking an appropriate word, they called it by the old name of "Byblos-boat." Thereafter the title equivalent to "admiral" appears in the form of "commander of Byblos-boats," or "commander of the king's fighting ships in the Mediterranean."

If Egypt was drawing inspiration from the outside world, that world was experiencing a reciprocal attraction to the revived kingdom of the pharaohs. Greek hoplites had proven their worth in Psamtek's fight for the throne, and had become aware of the wealth to be made by service in Pharaoh's army. For their part Psamtek I and his son Necho II welcomed these foreign mercenaries, and substantial numbers of them begin to turn up in Egyptian ranks. Strengthening native capabilities by superior training and mimicry of Greek troops was the obvious policy to adopt, though in the long run it enjoyed only mediocre success. While, after the fall of Gyges around 640 B.C., Greeks entered Egypt as freebooters, the Phoenicians, Syrians, Judaeans, and Carians who also entered into the service of the king of Egypt, did so as a result of reciprocal agreements with Asiatic cities. (Deuteronomy 17:16 suggests, in exchange for auxiliary troops, the king of Judah received horses). Organized under Egyptian liaison personnel, the foreigners nonetheless retained their own officers, and brooked little interference from the Egyptians. On one occasion, in fact, a group of disaffected mercenaries of Greek and Asiatic origin were barely prevented from defecting to the Sudan by the tactful intervention of the Egyptian officer assigned to them. The story, long known in a distorted version in Herodotus, has now turned up in the biography of the officer himself, who came from Mendes.

A combination of factors, not least racial tension between Egyptians and foreigners, led to assigning Greek and Asiatic mercenaries to garrison duty on the frontiers when not engaged in expeditionary campaigns. We hear of Asiatic troops assigned to the Thebaid early in the dynasty, as well as barracks of the "Shasu" (literally "nomads," but perhaps indicating inhabitants of the Negeb) near Sais itself. Aswan received a contingent of Aramaeans, and the island of Elephantine a garrison of Judaeans. These latter are very well known today, thanks to the German excavations over the past century, which have turned up their houses, family archives, and a temple to Yah(weh). Greeks were stationed at Daphnae and Migdol on the eastern frontier of the Delta and also at Sais and Memphis. The fortress at Migdol (modern Tel Kedwa), excavated by Eleazer Oren and the present writer, reveals clearly the adverse living conditions the Greek soldiers had to suffer. Situated on low-lying land (ᴇ), between a large lake to the south and the Pelusiac branch to the north, Migdol constituted a mud-brick fort 220 meters square, with walls 13 meters thick expanding to 17 meters at the bastions. Although communications with the Delta were regular, the mercenaries lived in virtual isolation in a humid climate prone to disease, insect infestation, and marauding bedu. Lean rations could be gleaned locally in the form of fish, quail, and goat, but all else had to be imported from Egypt. The presence of numerous wine jars of East Greek manufacture, sent from the Aegean islands, attests to the craving of these lonely men for the comforting things of home.

Nonetheless service to Pharaoh brought compensation. While we do not know how long a soldier might work in Egypt, the pay was reasonably good. Greek commanders whom the Egyptians thought had done a good job might receive even more. One such officer from Priene on the Ionian coast has left us an inscription in which he records that a "king Psamtek" honored him with rich rewards including an entire city to rule!

Fiscal Controls and Commerce

Early in the 7th century the kings of Lydia in Asia Minor had begun to issue pieces of precious metal of a fixed weight and value, stamped with an official symbol. This first coinage became popular in Greece, and soon Greek and Lydian merchant vessels began paying for their purchases in coined money, rather than in goods. Egyptians accepted coinage by weight (which was not much different from the way in which they had always carried on exchange), but they remained reluctant to use it themselves as a medium of currency. Only about 450 B.C. did coinage come into limited circulation.

Nevertheless the appearance of coined money signalled the beginning of a period of increased commerce throughout the world. Egypt enjoyed a "seller's market" as she had in the Ramesside age: all the world came to her borders seeking to trade. Those nomarchs whose jurisdictions lay on the east or west frontiers of the Delta, or at Elephantine, were also charged with the collection of import dues, calculated apparently at the rate of 10% of the value of the goods, and by virtue of the fact received the title "Superintendent of the Door of Foreign Lands," or customs agent. The regions whence Egypt had traditionally sought products continued with even greater frequency to send their flotillas of cargo vessels to the wharves at Sais and Memphis (see map). Timber, cedar oil, spices, alum, and wine came from Lebanon and Syria; cattle, sheep, dom-palm timber, ointment, fruit, and tropical products from the Sudan. Supplies of wine and fruit from the western oases were assured by the imposition of Egyptian control on Kharga and Dakhleh; and increasingly from Saïte times the routes through these oases were used as a convenient means of access to points further west and south. In a move that was partly strategic and partly economic, Necho II (610–594 B.C.) began a canal from the Nile to the Red Sea through the Wady Tumilat, and constructed docks and a fleet of ships on the coast of Suez. Obviously intent on reviving the age-old commerce with the land of Pwenet in Somalia, Necho despatched a flotilla of ships manned by Phoenician sailors to explore the coast of East Africa. According to the account of an unbelieving Herodotus, 150 years later, the ships re-appeared after the passage of three years via the Pillars of Herakles, i.e. Gibraltar! The Phoenicians had actually circumnavigated Africa!

Novel for the Egyptians of the 7th century B.C., and a harbinger of things to come, was the opening up of a lively trade with Greece. After the collapse of the Bronze Age civilization in Greece in the 12th century, the Aegean had been all but cut off from Egypt; and the few products of Egyptian manufacture to reach the region did so through the agency of sea-roving Phoenician merchants. By the early 8th century Greece was beginning to emerge from this (loosely termed) "Dark Age." The remote cities of the mainland were one by one rejecting government by local rulers (*basileus*, "king," but deriving from the Mycenaean term for "local governor"), or even aristocratic oligarchy. Faced with economic and social problems they could not handle, people were turning to capable, energetic men who disregarded traditional procedure and exercised authoritarian control. It was to these "tyrants" (unconstitutional rulers), many of whom had come to power by force, but who nonetheless enjoyed broadly-based support among the people, that Greece owed the first flowering of its classical culture in the "Archaic" period. The Greek tyrants of the 7th–6th centuries appreciated the importance of foreign alliances and the trade that accompanied them, and actively courted Egypt's friendship. Corinth under the family of the Kypselids was one of the first to make overtures. So close became the tie to Egypt that the nephew of the tyrant Periander was named "Psammetichus," after Psamtek I.

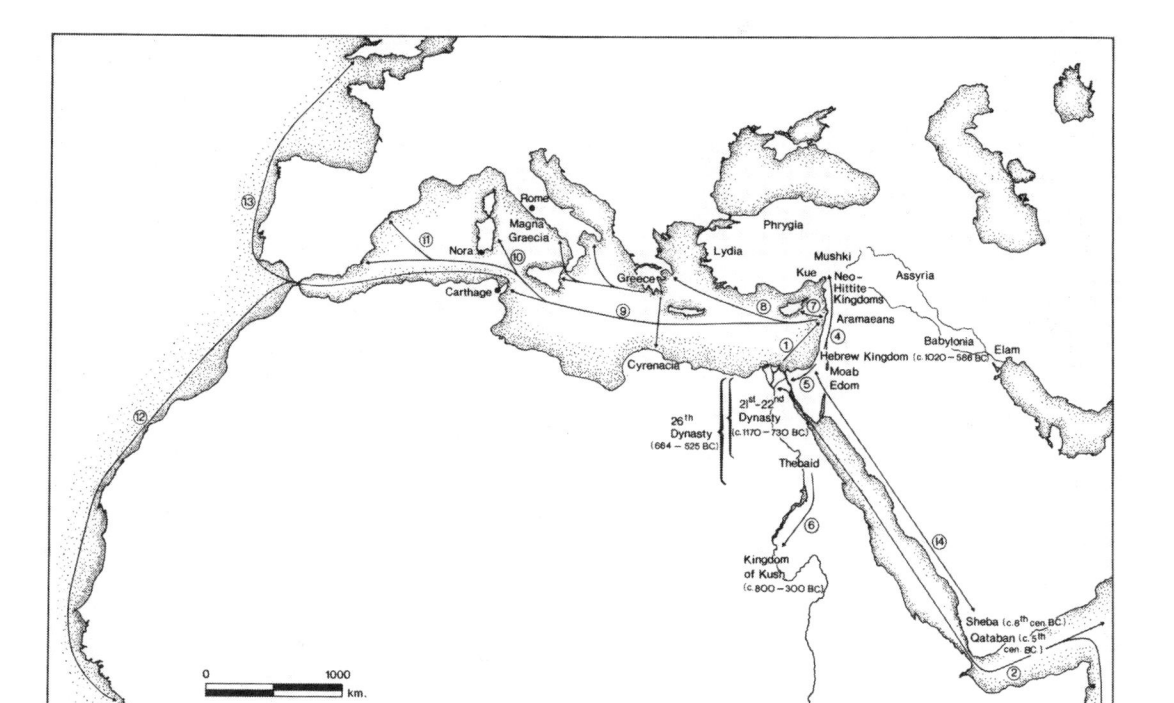

Map Key

1. Trade route between the Delta and Phoenicia.

2. Red Sea trade.

3. Route of the Phoenician circumnavigation of Africa.

4. Levantine trade with Anatolia and . . .

5. . . . with Egypt.

6. Egyptian trade with the Sudan.

Phoenician trade routes . . .

7. . . . with Cyprus.

8. . . . with Greece.

9. . . . with Carthage and North Africa.

10. . . . with Sardinia.

11. . . . with the Iberian peninsula.

12. . . . with West Africa.

13. . . . with Britain.

14. South Arabian corridor to Egypt and the Levant.

But it was the Ionian Greeks, in particular those from the city of Miletus, that took the lead in actively promoting trade. By 630 B.C. Milesian merchants had set up a trading post in the north-west Delta near the mouth of the Canopic Branch; and towards the close of the century a new city, Naukratis, was established near Sais as a Greek emporium where goods could be exchanged and dues levied. Naukrates soon became a flourishing town of Greek caste with Greek temples and Greek colonists from a consortium of Ionian cities. The city thrived for four centuries until finally overshadowed by Alexandria.

The Reassurance of Antiquity

The collective psyche of Egypt had, in the five centuries which had elapsed since the end of the New Kingdom, suffered the impact of momentous events totally at variance with the pre-suppositions on which the Egyptian state had been fashioned. That state and society had been created by Re-Harakhty and given to *men,* i.e. Egyptians; it was intended to continue in happy equilibrium to all eternity. It was in the very nature of *ma'at* that Egypt, god's land, should hold primacy of place everywhere. It was god's will that Egypt be strong, and that the king, his child, rule the earth for him. Pharaoh's eyes were on the entire world, his will prevailed universally; thwarting that will and contravening his law brought dire punishment. All "lesser breeds without the law" were obliged to abase themselves in his presence. But now those "lesser breeds" were everywhere in the ascendant: those whom the ancestors had dismissed as "the cowardly Labu" or "vile Kush" now dominated Egypt and had even assumed the kingship! To add to their chagrin the Egyptians themselves were castigated by these aliens as apostates in a back-slidden condition having abandoned the "true" lifestyle. The oath of Asshur had supplanted the oath taken in Pharaoh's name, and Egypt had suffered the renaming of its cities according to Assyrian style. The gods themselves, who deserved immediate obedience and respect, had been treated with contempt: Amun had been upbraided by a Libyan prince and his temple pillaged by an Assyrian; though professing piety, a Kushite had destroyed the city of Ptah.

To the increase of their own sense of shame, the Egyptians had to admit that the dismissive attitude of foreigners was not entirely unjustified. In general the divine cult had been bastardized and adulterated, sometimes for political reasons; religious literature was copied out in many versions, most of them inferior to the remote originals. Amun still represented the great symbol, nay the reality, of Egypt's strength and independence; but had been unable to act through the apostasy of his people.

But all was not lost! If today god seemed to have turned his back on the land, it was because of the nation's sin; salvation would come through repentance for sin and reform of lifestyle. But god had told them how to live, and they had a model *in the ancestors:* to conform to *ma'at,* to show forth love, and humbly to follow god's will. And so a respectful awe of the past, its works and society, all interpreted as manifestations of *ma'at,* took hold of the collective Egyptian psyche. National well-being and restoration would come from the ancestral past, not the present. To copy the past in all its forms became virtually a moral duty for Egypt.

It is interesting to note, in passing, that the same, almost desperate, turning to the past for models is exemplified in other communities around the eastern Mediterranean at about this time. The devastation wrought by Assyria or the depredations of Cimmerians and Scythians had wrought not only physical damage to older cultures, but also traumatic harm to national egos. In Phoenicia a priestly figure called Sanchuniaton is reputed to have collected the national lore, and worked the mythology of the coastal cities into a historified hermeneutic from creation on. In the 8th and 7th centuries Hebrew prophets ceaselessly assign Israel's discomfiture to the nation's abandonment of the "pure" law delivered to the ancestors in the wilderness; and King Josiah's discovery of Moses's "Book of the Law" is a blatant perpetration of pseudoepigraphic writing in an effort to reform the state after old models. In Greece too men looked to the past with a critical appraisal of the present, as the "historical" treatment of the gods by Hesiod and Pherycydes or the redaction of Homer under Peisistratus attest. Even Assyria, the cause of so much dislocation in the ancient world, and neo-Babylonia evinced their own fascination with antiquity in the form of restoration of buildings and recopying of texts (cf. the work of Ashurbanipal [667–626 B.C.] and Nabonidus [556–539]).

Egyptian use of the past as a model is most clearly, though not necessarily most significantly, seen in the realm of art. Whether one applies the term "archaism" involves a pointless debate: the works of the ancestors were to be preferred over those of the present. Beginning early in the Twenty-fifth Dynasty (although the origins may have their roots in Sais of the 8th century), Egyptian art turns to ancient prototypes from all periods, but especially those of the Old and Middle Kingdoms. Sculptors, although using very hard stone for the first time, used models from the Old Kingdom when sculpting likenesses of contemporary kings, and Amenemhet III's sphinxes became an inspiration for those of Taharqa. Certain statue forms, such as the cross-legged "scribal" pose, were revived, and the restrained style and basic costume of Old Kingdom reliefs re-introduced. Older forms of wooden coffins and *qeres*-box coffins are done in hard stone with great success from Saïte times on (E–E). Themes copy those of antiquity: the trampling sphinx, head-smiting, the mortuary meal (F), Isis and the child Horus, agricultural work on an estate (G). The people of Kushite-Saïte times knew the ancient tombs intimately through having visited them, not through "pattern-books" compiled for convenience, and the ink grids which they superimposed on the reliefs in them show that they intended to copy them. The tombs of Montu-em-hat and Petamenopet at Thebes, though eclectic in their choice of themes, draw heavily on earlier tombs in the Theban necropolis. One Saïte individual, a certain Aba, discovered that he had a namesake in the Old Kingdom, and pursuant thereto undertook to make exact copies of the older Aba's tomb reliefs for his own sepulchre!

But art and sculpture are only the most visible forms in which longing for antiquity manifested itself. Cult practices were "purified" based on ancient, written prescriptions discovered in old archives and libraries; and scribes became so adept at reading and even composing in Old Egyptian that they often boast that they are "able to restore lacunae (holes in the text)!" Cultic literature enjoyed an editorial clean-up. The Pyramid Texts were carefully copied, older versions of cultic formulae re-instated, and the Book of Going Forth by Day revised. Nothing would have delighted an Egyptian of Saïte times more than hearing it said of him that he was one who "restored (ancient) ritual procedures which had fallen into neglect." This is a period that witnessed the cleaning and refurbishing of many a dilapidated, half-buried mortuary chapel belonging to a bygone king, as the Saïtes undertook a wholesale resuscitation of royal cults, including those of Neferkasokar, Snofru, Khufu, Khafre, Menkaure, Pepy I, Senwosret III, Amenemhet III, Thutmose III, and a host of others. Graffiti in the pyramid temples of Old Kingdom kings attest the presence of all sorts of curious visitors, both Egyptian and foreign. Some even sought to build their tombs within the sacred precinct, as close to the pyramid as possible! Nor were the archaizing tendencies of Saïte times confined to private society. The government re-introduced the most archaic sounding titles, leaving us (and perhaps contemporaries!) to ponder what they signified. The royal chancery attempted, with success, to revive the language, form, and style of Old Kingdom decrees, and went so far as to try to revive the peculiarities of Old Kingdom dating, though it is doubtful whether the common man could understand it.

The Community of Proto-philosophic Thought

As part of her insistence on the old, Egypt of the Kushite-Saïte period revived its interest in the major systems of cosmogonic speculation. As will have been evident in earlier chapters of this work, the thought which lies behind this speculation achieved a fullness and sophistication at a very early period indeed. That it came to the fore once again in the 7th–6th centuries reflects the psychological needs of the time to establish the primacy of an old belief system. As in the case of every religion, not excluding Christianity, speculative thought is saddled with some very crass and embarrassing baggage; but in what follows it is not the "man-in-the-street" talking, but the intelligentsia that is thinking.

Basic to Egyptian thought is the concept of a primordial unit, "full of souls" as it were, in which all the infinite forms of existence are latent and as yet undifferentiated. The unit is called the *nun*, the primaeval sea, and is "unlimited" (Egyptian *nn ḏrw* or *iwty ḏrw.f,* "[the thing] whose boundaries do not exist"). Its component characteristics are given in terms of (implied) absolutes: unfathomable depth, infinite size, complete darkness, and impenetrable essence. For cultic purposes the four abstracts—the number four denoted totality to the Egyptians—were personified as four couples, male and female, and the resultant "Eight," the *Ogdoad,* had from the early Old Kingdom given its name to the town of Hermopolis (*Khmun,* "Eight-town"); but the abstraction of inherent quality is not to be confused with crude cultic practices.

The emergence from the "Unlimited" of "the All-Inclusive " (Egyptian *Atum*), signalizes the passage from latency to action: the All-Inclusive encorporates the entire cosmos, and by self-generative projection, a species of emanationism, gives it existence in all its multiplicity of form. The initial series of projections amounted to four, again the totality of elements, fiery heat/light, air, earth, and water, a construct which can be dated back to the formation of the king's pedigree (see above). As in the case of the Ogdoad, the crass demands of the cult created tangible and graphic personifications which, when complemented with females and augmented by the "All-Inclusive," created the *Ennead,* or "cycle of nine." The second element provided the rationale for the fact that all animal and human life share the same life force working within them. It derived from "air," or "breath," the first principle, conceived as a universal essence in the form of will and enunciated thought residing in every living creature. "I lead them (all living creatures)," says the numinous projection from the All-Inclusive, "I give them life through this utterance of mine, 'The Living One,' which is in their nostrils"; and "it is the divine utterance which is in every body." One can detect in this way of thinking the influence of the image of the Perfect God, the king, in the Old Kingdom, giving birth to concepts in his wisdom *(Sia)* and giving them concrete existence in his utterance *(Hu).*

These concepts crystallized in the doctrine surrounding the god Ptah of Memphis **(fig. 2).** Of Old Kingdom origin, Ptah had originally presided over the many technical crafts at home in the workshops of Memphis and the Saqqara necropolis, and his high-priest had early borne the appropriate title "Chief Manager of the Crafts." Later identified with the Greek Hephaestos and the Latin Vulcan, it was easy for Ptah to slip into the role of creator. He was also "earth" itself, the "risen land" pregnant with life. Ptah became "the August god

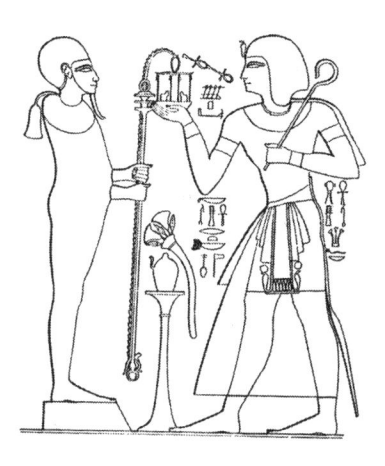

Figure 2 Ptah (left) bestows symbols of longevity upon the king.

of the primordial moment (the first point in time, when things began to be), constructor of men, progenitor of gods, the primaeval one who created all the living when it was spoken in his heart, who conceived their form and forecast precisely what had not (yet) been seen." There is good reason to believe that this interpretation of Ptah and his role go back at least as far as the Middle Kingdom, if not earlier; but the Ptah doctrine is most clearly set forth in a document known as the "Memphite Theology." The text is made up basically of three parts, the spoken formulae and rubrics of a mimetic presentation of the Osiris myth, glosses on this presentation, and a commentary on its meaning for Memphis and Ptah. Presently in the British Museum, the document was copied out on stone by order of Sabaco around 710–705 B.C., after he had discovered it in an old, moth-eaten manuscript in the temple library at Memphis. Scholars have debated whether this theological tractate (more metaphysical perhaps than theological) was a genuine copy or a pious forgery. But, be that as it may, the document certainly circulated in the Kushite-Saïte period and later spawned a daughter literature down into the Roman period. The ideas it propounded had a profound influence on the contemporary world.

In the process of formulating his ideas the unknown commentator became aware of an important reality and incorporated it as a corner-stone of his doctrine. "The sight of the eyes, the hearing of the ears, the smelling of the air by the nose, they report to the heart. It is this that causes every completed concept to come forth, and it is the tongue that announces what the heart thinks." The passage reflects an awareness of sensory perception and its implications: the senses report to the mind, the mind frames judgements, and the tongue gives expression to what the mind has conceived. The writer has, in fact, sensed what separates animate from inanimate. He has isolated two elements, which in typical Egyptian fashion, he designates by concrete terms: "heart," the intelligence or rational element in humankind which is able to think and bring forth ideas; and "tongue," the means of enunciating ideas, the purposeful expression and action of one's will. The essence of Ptah consists in a combination of heart and tongue and (implicitly) nothing more; the earth and the images of wood and stone are merely temporary habitations of something more ethereal. As "heart" and "tongue" Ptah came into being by himself; he was not created. The whole universe took shape in the beginning as a thought in the heart of Ptah, and by uttering the divine *fiat,* "let it be!" gave it concrete existence. The All-Inclusive, Atum, was simply a part of this intellectually-conceived universe: "there came into being as the heart and there came into being as the tongue (something) in the shape of Atum. . . . Indeed all the divine order really came into being through what the heart thought and the tongue commanded. . . . Everything came forth from him (Ptah), nourishment and provisions, the offerings of the gods, and every good thing. . . . And so Ptah rested after he had made everything. . . ." But coming-into-being and passing-out-of being involves the tension between opposites, the functional and the dysfunctional, "what is loved" and "what is hated"; life belongs to the harmony of the former, death to the injustice of the latter.

The author carried his metaphysical speculations one step further. If the sum of deity is Mind and Will, then wherever these are found, god exists. "Thus it happened that the heart and tongue gained control over every other member of the body, according to the doctrine that he (Ptah) is *in* every body and *in* every mouth, of all gods, all men, all cattle, all creeping things, and everything that lives, by thinking and commanding everything that he wishes." The animating principle thus pervades the universe and is identical with Mind, Egyptian *het* which Greek translates as *nous.* Unmixed with contaminants, Mind exists everywhere and was responsible for the separating out of entities from the All-Inclusive.

The activities of Mind, *nous,* i.e. conceptualizing and formulating, were tied into the notion of the basic substratum of the cosmos itself. Egyptians had long wrestled with the conundrum of Being and Not-being *(ntt iwtt)* as the expression of total reality and potentiality. Creation, "coming-to-be," and continued existence were all dependent on Ptah, who is himself not only *in* his creation, but *is* his creation. "O thou that didst engender himself," sang the hymnist, "ere any being had come to be, who fashioned the earth in his heart's design that his forms of being might come into being!" Of Ptah it became a constantly repeated declaration that "there is nothing that came to be without him. Coming-to-be is his being continually. . . ." Many other gods, such as Amun and Khnum, by appropriating this metaphysic, came themselves to be considered the universal substrate. All could be called "the Great God of the Primordial Moment," "the oldest god, the one that first-came-to-be," "the primaeval one who came-to-be at the first, the One without a second."

While for the mundane purpose of cult service Ptah, like so many other visions of the supernatural, is depicted as a life form, he has graduated in the thinking of the Memphite savant into a metaphysical concept. What precisely he meant in the scheme of things can be summed up by the following statement: "God is one. . . . Without effort he sets in motion by the thought of his mind. . . . All things come from earth." And again: "whatever things were to be, and whatever things were, as many as are now, and whatever things shall be, all these Mind arranged in order." Egyptians would have recognized a paraphrase of their own beliefs in these passages: the first comes from the Pre-Socratic philosopher Xenophanes (*floruit* c. 550 B.C.), the second from Anaxagoras (*floruit* c. 475 B.C.).

Further Readings

There is no comprehensive, up-to-date work on the history of the Twenty-sixth Dynasty, and in the absence of such treatments, one is thrown back on to somewhat tangential monographs.

The standard treatment of Herodotus's account of his visit to Egypt is that of A. B. Lloyd, *Herodotus Book II: An Introduction* (3 vols.), Leiden, 1975–88; see also N. Luraghi (ed.), *The Historian's Craft in the Age of Herodotus,* Oxford, 2001.

On the archaism of the period see J. Boardman, *Greek Sculpture: The Archaic Period,* London, 1985; B. V. Bothmer, *Egyptian Sculpture of the Late Period 700 B.C. to A.D. 100,* Brooklyn, 1960; P. Der Manuelian, *Living in the Past: Studies in Archaism of the Egyptian Twenty-sixth Dynasty,* London, 1994.

On the political history of the Saïte period, see J. Boardman, *The Greeks Overseas,* London, 1980; F. Ll. Griffith, *Catalogue of the Demotic Papyri in the John Rylands Library Manchester,* Manchester, 1909; M. F. Gyles, *Pharaonic Policies and Administration, 663 to 323 B.C.,* Chapel Hill, 1959; T. G. H. James, "Egypt: the Twenty-fifth and Twenty-sixth Dynasties," in the *Cambridge Ancient History III, Pt.2* (Cambridge, 1991), ch. 35; A. B. Lloyd, in B. G. Trigger and others, *Ancient Egypt: A Social History,* Cambridge, 1983; R. A. Parker, *A Saïte Oracle Papyrus from Thebes in the Brooklyn Museum,* Providence, 1962; A. M. Snodgrass, *Archaic Greece,* London, 1980.

On the "Memphite Theology" and the community of thought in the lands of the Eastern Mediterranean, see J. P. Allen, *Genesis in Egypt: The Philosophy of Ancient Egyptian Creation Accounts,* New Haven, 1988; J. Assmann, *The Search for God in Ancient Egypt,* Ithaca, 2001; *idem, The Mind of Egypt* (New York, 2001), ch. 23; J. Barnes, *Early Greek Philosophy,* London, 1987; W. Burkert, *The Orientalizing Revolution: Near Eastern Influence on Greek Culture in the Early Archaic Age,* Cambridge, MA, 1992; J. E. Coleman, C. A. Walz (eds.), *Greeks and Barbarians,* Bethesda, 1997; R. Waterfield, *The First Philosophers: The Presocratics and the Sophists,* Oxford, 2000.

CHAPTER SEVENTEEN
Egypt in the World of the Persian Empire

Twenty-seventh Dynasty	
Cambyses	525–522 B.C.
Darius I	521–486 B.C.
Xerxes	486–466 B.C.
Artaxerxes I	466–424 B.C.
Darius II	424–404 B.C.

Twenty-eighth Dynasty	
Amyrtaeus	404–399 B.C.

Twenty-ninth Dynasty	
Neferites I	399–393 B.C.
Psammuithis	393 B.C.
Akoris	393–380 B.C.
Neferites II	380 B.C.
Ahmose III (?)	380 B.C.

Thirtieth Dynasty	
Nektanebo I	380/79–362 B.C.
Tachos	362–360 B.C.
Nektanebo II	360–343 B.C.

When a nation loses the initiative, whether in domestic or foreign affairs, the consequences are serious. Even if, as in Egypt's case, the geographic location of the state enhances its ability to defend itself, nonetheless that nation is living on borrowed time under such circumstances. In spite of the ability and perspicacity of the merchant kings of the Twenty-sixth Dynasty, Egypt was struggling against impossible odds. Soldiering was largely in the hands of foreigners: the Egyptian element in the armed forces counted for less and less. Foreign commerce was a Phoenician or Greek enterprise, undertaken in foreign bottoms. Egypt was complacent with its bountiful harvests, and seemed in need of nothing. Long had Egyptians viewed foreigners with contempt: They could teach Egyptians nothing worthwhile. With this attitude pervading the court of the king of Egypt, the ultimate outcome was eminently predictable.

The Persian Conquest of 525 B.C.

By the year 626 B.C., when Psamtek I had long since established an independent Egypt, Ashurbanipal of Assyria was dead, and the end of his once mighty empire was not long in coming. Even Psamtek's *volte-face* in policy, which resulted in Egyptian military aid being sent to the upper Tigris to prop up the Assyrian regime, could not stem the growing tide. In 614 B.C. hordes of Medes from the Iranian plateau descended upon the plains of Assyria and laid waste Asshur, the pivot of the empire, from which the kingdom had taken its being. Two years later Nineveh fell to the concerted assault of Medes and Babylonians, and the last scion of the Assyrian royal family was forced to flee into western Mesopotamia. There, in 605 B.C., he suffered an ignominious defeat at the hands of a resurgent Babylonia under Nebuchadnezzar II, the villain of the Book of Daniel. The Egyptian army under Necho II, which had come to help him, was virtually annihilated. Although foiled in 600 B.C. in his attempt to invade Egypt, Nebuchadnezzar terminated the independence of many a buffer state in southern Palestine, including Ashkelon, Ekron, and Judah, and maintained a hostile presence in the Sinai for 60 years. Then in 539, abruptly and with little warning, Babylon was overthrown. Cyrus, the king of an incipient Medio-Persian Empire, marched unopposed into the Tigris-Euphrates valley, and in Babylon itself was hailed as a deliverer. A master of persuasion rhetoric, Cyrus took full advantage of the favorable political climate to claim to have elicited the approbation of all gods, and to fabricate *marriage stories* to bolster territorial claims. The entire Near and Middle East, from the recently conquered Kingdom of Lydia in western Asia Minor to the steppes of central Asia, was united into a single imperial sphere, under the authority of one man, Cyrus the Great, King of Kings.

For a century and a half Egypt had staved off three great empires: the Kushite, the Assyrian, and the Neo-Babylonian. Kush, never willing to concede primacy of place in the valley of the Nile, had posed a real and imminent threat to the Saïte kings until Psamtek II mounted a successful military campaign in the south, which resulted in the destruction of Napata, the enemy capital. Thereafter the Sudan receded from Egypt's southern horizon, but the northern outlook remained bleak. Attempts in 587 B.C. to aid Jerusalem against Babylon at the eleventh hour ended in disaster for Egypt and a loss of face among the peoples of southwestern Asia. When, after 539, the Medio-Persian Empire began to mobilize its forces,

Amasis, the last of the great Saïte kings, took steps to defend his eastern frontier, occupied Cyprus, and entered into alliances with the Greeks, in particular with Polycrates, tyrant of Samos. But it was to no avail. These acts were clearly construed as hostile by Cyrus and his successor Cambyses, and were considered a *casus belli*. Amasis died just as the long-expected Persian offensive got under way; and the Persian king Cambyses had only to face an untested youth, Psamtek III, and a defense force lacking in confidence. In the spring of 525 B.C. the Persian host appeared before the walls of Pelusium (A) at the mouth of the easternmost branch of the Nile (B). In the ensuing battle the Egyptian troops put up a half-hearted resistance, but their Greek auxiliaries failed to turn the tide. The Persians carried the day. Psamtek III perished, the border forts were abandoned, and Memphis was captured. By June of the same year Egyptian business documents were being dated to the reign of Cambyses. Egypt was to remain a Persian province for 120 years.

Egypt under Cambyses and Darius I

In Egyptian historiography, both ancient and modern, Cambyses is an equivocal figure. In contemporary texts he was portrayed as a pious "Egyptian" king, allowing himself to be introduced to the *recherché* aspects of the cult of Neith at Sais, by the former Egyptian admiral and turncoat Udjahoresne. Nevertheless, Cambyses survives in later tradition as a blasphemous madman who slaughtered the sacred Apis bull of Memphis. This is a curious indictment, as Apis worship seems to have continued throughout his reign without interruption. It may be that the specific accusation of tauricide has something to do with Mithraic mythology: after all, the slaying of the bull by the "unconquered sun" was a longstanding inaugural myth in an Iranian context.

But the vilification of Cambyses probably originated in his historic dealings with the temples and their priestly staffs. With the exception of three institutions only, Cambyses decreed that certain commodities, formerly supplied at the expense of the state, should now be made the responsibility of the temples themselves. In other words, the priests would be obliged to scrounge! One cannot imagine this fiscal belt-tightening sitting well with the priests; and the bad public relations that resulted may have haunted the memory of Cambyses ever after.

With Cambyses' unexpected death three years after his conquest of Egypt, the empire was plunged into a civil war from which it was rescued by an usurper, Darius, son of Hystaspes. A man of far-sightedness and intelligence, Darius emulated his predecessor Cyrus in the tact and imagination he brought to the running of such a vast imperial structure. In the case of Egypt, where the rebellion had never been serious, Darius sought to win hearts and minds by real gestures of conciliation. Late in 518 B.C. he visited Egypt, arriving, as luck would have it, just at the moment when an Apis had died. The Apis bull was sacred to Ptah, and the priesthood that served both deities reserved the unofficial right to countenance and confer legitimacy on a prospective power wielder. His reverential attitude at the obsequies (**fig. 1**) ingratiated him with his new subjects, and his decision to allow himself to undergo a Pharaonic coronation in Memphis sealed their acceptance of him. The legitimacy that was thus attached to Darius was in large measure responsible for Egyptian acquiescence, albeit grudgingly given, in the hegemony of these "foreign rulers" for over a century.

Figure 1 Adoration of the Apis at the time of the bull's funeral; probably Darius year 4.

Persian Administration

Throughout the course of the 120 years of the first Persian occupation the administration transmogrified from a lenient, symbiotic co-option, through the introduction of a foreign style, to ultimate neglect and incompetence. At the beginning an enlightened self-interest characterized the Persian approach to their Egyptian subjects. Egyptians, even those in military posts, retained their jobs under Cambyses and Darius; and it is often difficult, failing the presence of a cartouche, to date a private statue in the period between, say, 540 and 480 B.C. Inscriptions from the quarries (c) indicate a continuation of building projects. At first under Darius I Egyptians occupied the post of overseer of quarry and construction work; later, during the reigns of Xerxes and Artaxerxes I a Persian *ša rêši* is found occupying this office.

But this apparent leniency masked an iron resolve to quash dissent and nationalistic feeling, and to milk the country of its resources. The great city of Thebes, that center of patriotism, lost any favored status it might have enjoyed under the Kushites and Saïtes, and the institution of the Divine Worshiper of Amun was terminated. A relic of a time when a native regime in the north of Egypt controlled the Thebaid through a princess of the blood, the Divine Worshiper did not at all fit the Persian framework. The Persian administration was centered in Memphis where a governor and a garrison of Persian troops occupied the age-old *White Fort*. The old townships still retained their role as provincial units of political and juridical control, and Herodotus, who visited Egypt in the middle of the 5th century B.C., describes the function of the *nomarch* in some detail.

In fact, the roster of provincial officials reflected in Rylands IX, with its division between civilian, police, and military functions, and rooted in a bifurcation as old as the Twenty-second Dynasty, continued to be maintained throughout the Persian occupation. Moreover, the Persian authorities did not take over the general oversight of Upper Egypt and its riverine commerce, which the Saïte kings had bestowed on the governor of Herakleopolis. Instead, they grouped townships loosely into larger administrative districts, and Persian officials with Aramaic-speaking support staffs of *pkidm,* administrative officers, were gradually introduced throughout the countryside.

Aramaeans had long since lent their language and script to the great empires of the Near East, beginning with Assyria at the beginning of the first millennium B.C.; and it should come as no surprise that the Persian government issued its decrees and kept its records in Aramaic. Papyri still extant include letters and business documents from the garrisons at Elephantine **(fig. 2)**, Hermopolis, and Migdol, a customs officer's log book, a dockyard account book, and the private correspondence of one of the governors. Rarely, however, did the Egyptian business community resort to Aramaic, preferring to use its own vernacular, Demotic, and the cursive script in which it was written. The Egyptian business community retained the old Kushite-Saïte regnal-year system, backdated to New Year's Day, and now applied to the reigns of the Persian overlords.

The Persians naturally showed great interest in the riches of Egypt. The alleged codification of Egyptian law by Darius I, reflected in tradition centuries later, is in fact nothing more than an attempt by the Persians to translate tax- and contract-law relating to the endowments of temples into Aramaic for greater ease of perusal. The Persians occasionally confiscated temple land, and the business agent of each temple (the *lesonis*-priest) was placed under state control. Although Darius, in his accepted role of "Pharaoh," continued to make gifts to temples in the time-honored Egyptian tradition, after his reign donations by Persian kings almost completely dried up. The tax structure in place under the Twenty-sixth Dynasty was apparently left intact. This must have included the novel income tax instituted by Amasis, as well as those taxes

Figure 2   Elephantine: stratification in the quarter in which the Jewish garrison was housed.

and revenues attached to the running of Egypt's extensive necropoleis, a species of mortuary economics. In general, taxes paid to the state were by no means light. Farms paid a land tax as well as the harvest tax, amounting to 120,000 measures of grain; and other food-gatherers, such as fishermen, were obliged to hand in a portion of their catch. While these forms of tax find parallels in earlier times in Egyptian history, the tax burden of 700 talents of gold sent annually to the Great King in Persia was something new. Nor were the Persians going to risk the uncertainties of land travel in order to ensure that taxes reached Persepolis and Suza: Darius had the old eastern canal, begun by Necho II, completed and dredged so that cargo boats could make their way by sea from the Nile to the Persian Gulf.

The Denigration of the Monarch and the Folklore of Deliverance

In spite of the general calm that pervades the first half of the 5th century B.C., it cannot be said that the Egyptians bore their lot with equanimity. True, in general the decrees and reforms of the Saïtes had not been rescinded by the Persians. Nor was there a return to the parochial anarchy of the Libyan period. In fact there was some attempt at standardization throughout the country (e.g., in weights and measures that followed the standard of the temple of Ptah at Memphis). But Egypt was now a backwater, a conquered country. Big money was being diverted or left unused; few temples were erected. High tariffs on imports from Greece (in contrast to low import dues on Phoenician goods) were ostensibly intended to pursue a sort of economic warfare, but in fact redounded to Egypt's disadvantage. In spite of one or two notable exceptions, Persians settled in Egypt showed no interest in acculturating themselves to the ways of the country, and in general contemned Egyptian religion. Skilled natives were being taken to Suza and Persepolis as artisans or soldiers. In short, the Persian kings following Darius I displayed a studied indifference toward the country and its well being.

From the 7th century onward, one senses among Egyptians a wholesale, creeping disillusionment with the political forms by which they have been traditionally governed. Neither Libyans nor Kushites fit the ancestral roles called for by royal theology: the former had proven indolent and destructive, the latter pious, but foreign. We know little about the personalities, policies, or politics of Saïte kings, and it is fatuous to write on the concept of kingship under the Twenty-sixth Dynasty; they may have made the kingdom prosperous, at least for their followers, but Egyptians shed no tears when Psamtek III departed suddenly. Within a generation of the Persian occupation folklore was throwing up the concept of two monarchic types: the "good but weak" king, and the unprincipled tyrant. Giza became the type site, and pyramid size dictated the image. Khufu and Khafre had been monstrous despots who shut the temples and enslaved the people; Menkaure, while well intentioned, had been weak and unable to circumvent his fate. These were *men*, not gods.

Invasion from without, especially from the north, was becoming a familiar occurrence to the Egyptians. From c. 725 to 525 B.C. the land had witnessed at least nine attempts (some abortive) to break into the country by force: two from the Sudan, four by Assyria, two by Babylonia, and one by Persia. The concomitant destruction and dislocation of life may be imagined: if it was not the foreign soldiery that defiled the sacred fanes of Egypt, it was the lower classes squatting for protection within the unguarded temple courts.

Small wonder, then, that the period from the 7th to 5th centuries should have seen the genesis in Egyptian folklore of the "legend of the deliverer," although most surviving exemplars date from the Greco-Roman era. The plot pattern turns up in a variety of mutations, but all with the following basic ingredients: Egypt prospers under the rule of king so-and-so (usually a historical figure); then a prophecy is uttered by a wiseman, inspired peasant, or sacred animal with the power of speech, to the effect that the land is about to be invaded from the north (the prophecy in fact usually adumbrates the rest of the plot). The prophecy comes true, and "impure" Asiatics overrun the country, wreaking destruction for a set period of time (sometimes seven years). King and court flee south to the Sudan, where they remain safe until the predicted period comes to an end. Then, with divine assistance and a large army, the legitimate king re-appears, drives out the filthy foreigners and cleanses the entire land and its temples. The plot has the impress of events of the period of foreign invasions seen from a Theban perspective: The threat is from the north, salvation from the south. As it turned out, the pattern did not quite fit the events of the 4th century B.C., but the story line is a genuine reflection of the attitude of the Egyptians toward the northern world, and a pitiable expression of their forlorn hope for freedom.

The Last Period of Political Independence: Dynasties 28 to 30

Sporadic outbreaks of revolt in the Delta during the 5th century B.C. did not overtax Persia's ability to retaliate, although they did disrupt the everyday life of the country. Most were on a small scale. The consistent pattern involved Delta warlords, cast in a mold similar to the Delta dynasts of Libyan times, with distinctly piratical tendencies. Often they holed themselves up in their marshland strongholds, where it was difficult for the Persian authorities to operate effectively. They may have viewed themselves as divinely chosen to rid the sacred soil of Egypt of any trace of the hated foreigner; but their purview was parochial, their performance inept. All that is vouchsafed to us today are a few references in classical authors, and a handful of statues with names redolent of past glories—a "Psamtek" or "Petubastis"—which the rebels managed to have carved before their rebellions were suppressed. Only the revolt of Inaros (463 to 454 B.C.), with Athenian help, seriously threatened the Persian hold—a Persian governor was in fact killed—and was bloodily suppressed. But it proved to be a harbinger of things to come: The Persian Empire was about to crumble.

By the end of the 5th century the political climate and the *dramatis personae* had changed. Darius II now sat on the Persian throne, and his rule was weak and incompetent. In Egypt after 416 B.C. unrest took the form of uprisings and terrorist acts (which to us would approximate food riots, rather than politically motivated insurrections). And the results of mismanagement were felt elsewhere as well: Lydia, Syria, and even the Persian homeland flared into open revolt. In 404 B.C., upon the departure of the Persian governor, a certain Amyrtaeos, perhaps a descendant of the Twenty-sixth Dynasty, declared a kingship from the city of Sais; and when, two years later, a problem in the succession to the Persian throne produced an outright civil war between Artaxerxes II and his brother Cyrus, all Egypt threw off the Persian yoke. Amyrtaeos backdated his legitimacy to the accession of the "illegitimate" Artaxerxes II, and declared all Egypt independent.

Freedom had been won and was to be maintained with surprising ease, but one reason not yet considered is abundantly clear. With the end of the Peloponnesian Wars in Greece (404 B.C.) large numbers of highly trained hoplites from both sides found themselves without occupation, and thousands entered Egyptian service as mercenaries. It was largely due to their presence in Egypt that the two serious attempts the Persians made to retake Egypt (385 and 373 B.C.) were thwarted. Moreover, thanks in part to the incompetence of Darius II's administration, Egypt had retained a remarkable degree of real wealth, and was easily able to purchase both service and loyalty. Remarkable Greek generals such as Agesilaus and Chabrias accepted Pharaonic employment and contributed significantly to the country's defenses. With the weakening of the Persian Empire due to widespread rebellion, Egypt during the early 4th century B.C. was offered a golden opportunity to consolidate its political independence.

Curiously, the great Delta families who had led the revolt could not stop feuding among themselves. In 399 B.C. the short-lived Twenty-eighth Dynasty was toppled when Amyrtaeos was betrayed and arrested by Neferites, a former comrade in arms, who brought him to Memphis and had him executed. Neferites (**fig. 3**) came from the city of Mendes in the central Delta, and he and his four successors, ruling scarcely 20 years, constitute the Twenty-ninth, or *Mendesian,* Dynasty. This regime was toppled in turn by general Nektanebo, a grandson of Neferites from a cadet branch of the family. Although Mendesian in origin, Nektanebo (**fig. 4**)

Figure 3   Royal head, probably of the tomb-owner, from the tomb of Neferites I at Mendes.

Figure 4 Relief of Nektanebo I from Karnak; the pleasant expression and smiling mouth are characteristic of the art of the 4ᵗʰ century B.C. through Roman times.

Figure 5 Temenos wall of Nektanebo I at Mendes, demolished by the Persians in 343 B.C.

resided in neighboring Sebennytos, and with his two successors is counted as Dynasty 30. In spite, however, of the political prominence of Mendes, Sais, and the memory of the Twenty-sixth Dynasty continued to cast a spell over the land. In a sense the rulers of this period legitimated themselves at the shrine of Neith of Sais, and felt themselves to be true spiritual successors to the Psamteks.

Despite their internecine feuding, the last native rulers of Egypt had the time, money, and inclination to benefit Egypt in traditional, Pharaonic ways. A vast amount of architectural restoration was undertaken: new temples and palaces went up all over the country, and city and temple enclosure walls were rebuilt **(fig. 5)**. It is not uncommon on Ptolemaic sites to find that the earliest masonry still standing, if not the temple structure itself, dates to the Thirtieth

Dynasty, and was only finished off under the Ptolemies. Additional cultic benefactions extended to the renewal of shrines and naoi, cult statues in precious metals, offering tables, libation stands, ewers, and censers. It became common practice to list graphically all the gods and goddesses of a temple, along with their implementa. One senses an underlying concern for preserving cultic detail: for too long the authorities had neglected the world of the Egyptian temple and its denizens.

The Last Persian Conquest of Egypt

By the middle of the 4th century B.C. the reconquest of the Nile had become an obsession with the Great King. Nothing he attempted in this regard ever came to fruition, and had often ended in humiliating disaster. Artaxerxes III, in spite of initial setbacks before 350 B.C., was more dogged in his determination to bring Egypt to heel, and in the five years following the middle of the century made preparations on a vast scale for a showdown with Nektanebo II, the Egyptian king. The world seemed to sense what was in the offing: in far-away Arabia merchants were concerned that their trade with Palestine and Egypt might suffer, and Athenian politicians warned that if Egypt fell, Greece would be next on the list.

The Persian host, accompanied by a considerable navy, set out from Gaza in the early summer of 343 B.C. As though fated to reverses at every turn, Artaxerxes endured the consequences of poor logistics, unfavorable winds, and the ravages of quicksand (into which part of his army strayed). But he pressed on, and it was only the ineptitude of Nektanebo that saved him from a disaster comparable to those of his predecessors. For when the Egyptian commanders perceived the size of the enemy army, and detected an outflanking manuever by sea, they were unnerved and fell to cavilling with their Greek auxiliaries. To make matters worse, Nektanebo panicked, retreated to Memphis (where he hastily gathered up his treasure), and fled precipitously into the Sudan. The frontier defenses collapsed, and all Egypt lay open to the invader.

Folklore was being paralleled by history. Egypt was given over to plunder as the Persians defiled the temples and slaughtered the sacred animals. Mendes, in particular, was harshly treated. The Persian invaders destroyed the tomb of Neferites **(fig. 6–7)** (probably exhuming and destroying his corpse in the process), tore down the city wall erected by Nektanebo, and defiled parts of the sacred ram necropolis. Bubastis suffered a similar fate, and Memphis and Thebes probably were punished as well. Contemporary biographies speak of civil strife and mayhem engulfing the land from one end to the other, as the Persians wrought revenge. One act in particular was calculated by the Persian eunuch and henchman of Artaxerxes, Bagoas, to deal a fatal blow to the priests and temples, those institutions at the very heart of Egypt's socioeconomic system. Bagoas demanded that the priests hand over all the temple paraphernalia: cult images, altars, censers, wands, sacred vessels, vestments, and the like, and carried them off to Persia. In particular, he confiscated the contents of the temple libraries throughout the land, and cynically refused to return them until the priests had paid an exorbitant ransom. Since the cult of Egyptian temples heavily depended on this sacral implementa and the sacred books, this act was tantamount to an attempt to destroy the Egyptian belief system.

Figure 6 Burial chamber of Neferites I, Mendes, showing the sarcophagus box of limestone; destroyed in the Persian invasion of 343 B.C.

Figure 7 Swaths of shattered limestone from the destruction of Neferites' tomb in 343 B.C., cascading over the wall of Nektanebo I.

Expectantly, Egypt awaited the deliverer promised in the prophecy: would Nektanebo return from the south? In 332 B.C., after 12 turbulent years of servitude, the nodding plumes of the forces of salvation appeared on the horizon. But contrary to the prophecy, they came from the north, and their leader was not Nektanebo *redivivus,* but Alexander the Great.

Further Readings

In general, on the Persian Empire and Egypt's place in it, see E. Bresciani, *Nine Pharaohs,* Pisa, 2002; P. Briant, *From Cyrus to Alexander: A History of the Persian Empire,* Winona Lake, 2002; J. H. Johnson (ed.), *Life in a Multicultural Society: Egypt from Cambyses to Constantine and Beyond,* Chicago, 1990; A. T. Olmstead, *History of the Persian Empire,* Chicago, 1948; H. Sancisi-Weerdenburg and A. Kuhrt (eds.), *Acheamenid History VI: Asia Minor and Egypt: Old Cultures in a New Empire,* Leiden, 1991; J. W. Watts (ed.), *Persia and Torah: The Theory of Imperial Authorization of the Pentateuch,* Atlanta, 2001.

On the Jewish community and the Aramaic Papyri, see E. Bleiberg, *Jewish Life in Ancient Egypt,* Brooklyn, 2002; A. Cowley, *Aramaic Papyri of the Fifth Century B.C.,* Oxford, 1923; G. R. Driver, *Aramaic Documents of the Fifth Century B.C.,* Oxford, 1957; E. G. Kraeling, *The Brooklyn Museum Aramaic Papyri,* New Haven, 1953; J. M. Lindenberger, *Ancient Aramaic and Hebrew Letters,* Atlanta, 1994; B. Porten, *Archives from Elephantine: The Life of an Ancient Jewish Military Colony,* Berkeley, 1968; J. B. Segal, *Aramaic Texts from North Saqqara,* London, 1983.

CHAPTER EIGHTEEN

"No Longer Masters of Their Own House"

Egypt under the Ptolemies

--------------- ψ ---------------

Unlike Egypt, which succumbed to Persian conquest in 525 B.C., Greece had resisted success-fully. When the Persian ambassadors in 492 B.C. asked for tokens of submission from the Greek cities, the Greeks insulted the envoys and brought upon themselves an armed invasion. In 490 and again in 480 Persian expeditionary forces of overwhelming size invaded Greece, and Athens and other Greek cities were devastated; yet the Persians ultimately suffered defeat. Thereafter, the Great King adopted a subtler approach, dabbling in the internecine strife of the Greek cities, backing one against the other and ultimately, in the King's Peace (387 B.C.), negotiating a general truce throughout the region. Yet the Greeks never forgot nor forgave the outrages perpetrated on their homeland in the early 5th century, and nursed a great purpose someday to retaliate. If it did not involve an anachronism, we might say the idea of a crusade against Persia had been born; and with the rise to ascendancy over all Greece of Philip of Macedon, the idea was well on its way to becoming reality.

The Arrival in Egypt of Alexander the Great

The untimely assassination of Philip (336 B.C.) did nothing to deflect the fixation of policy on pursuing the grand design, as in this respect Philip's son Alexander was one with his father. In 334 Alexander crossed the Hellespont with his army and defeated an advance guard of the

Persians at the river Granicus. In the next year he moved eastward through Anatolia, intent on annexing the eastern coasts of the Mediterranean and Egypt; and in the fall of 333 he routed the enormous host that Persian King Darius III had mustered to block his way at Issus in northern Syria. Thereafter, Alexander moved south, reducing the island fortress of Tyre after a siege of eight months, and the border stronghold of Gaza after two months. Then, in the late fall of 332, the Macedonian troops arrived on the Egyptian frontier at Pelusium. Since many Persian soldiers had been withdrawn from Egypt to take part in hostilities in the north, the deputy of the satrap in charge wisely conceded defeat and handed the country over to Alexander.

In the decade since Artaxerxes III had reconquered the country, Egypt had been seething with discontent. Fugitive rebels against the Great King had been welcomed in the streets of Memphis, and reluctant recruits to the Persian forces had absconded quickly. In the Delta a rebel warlord, Khababash, successfully evaded arrest, and even set up his own administration. In consequence, when Alexander and his Macedonians arrived at the outskirts of Memphis, the populace hailed them warmly as deliverers, not conquerors.

Alexander's short stay in Egypt was dominated by the need to fulfill two vital purposes: to legitimize the passage of suzerainty from Darius III to himself and his successors, and to confirm by divine approbation his own status and destiny. To these ends he honored Memphis and its cults, and celebrated games at this "royal city of the Egyptians." Then he was off down the western branch of the Nile to make the long trek to the temple and oracle of Amun in the western oasis of Siwa. The questions he put to the oracle, one that was well known to the Greeks, were not divulged by either Alexander or the priests; but they undoubtedly had to do with the king's view of himself, his destiny, and his identity. The priestly respondent addressed the royal supplicant as *si-onsi* (king's son), *ensi* (king), and *si-Amun* (son of Amun), embodying concepts long known and well used by Egyptians, but rather novel in the Greek world. Alexander was clearly immensely impressed and carried this assurance of his divinity to the grave—and beyond. In fact, he purposed to locate his grave at Siwa close to the shrine of Amun, his father.

Alexander's route to and from the oasis took him past lake Mareotis and the rocky coast of the northwest Delta. Here, for several centuries, a fishing village had been located called Rakotis (Egyptian "Lake-entry"), adjacent to a natural harbor. Although Alexander saw the terrain only briefly, he realized that here was an ideal location for a major port that could provide a link between Egypt and Greece. He himself laid out the plan of a city, in concert with the architect Deinocrates of Rhodes, to be named *Alexandria* (with later distinguishing tag *ad Aegyptum*). Twelve years later the city was sufficiently completed for occupancy, but by then the political situation had drastically changed. Alexander had died suddenly at age 33, and his generals, faced with the exigency of continuing the empire in the name of a demented brother of the great conqueror, had opted for a division of the provinces under their own control. To general Ptolemy Lagus fell the satrapy of Egypt, and he set about to ensure his political control of the country. By skulduggery he diverted the funeral cortège of Alexander on its land journey to Macedonia, and brought it first to Memphis and later to Alexandria, where a magnificent tomb was prepared for the body. After successful engagement in the intestine feuding of his fellow generals, Ptolemy in 306 B.C. declared himself king and occupied Alexandria as his permanent seat. A new dynasty had begun.

A Note on Sources

Traditional histories of Ptolemaic Egypt (306–30 B.C.) are heavily dependent on those sections of classical historians, such as Polybius and Diodorus, which touch upon Egypt. To a great degree these historians are concerned with Egypt's place and activity within the melee of the political fragments into which Alexander's empire had quickly broken up. Marching and countermarching, fleet sailings and sea fights chart the course of Egypt's external relations during this period. A prior concern from the 2nd century B.C. is the need to describe how Rome impinged on these Hellenistic states and eventually absorbed them.

Little of this touches on the internal history of Egypt. The voluminous archives of Greek papyri that begin to appear, especially in the towns of the Fayum and Middle Egypt, occupy the historian only insofar as they shed light on the life of the *Greek settlers,* and the workings of the government machinery the Ptolemies are supposed to have imposed on the country. Few classical historians have in the past paid attention to the equally voluminous Demotic sources that cast invaluable light on the life of the autochthonous inhabitants and their relations with the invaders; although French and German scholarship began over a generation ago to make equal use of Greek and Demotic texts. A similar divide often separates the classical historian from the information contained in hieroglyphic inscriptions on the well-preserved walls of Ptolemaic temples. In light of the continuing importance of the priestly class under Ptolemaic rule, such an omission has a distorting effect on any history of the period.

The Government of the Ptolemies

Governing a country that is located on a seasonally inundated flood plain does not present rulers with many options. There is one way only to maximize yield, collect revenues, organize agriculture, and administer justice, and both a Pharaoh and a Macedonian king would have been constrained to employ the same methods. The highly praised administration of, say, a Ptolemy II, is but the system of the Pharaohs running to perfection.

The center of government, however, was now in Alexandria, which the native Egyptians, at first excluded from residency in the city, called the "*Itj-towy* of the Greeks," in imitation of the name of Amenemhet I's capital 17 centuries before. Memphis retained a certain aura and continued to be called the "royal city of the Egyptians," but it was now simply the bailiwick of the high priest of Ptah, a sort of ethnarch with responsibility for the native population as well as the priesthood. This high-priestly family over the three centuries of Ptolemaic rule reserved the right to crown the king and advise him on native matters; but otherwise exercised little power. Under the king in Alexandria the old function of vizier was discharged by the manager (*dioiketes),* and the old office of treasurer by the chief accountant (*eklogistes*). The "Letter-scribe of Pharaoh," a post that had gained prominence in the Twenty-second Dynasty, was carried over into the Greek administration as the letter-scribe (*epistolographos*); while the centuries-old office of king's herald appears under exactly the same rubric (*eisangeleus*). The king's privy purse, which we have seen growing from the middle of the second millennium B.C., survives in the private account of the Ptolemies. Mechanisms of government followed Pharaonic prototypes down the line. The all-important harvest tax (*epigraphe*) was carefully monitored and collected, and the tax on forced labor, 27 centuries old when Ptolemy I reigned, continued on in the form of the *corvée*. The scribal penchant for recording everything, which we have identified as a hallmark of Egyptian archivism from time immemorial, shows up in the voluminous inventories, draft-lists, and census figures the Ptolemaic bureaucracy has left behind. Even in the more subtle mechanics of governance the Pharaonic model is adhered to: the typical instructions (*tp-rd*) that every Pharaoh gave to a newly appointed office holder appear in exactly the same form and style, rendered into Greek, under the Ptolemaic kings. Even in the edicts in which the king speaks in his own name (*prostagmata*) we can clearly discern the standard king's command of the earlier, native, period.

The provincial administration likewise remained largely unchanged from the Pharaonic prototypes of the immediate past. The nomarch continued to be responsible for the individual township, although as time went by the commander of militia (Greek *strategos* = Egyptian *mr mš*ᶜ) tended to overshadow him. A justice of the peace, bailiff, and treasury official augmented the roster. A king's scribe, a title with excellent Egyptian credentials, assisted the nomarch and militia commander. The mass of the native Egyptian population on the land remained in the status they had suffered under from of old: they were sharecroppers, leasing royal land as king's tenants. Like the *khato*-land of Ramesside times (see above), unworked and unowned land became an extra burden for local landowners and officials. A tight control of coinage and taxation endeavored to maximize royal profits at every level, from the affairs of the smallest local village to the elevated issues of international commerce.

Apart from Alexandria, Ptolemais, and Naukratis, very few towns of purely Greek composition existed in Ptolemaic Egypt; and the Macedonian troops who accompanied the Ptolemies had to be accommodated in other ways. They were settled on the land and interspersed among the native population. Adopting the practice in vogue from the outgoing New Kingdom, the Ptolemies gave the soldiery small farms for their upkeep and homes in the villages where they lived cheek-by-jowl with the Egyptians.

The Ideology of Kingship

It remains moot as to what extent, if at all, the family of the Ptolemies made conscious use of the Pharaonic model of kingship. True, the temple reliefs portray them as bona fide Pharaohs, with the requisite costume and crowns, performing the cultus in time-honored fashion; but in most temples of the period the focus of attention has shifted away from the royal celebrant to fasten upon the resident god of the place and his birth and rejuvenation. In Alexandria, Ptolemy and his court lived entirely by Greek standards, donning Greek clothing, enjoying Greek entertainment, and speaking and reading the Greek language. If they occasionally repaired to Memphis to undergo a coronation or participate in the obsequies of a deceased Apis bull, they did so, for the most part, with an eye to placating their native subjects, rather than in pursuance of sincerely held beliefs. In all probability they knew and cared little about how they were being portrayed in detail by their barbarian subjects.

If the court of the Ptolemies were largely dismissive of the native culture, the latter's exponents, the priests, could not afford to be oblivious of their Greek masters. They fashioned a formal titulary in the hieroglyphic script for each Ptolemy, after Pharaonic style, and by their choice of epithets show that they were well aware of royal policy and achievements even at the international level. Thus hieroglyphic epithets credit Ptolemy II with many victories and sur-passing naval power, and his son with far-flung conquests in reliefs employing the age-old array of conquered place names.

And yet, in spite of the fact that Greeks and Egyptians occupied two solitudes, traces of the Egyptian character of the foundations of the state show through unmistakably in the Alexandrian kingship. The royal ancestor cult with its focus on the ancestral statue, a hallmark of Ptolemaic kingship, parallels and probably derives from the similar cult under the last native kings. Statues **(A; fig. 1)** and reliefs **(fig. 2)** from the Greco-Roman period tend to depict the ruler in Pharaonic guise. The prominence of royal sister and royal mother likewise recalls ancient prototypes, and it is no accident that the one Egyptian deity who captivated the Ptolemies from the beginning, and who alone fulfils these mythological roles, was Isis.

Figure 1   Classical figure in Egyptian accoutrements (Alexandria museum).

Figure 2   Roman emperor depicted in pharaonic guise (Elephantine).

The Egyptian Temples under the Ptolemies

From time immemorial the great temples of Egypt and their landed endowments had formed both an economic and cultural bulwark that guarded the very essence of "Egyptianness." On the morrow of Alexander's arrival they constituted a power block that no conqueror could ignore, if he wished, using the agency of the natives, to exploit the country's natural resources. In this light must be viewed the deference shown by Ptolemy I to the high priest of Ptah who, the new regime hoped, would represent and speak on behalf of the Egyptian priesthood at large; and to that end synods of all Egyptian priests were organized from time to time to convey desiderata and confirm honors.

The Ptolemies could not, nor did they wish to, curtail drastically the wealth and influence of the temples, so valuable were they as intermediaries with the native populace. They continued, moreover, to be useful and dynamic centers of manufacture and food production. Therefore, the priests were allowed to keep their estates and endowments; and nothing was done to impede the normal workings of priestly society. Priests and temples enjoyed exemption from certain taxes, and were granted monopolies in the production of oil and the manufacture of linen. As in Pharaonic times, even the temple of Amun, the most fractious center of nationalism, received the benefit of tax reversion. Occasionally a royal donation might be made, in cash or paraphernalia, to a particular cult that for some reason had caught the king's eye. The expense of burying the sacred animals was sometimes covered in this manner.

Temple building during the three centuries of Ptolemaic rule poses a number of questions difficult to answer at this point in time. Some of the largest and best-appointed temples to be seen today in Egypt are "Ptolemaic" **(fig. 3–4)**, but they reflect an imbalanced record of the cult of the times. First, with one or two exceptions, the surviving Ptolemaic temples are to be found in Upper Egypt: Lower Egypt, which we know to have had major shrines at such places as Buto, Sais, Busiris, Bubastis, and Mendes, suffers by comparison. Second, in some cases the cost of construction of these buildings does not represent an outlay of Ptolemaic wealth. The great building program of the Thirtieth Dynasty had thrown up a number of temple structures that, because of Nektanebo II's precipitous flight, had been left to the succeeding generation to decorate. In a number of cases the temple construction of such-and-such a Ptolemy amounts to the filling in of wall surfaces already in existence. Moreover, in some instances, such as the temple at Kom Ombo, the costs of construction were met by private individuals rather than the government. Third, over the three centuries of Ptolemaic rule a slackening of interest is apparent in rebuilding standing structures. The temples of Edfu and Philae begun in the 3rd century, and those of Kom Ombo, Esna, and Dendera begun in the 2nd, would never be substantially extended or rebuilt; and the priests would have to make do with available space if they wished to carve new inscriptions.

What is lacking in all this is a central authority concerned solely with the promotion of the worship of the gods. Pharaonic times had created such offices as "overseer of all priests of Upper and Lower Egypt," or "overseer of the temples of all the gods," whose purview included temple maintenance and the promotion of the divine service. The *Great Inventory*, a sort of blue book containing the only authorized regulations regarding the detailed minutiae of the cult, had been kept in the capital at Memphis. Its existence and constant use had helped to unify and regularize the worship of the gods and the texts of the hymns and liturgies. Now neither Memphis nor Thebes exerted any such regulatory control over the cults—the priesthoods of

Figure 3 Temple of Hathor, Dendera (2nd century B.C.); intercolumnar screens designed to conceal the mysteries are common in the Late Period.

Figure 4 Egyptian goddess, Dendera; the bold, high relief is characteristic of Egyptian art during the Ptolemaic and Roman periods.

these two centers were, in fact, at loggerheads—and Alexandria found this function strange and alien. The lack of a unified cult shows most clearly in the hieroglyphic tradition in Ptolemaic temples, each of which develops its own peculiar orthography different from that of its neighbors. New signs are manufactured in quantity, and old signs given new phonetic values or functions. In addition to these changes, the temple decoration of Ptolemaic times favors transferring to the walls whole ritual books, the papyrus originals of which continued to reside in the temple library.

The first three Ptolemies prided themselves on having, on their military campaigns, scoured the former territories of the Persian empire to recover the sacred literature and cult equipment which had been stolen at the time of the second Persian invasion of 343 B.C. Perhaps now that their literature had been restored, the priests were not going to risk a repetition of the loss: copies on stone would act as a visible back-up.

Race Relations between Egyptians and Greeks

Reckoning from the archaic period of Greek history, Greeks had been coming to Egypt for nearly four centuries when Alexander and his men entered the land. Initially the reaction of the visitors to the strange and wonderful land of the Nile was one of awe and admiration for the architecture and art. Already reflected in the writings of Hecataeus and Herodotus (5th century B.C.), the myth of Egyptian wisdom had taken root, and its stubborn refusal to conform itself to the facts was to bedevil serious interest in Egypt for millennia.

During the 4th century, however, a new and jaundiced view of Egypt began to appear among the Greeks. The wholesale hiring of thousands of Greek mercenary soldiers by the kings of the Twenty-sixth, Twenty-ninth, and Thirtieth Dynasties had brought large numbers of Hellenes, now long-term employees rather than tourists and merchants, into close contact with Egyptians of all classes. The newcomers could not help but become uncomfortably familiar with the day-to-day Egyptian lifestyle, and what they saw and heard they found repugnant. Many Greeks at first did not understand the Egyptian penchant for worshiping animals, whether single avatars or whole species, and either contemned or ridiculed this trait: Even their kitchen gardens produce gods, scoffed one Roman writer. Unwilling for the most part to learn the Egyptian language, the Greeks persisted in misunderstanding Egyptian society and culture, misconstruing, for example, the tendency to keep professions within the family as a caste system. At the level of royalty, the macho image and bravado required by the Pharaonic model were passed off by Greek generals as acts of foolhardiness.

For their part the Egyptians rapidly developed a love–hate relationship with the Greeks. Already in the Twenty-sixth Dynasty friction had occasionally arisen between mercenary soldiers and the native population, but the Saïte kings had been careful to put in place a cadre of liaison officers to act as a buffer. With the arrival of the Macedonian troops as liberators, the Egyptians at first experienced a change of heart. Some, like Padi-Osiris, the high priest of Thoth at Hermopolis, tried to imitate the art of the Greeks in their tombs (B), and in the process produced a fascinating hybrid style of relief, combining Egyptian themes with classical treatment (C, D, E). Others attempted, with indifferent success, to compose literary pieces in the Greek language, although their first language, Demotic, shows through clearly. For the most part, the first three Ptolemies attempted, with enlightened self-interest, to cultivate their native subjects by commissioning works in Greek, from Egyptian professionals—the context undoubtedly was the new library at Alexandria—intended to introduce the incoming Greeks to Egyptian history, religion, and the calendar.

But there could be no doubt that the 3rd century B.C. was the heyday of the Greeks in Egypt. Colonists were invited to the land of the Nile from all over the Greek-speaking world, and *koine* Greek became the official language of government. Greeks began to be assigned, or to buy up, land throughout Egypt, and by 288 B.C. Greek landowners had appeared in the southernmost townships. While the first three Ptolemies were careful to patronize Egyptian cults to a limited extent and to cultivate native sensibilities in general, for the most part Greek art, architecture and language were distinctly in favor. The native Egyptians, initially forbidden to marry Greeks, were free to use their own language and script, Demotic Egyptian, among themselves and in their own courts, but all Demotic contracts had to have a résumé of the contents in Greek appended to the document. While no formal attempt was made to Hellenize the Egyptians, their language, culture, and way of life was deemed second rate, and was held up to derision upon occasion as barbaric. The vast majority of them remained, as they had always been, sharecropping peasants overworked and overtaxed. Although some military officers were held over from the earlier administration, very few Egyptians in the 3rd century entertained any hope of breaking into the ranks of the ruling elite.

The social tension inherent in this situation reached a point of crisis after 217 B.C. In that year a hastily recruited and trained phalanx of native Egyptian troops had been instrumental in winning the battle of Raphia, and thwarting the attempts of the Seleucid king to invade Egypt. In the generation following, the native population seemed to sense its real strength, and rebellions began to break out all over Egypt. In the Delta, uprisings continued until 184 B.C., and dislocated commercial life. Excavation has shown that the great harbor at Mendes suffered a drastic reduction in its traffic after the reign of Ptolemy IV, and, in fact, with the drying up of the Mendesian branch, never fully recovered. In 205 B.C. the Thebaid broke away and declared independence under a native king, and it was not until 186 B.C. that Ptolemaic troops managed to regain the territory. But rebellions in the south continued to plague the Alexandrian government down to the middle of the first century.

Despite the failure of overt rebellion, there could be no return to the servile status the Egyptians had suffered from before the battle of Raphia. In the 2nd and 1st centuries B.C. an increasing number of native Egyptians appear in the Ptolemaic administration, both in local townships and also in the army. In fact, the Ptolemaic commander who put down a Theban uprising in 130 B.C. was himself Egyptian. By the 1st century B.C. this upward mobility combined with intermarriage had created a Hellenized Egyptian element in the population, which spoke Greek in the business world and understood Greek culture, but spoke Demotic Egyptian at home and perpetuated the Egyptian way of life.

But there could be no doubt that Egyptian culture was being progressively marginalized. Increasingly, the native Egyptian temples and their staffs were being identified as the sole repositories and guardians of the pristine aspects of Egyptian civilization. *Pharaoh* and *temple* had from time immemorial constituted an axis around which the people and their culture had revolved; now, with the elimination of the unifying figure of *Pharaoh,* the temple stood alone as a bastion against the foreign influences that were bombarding Egypt as never before. With no centrally preserved standards for script, iconography, and cult, the temples in the Hellenistic age show considerable local variations in their decoration; but they at least survived in a symbiosis with the Ptolemaic authorities, which proved beneficial to all concerned.

Egypt under the Roman Empire

During the 1st century B.C. a weakened Ptolemaic regime, shorn of its foreign empire and suffering from intestine feuding in the royal family, fell within the penumbra of expanding Roman influence. The last Ptolemaic ruler, Kleopatra VII, to Egypt's ultimate disadvantage, threw in her lot in the republican civil war by supporting Mark Antony against Octavian. Mark Antony's defeat at the battle of Actium (September, 31 B.C.) was followed within the year by his suicide and that of Kleopatra. By the end of 30 B.C., Octavian, later to be honored with the title *Augustus,* had come to Egypt and transformed the country into a Roman province.

The advent of Rome drastically modified the situation to the detriment of Egypt and her temple communities. Upon his arrival in Egypt pursuant to his victory at Actium, Augustus went out of his way to show contempt for the now defunct Ptolemaic regime, as well as manifestations of native culture. If Augustus allowed himself to be portrayed as a Pharaoh in temple art, it was only insofar as normative Egyptian religion required it. The comparative leniency of the Ptolemies toward the native priests now came to an end. Temple land was confiscated, and temple communities were subject to regular audits. Funds for the construction of new temples were withdrawn, and the communities of priests were obliged to survive on a niggardly grant. Only hereditary priests **(fig. 5)** were allowed to function (thus eliminating recruitment), and immunity from taxation was withdrawn. If an office fell vacant because it lacked a hereditary claimant, it was sold to the highest bidder. Occasionally, Roman emperors displayed a fleeting interest in one of the exotic cults from the Nile, but it was always in its "Mediterranean Hellenized" form. These same emperors felt no qualms in raping away to Rome numerous Pharaonic monuments that once had graced Nilotic shrines, or in outlawing various aspects of native religion. The result was a dwindling number of knowledgeable priests. While in the last decades before Christ priests were still being taught hieroglyphic, hieratic, and Demotic scripts, in 19 A.D. it required one of the older priests to translate the battle inscriptions of

Figure 5   Egyptian priest, Greco-Roman period (Alexandria museum).

Ramesses II at Karnak for the benefit of Germanicus and his Roman tourists. By the end of the 1st century A.D., the cult of Amun had ceased and Karnak was lying derelict. By Trajan's time (107 A.D.) only five hieroglyph carvers were operating in the temple at Oxyrrhynchos (dedicated to Osiris), and these are explicitly stated to have no apprentices. The latest text at Diospolis Parva belongs to the floruit of Hadrian, while the Esna temple continued to be decorated in fits and starts from c. 150 A.D. until its abandonment some time after the time of Decius (249–251 A.D.). By the close of the 3rd century A.D. the temple of Arsaphes at Herakleoplis had been abandoned, and was being used as a quarry, while the Luxor temple had been turned into a legionary camp. By the first half of the 4th century A.D. worship had ceased at Deir el-Bahari, although unofficial festivals patronized by the common people continued. Although some cults clung to life tenaciously—Thoth and Serapis at Memphis, Thoeris at Oxyrrhynchos—the 4th century A.D. witnessed the effectual demise of the gods of Egypt.

On the socioeconomic level, Egypt languished. The second half of the 2nd century A.D. was marked by a disastrous plague that swept over the entire empire, and was especially virulent in Egypt. As the government imposed increasingly severe tax- and service-obligations, many people fled from their towns and villages, or took to brigandage. The only townsmen who could survive were the very rich, and as time went by they accepted the new role of patron for the poor and disenfranchised. A new and rudimentary social classification gradually appeared, separating the "haves and have-nots" *honestiores* from the *humiliores* on the basis of obligations, immunities, and punishment. A new configuration appeared in the provincial administration of the land at the end of the 3rd century A.D., as the age-old townships or *nomes* were abolished. Egypt was divided into three divisions, each supervised by a *dux,* and a parochial organization of *pagi* was introduced. These rural subdivisions, where non-Christian beliefs were to survive longer, eventually gave us the adjective *pagan.*

It would be easy to appreciate how the relentless downsizing of the state imbued the dwindling priestly class with a sense of paranoia and a siege mentality. References to "priests" in day-to-day documents tend to die out after c. 250 A.D., and by the end of the century there could have been only a few hundred surviving celebrants. The more their numbers declined, the more they considered themselves the embattled guardians of the true religion. They and they alone could preserve the world by celebrating the mysteries in the original, hallowed forms; and they could only do this if separated from the defiling gaze of the populace at large. Self-consciously, they fashioned a stoical pattern of behavior for their regimen, and self-serving eschatology for their comfort: "Divine Egypt will suffer evils. . . . Egypt, lover of god and dwelling-place of the gods, school of religion, will become an example of impiety. . . . Darkness will be preferred to light and death will be preferred to life. No one will gaze into heaven. And the pious man will be counted insane, and the impious will be honored as wise. . . ." (Hermetic corpus)

Egypt's Spiritual Bequest to the Roman World

Despite the irreversible isolation of the priests in their temples, Egyptian religious concepts in a transmogrified form were in fact bequeathed to posterity. From Ptolemaic times the cult of Isis had thrived among Egyptians and resident Greeks alike; and with Serapis (Osiris-Apis), a Zeus-like god, her consort, and the baby Horus, she offered to worshippers the warmth of family affection. Serapis had in part been foisted upon Egypt as a creature of the early Ptolemies, eager to find a spiritual means of uniting their realm; but as his name implies, he had his roots deep in Egyptian religion. In the 1st and 2nd centuries after Christ, the worship of Isis spread like wildfire all over the Roman Empire, promising an Osirian salvation to all, both men and women. In the major cities of the empire Isis-shrines (*Iseia*) sprang up, in which the cult was carried on in imitation of native Egyptian rites, and amid a physical ambiance reminiscent of that of an Egyptian temple. The character of the goddess, which shows through in the hymns and aretalogies translated into Greek (or composed in that language in paraphrase of Egyptian originals), reveals a powerful concept, well on its way to universal status.

While initially banned, intermarriage between Egyptians and Greeks could not be prevented, and from the mid-3rd century B.C. began to become more common. By the end of the 2nd century B.C. a class of Hellenized Egyptians had emerged, the product of intermarriage (especially between Greek soldiers and Egyptian women). The size of this class is difficult to determine, but it is clear that its members were bilingual in Egyptian and Greek and could often write in both Greek and Demotic scripts. In Roman times Egypto-Greeks were not allowed to change their economic status, and false declarations of nationality or descent were severely punished; yet it was to this class that antiquity owed the transmission of certain basic Egyptian concepts. Egyptian religion had exerted an almost irresistible attraction on the Greeks (less so on the Romans), and it was this half-breed class of Egypto-Greeks that we must imagine as the essential mechanism of transmission of Egyptian religious lore. Their presence and agency must be posited in any case to explain the essentially Egyptian content (and even style) of liturgical and hymnodic texts done into Greek. Once having been rendered into Greek, however, the original Egyptian concepts in their pristine form in hieroglyphic or Demotic counted for little. Educated Greeks (even Alexandrians) might know vaguely of native Egyptian priests of legendary repute, such as the Denderite Sminios, Nephotes, Pibekheos, Pituos, Pachrates, Pnouthis, Nechepso, or Petosiris; but it was only through "translated" texts that they had access to what purported to be their works.

The future transformations of Egyptian material lay in a truly syncretistic process in which oriental combined with Greek notions provided the informing principle. The chief example of this process is the Hermetic literature, a corpus of quasi-theosophical material that came to birth in the 1st century A.D. and enjoyed expansion through the 5th in Greek-speaking Alexandria at the hands of the educated middle and upper classes, the spiritual descendants of the Egypto-Hellenics of late Ptolemaic times. Behind the alleged author, the Greek Hermes Trismegistos, lurks the figure of the Egyptian Thoth, "the thrice-great," who, as traditional inventor of the script and author of wisdom lent himself admirably to the role of philosopher-interlocutor. Debate over the past decades has centered upon the extent to which genuine Egyptian material is to be found in the *Hermetica,* but by and large the exercise has been misguided: Egyptian ideas have been identified where in fact none exists, while concepts of possible Nilotic origin have been passed over in silence. In its current form, however, the whole is several steps removed from its putative Egyptian (or for that matter, non-Egyptian) origins.

An equally recondite belief system that came to the fore in Roman Egypt has been assigned the identifying label *Gnosticism.* Although eclectic in its sources and purview, this movement had a deep root in the culture of Egyptian "mysteries," which offered the devotee initiation and salvation through the acquisition of mystic knowledge (*gnosis*). While "knowing the manifestations of . . ." was a phrase redolent of ancient Egyptian esotericism and correctly stressed the widespread claim to secret knowledge by devotees in Pharaonic times, Gnosticism in Egypt early attached itself to nascent Christianity and for two centuries rivaled orthodoxy. Although declared a heresy and persecuted by the church, Gnosticism survived and in its broad concepts continues to exist in modified form among Masons, New Agers, Rosicrucians, and their congeners.

Ancient Egypt in the Writings of Classical Authors

Ancient Egypt suffered an equivocal treatment at the hands of classical authors, most of whom witnessed Egyptian civilization in the final throes of its decline and slow extinction. On the one hand they had all, as members of a Greek-speaking class, fallen under the spell of traditional Greek admiration for Egyptian "science and wisdom;" on the other, they had all (or most of them) experienced at first hand the crassness of the day-to-day manifestations of Egyptian religion. But none of the (surviving) literary pieces of these authors show the slightest awareness of the need to consult surviving records in the Egyptian language; and none of the authors themselves took the trouble to learn the language or script of the natives. They showed a willful preference for those early Greek authors, like Hecataeus and Herodotus, who had (themselves ignorant of the Egyptian language) written tomes on Egypt that reflected native folklore and oral tradition.

Apart from the known fact that from Saïte times on Egypt was a favored destination for philosophers, poets, proto-scientists, and other Greek intelligentsia, there developed an appetite of Greek speakers for an account of Egypt in their own language. Failing any inclination on the part of the Egyptians to satisfy this appetite, Greek visitors themselves wrote of their travels, replete with information from the only sources available to them: their own eyes, bilingual dragomans, and purveyors of local folklore. What began as a necessity became a virtue: Hecataeus, Herodotus, Diodorus, and Strabo had no interest in tapping into native sources. Those Egyptians who realized the need to promote their own culture and wrote in Greek (e.g., Manetho and Chaeremon) were ignored; and those whose works in Egyptian were translated into Greek were valued more for the esoteric quality or titillation of their work. From the 4th century B.C. a strong historiographical tradition is in evidence among Greeks born in Egypt, centering upon the cities of Naukratis, Mendes, and Memphis. But almost all this writing is lost, and it remains doubtful how much native source material these writers were willing or able to transmit. With the rise of the Judaeo–Pagan polemic in Ptolemaic Egypt such native writings as could be accessed were wrenched from their contexts and used in distorted and irrelevant ways to assist in triumphing in debate. Nonetheless, the debate was in *Greek,* and Greek authors were deemed as reliable as sources as Egyptian.

The dominance of this Greek tradition wholly oblivious to the Egyptian language and ignorant of its script proved fatal to the accurate transmission to Europe of a faithful record of Egyptian history and culture. Although some early Greek authors were aware of the nature and operation of the hieroglyphic script, the vast majority of them mistook this writing system as a symbolic mode of expression created on allegoric principles. To Diodorus (1st century B.C.) they were "Ethiopian letters . . . hieroglyphs among the Egyptians . . . not built up in syllables to express the underlying meaning but from the appearance of the things drawn and by their metaphorical meaning." Philo Judaeus (1st century A.D.) refers to them as "philosophy which is expressed in symbols, exemplified in the so-called 'Sacred Letters'. . . ." Tacitus

(2nd century A.D.) perpetuates the error: "the Egyptians in their animal pictures were the first people to represent thought by symbols." Even the usually well-informed Clement of Alexandria can speak of a variety of "symbolical methods" inherent in the hieroglyphic script, one of which "speaks literally by imitation, a second writes as it were 'metaphorically,' and a third is outright allegorical by means of certain enigmas." The Neo-Platonism of the late 3rd and 4th centuries A.D. capitalized on the supposed cryptic, symbolic nature of the hieroglyphs: Iamblichus discerned "an intellectual, divine, and symbolic character of divine resemblance," and Plotinus believed that "each carved image is knowledge and wisdom grasped all at once, not discursive reasoning or deliberation." And this was the common Gnostic misinterpretation: "(The signs) are not vowels nor are they consonants . . . they are the letters of the truth which they alone speak who know them. Each letter is a complete <thought> like a complete book."

The Impact of Christianity

The coming of Christianity to Egypt filled the void created between the mass of the population and its ever-more-isolated and dwindling priests; but it also contributed markedly to the demise of the native hieroglyphic script. Traditionally, Christianity was introduced into Egypt by St. Mark, two decades after the execution of Jesus. How accurate this tradition is cannot be assessed at present; it is only with the 2nd century A.D. that a Christian presence can be verified. A catechetical school existed in Alexandria in the second half of that century, but it was not until the third that any great strides were made in converting the countryside. Critical, perhaps, was the church's adoption of a mode of writing that had been developed in an experimental fashion as early as Ptolemaic times, viz. the writing of the Egyptian language in a modified Greek alphabet. By the mid-3rd century A.D. Christian literature of all sorts was being translated into Egyptian employing this new "Coptic" (Egyptian) script.

In other ways, too, the time of the Pharaohs was receding from men's minds. Beginning with the visit of Septimius Severus to Egypt in 197 A.D., books of magic and magic practices in general fell under suspicion. A century later, the age-old system of townships (or nomes) was finally done away with. As mentioned earlier in this chapter, Egypt was divided into three sections, each under the administration of a *dux*. New systems of annual census and taxation were introduced in the early 4th century, and numbered on a 15-year cycle. Finally, under Emperor Constantine the Christian sect, which had no root at all in the ancient Nilotic culture and was by its very nature antithetic to the gods, achieved a victory that catapulted it to a supremacy no other religion had ever experienced.

And so the ancient Egyptian culture and the script used for three millennia to express it were finally and effectually lost. In the 50 years following Constantine's edict of toleration (313 A.D.), most temples and their belief systems fell into abeyance, and their doors were officially closed by the Edict of Theodosius in 391. Within four years the last known hieroglyphic inscription was carved. Demotic, which had been in decline since the 2nd century A.D., experienced its final demise in the middle of the 5th century. The Christian church could never forget that the ancient scripts were tied to a pagan, heathen religion, a realization that made it easier to commit the temple libraries to the flames. The speed with which an accurate knowledge of the hieroglyphic script was lost can best be appreciated from the *Hieroglyphica* of Horapollo. A dilettantish work written by an Alexandrian in the second half of the 5th century, this primer of the defunct script combines outlandish explanations with half-remembered, though misunderstood, facts.

The end was ignominious. Beginning in the 5th century, the old temples of the gods were either demolished or turned into churches. Much of the arable land passed into the possession of large landed estates whose owners exercised control, both politically and socially, over a peasant mass. Through the weakness of the empire Egypt fell prey to invasion from the outside, Blemmys from the south, Persians from the northeast. Around 200 A.D., Alexander's tomb was sealed, then forgotten; the library and museion of Alexandria suffered progressive destruction, beginning with Julius Caesar's war in 46 B.C. By the 6th century it was defunct. In 641 A.D. Amr ibn el-As conquered Egypt for Islam, seizing it from the Byzantine Empire scarcely a decade after the death of Muhammed. The last vestiges of Ancient Egypt had perished.

APPENDIX I
Textual Sources for Egyptian History

ψ

Histories written in a traditional narrative style are not cast in a format conducive to naming and analyzing all the sources used. By not bringing the reader constantly back to the primary source material, such works run the risk of giving false impressions as to how much documentation actually exists for a given period, and where and how wide the gaps in our knowledge are. This appendix attempts to remedy that failing.

Our Sources for the Old Kingdom

As pointed out in Chapter 2, the invention and development of the script in Egypt was designed to meet the need to keep accounts, to commemorate events, to identify individuals, and to specify ownership. These were needs felt by a self-conscious administration seeking to centralize political authority in the country. It follows that most, if not all, of the earliest examples of writing come from the Memphite capital, where that administration was centered. Any written material originating outside the capital was at first due to the presence of an agent of that administration in that particular province.

One of the earliest types of document known to us is the *year record* or *annal* (Egyptian *gnt*), carved on rectangular pieces of wood or ivory. Although the examples vouchsafed to us are adaptations of an original master format now lost, it is probable that the latter contained three types of information:

1. The name of the king
2. The salient event (or events) of that year
3. The height of the annual inundation

When adapted in a mortuary context to identifying and dating commodities placed in a tomb, the third piece of information was replaced by the specification of the commodity in question and the name of the official in charge. Not a few of these dockets have been found, especially at Saqqara and Abydos, although not nearly enough to provide a connected sequence for any reign. Of the master set of annals kept in the palace archives, none have survived; but a fortunate publication on stone of those from the beginning of the First Dynasty to midway through the Fifth Dynasty has come down to us in fragments. Other "publications" seem to have been undertaken in the Sixth Dynasty.

Texts from the high Old Kingdom give a glimpse of a large and well-ordered chancery and archives. The latter contained *inter alia* copies (and presumably originals) of royal decrees (*wḏ-nsw*) issued to temples and private individuals, royal charters (*ˁ-nsw*), orders for conscription (*srw*) of labor, and work orders, or commissions (*wpt-nsw*) to high officials to carry out tasks, usually in the provinces. Various records were also deposited in the archives: Besides the annals may be mentioned the "count-records" (*ṯnwt*) or census lists (of livestock as well as humans), copies of all deeds or property transfers (*imyt-pr*), and copies of all notices and rescripts (*mḏȝt*). In addition to these prosaic records of a civil service, medical treatises, many of which tradition insists were composed early in the Old Kingdom, must have been found in the royal archives.

We hear of parts of the archives called "the House of Rescripts" (*pr-mḏȝt*), "the House of Divine Rescripts" (*pr-mḏȝt nṯr*), and "the House of Rescripts of the King's Business" (*pr-mḏȝt ḥt-nsw*). These were registries to which scribes were attached who were responsible for drawing up the lists of workers, royal decrees, and so on. A group of letter carriers delivered state letters and documents to recipients throughout the kingdom. They were also responsible for the filing and storage of all the documents in the archives.

None of these precious documents has come down to us in the original. Only in cases where it was expedient to "publish" a text on stone has any survived; but these are relatively few. Royal decrees in favor of a provincial mortuary temple were copied on stelae set up at the gates of the institutions in question, in the interests of easy reference. Some 30 stelae (standing stone slats) containing decrees (more or less intact) have come down to us from the Old Kingdom, the largest number constituting a lucky find in the temple of Min at Coptos. Work orders sometimes found their way onto hieroglyphic records left by leaders of quarrying or mining expeditions in the rocky fastnesses of the Sinai, the Wady Hammamat, Aswan, or Hatnub. As the Old Kingdom wore on, and officialdom sensed its own worth, such records proliferated: Any royal emissary could carve the date, his name, and the purpose of his trip at certain customary points on traveled routes.

By the time that the Giza pyramid group was being built, the sense of achievement felt by royalty was being translated into art. The causeway and mortuary temple offered much wall space on which to depict in relief the king in the company of the gods, conquering his enemies, or engaging in building activities. Very few fragments of such scenes have come down to us. Better represented is that genre of propagandistic scenes, of prophylactic intent, which show Pharaoh, with appropriate texts, smiting his enemies. The best extant series of such reliefs was set up at the turquoise mines in Sinai.

Although royal records are conspicuous by their absence from Old Kingdom remains, private records are relatively numerous, at least in Dynasties 5 and 6. At the very outset of the Third Millennium, two genres of text made their appearance: the *name stone,* showing a crude figure of the deceased with his name, which was set over the private grave, and the slab stela incorporating a scene of the *funerary meal* in which the dead man with name and titles sat at a table spread with food. The funerary meal evolved into the nucleus of all those texts and reliefs of a specifically mortuary nature which adorned the walls of the mastaba-tombs of the nobles from Dynasty 4 through 6; while the slab stela developed into those representations of the deceased, in relief or the round (usually the former) but always mortuary, which gloss the figure with name and titles. These latter are often the vehicle, especially from Dynasty 4 on, for an extended text embodying a statement by the deceased. The common format is as follows: (a) titles, (b) name, (c) formula "(he) says," (d) statement by the deceased to visitors. Section (d) can comprise either a testamentary statement, in which the deceased makes his will (or transfer of property), or contract with mortuary priests, or a biographical statement in which he sets forth his *Lebensgeschichte* (or part of it). Titles are *very* common in Old Kingdom mastabas, biographical statements much less so. But it is largely upon the latter that we rely for what little we know of the political history of the period.

Another type of repository for documents was the temple archive. From scattered allusions we know that, on its "cultic shelves" as it were, the temple library counted such things as books of ritual (*ḥbw*), magic spells (*ḥkꜣw*), and beatifications (*sꜣḥw*), the latter being used in mortuary services for the benefit of the deceased spirit. Again, none of this has come down to us in the original, but large extracts from the magical and beatific literature found their way into the Pyramid Texts, a corpus of spells that from the end of the Fifth Dynasty into the Eighth was carved into the pyramid chambers for the benefit specifically of the royal owner. These texts have been preserved largely intact, and constitute the largest single body of inscriptional material from the Old Kingdom. They cast a flood of light, as might be expected, on the cult and mythology of the Third Millennium B.C.

In the business offices of the Old Kingdom, different sorts of text would have been found. A lucky find in the mortuary temple of Neferirkare (Fifth Dynasty, c. 2500 B.C.) at Abusir has brought to light the "waste basket" of the temple administration. Preserved are fragments of service regulation books (*sšm r imy-st-ꜥ,* or *sšm iꜣt*) in which the duties of temple personnel are set forth for all days of the month, offering lists (*ssnt*), distribution lists (*mḏd*) apportioning the income of the temple to the priests as stipend, grain receipts (*šsp ꜣwt*), and gift receipts (*sš n nḏt-ḥr*).

Our Sources for the First Intermediate Period

The anarchy that followed the death of Pepy II resulted in the wholesale destruction of many archives, and contemporaries of these events knew well the extent of their loss. Along with the archives, the cadres of scribes and other servants suffered diminution, if not outright disband-ment, and the scribal art on which the capital had prided itself began to be lost. The result was that, with no standard of excellence on which to model themselves, the provincials produced texts of a markedly uneven nature, but all of barbaric taste and atrocious orthography. It is the product, often, of men who were barely literate. Cut off, moreover, from the unifying influence of a central authority, the townships rapidly developed regional styles of orthography and iconography.

One trend that did not disappear with the collapse of the Old Kingdom was that toward the writing of private memorials by the upper and middle classes in the provinces. In fact, if anything the biographical statement increases with the advent of the First Intermediate Period. Biographical texts occur mainly on the small, crude slab stelae, placed in tombs, which are common during the period; less often they decorate the walls of the rock-cut tombs in the necropolis adjacent to the provincial capitals. As in the Old Kingdom, the owner's name and titles gloss his representation. Titles evoke standard relationships with the king or the royal house; but the biographical section rarely mentions the king. The authors revel in their appel-lation "excellent commoner," and delight in stressing their social independence and resource-fulness. It is thanks to these texts that we get a view, albeit shot through with lacunae, of the period of the civil war between north and south; and for once, our sources come from both sides. The rock tombs of the powerful nobles of Asyut and Hermopolis give a perspective from the followers of Herakleopolis in the north, while the crude slab stelae from the incipient king-dom of Thebes provide the view of the southern rebels.

It is out of this genre of private biographical texts that our earliest royal inscriptions emanate. The Old Kingdom had produced "royal" stelae only in the case of royal edicts, the publication of which was occasioned by a practical need. In the First Intermediate Period the rebel king of the south speaks to us candidly for the first time, in a way that reveals that he appreciates the value of propagating his views, and his reputation among contemporaries and to posterity. His statements are at first biographical, and are couched in the same format as are those of commoners. Like the latters' stelae, the king's are set up in a mortuary context, and like a private citizen the king boasts of his mighty deeds, his strong arm, and his piety toward the gods. Nothing points up the common origin of the Theban Eleventh Dynasty like the inscriptions they have left us: These upstart kings who eventually unified Egypt thought, talked, and wrote like the provincial nobles they really were.

Egypt was buoyed by its reunification under Montuhotpe I, and the solemnity of the event called forth more dignified memorials. On the walls of their mortuary temples at Thebes, and probably elsewhere in provincial temples, Montuhotpe and his successors carved scenes and texts commemorating the triumph of Thebes, and their devotion to the gods. It was a crude but sincere attempt to place themselves within the kingly tradition by aping the decoration of the Old Kingdom mortuary structures in the north.

The First Intermediate Period throws up what the Old Kingdom does not seem to have cherished, or perhaps even produced—a *literature*. Though the word does not do credit to the parallel role played by oral tradition, nevertheless it is true that the phenomenon in question enjoyed a written form that provided the ancients with a quasi-canonical standard. The cataclysm of the collapse of the ordered society of the Old Kingdom produced a type of lament in which a wise man who witnesses the anarchy of the time describes it in poetry, decries it, and lays the blame (cf. the Admonitions of Ipuwer). Flowery rhetoric was much valued: the *speech* (*mdt*), whether by an illiterate peasant claiming his rights before the law (cf. the Eloquent Peasant), or the declamation of a wise man slighted at court, was a favored vehicle of conveying a moral. People longed for better things to come, and so the "Prophecy" (*srt*) became a popular genre; but others were jaundiced by it all, and gave expression to their skepticism regarding the reality of the afterlife in hedonistic songs (*ḥst:* cf. the Song of the Harper). The most striking new genre is the dialogue: A man speaks with his soul on the efficacy of the afterlife, gods discourse on the imponderables of the universe. Most popular seem to be the *Books of Wisdom* (*sb³yt*). These are collections of aphorisms and worldly wisdom that purport, much in the vein of *How to Win Friends and Influence People,* to teach the young how to get along in society. Often the collections are alleged to go back to some illustrious figures of the past—Hordedef, son of Khufu, or the viziers Kagemni and Ptahhotpe; once a king Wahkare Akhtoy of the Tenth Dynasty writes on statecraft for the benefit of his son, Merikare.

The Middle Kingdom

The outgoing Eleventh Dynasty had witnessed a return of peaceful conditions to the Nile Valley; and with them came a revival of the scribal arts. A writing school was formed at the capital to provide the unified state with bureaucrats, and efforts were made to reorganize and develop state archives. Contemporary texts evince a keen interest in old documents. They were examined for the setting up of laws, for evidence of where old survey lines ran, dividing townships and estates, and even for such esoteric "historiography" as establishing lists of predecessors in office.

With the centralization of the kingdom in the new capital at Itj-towy, the amassing and organization of state archives once again became paramount. Only a few scraps of papyri have come to light, mainly from the close of Dynasty 12, to elucidate the contents of the archives; but allusions in various texts apprise us of a fair number of the genres involved. The word *annals* still appears, though in a stereotyped formula only, suggesting that its pristine purpose was no longer being served. Nonetheless, some sort of record of a king's reign was undoubtedly written up; and there is good evidence that the scribes of Itj-towy began a formal king list of all kings with their lengths of reign, from the primeval gods to the contemporary monarch. Royal decrees, comprising *in toto* "the king's law" (*ḥpw nsw*), continued to be copied and deposited in the archives, along with property transfers, draft lists (*imy-rn.f*) of all those eligible for taxes or state service, official correspondence, and census lists. The early kings of the Twelfth Dynasty had undertaken a monumental survey of the land of Egypt, and the great cadaster that resulted was duly deposited in the archives, along with the annual tax-assessment records, which depended on the cadastral survey. In typical Egyptian fashion, copies of all sorts of information were kept in the archives, under the seal of the vizier: transcripts of trials, criminal registers, copies of provincial records, transcripts of oral petitions (*sprt*), even the doorkeepers' records of everyone who daily entered or left the palace!

One genre of text that appears in the Middle Kingdom for the first time is the journal or *day book* (*hrwyt*). Most large institutions (the king's house, temples, the granary, etc.) kept such a master log, possibly to facilitate reference and bookkeeping. All important transactions of the institution in question—receipts and disbursements of commodities, copies of important letters, the going and coming of personnel, salient events, and the like—were duly entered under the day, month, and regnal year of the reigning king. Journals were stored away and carefully preserved for posterity: they were, in effect, a great source of historical information.

The Middle Kingdom administration manifested a thinly disguised self-consciousness about its own importance. In the turmoil that followed the close of the Old Kingdom, sophistication and etiquette in government were nowhere to be found, and these the Twelfth Dynasty now attempted to reintroduce. Wisdom texts partly fulfilled the need for "How to . . ." books, but they did not cover the niceties of court protocol. We have allusions to some courtly instructions that must have circulated during this period; and from the Empire period there survive extracts copied from ancient documents of the rules governing the operation of the vizier's importance.

As was the case in the Old Kingdom, few of these precious papyrus archives have been vouchsafed to us. Scattered pieces, of inestimable importance admittedly, are all that we can show: the private correspondence and notes of a small Theban farmer, a scribe's ledger from a royal construction project, a shipyard ledger, the tattered remnants of a temple waste basket, dispatches from a border fort, fragments from a government office, and a fragmentary tax assessor's journal. As ever, we are forced to rely on those records and pronouncements, written or oral, that were thought fit to be committed to stone.

As we have seen, royal stelae of historical purport had come into being as mortuary texts of the same genre as that employed by private individuals to invoke offerings, laud their own accomplishments, and set on record their names and titles. In fact, they were addresses to the visitors who might pass by and visit their tombs, and when in Dynasty 12 the royal stela comes into its own it is used principally to publish a royal speech to a specified and assembled group. One genre is a formal record of a "king's sitting," noting the date and place of the audience and who was addressed (usually the court), and giving the text of the royal speech ostensibly verbatim (though perhaps literary reworking is at times evident). Another type contains the words of the king, addressed to all and sundry, without the framework of a sitting. The tone is variously apologetic or admonishing; often, the king uses this vehicle to state a policy or announce a decision to undertake a public work. Upon occasion the setting of the speech might be elaborated upon by a skillful scribe: a king announces he will restore a certain temple, but the accompanying framework will tell how he learned that the temple was dilapidated and how he sought expert advice.

Only a few such royal stelae have come down to us from the Middle Kingdom; much more numerous—in fact the single most common Middle Kingdom texts—are the private memorials on stone. This is the heyday of the family stela, a slab set up in the neighborhood of a shrine (the environs of the Osiris temple at Abydos have produced the most) on which the owner, his family, and friends are depicted and named. Useful for prosopography, genealogy, and titles, such stelae are of limited historical use. Until Senwosret III large and well-decorated tombs continued to be carved by the upper classes in the provinces. El-Berseh, Beni Hasan, Asyut, Kan el-Kebir, Akhmim, Naga ed-Deir—all situated near the metropoles of townships, have yielded sequences of nobles' tombs replete with painted scenes and texts. As in the Old

Kingdom, the life of a noble's estate is depicted, along with biographical texts of no little historical importance.

Government officers would often, as had their forbears in Dynasty 6, commemorate their official missions by carving a record in the rocks at a particular site with or without royal authorization. Such texts are found in quarries (Hatnub, Wady Hammamat), mines (Sorbut el-Khadim), border forts (Semna-Kummeh), temple environs (Deir el-Bahari), or rest areas (Qosseir, Dehmau). At worst a simple graffito, at best a well-cut stela with vignette depicting the king and gods, such records of missions are often extremely informative with respect to military campaigns, trading ventures, and building activity.

The circumstances under which Dynasty 12 seized power called forth a variety of measures taken in the interests of maintaining the hard-won peace and prosperity they had achieved. There were sanctions, of course, and acts of conciliation, as well as the fostering of honest government; but this gifted family must also and especially be remembered for its skilful use of literature of persuasion. A number of works have come down to us, the intent of each being to bolster loyalty toward and promote confidence in the royal family and the prosperous regime that it had inaugurated. In the story of Sinuhe, the most popular (among ancient Egyptians) of all Egyptian tales, a naïve servant who fancies himself on the wrong side of an impending civil war flees to Syria, only to be pardoned by a magnanimous Senwosret I and welcomed back to court with open arms. In the *Ship-wrecked Sailor,* a mariner (the prototype of Sinbad) is cast upon a fabulous island ruled by a great snake; eventually the sailor reaches home with the snake's advice still ringing in his ears to remain in Egypt and live out his life there. Both texts employ the first person and employ a form grounded in the address to an audience, and probably would have been labeled *sdd,* "narrative folk-tale," a genre noted by the Egyptians themselves for its extraordinary exaggeration. But more respected forms are also found in the repertoire. A thinly disguised prophecy (*srt*) in the form of the oratorical delivery (*mdt*) placed in the mouth of a wise man of Snofru's time (Fourth Dynasty) forecast the time of troubles that followed the Sixth Dynasty and exhorted all men to support "Ameny" (Amenemhet I), who would restore order. A father discourses with his son in the time-honored vehicle of the "teaching of wisdom" (*sb³yt*); but the wily adult does nothing but satirize all callings and professions save that of the scribe in an effort to influence his son in his eventual choice of career. A motif that recurs in several contexts (some albeit fragmentary) describes the plight of the wronged poor or the wise man who attempts to address a petition to an unfeeling bureaucrat, or a government officer more interested in frivolous entertainment. Again, the essential injustice of this situation is stressed and implicitly condemned. Finally, the propagandistic intent is but thinly disguised in those royal records, which record the divine birth and coronation of the king, and the hymns that laud the monarch and his kingly regalia.

But with increased sophistication in court life, interest in literary composition for its own sake increases. Etiology proliferates and is dignified by inscripteration: Thus and so did the Fourth Dynasty give place to the Fifth, here is the true story of Pepy II's excesses and the end of the dynasty. Stilted, rhetorical texts describe the pleasures of fowling and fishing indulged in by king and court. The lament becomes a cliché-ridden form much used by poor composers, and the serious artist who indulges therein longs for fresh words and figures.

The existence of this body of *written* narrative, prophecy, and aphorism should not make one forget the existence of a strong *oral* transmission of verbal composition. We have no figures on illiteracy, but it must have been very high: people *told* and *listened* to composed pieces.

Even stelae were read aloud by the scribe to an audience. Pieces like Ipuwer and the Middle Kingdom model letter show clear traces of mnemonic devices and phraseology meaningful only if spoken, indicating that the original form of composition was oral. But some of the texts we have reviewed (like Sinuhe) were certainly written first, and the oral transmission was secondary. Any characteristics that point to oral tradition arise out of the fact that the society in which the scribe lived was heavily indebted to such a tradition, and mimicking its forms in written composition came as second nature. In fact in Egypt, scribe and orator being highly respected authors, the interplay between the scribal and oratorical arts was close and subtle. Genres like proverb and aphorism, which we might think to have been wholly within the oral tradition, show the strongest reliance on written forms of almost canonical authority, while such records as those of a bygone king and his fame and the mighty acts of the gods, which we know to have been written on temple walls and stelae, are most often said to have been passed on by word of mouth!

The New Kingdom

Written records gradually diminish in numbers during the 18th century B.C.; by 1700 B.C. they have almost failed us. The next century preserved scattered texts only, and those are of a rather crude nature (though the depth of incompetence reflected in the First Intermediate Period is rarely reached). Private stelae from Edfu, tombs at El Kab, a few stelae, buildings, and tombs from the Theban region are the sole survivors from Upper Egypt. From Lower Egypt there is some evidence that the later Hyksos were responsible for monuments and buildings of a respectable nature, and that hieroglyphic records were kept; but the warfare and destruction that attended the expulsion of the Asiatics has deprived us of all but a few scattered examples.

With the reunification of Egypt under the Eighteenth Dynasty and the return of prosperity, our written sources burgeon. The family of the Thutmosids considered themselves the heirs and successors of the Twelfth Dynasty, and it is therefore not strange to find the bureaucratic and scribal traditions of the empire strongly reminiscent of the Middle Kingdom. Scribes are encountered everywhere in the new administration, and to every government department are attached "the keepers of the writings" and their superiors (i.e., a cadre of archivists-*cum*-file clerks). The accepted literary dialect of the Eleventh and Twelfth Dynasties, Middle Egyptian, as it is known, continued to be used under the Eighteenth Dynasty, until replaced at the end of the Amarna period by a contemporary vernacular (a Lower Egyptian dialect?) called by scholars Late Egyptian.

In the two major administrative centers, Thebes and Memphis, great archives called offices of writings grew up under the authority of the two viziers. As in the Middle and Old Kingdoms, these archives contained originals or copies of all official documents, petitions, and private contracts. The originals of all royal decrees, sealed in the king's presence, were deposited there along with copies of the king's *communiqués* and encyclicals. Of special importance was the diary-ledger, "the day book of the king's house," which recorded day by day the king's movements and the doings of the court, especially receipts and disbursements of food. The vizier's hall of writings was also the repository for legal records such as the transcripts of trials (*smtr*), legal depositions (*ꜣwty ḏdt.n* N, literally, "document of that which N said"), and property transfers. Work assignments (*shnt*), special reports by provincial officials (*smit*), and simple memoranda (*sḥꜣ*) were also stored here. Less numerous, but of great importance, were the inspector's reports or inventories (*sipty*) filed by some high official assigned by the king on a sort of royal commission to investigate some problem of state.

Other government departments kept their own archives. In the Department of Pharaoh's Granaries were kept the yearly grain assessments, filed by the tax assessors, registers of grain receipts recording the arrival of grain taxes at the granaries, lists of arable land, and conscription lists of cultivators. The treasury had its own archives in which were to be found the treasury records, the land-cadastre of Egypt (*dnyt nt Kmt*), the records of annual imposts and quotas, lists of estates and tax-bearing institutions, and census records. The Department of Pharaoh's Correspondence kept copies of letters dictated by the king, and where necessary translated into cuneiform upon clay, and also kept copies of letters sent to him. The keepers of the writings of the army kept draft lists of people eligible for military service, and a register of professional soldiers was kept in the royal stables. As the empire grew, and the numbers of foreign captives within Egypt multiplied, a special department was set up to register and assign this new manpower within Egypt.

Under the empire, temples and their estates prospered as never before. In fact, they had become complex, land-owning institutions, the operation of which required as much bookkeeping as a government department. Temples kept their own archives containing inventories of cult paraphernalia and real estate, registers of workers, day books (*hrwyt*) or logs, assessments and receipts, and that great *Blue Book* of regulations for the manufacture of cult objects and the running of the cult, the Great Inventory (*sipty wr*).

More in keeping with what we expect from an Egyptian temple archive are the contents of the House of Books (*pr mdꜣt*), variously called the Chamber of Writings or the Mansion of (the goddess) Seshat. The *House of Books* was a term now applied, in contradistinction to its use in the Old Kingdom, to the repository for cultic literature. Attached to each of the main temples was an institution known as the House of Life. Here were copied out and stored the writings of the House of Life, "the hidden things of heaven and all the mysteries of earth," called collectively *The Manifestations of Re.* The highest grade of scribe was trained in their contents and use. Here, too, certain mystic rituals prescribed by writings were performed. In Ptolemaic times inscriptions on the walls of the temple apprise us of the contents of such temple libraries, and the catalog must have changed little since the New Kingdom. Magic spells of prophylactic import, medical books, propitiatory hymns, and of course the very ancient mortuary beatifications of the lector priest's art, make up the vast majority of the contents of the "stacks" of these libraries. Especially numerous as time goes on are books dealing with the minutiae of the embalmment procedures: *The Book of Going Forth by Day, The Book of Breathing, The Book of Amulets,* and so on. The priests also kept dream books, hemerologies, and records of the oracles delivered by the god. The word *annals* (*gnwt*) still occurs in the New Kingdom in the context of the House of Books, but it now seems to be applied as much to mythological stories of the gods and cosmogonies as to genuine records of past reigns.

The euphoria of empire inevitably gives rise to an interest in the past, if only to contrast the magnitude of current accomplishments with the poverty of monuments of bygone days. This certainly was the limit of interest of Eighteenth Dynasty kings, but by the Nineteenth Dynasty a genuine admiration for the past is displayed by the Ramessides. Loyal and devoted to their own family, and aware of their direct succession to the illustrious Thutmosids, the Nineteenth Dynasty monarchs revived interest in the king list tradition. This had survived the vicissitudes of the Hyksos and Amarna periods, probably through the scribes first of Itj-towy and later Memphis, and appears in surprising detail and accuracy in a fragmentary papyrus of Ramesses II's reign, now in the Turin museum. The offering to the royal ancestors was part of the daily services of the great state temples, and statues of the king's fathers regularly appeared in procession at the festivals of Min and Amun. Several *pseudo king lists* of the New Kingdom take the form of assemblages of statues of royal ancestors (sometimes cartouches) to which the king makes an offering: the Karnak list of Thutmose III, the Abydos lists of Sety I and Ramesses II, the lists at the Min festivals of Ramesses II and III. In imitation of their Pharaoh, the great nobles of the Ramesside Age were fond of depicting themselves in their tombs piously revering or offering to a selection of bygone kings.

The written material reviewed in the foregoing paragraphs was almost exclusively in papyrus form. The documents (*ȝwty*) favored by the chancery were papyrus rolls often of 16 pages in length, though it is by no means uncommon to find much longer rolls. Very occasionally animal skin was used for documents of great importance. In the routine business activity of daily life, memoranda, bills, receipts, accounts, and even letters were often written in ink on ostraca or chips of stone. Schoolboys did their exercises on the same material, or occasionally used a scribe's wooden palette (*gsty*) for a copy that could easily be washed off.

The New Kingdom has bequeathed to us more papyri and ostraca than earlier periods, and these almost exclusively from Thebes. As in the case of stratified remains at an archeological site, the largest number of papyri come from the latest century of the period (viz., the 12th century B.C.). From the Eighteenth Dynasty very little has survived beyond three account papyri from government departments, caches of business ostraca from Deir el-Bahari, Molkata, and Amarna, and a handful of private letters. Some day books have survived, along with one or two account papyri; private letters appear here and there, and toward the close of the Dynasty the large caches of ostraca (of an administrative character) begin at such sites as the Ramesseum and the workmen's village at Deir el-Medina. But it is the Twentieth Dynasty that abounds, relatively speaking, in papyri and ostraca. From the reign of Ramesses III comes the Great Harris Papyrus (complete), recording the king's benefactions to the gods and their temples throughout the three decades of his reign. The circumstances surrounding the passing of the same king have produced the fragmentary transcripts of the treason trials (Papyrus Lee and Rollin); while the inquest into the spate of tomb robberies beginning in the reign of Ramesses IX is responsible for the official transcripts contained in Papyrus Abbott and Papyrus Mayer. A tax assessor's journal, Papyrus Wilbour, survives from the reign of Ramesses V, a report on a worker's strike (Turin Strike Papyrus) from Ramesses III, a memorandum of indictment again from Ramesses V, and substantial numbers of letters, tax collectors' journals, and the like from the entire century and a half during which the last Ramessides held sway. Covering the same span, moreover, is the vast collection of ostraca—the waste baskets of an entire community—from the workers' village of Deir el-Medina.

In spite of the relative wealth of papyri, textual sources engraved on stone remain the primary source for the historian. In the main these are royal publications, and three types we have encountered before. Stelae recording royal decrees (*wḏ-nsw*)—whether charters of immunity, endowments, or new laws—belong to one of the oldest genres of inscription, and continue to be erected during the course of the New Kingdom. Speeches at royal sittings, rare under the Middle Kingdom (although of Middle Kingdom origin), become rather more common in Dynasty 18. The intent, as before, is to publish the king's account of an event, his voiced desire to embark on such-and-such an enterprise, or his explanation of why he is doing a certain thing. The text is in the first person, and may be introduced by some such phrase as "the king himself speaks." The personal nature of this type of oration is shared by the direct royal address, in which the king addresses his audience or readers, with the intent to inform them of his will. Although lacking the formal setting, it is the assembled court, listening intently, that we should imagine as the recipient of the spoken address. Of a less embellished nature, and with a format set by the chancery, was the "Palace Order" literature, "that which was said in the Majesty of the Palace." This was a formal pronouncement of intent to undertake an expedition or a construction program, to engage in battle, to promote an official, or the like. Such a statement had the force of law, and in written form constituted a legal permit.

Seldom were raw extracts from royal journals translated into inscriptions in stone: Only Thutmose III, his son, and great-grandson excerpted their military annals. The longest such text, that of Thutmose III, was part of an extensive scene with accompanying text that recorded in an ambulatory around the god's shrine the dedication of booty and gifts to the god Amun. The record was for the eyes of the gods and priests, not the people. The rhetorical embellishment that normally informs a text for public consumption is therefore not in evidence, and the annals sound very sober indeed.

The day book of the king's house was also the ultimate source for a wide variety of adulatory stelae that popularized the king's mighty acts. These usually, but not always, begin with a date and the king's titulary. The body of the text is often taken up by a royal encomium of extravagant proportions, only at the end of which will the specific victory that occasioned the text be mentioned. Sometimes the text will employ a stereotyped motif to heighten the brilliance of the king's accomplishment. A messenger suddenly arrives at the royal palace with news of a foreign invasion, a rebellion, or some other disaster, and after a fit of righteous indignation, Pharaoh will take the necessary steps immediately and without consultation to put the situation right. Another recurrent plot pattern describes the king in council rejecting the timorous advice of his ministers in favor of his own daring policy of action. Such inscriptions glorifying Pharaoh smack of poetry, and usually go under the loose designation "victory stela." They were often set up on the avenue leading to the temple, within the temple precincts themselves, or at "the station of the Lord/Ruler" where the king stood during the temple ceremony. Stelae set up along the frontiers to overawe the natives could also be called victory stelae.

Temple walls and pylons during the New Kingdom abound in texts and reliefs of a military nature. The age-old scene of the king smiting his enemies is the earliest to appear, appropriately enough on the exterior faces of pylons where the populace could see it. Long lines of ovals inscribed with the names of foreign toponyms and surmounted by the torsos and heads of bound captives accompany the smiting scenes from the reign of Thutmose III on. The captions state that this is the list of places His Majesty conquered, but in fact they seem to be place names drawn from known itineraries in western Asia and the Sudan. Beginning in the late Amarna period, external temple walls are decorated with sequences of military scenes showing the stages of the battle: the god's commission, mounting the chariot, riding into battle, the *mêlée,* and the return, all glossed by explanatory texts of varying worth to historians.

The high-flown language of poetry used in royal encomiums gives evidence of the importance attached to rhetorical style in court circles during the New Kingdom. Hymnodic stelae become increasingly common as the Eighteenth Dynasty progresses, and scribes became more practiced in the art of formulaic composition. As the form and content indicate, as well as the presence of the recurring formulae, an oral use of this genre seems beyond question. The

Eighteenth Dynasty familiarizes us with the *Collection of Deeds,* a text in which the prowess of the king as a warrior and a sportsman is described by reference to specific acts. The form died out early in the Nineteenth Dynasty, but a more stereotyped hymn of praise replaced it and soon became very common. This latter is a formal song to be sung to the harp, in which each verse ends in the names of the king. The type belongs to the broader genre of "Hymns of Adoration," a litany used by king or commoner, in which the object of adoration is either the king or a god.

Adoration stelae are frequently placed by private individuals as votive offerings in temples and shrines; they invoke the god in language redolent of oral formula, and often constitute testimonials on the part of a sufferer of healing from sickness. A special type of royal apologia to the god were the adorations and supplications carved on stelae and set up close to the deity's shrine. These were prayers and statements of benefactions, and were sometimes coupled with the god's address to the king, promising him glory and power.

A very common genre of text, to be found on all edifices, was the building inscription, a sort of text of dedication. The simplest form involved the name of the king, followed by the formula "he made (it) as his memorial for his father (god N)." Then follows the name of the specific building or object in question. Occasionally, the simple formula may be expanded into, or replaced by, a long text (sometimes dated) in which the king lists and describes the structures and cult paraphernalia he has built for a god or gods.

Another source of historical information, not quite as important as texts of royal authorship, is the private necropolis. The tombs of the nobility, especially at Thebes (to a lesser extent at Saqqara), yield historical and biographical, as well as mortuary, inscriptions. Nobles in the Eighteenth Dynasty are fond of setting on record for posterity what they considered their most notable achievements during life: a military campaign, their reception of tribute, their service in office, their relationship to the king, and so on. During the long reign of Ramesses II, however, it became increasingly fashionable to devote more and more wall space to mortuary and cult scenes; and the biographical content (except for strings of titles) virtually disappears.

Like the high Middle Kingdom, the New Kingdom from the morrow of the Amarna experiment throws up a literature of sorts. But although some of the same genres are represented, it differs from the illustrious classics of the past in several ways. New Kingdom tales and poetry emanated from a different *Sitz im Leben* from the Middle Kingdom pieces. The latter by and large emerged from the hands of learned scribes or orators, reflecting, broadly speaking, the official attitudes of the court. Not unexpectedly, they had by the Eighteenth and Nineteenth Dynasties come to dominate the school curriculum. (One of the reasons we are so well provided with copies of Sinuhe, the Instruction of Amenemhet or of Ptahhotpe, to name but a few, must be sought in the practice of New Kingdom scribes of setting these pieces before their pupils to be copied and studied.) Late Egyptian stories, by contrast, display marked folkloristic characteristics; our copies did not originate in the classroom, but most often the private collection of a trained scribe. Unlike Middle Kingdom literature, they lack propagandistic intent, being rather in the category of pure entertainment. On the whole, one would have to say of the Late Egyptian stories, in contrast to those of the Twelfth Dynasty, that they are more firmly rooted in the oral tradition of narrative (*sḏd*, "oral narrative," often with the overtones of "tall tale"); although this should not prejudice the question of origin, written or oral, of the individual stories. Some new genres, scarcely represented by classical Middle Egyptian, make their appearance in the Late Egyptian corpus (e.g., love poetry, mythological stories, and allegory).

Fairytales, "*Märchen,*" are still very much to the taste of Egyptians in the Nineteenth Dynasty. Like examples of this genre wherever it is found, the fairytale of the New Kingdom is built around a simple though often ingenious plot, divorced from historical reality. Personal names and toponyms are eschewed in favor of terms of relationship and the most general geographic terms; the setting is not specified, nor is the time set, and miraculous elements are nearly always present. A prince, doomed to death by the bite of a crocodile, snake, or dog, seeks his fortune in a far-off land where he wins the hand of a princess locked in a tower, and defies his fate. Two brothers lived together in peace until the wife of the elder, passionately in love with the younger but rebuffed by him, accuses him of improper advances and sets her husband against him. The son of Truth avenges his father for the wrong done to him by his uncle Falsehood by resorting to the same kind of lie Falsehood had used in his incrimination of Truth.

Perhaps more popular among the masses were the tales told about great figures of the immediate past. The Middle Kingdom had woven its legends around the greats of the Old Kingdom—Snofru, Khafre, Pepy II; the Egyptian of the Nineteenth Dynasty, basking in the glory of the empire, fabricated his yarns about the builders of that empire—Seqenenre, Thutmose III, Djehuty the general. The stories are simple and center on the interest inherent in the deeds of the clever trickster. The subject matter is always basically historical, though often wildly embellished, and no miraculous element is present. Nevertheless, these tales are in no way to be construed as sober history: they are at home in the storytelling of the illiterate and the etiologies that center on the interpretation of a known monument.

Much more frequently preserved, if not more popular, were the stories that circulated about the gods. These were not in the nature of the originals of *myths*—by definition, originals did not exist, myths constituting simply "notional wholes"—but rather theme and variation on a well-known mythical situation or episode, or a free embellishment of the same. The *dramatis personae* are well known and the incidents are familiar, but the treatment is innovative and even inclines toward the picaresque. The *Book of the Heavenly Cow,* a rambling collection of etiologies, tells how, in order to punish mankind for sin the sun-god sent to earth his "Eye" in the form of a lioness. Unable eventually to stop her slaughtering, Re was obliged to invent a very potent liquor as red as blood; inebriated, the goddess proved easily subdued. Another tale told how the wise Isis contrived to learn Re's hidden name of power. She created a snake with a virulent venom that bit Re in the rump, and she refused to administer the antidote until the sun-god divulged his name to her. Other tales told how Anhur ("He who brings the far-off one") brought back the wandering "Eye" of Re; how Seth defeated the celestial dragon Apophis; how the inquisitive Shu was bitten by a uraeus, and so on. The largest group of tales arises out of the plot structure of the Osiris myth. Egyptians were especially fond of that part of the tale in which Isis with the baby Horus is hiding from Seth in the marshes of the Delta: They tell how he was bitten by snakes, scorpions, and dogs, and how his mother or her helpers devised cures for him, or how he evaded Seth and his accomplices. The longest such story concerns itself with the Trial of Horus and Seth for the rule of Egypt, and in a series of largely unrelated episodes pits the canny youth Horus against his dim-witted uncle. In a real sense, it is a prototype of such contests as Bugs Bunny vs. Elmer Fudd, Road-runner vs. Coyote, Br'er Rabbit vs. Red Fox. If casting religious tales in the mold of such entertainment literature smacks of sacrilege, it should be clearly understood that the mythological tales of the New Kingdom belong in the same basket and are imbued with the same bawdy spirit as the miracle plays of the Middle Ages. That relatively speaking so many have come down to us is largely explained by their widespread secondary use as magic spells.

The period following the collapse of the Thutmosids in the twilight of the Amarna Period produces for the first time in the history of Egyptian *Belle Lettres* the phenomenon of love poetry ("delectation of the heart," or "sweet saying[s]"). Three great collections and some miscellaneous ostraca range over the two centuries from c. 1300 B.C.; and the content of each conforms to a widespread genre known all over the Near East and the Levant. In form the couplet preponderates, each line comprising a 3:3 or a 3:2 beat structure; the contents, like the biblical Song of Songs, alternates between passionate outbursts of the boy and of the girl. Most of the repertoire of later love poetry—biblical, classical, Petrarchan—is already present, and the themes and settings are familiar: the catalog of the loved one's charms, the sickness of the lover, the locked door, lovers at dawn, lovers separated, and so on. Sensual love is never explicit in this poetry—an erotic papyrus and some ostraca exist, but differ in form from the current genre—but the figured ostraca from the Nineteenth and Twentieth Dynasties showing scantily clad females at their toilet provide a fitting graphic complement.

The Period of Libyan Hegemony

In the second quarter of the 11th century B.C. the wealth of written material we have relied on in our reconstruction of the history and society in the New Kingdom begins to dry up. There are two reasons for this. First, the Twenty-first and Twenty-second Dynasty kings did not build as extensively as their predecessors, nor did they erect as many triumphal inscriptions. Second, Thebes, which had supplied so much of the inscriptional material for the New Kingdom, was no longer a center of the government or royal family. Whether the Libyan Pharaohs erected historical stelae at their residences of Tanis and Bubastis is not known; but it is probable that the practice gradually fell into abeyance. Thus, the writing of a history of the Libyan period is fraught with difficulties.

In the absence of stelae, reliefs, or papyri, we are thrown back on whatever the society of the times chose to memorialize on material of permanence. Statue inscriptions with genealogies are fairly common, especially in priestly circles. Faintly cut restoration inscriptions at Karnak contrast with the bold reliefs of former ages. Available space on architraves and walls erected by the mighty kings of the Middle and New Kingdoms is employed by the priests to inscribe their annals—really, a set of records of official acts, like the induction of individuals into office. The annals (with the exception of those of the High Priest Osorkon) thus do not constitute a set of records inscribed at regular intervals, nor do the Karnak quay inscriptions, much used by historians. These are notations on the face of the dock before the Temple of Amun, recording the height of exceptional inundations, year and name of the king, and later the name of the incumbent high priest. For any other endeavor than the ascertaining of relative chronology, the Karnak quay notations are of little use.

At the beginning of the period under discussion, and to a limited extent later, it was deemed important to inscribe on stone the results of a favorable oracle. Such records are nearly always of a quasi-legal nature and have to do with the real estate or the inheritance of the very rich. More common, but of more use to the economic historian than the Egyptologist, are the donation stelae. These detail the extent and character of a tract of land given by prince or private individual to the temple, and were apparently set up as a sort of boundary marker on the land in question. The texts are stereotyped and often contain nothing more for the political historian than prosopographical information and a regnal year date.

The same information—prosopographical and chronological—is about the extent of the contribution to our knowledge made by another sizable group of texts, namely the Serapeum stelae. Beginning in the late New Kingdom, the king and the grandees of the kingdom took to memorializing the interment of the sacred Apis bull at Memphis by including in the burial chamber in the Serapeum at Saqqara a number of pious stelae of private donation. This great cache of texts, discovered by Auguste Mariette in the 19th century and now in the Louvre, are only now being published properly. Ironically, textual material from *human* burials during this period is of negligible significance.

Rather common in the Twenty-second Dynasty and extending to the Twenty-sixth are *donation stelae.* These record the donation to a temple of a private tract of land by its owner, usually a grandee of the realm. Of importance in reconstructing the economic life of the times, donation stelae that are dated to specific kings' reigns often help in solving problems of chronology.

The Kushite, Saïte, and Persian Periods

It would be a fair assessment of the scarcity of historical inscriptions during the 1st millennium B.C. to say that we gain more insight into the political history of the Nile Valley from biblical and Assyrian sources than from those of native authorship. The Books of Kings, Isaiah, and Jeremiah, and the annals of Shalmaneser III, Tiglath-pileser III, Sargon, Sennacherib, Esarhaddon, and Ashurbanipal, often shed a great deal of light upon Egyptian history, at least when it impinges on the rest of the Near East.

But the capitals of Napata and Sais are silent. The great record of Piankhy's invasion, the stela of the miracle in Taharqa's year 6, or the record of Psammetichus II's victory over Kush, are exceptional: In spite of the objection that Sais is wholly destroyed and Napata laid waste, the kings of the period clearly were not in the habit of inscribing their triumphs on stelae. In keeping with the tenor of the times, there was considerable temple building and relief decoration of a pious nature, and a few edicts done in archaic style. As in the Libyan period, the stela form lent itself to the practical purpose of inscribing a legal text on permanent material. The best example of this, the Adoption Stela of Nitocris, records the legal adoption of Psammetichus I's daughter by the Divine Worshipper Shepenwepet at Thebes.

A type of text more frequently met with is the pious statue inscription already common in the Twenty-second Dynasty. Of a private and often biographical nature, these texts were carved on statues set up in tomb chapels or temple ambulatories. The grandees to whom they belong loved to give lists of titles, and sometimes recount snippets from their life histories, such as the refurbishing of a temple, the restoration of a cult, or a successful mission for the king.

The 7ᵗʰ and 6ᵗʰ centuries witnessed in the Delta the introduction and early evolution of a new and cursive script now called Demotic. Derived from the late cursive hand of the late Libyan period *(abnormal hieratic)*, the script is known to us in its earliest form by an increasing number of business documents: deeds of sale mainly, but also contracts, memoranda, receipts, and letters. During the Persian and Ptolemaic periods Demotic texts proliferate everywhere— the script is even used, although a trifle bizarrely, on stone.

Decorated tombs are present in some numbers in the major necropoleis at Thebes and Saqqara. Indeed, some of the most impressive sepulchres ever constructed are to be found at the former site. The mayor Montemhet, the majordomos of the Divine Worshipper Pabasa, Aba, and Sheshonk all have monumental tombs; but although lavishly decorated, their contents prove of little use to the political historian. Pious religious scenes and texts drawn from traditional mortuary literature (including copies of the *Pyramid Texts* and a new edition of the *Book of Am Duat*) are the favored repertoire from which the tomb owner chooses his material.

Were it not for Herodotus, the chapter on the Twenty-sixth Dynasty in modern history books would be considerably slimmer than it now is. Herodotus probably visited Egypt in the mid-5ᵗʰ century, two or three generations after it had been reduced by Persia, when the memory of the Saïte kings was still vivid in Egyptian memory. Although he drew on his predecessor Hecataeas, Herodotus certainly saw the monuments of the Delta and Memphis (if not the Thebaid), and had opportunity to discourse with native Egyptians. Nevertheless, his informants were, in the main, out of touch with the written sources then extant, and they reflect the popular tradition, largely oral and with etiological intent. In contrast to the remainder of his Book II on Egypt, the chapters on the Twenty-sixth Dynasty have preserved the names and correct order of the Saïte kings and give a fair *résumé* of their reigns.

The paucity of royal inscriptions from the 5ᵗʰ and 4ᵗʰ centuries makes it difficult to base oneself solely on Egyptian monumental sources in writing a history of Dynasties 27 to 30. For the beginning of this period, and sporadically throughout Dynasties 29 to 30, the records from the Serapeum help to fill the void. But, except for the reign of Darius I and the Thirtieth Dynasty, biographical stelae and statue inscriptions are comparatively rare. Inevitably, one must again turn to the incidental passages mentioning Egypt in such Greek historians as Thucydides and Diodorus.

Basis of Our Chronology

———————— ψ ————————

A basic question that might be put to anyone is, how can I date anything that happened before I was born, or, more to the point, before I became conscious and knowledgeable enough to count? One answer might be: from identifiable events that I observed or from what my family and older contemporaries told me. Thus, I *know* my eldest son was born in the year Kennedy was elected president; I *was told* I was born two years after FDR was elected president and one year after Adolph Hitler was appointed chancellor. My father indicated he was born 5½ years before the outbreak of WW I, and my great aunt told me she was born two months before Charles Dickens died. By consulting the family Bible and totting up ages at the birth of the next generation, I can carry my personal history back about 190 years. But the *about* is important: I cannot achieve accuracy. Moreover, I can only proceed by *naming* years after events, and any time reckoning using this mechanism would necessitate a truly phenomenal memory.

A moment's reflection will indicate that, ironically, a better frame for history is one that ignores historical content: a simple linear sequence of units corresponding to years, *numbered* from a single event. Once such a sequence has started the event whose commemoration was chosen to begin it need not be remembered for the mechanism to work. Society need only remember the current number in sequence, and society never suffers the collective amnesia that would blot out an entire time span! We today are fortunate to use such a linear sequence, an *era* in fact, by which to date events. But how far back in time does such a sequence permit accuracy?

1. Medieval Chronicles

Popular impetus in Christian attempts at prediction, and belief in number-significance, led early to close attention to numerology. The 17th and 18th centuries witnessed the formal publication of medieval chronicles and annals in most European countries, carefully annotated. These include the Anglo-Saxon chronicle, begun by Alfred the Great and continuing to1154; Norman chronicles from the 11th century; Annals of the Franks down to 829; the Liber Pontificalis of the Vatican.

The early Church Fathers (2nd through 4th centuries A.D.), while they spurned non-Christian literature as heathen, nonetheless attempted to emulate non-Christian historians in compiling tables of dates to interlock biblical and secular history (Africanus, Eusebius, Jerome). This was often done in the heat of Christian-pagan polemics, and no one was beyond distorting the facts. Therefore, caution is called for in using these sources.

2. The Common (Christian) Era

All of the preceding examples, whether accurate or not, are dated and extended on the basis of a single era: the Common (Christian) Era. Other era-dating mechanisms exist (e.g., Muslim dating from the Hejira), but by consensus, C.E. (earlier A.D.) has been adopted by almost all scholars working around the world. Stimulated by the controversy surrounding the date of Easter, Pope John I, 1,479 years ago, commissioned a monk, Dionysius Exiguus, to undertake a new computation. His research issued in dating by a new era in which years were numbered from the putative birth of Christ (which Dionysius believed had taken place 525 years before his time of writing). Although he may well have been incorrect, a year sequence had been inaugurated that admitted of no hiatus, and was followed by all the chronicles mentioned above—as well as, eventually, by civil governments in Europe. It is still followed today.

3. Greco-Roman Era-dating

What chronological data, era-linked or otherwise, did Dionysius himself have access to in his own time? How do we get back before the year 525 with any attempt at accuracy? The following are some of the material Dionysius used:

- *The Era of Diocletian* (a Roman emperor). This was still being used by the Church in Egypt, and was in its 242nd year when Dionysius composed his new era.

- Indiction tables (taxation at 15-year intervals). They were still in use in Dionysius' time, dating from Diocletian and before.

- *A(b) U(rbe) C(ondita)* dating, an era dated from the putative founding of Rome (in use or easily computable in 525).

- Olympiads (four-year units tied to successive performances of the Olympic Games). The games themselves had been abolished 132 years before 525, but the lists extended over 1,169 years.

- *Annales Maximi,* published a.u.c. 623 (130 B.C.). These were derived from earlier consular, annual records kept at Rome, but were unreliable because of gaps in the ancient sources.

- *Liber Annalis.* These were chronological tables published in the middle of the first century B.C., allegedly based on records now lost.

- Roman Consular years. These are accurate from the end of the 2nd century B.C.

- *Constantinople City Chronicle.* This had been begun 195 years before Dionysius, and could be used as a bridge to older chronological mechanisms.

4. *Hellenistic Era-dating*

In the aftermath of the collapse of the empire of Alexander the Great, Seleucid Syria had instituted an era based on the assumption of power by Seleucus I, one of Alexander's generals. Pompey terminated the Seleucid kingdom in the 249th year of its existence, and since this event can easily be computed in relation to the Roman and Dionysiac systems as 64 B.C., the Seleucid Era must have been dated from 312 to 311 B.C. Many Levantine cities used their own eras, reckoned from their liberation by Alexander's advance into Asia.

No Hellenistic era-dating was adopted in Egypt, but the wealth of dated papyri has made it possible to establish lengths of reign, sometimes to month and day, back to Ptolemy Lagus. Kleopatra VII died in late summer of the 21st year after coming to power and one year after the battle of Actium (established independently by the Roman sources as September 2, 31 B.C.); she thus came to power in 51 B.C. Sources are full enough to establish Alexander the Great's presence in Egypt 301 years before Actium (i.e., 332 B.C).

5. *Ptolemy's Almagist (Greek* Μαθηματικὴ σύταξις*)*

This monumental work has been described as "a complete textbook of astronomy in thirteen books . . . using carefully selected observations . . . [and producing] tables necessary for describing and computing the positions of the sun, moon, the five planets, and the fixed stars" (G. J. Toomer, OCD, 1274). In order to compile such tables necessary for precise predictions, Ptolemy required the records of as many astronomical observations as he could lay hands on, distributed as far back in time as possible. Ptolemy worked in Alexandria in the 2nd century A.D. but, while Egypt had no long-standing tradition of recorded astronomical observations or omina texts, in his day Egypt had long been in receipt of such texts from Babylonia, rendered into Demotic and Greek. These had been brought into Egypt either in Saïte or early Persian times: surviving manuscripts refer to the "new writings" and associate them with Darius, and Roman Demotic copies exist that are contemporary with Ptolemy, and of which he undoubtedly made use.

On the basis of this material Ptolemy was able to reconstruct a king list (κανων Πτολεμαιου) dating back to one Ναβουασσαρος, a Babylonian king of the 8th century B.C. While the accuracy of the list depends on Babylonian eclipse observations, Ptolemy betrays an Alexandrian/Egyptian perspective: When he pushes his list beyond Alexander the Great, he uses the lengths of reign of the Ptolemies, not the Seleucids or Macedonians. It is important to note that Ptolemy's purpose in reconstructing a king list with lengths of reign and no gaps was practical, not dilettantish or historical. He *had* to know how much time separated him from the individual observations in the past, the records of which he was using. Errors in the list would have been immediately apparent, since they would have affected the precision of computations.

Ptolemy's king list was so valuable a tool that it did not pass into oblivion. Theon Alexandrinus updated the list after Ptolemy's death in his *Handy Tables* (dated by the solar eclipse of June 16, 364 A.D.). With this update we are well within the range of the indiction lists, the *Constantinople City Chronicle, The Era of Diocletian,* and the a.u.c. dating scheme.

6. *The Early First Millennium*

Making use of the relatively rich sources of Demotic business documents (dated to specific reigns) and hieroglyphic inscriptions, it is possible to reconstruct Egyptian chronology with accuracy from the arrival of Alexander in Egypt in the summer of 332 B.C. and the beginning of the reign of Taharqa in 690 B.C. Before this date, however, the task of the student of chronology is beset by the following problems: First, dead-reckoning on the basis of known lengths of reign becomes impossible due to gaps in the surviving record. In particular, we do not know how many years elapsed between the demise of the last Twenty-second Dynasty king and the Kushite invasion. Of the Twenty-second Dynasty kings, only Sheshonk III has a known length of reign (52 years); Pemay and Sheshonk IV can be shrewdly reckoned at 47 years. Earlier reign lengths are educated guesses: Sheshonk I at 33 on the basis of mummy-bandage dates, Osorkon II at 30 or more on the basis of his sed-festival. The Twenty-first Dynasty gives a quite plausible 25 years to Smendes and 50 to Psusennes I, but for the rest we are thrown back on to Manetho. Second, precise synchronisms between Egyptian history and the better-dated histories of Assyria and Babylonia are virtually nonexistent between c. 1190 and 701 B.C. The dating of Sheshonk I's attack on Palestine, equated in the Bible with Rehoboam's fifth year, would be invaluable if we knew the regnal year in which it occurred. Third, astronomical observations are rare in the extreme—and are not free of controversy. Of two passages that might refer to celestial observations, one (a lunar eclipse) has been proven to be illusory, and the other (the appearance of a comet) is highly debatable.

7. *Astronomical Observations and the Chronology of the Second Millennium* B.C.

Unlike the Babylonians, the Egyptians were woefully lax in recording celestial events. Only one sure solar eclipse appears in our sources, although it may be we that are at fault in our inability to appreciate a formulaic turn of phrase. Although textual references indicate an appreciation of lunar eclipses—"the sky swallows the moon"—few were set down in the records because they were regarded as evil portents. From time to time, though in high-flown rhetorical contexts, texts speak of "stars" (*sb3w*) dashing across the heavens. Since any celestial body, apart from the sun and the moon, could be termed *sb3*, one wonders if these are not allusions to comets. Two that might possibly be of use in confirming or establishing a chronology are (a) the dashing star that is said to have discomfited Thutmose III's enemies on an unspecified military campaign (Gebel Barkal stela), and (b) the personal name of the second king of the Twenty-first Dynasty (obviously given at birth) *P3-sb3-ḫꜥ-m-niwt* (Psusennes), "the star rises in (over) the city."

Scholars have had better luck working with records of *psḏntiw* (i.e., the day before the new moon when no part of the lunar orb is visible). These sightings can be computed, but often several absolute dates are possible. Thus two famous observations in the reigns of Thutmose III and Ramesses II have yielded three possibilities, narrowing the margin of error to 25 years, within which a "high," "middle," and "low" absolute chronology is possible; but beyond this the continuing and acrimonious debate has been unable to produce a consensus. As stated in the Preface, this history follows the "high" chronology for the New Kingdom.

As pointed out at the outset of this work, the Egyptian calendar, when first created in the Archaic Period, began with the heliacal rising of Sirius (July 18/19), and spanned 365 days. In view of the quarter day (or so) unaccounted for, this calendar, if unadjusted, would move slowly forward one whole day every four years, and one whole year in 1,460 years. It has become one of the cornerstones of Egyptian chronology that the Egyptians never saw the need to adjust this calendar; but this would mean that the rising of Sirius would occur anywhere but when it should—that is, on New Year's Day. Fairly often the Egyptians recorded "the Going Forth of Sothis" when it actually occurred in the civil calendar, which is a godsend for chronology. Observations under Senwosret III (18th century B.C.) and Amenophis I (16th century B.C.) are prime evidence in the debate over Middle and New Kingdom chronology. It should be noted, however, that although records based on observation might seem to offer hope of exact computation, the place and circumstances of observation must be addressed. A wide variety of conditions, ranging from haze on the horizon and cloud cover to observer error brought on by failing eyesight, sickness, oversleeping, or inebriety, could easily account for discrepancy. Different results can be obtained by locating the observers at several spots along the Nile and Delta: observations made in the latitude of Heliopolis or Memphis will differ from those made at Thebes or Elephantine. Since we have no evidence as to where they were made, inferences will have to be drawn from historical conditions at the time.

Although an absolute chronology may be yet beyond our powers to reconstruct, historical sources from the New Kingdom are full enough to create a relative chronology. The exact lengths of the reigns of Thutmose III, Ramesses II, and Ramesses III are known, and totals for Ahmose, Amenophis I, Amenophis II, Thutmose IV, Amenophis III, Akhenaten and Tutankhamen can be argued with a fair degree of precision. For the Twentieth Dynasty the ostraca and papyri from Deir el-Medina are useful in establishing totals with which scholarly consensus is content.

8. *The Chronology of the Third Millennium B.C.*

There is no evidence available at present to reckon, even within a reasonable margin of error, the number of years elapsing between the end of the Twelfth Dynasty and the beginning of the reign of Ahmose (although a rough generation count may be possible). Thus, the Sothic rising in Senwosret III's seventh year, recorded in the Kahun papyri, becomes all important. This event can be dated by means of the Sothic cycle to 1872 B.C., and pursuant thereto, the beginning of the dynasty to 1991 B.C. If the Turin Canon's plausible figure of 143 years for the Eleventh Dynasty is accepted, we arrive at 2134 B.C. for the declaration of independence by Thebes and the commencement of that regime.

Our problems increase as we move back from this date. We do not know how many years separate 2134 B.C. from the end of the reign of Pepy II. For the Old Kingdom, moreover, few exact lengths of reign are known, and the archeological recovery of a complete set of annals is but a dream. The scribes who in the Middle Kingdom drew up the first king list worked with uneven evidence and presuppositions that we now know to be in error; and the garbling of names and figures through their inability to control the early archaic writings contributed to distorting their efforts.

APPENDIX III
The King List

$$\Psi$$

It was probably in the Twelfth Dynasty (1991–1786 B.C.) that government scribes began and maintained, as part of the dynastic legitimation for which this dynasty strove, a true running king list. From the Twelfth Dynasty on each reign was recorded to the year, month, and day of a king's death.

For the Third Millennium the list is not always reliable, because of the lacunae (which the scribes acknowledge!) in the annals and other sources of the Old Kingdom of which they made use. Leaving aside the mythological introductory section, the following unlikely entries, if not downright errors, can be detected in the historical list:

1. In the section devoted to the first two dynasties, reign lengths are fantastic, and alternate between 70 or 94 (or 95) years.

2. A like fixation with a number, 19 (twice), 6 (twice) and 24 (three times) dominates the list from Djoser to Khafre. Since we now know that Snofru reigned 48 years, the 24 with which the king list credits him betrays the scribes' ignorance of the old biennial nature of the cattle count.

3. Here and there, and especially in the section devoted to the Archaic Period, names are distorted from the original, as though transmission through hieratic lists has fostered misinterpretation.

Two exemplars of the list survive: the Turin Canon, on the verso of a papyrus dated to the reign of Ramesses II, and the *Aegyptiaca* of Manetho (3rd century B.C.). The canon is clearly a copy, and the copyist tells us when he was confronted by missing information in the original. It purports to list all the kings from Re, the creator, down to the time of Ramesses II but, as it survives today, the page containing the names from Seqenenre of Dynasty 17 to Ramesses himself is gone. The edition represented by the Turin Canon was treated in part as a "final edition," even though the addition of royal names continued with each reign, and later it suffered partial conflation.

Only a digest (the *Epitome*) of Manetho's three-volume work survives, which took the form of a king list fleshed out by notations of events. The principal authors who quote the *Epitome* or the original are the Jewish historian Flavius Josephus, and the early church fathers Africanus and Eusebius. The events included by Manetho derive largely from folklore and legend, rather than readings of original monuments. Thus, in using Manetho, one should note the following:

1. The process of periodization has accelerated in the thousand years since the Turin Canon and has resulted in a division (frequently artificial) into 30 dynasties. These dynasties are not always qualified by the historical place of origin of the family, but by the place where most of their monuments survive. Thus, the First Dynasty is said to be "Thinite," though it hailed from Hierakonpolis; the Twelfth Dynasty "Diospolitan (=Theban)," though it ruled from Itj-towy; the Nineteenth "Diospolitan," though it came from the east Delta, and so forth.

2. Divisions of dynasties are heavily influenced by the mythological "Ancestral dynasty," the *Ennead,* and so artificial groupings of nine kings are frequent, though unhistorical. The Second, Third, Fourth, and Twenty-sixth Dynasties are thus distorted in Manetho.

3. Lengths of reign are not always reliable, as "number games," copying errors, and the prior needs of church fathers have influenced the copies of the *Epitome.*

4. A major prior consideration of Manetho is that, since the Pharaonic monarchy is unitary, there must have been only one king on the throne at a time. Regimes that were, in fact, contemporary, must be placed end to end. The classic example of the wholesale distortion to which this can lead is the Second Intermediate Period.

5. Sometime during the transmission of the king list misinterpretation has crept in: Dynasty 7 ("seventy kings for seventy days"), Dynasty 14 (really the ancestral pedigree of the Hyksos), Dynasties 17 and 18 (same family).

6. Since it was pressed into use in the ongoing Judeo-pagan polemic, the *Epitome* has at times been wildly distorted.

    Ancestral Offering Lists, inscribed on walls in the context of temple or private tomb, are often mistakenly called king lists. These comprise series of royal names, almost always presented in correct chronological order, invoked in the offering liturgies. Beyond providing evidence of sequence, their value is limited because no lengths of reign are included.

Death and accession notices were fully available to the keepers of the king list, but they have survived only sporadically. In the Old and Middle Kingdoms, and again in the Kushite-Saïte period, a king's accession was always backdated to the preceding New Year's Day. But in the New Kingdom, the regnal year ran from the calendar date of accession to its anniversary 365 days hence, and was numbered separately from the civil calendar year. The need to carefully note the accession day, for example in the practical world of the business community, led to its being mentioned fairly frequently in government, business, and private documents. Death notices were also issued, but not many of these have survived.

INDEX

A

Aba, 78, 251
Aba-sonbu, 241
Abassid Pluvial, 12
Abnormal hieratic, 242, 300
Abraham, XIV
Abu Simbel, 165, 231
Abusir, 287
Abydene, 60
Abydos, 37, 50, 59, 83, 90
Abyssinian, 3
Achaea, 194
Actium, 278
Adanirari I, 167
Addu-nirari, 159
Admonitions of Ipuwer, 85
Adoption Stela of Nitocris, 299
Adoration stelae, 296
Aegean islands, 137
Aegyptos, 118
Africa, 3, 7–9, 12
Africanus, 309
Afro-Asiatic family, 124–25
Afterlife, 27, 221–22
Agesilaus, 264
Agricultural revolution, 13–15
Agriculture, 4
Ahhiyawa, 193
Ahmes-Nofretari, 127
Ahmose, 123, 124, 126, 305
Akerblad XV, 146–55, 158–63, 165, 166
Akhenaten, 215
Akhmim, 290
Akhtoy, 87
Akhtoy I, 93
Akhtoy III, 219
Akizzi, 159
Akkad, 34
Akkadian (language), 168
Akkadian roots, 37
Akwoos, 196

Alalakh, 199
Aleksandros, XVII
Alexander the Great, 268–69, 303
Alexander VI (Pope), XIV
Alexandria XIV, 3, 5, 270–73
Aleyan Ba'al, 117
All-Inclusive, 252, 254
Amarna (city), 151–54, 158–59
Amarna family (Nineteenth Dynasty), 147
Amasis, 243, 245, 259
Amenemhet, 97
Amenemhet I, 98–99, 107, 296
Amenemhet III, 103, 104–06, 111, 114, 250–51
Amenemhet IV, 111
Amenmesse, 195
Amenophid family (Nineteenth Dynasty), 147
Amenophis, 201–02
Amenophis I, 126–27, 132
Amenophis II, 133, 136, 139–40, 182
Amenophis III, 140–43, 145, 146, 148, 175, 181, 196
Amenophis IV. *See* Akhenaten
Amenophis of the Forecourt, 216
Amenophis the Image, 216
Amorites, 113–14, 141
Amr ibn el-As, 283
Amun, 94, 98, 123, 143–46, 151, 152, 164, 178, 185, 203, 209, 213, 214, 233, 234, 241, 245, 250
Amunirdis, 232–33
Amurru, 161, 165, 199
Amyrtaeos, 263, 264
Anat, 117
Anatolia, 13, 35, 125, 158, 159, 165, 194, 196, 241
Anaxagoras, 254
Ancestral Offering Lists, 308
Andjety, 20, 90
Anii, 211
Animal husbandry, 24
Animal life, 5
Animals, artistic representations of, 19
Animal worship, 215, 278
Akhesenamun, 162

Ankhes-en-aten, 160
Ankhtify-nakht, 94
Annals, 286, 289, 293, 294, 299
Anti-life, in mythic narrative, 23
Antin, 114
Antiquity, XIV, 2, 245
Anubis, 92
Aper-el, 142
Aphorism, 291, 292
Apis worship, 259
Apophis, 116, 117, 132
Appearance of the King of Upper and Lower Egypt, 44
Apries, 243
Arabah, 7, 8
Arable land, 4
Aramaeans, 207, 247, 261
Archaic Period, 59
Archaism, 236
Archeology, XVIII
Archers, 179, 180
Acheulian, 12
Archives, 42–46, 286
Aristotle, XIV
Arkinian of Nubia, 13
Arkinian stage of culture, 13
Armed forces, in Twenty-sixth Dynasty, 245–47
Armenia, 35, 125, 232
Army
    during Ramesside Age, 181
    in Twentieth Dynasty, 201–02
Arpad, 207, 232
Arqata, 167
Arsaphes, 21, 279
Artaxerxes I, 257, 260
Artaxerxes III, 266, 270
Artisan concept of creation, 26
Arvad, 207
Ashdod, 234, 236
Ashkelon, 258
Ashurbanipal, 237, 239, 241, 251
Asia, 8, 107, 207–08, 236–37
Asia Minor, 258
Asiatic occupation, 115
Assassif district, 236
Asshur, 258
Assimilation, 22
Assyria, 35, 167, 193, 207, 214, 236, 237, 241, 258, 261, 267
Astarte, 117, 172
Astrology, XIV
Astronomical observations, 303, 304
Aswan, 1, 247
Aswan dams, 2

Asyut, 2, 7, 203, 233, 288
Atbara, 1
Aterian culture, 13
Atfih, 2, 7, 21
Atum, 242, 252, 254
Augustus, 5, 278
Auputa, 208
Authority, historical, 56
Avaris, 118, 122, 132, 171, 180
Ay, 153, 160–63, 172

B
Babylonia, 193, 262
Bagoas, 266
Bahr Yussef, 2
Bai, 56, 86
Banebdjed, 24
Bankes, W.J., XVI
Barley, 4
Baronies, 244
Bast, 209
Bast of Bubastis, 214
Battering ram, 234
Beatification literature, 219
Beatification spells, 46, 77
Beer, 5
Beit el-Wali, 165
Belief systems
    Afterlife, 221–22
    animal worship, 215
    artificial consistency in, 70–72
    invention of Heaven and Hell, 224–27
    island with no name, 227
    personal piety of the masses, 216–17
    in prehistoric Egypt, 17–22
    reward and punishment, 222–24
    sickness and prophylactic, 217
    syncretism of Amun theology, 213–15
    trial after death, 217–21
Belle Lettres, 298
Belos, 118
Benben-stone, 74
Benevolences, 184
Bene Yisrael, 118
Beni Hasan, 290
Benteshina, 165
Bent Pyramid, 61–62
Berenike, 7
Berlin and Mirgissa bowls, 113
Bethshean, 179
Beya, 195
Beyrut, 207
Big Man, 48, 49

Biographical texts, 288
Birds, artistic representations of, 20
Black Land, 4
Blue Nile, 1, 3
Bocchoris of Sais, 234, 241
Boghaz-keui, 168
Book of Am Duat, 300
Book of the Dead, XVI
Book of the Heavenly Cow, 297
Books of Wisdom, 289
Bouza, 5
Bowmen, 84
Bronze Age, 117
Brussels figurines, 113
Bubastis, 215, 266, 275
Bubastite royal house, 210
Buhen, 69, 107, 200
Building inscription, 296
Burial customs, in 8th Century B.C., 232
Burials at Merimde, 26
Busiris, 25, 89, 274
Buto, 2, 23, 34, 196, 274
Buto-Ma'adi culture, 31, 32
Buyuwawa, 207
Byblos, 14, 69–70, 92, 114, 208

C
Cadaver, preservation of, 56
Cairo, 7
Calendar, inception of, 40–42
Cambyses, 259
Canaanites, 9
Canopic Branch, 250
Capital city, 16
Carchemish, 168, 207
Cartouche, XVI
Cataracts, of the Nile, 1. *See also* specific cataracts
Cattle census, 46
Caucasus, 125
Causeway, of Valley Temple, 76, 77
Cemeteries, 83
C-group people, 84, 107
Chabrias, 264
Chaeremon, 281
Chamber of Writings, 293
Champollion, Jean François, XVI–XVII
Chancery, 294, 295
Chariotry, 130, 245
Chellean, 12
Chief Manager of the Crafts, 252
Chief of all construction work of the king, 67
Chief Royal Herald, 175
Chief taxing master, 184

Children, in New Kingdom, 187
Christianity, XIV, 225, 282–83
Chronology, basis of, 301–05
Cimmerians, 241
Cities, 34–36
Civil servants, 68, 84
Civil service, 39–42
Civil war, 85, 93–94
Classical authors, 281–82
Clement of Alexandria, 282
Closed system, 40
Coffin Texts, 87–89, 220
Collection of Deeds, 296
Colonies, 35
Commander of militia, 272
Commerce, in Twenty-sixth Dynasty, 258
Commercial agents, 193
Common (Christian) Era, 302
Common man, social phenomenon of, 86–87
Communication, 15
Communities, 13, 15–17
Consonantal sounds, 42
Constantine, 282
Copper, 8, 102
Copper mines, 69
Coptic language, XIV, XV, XVII, XVIII
Coptic script, 282
Coptos, 21, 94
Corinth, 248
Corvée, 272
Cosmogony, 26
Council of Thirty, 103, 176
Creation, 254
Creation myths, 24–26
Crete, 117, 118, 192
Crocodile, in predynastic art, 19
Cult center, 17
Cultic literature, 251, 293
Cultivation, 5
Cults, 231
Cultural exchange, during Eighteenth Dynasty, 135–37
Cursing, 113
Cycle of nine, 252
Cyprus, 110, 193, 259
Cyrenaica, 8, 13, 193
Cyrus the Great, 258

D
Dahshur, 61, 77, 102
Daily life, during Ramesside Age, 184
Dairy-ledger, 292
Dakhleh, 248
Damascus, 182, 207, 208, 235

Damietta branch, 2
Danaus, 118
Danuna, 199
Daphnae, 247
Dapur, 167
Darius I, 240, 259, 262
Darius II, 263
Darius III, 270
Day book, 293
Day book of the king's house, 295
Death
    in mythic narrative, 26–27
    trial after, 217–21
Decentralization, 83, 84
Decipherment, XV–XVI
Decius, 279
Deinocrates of Rhodes, 270
Deir el-Bahari, 164, 200, 279
Deir el-Bahri, 122
Deir el-Medina, 185–186, 187
Deities
    list of, 21–22
    personal piety and, 217
    in predynastic art, 18
Delta, 5, 6, 8–9, 31–32, 232–34, 237
Demography, 6–7
Demotic script, XV–XVI, XVIII, 277, 278, 280, 282, 300
Dendera, 274, 275
Dendereh, 71
Department of Manpower, 67
Department of Pharaoh's Correspondence, 293
Department of Pharaoh's Granaries, 293
Department of Revenue and Storage, 68
Deportation, 182
Description de l'Egypte, XV
Desert palaces, 59
Deserts, 7, 13
Determinatives, XVI
Dialogue, 289
Diodorus, 281
Diorite quarries, 69
Diospolis Parva, 279
Divine Worshipper of Amun, 235, 245
Divorce, 186
Djaw, 85
Djedef-re, 75
Djed-Hor, 215
Djeme, 235
Djoser, 59–61, 74, 75–76
Domesticated animals, 6
Donation stelae, 299
Dongola province, 231
Dues, of taxpayers, 184
Dynastic Race hypothesis, 34
Dynasties. *See* specific dynasties

E
East Africa, 7, 248
Eastern Desert, 7, 8
Eastern River, 2
Ebla, 70, 84
Economy, in Twentieth and Twenty-first Dynasties, 200
Edfu, 274
Edict of Theodosius, 282
Edicts of the king, 185
Edjo, 23, 36, 172
Egypte sous les Pharaons (Champollion), XVI
Egyptian mythology, 23
Egyptian wisdom, XIV
Eighteenth Dynasty
    creation of African empire, 132–33
    cultural exchange during, 135–37
    empire vs. retrenchment, 126
    end of, 159–61
    Hatshepsut, 127–29
    as heir to Middle Kingdom, 124
    Indo-European arrival, 124–26
    influence on Nineteenth Dynasty, 171
    kings of, 121
    Kush administration, 133–35
    Thutmose III, 129–32
Eighth Dynasty, 93
Ekron, 258
El-Berseh, 290
Elderly(?) land, 4
Elephantine, 2, 3, 69, 242, 261
Eleutheros Valley, 130, 165
Eleventh Dynasty, 95
El-Hibeh, 211
Elkab, 36
El Kab, 71, 292
Elkabian of Upper Egypt, 13
Elkabian stage of culture, 13
Eltekeh, 236
Emar, 117, 193
Emmer wheat, 5
Ennead, 48, 252
Ensi (king), 270
Eocene, 11
Epaphos, 118
Ermant, 21, 94, 95
Esarhaddon, 236, 237
Esdraelon plain, 130
Eshnunna, 113
Esna, 2, 21, 274
Esna temple, 279
Etiology, 291
Eusebius, 308
Event clusters, 44
Exchange, international, 193–94
Eye of Re, 71

F

Fairytales, 297
Falcon, 19
Falcon cults, 231
Family, as social unit, 22
Family compact, 203
Family life, during Ramesside Age, 186–87
Family stelae, 290
Famine, 84, 232
Farming villages, 16
Faubourgs, 245
Fayum, 2, 102, 103, 215, 271
The Fenkhu, 207
Fertility, 90–93
Fertility overtones, in predynastic art, 18
Fiefdoms, 229
Field of Rushes, 27
Fifteenth Dynasty, 115, 116–17
Fifth Dynasty
    annals of, 46
    collapse of, 85–86
    the "common man," 86–87
    downsizing of the state, 84–85
    magic and the coffin texts, 87–89
    Osiris, 90–93
    townships and manors, 82–83
Fifth Millenium B.C., 26
First Cataract, 1, 36, 84, 107, 132, 242
First Dynasty, 18, 36–38, 40
First Intermediate Period, 6
First Millennium, 304
First Occasion, 24
First-of-Westerners, 92
Fiscal controls, in Twenty-sixth Dynasty, 248–50
Fishstocks, 6
Flavius Josephus, 308
Flax, 5
Flooded Land, 4
Flooding, of the Nile, 3
Flower gardens, 5
Following of Horus, 44
Foodstocks, 5–6
Foreign rulers, 115–16
Fortified enclosure, 16
Forts, protective, 107
Four, importance of number, 252
Fourth Dynasty
    annals of, 46
    apogee of royal power, 63–66
    cult of Re, 74–75
    king as perfect god and man, 72–74
    Pharaoh's foreign influence, 69–70
    Pharaoh's government, 67–68
    pyramid texts, 77–78
    royal mortuary temple, 75–76

    social class and reward system, 68–69
    syncretism, 70–72
Fourth Millenium B.C., 22
Frieze, 89
Functionaries, 68
Funerary meal, 58, 287

G

Galilee, 167
Gardens, 5
Garrison of Kush, 230
Garrisons, 179
Gaza, 8, 133, 179, 270
Geb, 25, 26
Genealogy, 203
General officer, for townships, 83
Geography (of Egypt)
    arable land and agriculture, 4
    coast east and west of the Delta, 8–9
    demography, 6–7
    deserts, 7
    foodstocks, 5–6
    the Inundation, 3
    the Nile, 1–2
Gereg, 66
Gerf Hussein, 231
Germanicus, 279
Gibraltar, 248
Gilf System, 11
Gilgamesh, 221
Giza, 62, 262
Giza plateau, 2, 172
Giza pyramid, 287
Gnosticism, 280–81, 282
"God," artistic sign for, 19
Goddesses, 22
Gonfalon, 18
Government, of Pharaoh, 67–68
Government archives, 42–46
Government officials, in Ramesside Age, 174–76
Grain tax, 184
Grammar, exploration of, XVI
Grandees of the realm, 174–76
Granicus, 270
Granite quarries, 69
Graphic icons, 42
Great Chief of the Me(shwesh), 209
Great Chief of the Township, 83
The Great God, 63
Great Harris Papyrus, 6, 178, 200–01, 294
Great Inventory, 274, 293
Great One, 36
Great Pyramid of Giza, 62
Great Reckoning, 68
The Great Reckoning, 219

Great River, 2
Greco-Roman Era-dating, 302
Greece, 136, 192, 248–49, 251, 264, 269–70
Gulf of Suez, 7
Gyges of Lydia, 241

H
Hadrian, 279
Hammamat, 7
Hammurabi of Babylon, 125
Hapu, 142
Hapusonb, 127
Harkhuf, 84
Harmonization, 70
Harvest tax, 262, 272
Hasor, 113
Hathor, 22, 48, 71, 216, 275
Hatshepsut, 127–29, 133, 145
Hattusas, 158, 161, 198
Hattusilis, 167–69
Hau-nebu, 192
Hawara, 105
Hazor, 129
Heart, 254
Heaven, 224–25
Hebrews, 118
Hecataeus, 276, 281
Heliopolis, 24, 78, 115, 149
Helipolis, 65
Hell, 224
Hellenistic Era-dating, 303
Hellenized Egyptians, 280
Hemaka, 45
Hephaestos, 252
Hera, 118
Herakleopolis, 37, 81, 205–06, 209, 244, 260
Hereditary rights, 68
Herihor, 202–03, 209, 231
Hermeneutic, 23
Hermeneutic of Horus, 47
Hermes Trismegistos, XIV, 280
Hermetica, XIV
Hermetic literature, 280
Hermopolis, 21–22, 209, 230, 252, 261, 276, 288
Hermotybies, 245
Hero and monster myth pattern, 25
Herodotus, 105, 206, 215, 240, 245, 260, 276, 281, 300
Heroonpolis, XIV
Hesiod, 251
Hetepheres, 62
Hezekiah of Judah, 236
Hidden One. *See* Amun
Hierakonpolis, 36–38
Hieratic script, 242

Hieroglyphic script, 272
Hieroglyphica (Horapollo), XIV, 283
Hieroglyphic script, XIV–XV, XVII
Hieroglyphs, 88
High ground, 4
High Old Kingdom, 55
Hittites, 126, 129, 192
Hittite war
    Egypto-Hittite entente, 167
    resumption of hostilities, 165
    threat to Syria, 158
Holocene, 13
Holocene Wet Phase, 13
Homer, 251
Homonyms, 42
Homophony, XVI, 26
Hor-Aha, 72
Horapollo, XIV, 283
Hordedef, 100
Hor-den, 51
Horemheb, 161–62, 172, 231
Hor-Qa'a, 51
Horse, 113
Horus, 20, 36–37, 47, 91, 145, 173, 213, 251, 279
Horus Lord of Heaven, 22
Horus of Hierakonpolis, 22
Horus Qa'a, 52
Hotep-sekhemwy, 52
Hours, 40–41
House of Amun, 178, 230, 235
House of Books, 293
House of Herdsmen of the Residence, 68
House of Life, 88, 293
House of Rescripts, 286
House of the God's-Book, 88
House of the God's Book(s), 46
House of the Great One, 36
House of the Ku, 57
House of the Plow, 67–68
House of the Weavers, 68
Hu (authoritative utterance), 63
Huny, 61, 76
Hurrians, 125–26
The Hyksos
    impact of, 126–27
    occupation by, 122–23
    Thutmose III and, 129–31
Hymnodic stelae, 295
Hymns of Adoration, 296
Hystaspes, 259

I
Iamblichus, 284
Inachos of Argos, XIV

Inaros, 263
Income tax, 261–62
Indo-Europeans, in Eighteenth Dynasty, 124–26
Infantry, 179, 245
Influence, of Egypt in Fourth Dynasty, 69–70
Inscriptions, XIV–XVIII, 92–93
Insects, artistic representations of, 19
Instruction for Merikare, 25
Inter alia copies, 286
International trade and exchange, 193–94
Inter-nome strife, 70
In toto decrees, 289
The Inundation, 3, 23
Inyotef, 93–95
Inyotef II, 94
Io, 118
Ipuwer, 85, 88, 100
Iran, 112
Iraq, 14
Iron Age, 207–08
Isaiah, 230
Ishtar, 143
Isin, 113
Isis, XIV, 22, 48, 71, 90, 91, 209, 214, 251, 273,
    279–80
Israel, 207–08, 234
Issus, 270
Ithyphallic deity, 18
Itj-towy, 98, 99, 102, 103, 112, 117, 289

J
Jericho, 14
Jerusalem, 14, 70, 207–08
Jordan Valley, 207
Joseph's granaries, XIV
Journal, 290
Jubilant summons, 57
Jubilee, 72
Judah, 208, 233, 234, 258
Julius Caesar, 283

K
Kadashman-turgu, 168
Kadesh, 161, 164, 166–67, 196
Ka-gemni, 100
Kahun papyri, 113
Kalasiris, 245
Kamose, 122–23, 132, 135, 180
Kan el-Kebir, 290
Karkar, 208
Karnak, 90, 112, 142, 206, 279
Karnak quay inscriptions, 298
Karoy, 133
Kasr es-Sayyed, 2

Kassites, 125
Kawa, 200
Keftiu, 192–93
Kerma, 107, 112, 113, 124, 132–33
Khababash, 270
Kha-em-hat, 142
Khafre, 63, 64, 75, 262
Khamwese, 172
Khanigalbat, 126, 167
Kharga, 248
Khargeh depression, 7
Khartoum, 3
Khasekhemwy, 56
Khato-land, 183
Khatte, 125, 139, 158, 164, 193, 196
Khemmis, 23
Khendjer, 112
Khentiamentiu, 27, 36, 90
Kheruef, 175
Khnum-khuf-w(y), 62
Khonsu-em-heb, 221
Khonsu (moon), 94
Khufu, 46, 62, 63, 75, 262
Khyan, 116
Kingdom of Kush
    annihilation of, 132
    in early Eighteenth Dynasty, 124
    garrisons in, 179
    rise of, 230
Kingdom of the West, 233
Kingship, mythology of, 72
King-in-death doctrine, 87
King Josiah, 251
King list, 307
King list tradition, 303
King of the Gods. *See* Amun
King's commands, 66
King Scorpion, 38
Kingship, ideology of, 272
King's Peace, 269
King's scribe, 272
King's son, title, 135
Kircher, Athanasius, XIV
Kiya, 160
Kleopatra, XVI, XVII
Kleopatra III, XVI
Kleopatra VII, 278
Knossos, 117, 192
Kom Ombo, 2, 274
Koptos, 7
Kubbaniya, 13
Ku (life force), 57
Kullani, 232
Kumidi, 133, 179

Kusae, 117
Kush. *See* Kingdom of Kush
Kushite period, textual sources for, 299
Kushites
    hold on Egypt (712–664 B.C.), 234
Kypselids, 248

L
Labor tax, 272
Labu, 196, 199, 205
Labyrinth (pyramid of Hawara), 106
Laetus, Pomponius, XIV
Land-holding, during Ramesside Age, 183
Landing stage, 76
Land of Ramses, XIV
Land of the Flood, 4
Land of the shma-plant, 4
Land tax, 262
Larsa, 113
Late Egyptian, XVIII, 236, 292
Late Egyptian stories, 296
Late Period, 209, 213
Late Roman Empire, XIV
Law
    after death, 217–21
    during the New Kingdom, 184–86
Law Code of Hermopolis, 186
Laws, in Fourth Dynasty, 66
Laws of the land, 66
Lebanon, 113, 130–31
Legal doctrine, 185
Legend of the deliverer, 263
Leontopolis, 209
Lepsius, Richard, XVII
Letter-scribe, 271
Levalloisian, 12, 13, 14
The Levant, 14, 110, 113, 208
Levant communities, 15
Libya, 8, 214, 236
Libyan hegemony, textual sources for, 298–99
Libyan kings, 205–11
Libyarch, 299
Life force, 56–57
Life forms
    artistic representations of, 19
    in mythic narrative, 23
Linear B script, 193
Lioness, 22
Lisht, 102, 244. *See also* Itj-towy
Literature
    from First Intermediate Period, 288–89
    of the New Kingdom, 188–89
    of persuasion, 100–02, 291
Love poetry, 297, 298

Lower Egypt, 2, 6, 22, 36, 62, 292
Lower Nubia, 231
Lukka, 196
Luxor, 142, 165
Lydia, 241, 258, 263

M
Ma'at, 66, 250
Macedonian troops, 270
Magic, 58, 87–89, 222, 282
Magic spells, 113
Mahaswen, 205
Man, appearance of, 11–12
Manetho, 60, 85, 281, 308
Manfalut, 7
The Manifestations of Re, 88, 293
Manor-lords, 103
Manors, 82–83
Mansion of Seshat, 293
Märchen, 189
Mari, 117
Mariette, Auguste, XVIII, 299
Maritime traffic, 194
Mark Antony, 278
Market gardens, 5
Marriage stories, 258
Maryannu, 125
Mastaba, 59, 60, 75
Material culture, of late Naqada II, 34
Maternal overtones, in predynastic art, 18
Measurement, 40–41
Medes, 258
Medieval chronicles, 302
Medinet Habu, 198–99
Medjed, 68
Megiddo, 130, 131, 179–80
Meidum, 61, 76
Memphis
    Alexander and, 270
    annals at, 46
    archives in, 292
    civil war and, 93
    craftsmen in, 181–82
    deserts and, 7
    Greek occupation and, 242–43
    mortuary temples at, 142
    overshadowed by Sais, 243
    pillage by the Hyksos, 115
    as "place of ascent," 60
    population distribution and, 6
    Ptah and, 210, 252
    settlement of, 39–40
    townships and, 82–83
    under Persian occupation, 262

under Roman Empire, 279, 281
under the Ptolemies, 271–72
Memphite Theology, 253
Mendes, 2, 5, 22, 90, 264–65, 266, 274, 277
Mendesian Dynasty, 264
Menkaure, 55, 76, 262
Merenptah, 195, 196, 205, 207
Merenre, 77
Meret-seger, 216–18
Merikare, 87, 94, 219
Merimde, burials at, 26
Merimose, 142
Merit-aten, 160
Meroe, 242
Mersa matruh, 193
Meshwesh, 8, 196, 199, 205–06
Mesopotamia, 35, 112–13, 125–26, 158, 167, 221
Metjen, 82
Middle Ages, XIV
Middle Bronze II, 113
Middle East, 258
Middle Egypt, 3, 234
Middle Egyptian, scholarly grammars in, XVIII
Middle Egyptian dialect, 292
Middle Euphrates, 125
Middle Kingdom
    Amenemhet I, 98–99
    Amenemhet III, 104–06
    as art prototype for Twenty-fifth Dynasty, 251
    decline of, 111–14
    external world and, 106–10
    persuasion literature, 100–02
    reorganization of Egypt, 102–03
    student knowledge of, 176–77
    textual sources for, 289–92
    writing-school, 99–100
Migdol, 247, 261
Miletus, 250
Military annals, 295
Militia commander, 272
Min, 286
Mind, 253
Minshat Abu Omar, 27
Miocene, 11
Mitanni, 126, 127, 129–30, 139, 143, 189
Mokattam hills, 2
Montemhet, 300
Montu, 95, 98, 142, 143, 214
Montu-em-hat, 236, 241, 251
Montuhotpe, 124
Montuhotpe I, 98, 128, 288
Montuhotpe III, 97
Montuhotpe the Great, 107
Monument of Djoser, 59–61

Mortuary economics, 56–59
Moschion, 198
Moses, 251, XIV
Mother-goddess cults, 71
Mound of creation, 24, 227
Mound of Wēse, 235
Mount Bishri, 112
Muhammed, 283
Mullos, 198
Mursilis, 164
Mursilis I, 126
Mushki, 207
Mutara, 167
Mut (the mother), 22, 71, 94, 142
Muwatallis, 165, 167
Mycenae, 196
Mycenaean Age, 193
Myos Hermos, 7
Mystic knowledge, 280
Mythic narrative, 22–27
Mythology
    Akhenaten's attack on, 153
    Amun theology and, 213–15
    of Egyptian kingship, 47
    of kingship, 72–74
    royal, 47–50

N
Nabonidus, 251
Naga ed-Deir, 290
Naga Hammadi, 2
Nag Hammadi, 94
Nahr el-Kelb, 167
Name stone, 287
Namlot, 206
Namlot of Hermopolis, 233
Napata, 200, 209, 231–32, 233, 234, 258
Napoleonic expedition (1798), XV
Naqada II period, 34–35, 36, 37
Naqada (town), 36
Narmer, 38–39
Narrative folk-tale, 291
Narrative myths, 22–27
Narratives, 291
Nascent state, 51–53
Natufian culture, 14
Naukratis, 250, 281
Near East, 261
Nebuchadnezzar II, 258
Necho, 237, 239
Necho II, 242, 247, 248, 258, 262
Nefer-hotpe, 112
Neferirkare, 67, 76, 287
Neferirkare I, 46

Nefertiri, 155
Neferites, 264, 266
Nefertity, 151, 160
Neferty, 101
Neferu-Sobek-re, 127
Negeb, 8, 13, 14, 117
Neheb-kau, 25
Nehsi, 116
Neith, 214, 242–43
Neith of Sais, 259
Nekhbit, 36
Nektanebo, 264, 266, 268
Nektanebo I, 248, 265
Nektanebo II, 248, 266, 274
Neo-Hittite states, 207
Neolithic communities, 15
Neolithic period, end of, 32–34
Nephthys, 48
Nespakashuty, 241
Nesubanebdjed, 202–03
New Kingdom
    dynastic succession of the Twentieth Dynasty, 200–01
    economic hardship and social protest, 199–200
    end of Nineteenth Dynasty, 195
    international trade and exchange, 193–94
    Keftiu and the Hau-nebu, 192
    laws during, 184–86
    literature of, 188–99
    piracy and the Sea Peoples, 195–99
    priesthood during, 177–79
    priesthood of Amun and the army, 201–02
    Tanite period, 202–04
    textual sources for, 292–98
New land, 4
Niching, 34
Night of the Great Sleep, 92
The Nile, 1–2
Nile Valley, 12–13, 37
Nineteenth Dynasty
    accession of Ramesses II, 164–65
    army's assumption of power, 162–64
    Egypto-Hittite entente, 167–69
    end of, 195
    Hittite threat to Syria, 158–59
    kings of, 157
    resumption of hostilities with the Hittites, 165–67
    royal house of, 171–74
Nineveh, 143, 258
Ninth Dynasty, 93
Nitokerty, 127
Nitokris, 241
Nofer, 43, 46
Nofret, 43, 65
Nomarchs, 103, 248, 260

North Syria, 14
Nubia, 7, 32, 69, 70, 107, 135, 230–31, 235, 242
Nubian Levallois, 13
Nun (ocean), in mythic narrative, 24
Nun (primaeval sea), 245
Nut (sky), in mythic narrative, 25
Ny-neter, 52, 60

O
Obelisks, 149
Octavian, 278
Offering table, 58
Office of king's herald, 271
Offices of the Residence, 67
Offices of writings, 292
Ogdoad, 252
Old Egyptian, scholarly grammars in, XVIII
Old Kingdom
    ancestral worship and mortuary economics, 56–59
    apogee of royal power, 63–66
    art models from, 251
    collapse of, 81–95
    cult of Re, 74–75
    king as perfect god and man, 72–74
    kings of, 55
    Pharaoh's government, 67–68
    Pharaoh's influence, 69–70
    pyramid construction advancement, 61–62
    Pyramid Texts, 77–78
    royal mortuary temple, 75–76
    social class and reward system, 68–69
    syncretism, 70–72
    textual sources, 285–87
    tomb evolution and monument of Djoser, 59–61
Ombos, 36
Onkhsheshonky, 211
Opening-the-Mouth ceremony, 57
Opet, 171
Oracles, 293
Oral culture, 188
Oral transmission, of verbal composition, 291–92
Orchards, 4
Orontes, 28, 129
Orthography, 288
Osiride chapels, 214
Osiris, 48, 71, 72, 74, 90–91, 219–20, 223–25, 227, 279
Osiris-Apis, 279
Osiris myth, XIV, 253
Osorkon, 209
Osorkon I, 206, 207
Osorkon II, 208
Osorkon III, 210
Ostraca, 294, 298
Overseer of ploughland, 103

Overseer of township, 68
Overseer of Upper Egypt, 83
Overseer positions, 230
Ownerless land, 4
Oxyrrynchos, 244, 279

P

Pacified southerners, 70
Padi-amenemope, 241
Padi-Osiris, 276
"Palace Order" literature, 295
Palermo Stone, 62
Palestine, 123, 124, 125, 129–30, 207, 208, 221, 232, 266
Papyri, 5, 294
Papyrus Abbott, 294
Papyrus Mayer, 294
Papyrus Wilbour, 294
Paramses, 162
Parennefer, 146, 151
Parlando, 100–01
Parochial settlement, 16
Pax Aegyptiaca, 231
Paynehsi, 202, 231
Paynodgem, 209
Peasants, in Ramesside Age, 181–83
Pediese clan, 240
Peisistratus, 251
Peleset, 199
Peloponnesian Wars, 264
Pelusiac branch, 2, 5, 8
Pelusium, 237, 259, 270
Pepy I, 39, 77, 84
Pepy II, 85
The Perfect God, 63
Periander, 248
Peribsen, 52–53, 60
Persepolis, 262
Persia, 269
Persian Empire
    administration by, 260–62
    Cambyses and Darius I, 259
    conquest of 525 B.C, 258
    end of, 263–64
    last conquest of Egypt, 266–68
    last period of political independence, 263–66
    monarch denigration and folklore of deliverance, 262–63
Persian occupation, XIII
Persian period, 299–300
Personality, of ethereal being, 56
Personal piety, 216–17
Persuasion literature, 100–02, 233, 291
Petamenopet, 251
Petrie, William Matthew Flinders, XVIII

Petubastis, 210
Pharaoh
    foreign influence of, 69–70
    government of, 67–68
    Kush and, 133
    as land-holder, 183
    power and authority of, 63
    relations with Greeks, 276–78
    relations with Western Asia, 116
Pharaonic model, 272
Pherycydes, 251
Philae, 274
Philip of Macedon, 269
Philistines, 232–33, 236
Philo Judaeus, 281
Phoenicia, 232
Phoenician coast, 69
Phoenicians, 207, 247
Phrygia, 241
Piankhy, 209, 232, 233–34
Pillars of Herakles, 248
Piracy, 195–99
Pi-Ramesses, 168, 172, 179, 202
Plague, 161, 279
Plants, artistic representations of, 19
Plato, XIV
Pleistocene, 11–12
Pliocene, 11
Plotinus, XIV, 282
Ploughland, 4
Plutarch, XIV
Poetry, 295
Policy decisions, 185
Polycrates, 259
Population, 6
Pot decorations, 41
Pottery, 14, 31
Powerful One, 22
Precis (Champollion), XVI, XVII
Predynastic art, 18
Prehistoric Egypt
    agricultural revolution, 13–15
    appearance of man, 11–12
    belief systems, 17–22
    mythic narrative, 22–27
    sedentary community, 15–17
Priest, 18
Priesthood
    during New Kingdom, 178
    under Roman rule, 271, 274
Prime minister, 67, 112
Prisoners-of-war, 182
Private necropolis, 296
Privy council, 103

Privy purse, 271
Processional temple, 178
Production units, 67
Prophecy, 289, 291
Proto-philosophic thought, 252–54
Provincial administration, 244–45, 272, 279
Provincial governors, 85
Provincial officials, 292
Prussia, XVII
Psammetichus, 299
Psamtek, 237, 239, 340–41
Psamtek I, 244, 245, 340
Psamtek II, 258
Psamtek III, 259, 262
Psuedo king lists, 294
Psusennes II, 206
Ptah, 46, 171, 177, 271
Ptahhotpe, 100
Ptahmose, 142
Ptah of Memphis, 143, 252
Ptahshepses, 82
Ptolemaios, XVII
Ptolemies
    Egyptian temples under, 274–76
    government of, 271–72
Ptolemy, Claudius, XIV
Ptolemy I, 272
Ptolemy II, 271
Ptolemy IV, 277
Ptolemy Lagus, 270
Ptolemy's Almagist, 303
Ptolemy signs, XV
Ptolemy V, XV
Ptolemy VII (Physcon), XVI
Pudu-hepa, 169
Punishment, 222
Purukuzzi, 207
Puyemre, 127
Pwenet, 7, 128, 248
Pylons, 295
Pyramid City, 67
Pyramids
    for Christians, XIV
    construction of, 61–62
    largest, 62
Pyramid Texts, 18, 77–78, 88, 219, 251, 287

Q
Qa'a, 75
Qatanum, 113, 129
Qatna, 159
Qena System, 11
Qenbet, 185

Qoseir, 7
Quota tax, 184

R
Ra-hotpe, 65
Rainfall, 3
Rakotis, 270
Ramesses I, 162
Ramesses II
    accession of, 164–65
    disturbance of tomb of, 202
    Hittite hostilities and, 165–67
    as leader of army, 181
    legacy of, 192
    life and times of, 171–89
    piracy and the Sea Peoples, 195–99
    shrine for, 231
    tomb desecration of, 200
Ramesses III, 6, 178, 191, 195, 198, 199, 205, 236
Ramesses IV, 201
Ramesses IX, 200
Ramesses the Great. *See* Ramesses II
Ramesses VII, 200
Ramesses XI, 200, 201, 231
Ramesside Age, 1, 174
Ramesside family (Nineteenth Dynasty), 171
Ramess(u), XVII
Ramose, 142
Ra-nebi, 52
Rape, 186
Raphia, 277
Rebellion
    in 2nd and 1st Centuries B.C., 277
    in Seventeenth Dynasty, 122
Red Sea, 7
Reform, beginnings of, 98–99
Re-Harakhte, 219
Re-harakhty, 250
Residence City, 69
Restoration inscriptions, 298
Re (sun god), 48, 74–75, 173, 223, 224
Reunification, 288
Reward system, 68–69, 222–24
Riparian land, 4
Roman Empire, 278–79
Roman period, XIV
Rosetta branch, 2
Rosetta stone, XV–XVI
Royal decrees, 286, 289, 292, 294
Royal inscriptions,
Royal law, 66
Royal mortuary temple, 75–76
Royal mythology, 47–48

Royal stelae, 288
Rubrics, of a spell, 89
Rylands IX, 245

S
Sabaco, 234, 253
Sabni, 84
Sahara, 12, 94
Sai, 231
Sais
    Amun theology and, 214
    Amyrtaeos and, 263
    armed forces, 245–47
    government and court of, 242–44
    history of, 241
    Meshwesh tribes in, 205
    shrines at, 274
    Tefnakhte in, 233, 234
Saïte kings, 258
Saïte period, textual sources for, 299–300
Sakhmet, 143
Salitis, 114, 115
Salvation, 90
Samal, 207
Samos, 259
Sanchuniaton, 250
Sandy Cliffs, 4
Saqqara, 43, 60–62, 112, 210, 252
Sarbut el-Kadim, 8, 116
Sardinia, 199
Sardinian plain, 196
Sargon II, 241
Sargon of Akkad, 84
Sat-Amun, 146
Satuna, 167
Scholarly grammars, XVIII
Scribal arts, 289
Scribes, 176–77, 231
Scythians, 241
Sea Peoples, 195–99
Sebennytos, 205, 265
Sebilian stage of culture, 13
Seboyet, 100, 102
Second Cataract, 13, 69, 107, 112, 133, 231, 242
Second Dynasty, 59, 60
Second Millennium, 304
Security, of graves, 60
Sedentary communities, 14, 15–16
Sed-festival, 74, 143, 195
Semna, 3, 107
Senenmut, 127, 128
Sennacherib, 236
Senwosret I, 98, 99, 101, 107, 112, 124, 143, 149, 291

Senwosret II, 103
Senwosret III, 98, 103, 104, 107, 290
Septimius Severus, 282
Sepulchres, 300
Seqnenre Ta'o I, 122
Serapeum stelae, 299
Serapis, 279
Serpent stone, 43
Sesostris, 171
Seth, 36, 37, 47–48, 71, 90–91, 122, 171
Seth (Ash) deity, 18, 23
Seth Rebellion, 52
Setna-Khamois, 224
Sety, 162, 164
Sety I, 172, 207
Sety II, 195
Seventeenth Dynasty, 122–23
Seventh Dynasty, 85
Sexagesimal system, 41
Shalmaneser III, 208
S(h)arakhu, 34, 36
Shardana, 196, 198, 199
Shardona, 165
Sharuhen, 117, 180
Shasu, 207, 247
Shebitku, 234, 236
Shekelesh, 196, 199
Shepenwepet I, 210
Shepenwepet II, 241
Shepseskaf, 75, 82
Sheshonk, 207
Sheshonk I, 206–08
Shespe-ankh, 57
Ship-wrecked Sailor, 291
Shu (air), 25, 26, 48, 71
Sia (intelligence), 63
Si-Amun (son of Amun), 270
Sicily, 199
Sickness, 217
Sidon, 207, 236
Siege tower, 113
Sile, 179, 237
Sin, 223
Sinai, 13, 69, 102, 234, 258
Sinai peninsula, 8
Sinaitic alphabet, 116
Sinuhe, 101, 107, 291
Si-onsi (king's son), 270
Si-osir, 224
Siptah, 195
Sirius, 40
Sitz im Leben, 188
Siwa, 270

Six Great Halls, 67
Sixteenth Dynasty, 117, 122
Sixth Dynasty
    collapse of, 85–86
    the "common man," 86–87
    downsizing of the state, 84–85
    magic and the coffin texts, 87–89
    Osiris, 90–93
    townships and manors, 82–83
Slave raid, 70
Smenkhkare, 160
Snofru, 61, 62, 70, 76, 101
Sobekhotpe I, 111
Sobek-hotpe III, 112
Sobek-mosi, 142
Social class, 68
Social classification, 279
Social revolution, 85, 87
Social tensions, 277
Soleb, 142, 231
Sollum, 8
Solomon, 207–08
Somalia, 248
Somaliland, 7
Songs of the Harpers, 86
Son of the sun-god, 75
Sothis, 40, 124
Speech, 289
Spells, magical, 88, 92, 189
Speos Artemidos inscription, 128
State library, 46
Statue inscriptions, 298, 300
Statute law, 66, 184
St. Augustine, XIV
Stelae, 286, 288. *See also specific types*
Step Pyramid, 60, 61, 62, 74, 172
St. Mark, 282
Strabo, 7, 281
Sudan, 11, 70, 85, 107, 124, 258
Suez frontier, 8
Sumer, 34
Sumur, 179
Sun-disc, 152–54, 160, 172
Sun-god, names of, 71
Sun's eye, 23
Suppiluliumas, 159, 161, 165
Suppiluliumas I, 158
Support staffs, 69
Surer, 142
Suza, 262
Syncretism, 70, 213
Syntax, exploration of, XVI
Syria, 14, 36, 70, 84, 112, 124, 125, 158–59, 161, 207, 221, 263

T
Tacitus, 281
Taharqa, 236, 237, 251
Takelot II, 208
Tanis, 202, 206, 208, 230, 243
Tanite period, 202–04
Tanwetamani, 237, 239, 242
Tawosret, 121, 195
Taxation
    of Old Kingdom, 68
    during Ramesside Age, 183–84
Tax structure, 261
Teaching wisdom, 291
Tefnakhte, 233, 234, 237, 241
Tefnut, 22, 48
Tehneh, 208
Tel ed-Dab'a/Avaris, 113, 115
Tel el-Yehudiya, 115
Tel Haroer, 117
Tel Kedwa, 247
Tell el-Amarna, 157
Temple archive, 287
Temples, 272–74, 276–79
Temple walls, 295
Tenth Dynasty, 289
Testament of my Father, 73
Tety, 84
Teucrians, 199
Thebes
    archives in, 292
    during Assyrian occupation, 232–34
    early years at, 149–50
    independence in 205 B.C., 277
    kingdom of Kush and, 230–32
    under Kushite rule, 234–36
    Meshwesh tribes in, 196
    as model for Tanis, 202
    mortuary temples at, 288
    under Persian administration, 260–62
    in Ramesside Age, 171–74
    reunification and, 241–42
    revolt of, 208–09
    secession from Herakleopolitan kingdom, 93–94
    in Sixteenth Dynasty, 117, 122
    textual sources for First Intermediate Period, 288
    as theocratic state in 8th century B.C., 231
    in Twelfth Dynasty, 98–99
    wines of, 5
Third Cataract, 107
Third Dynasty
    ancestral worship and mortuary economics, 56–59
    monument of Djoser, 59–61
    pyramid construction advancement, 61–62
    tomb evolution, 59–61

Third Millennium, 8, 305, 307
Thirteenth Dynasty, 111, 112, 113, 116, 122, 135
Thirtieth Dynasty, 240, 274
Thirty-year festival, 72
Thoeris, 279
Thoth, XIV, 21, 25, 71, 184, 219, 225, 279, 280
Thutmose, XVII, 181
Thutmose I, 121, 124, 127, 129, 132
Thutmose II, 127, 133
Thutmose III, 117, 121, 127, 129–31, 132, 173, 180, 182, 192, 231, 295
Thutmose IV, 121, 139, 148
Tiberius Caesar, XVII
Tiglath-pileser III, 232
Tigris, 169
Tigris-Euphrates, 34, 35, 36
Tired land, 4
Tiy, 140
Tjehenu, 8
Tjekel, 207
Tombs
    evolution of, 59–61
    offerings to, 57–58
    as textual sources, 296
Tongue, 253–54
Town god, 17, 27
Towns, 21, 22
Townships, 68, 82–83
Transformation Spells, 89
Transit corridors, 35
Transliteration Alphabet, XIX
Transportation, in Naqada period, 32
Triad of gods, 94
Trial after death, 217–21
Trireme, 247
Tudkhaliyas IV, 196
Turesh, 196
Turin Canon, 52, 115, 116
Turin Strike Papyrus, 294
Turquoise, 8, 102
Turquoise mines, 69
Tushratta, 143, 158, 159
Tutankhamun, 160, 161, 162, 163, 172
Tut-ankh-aten, 160
Tuya, 140
Twelfth Dynasty
    Amenemhet I, 98–99
    Amenemhet III, 104–06
    external world and, 106–10
    impact of, 111
    persuasion literature, 100–02
    relations with Western Asia during, 112–14
    reorganization of Egypt, 102–03
    writing-school, 99–100

Twentieth Dynasty, 191–204
Twenty-eighth Dynasty, 257, 263–66
Twenty-fifth Dynasty, 229–38
Twenty-first Dynasty, 191–204
Twenty-fourth Dynasty, 205–211
Twenty-ninth Dynasty, 257, 263–66
Twenty-second Dynasty, 205–12
Twenty-seventh Dynasty, 257–63
Twenty-sixth Dynasty
    central government and the Saïte court, 242–44
    fiscal controls and commerce, 248–50
    proto-philosophic thought, 252–54
    reassurance of antiquity, 250–52
    relations with Greeks, 276
    reorganization of armed forces, 245–47
    restoration of provincial administration, 244–45
    reunification, 241–42
    Saïte history, 240
    triumph of Psamtek, 240–41
Twenty-third Dynasty, 210, 215
Two Banks, 4
Two Lands, 60, 62
Tyre, 208, 271

U
Udjahoresne, 259
Ugarit, 117, 198, 199
Ullaza, 133, 179
Ullubu, 232
Ulun Buru, 194
Underclass citizens, 183
Underworld, 221–27
Upliftings of Shu, 25, 26
Upper Egypt, 2, 21, 37, 68, 274
Ur, 113–14
Urbanism, 35
Urhi-teshup, 167–68
Ur-Nile, 11
Uruk period, 34–36
Userkaf, 75, 82

V
Valley Temple, 76, 77
Via Maris, 8
Viceroy of Kush, 230
Victory stelae, 295
Vineyard, 5
Vizier, 67–68, 113, 174–75, 271
Vulcan, 252

W
Wady Arabah, 7
Wady el-Arish, 234
Wady en-Natuf, 14

Wady Hammamat, 7, 35, 36–37
Wady Mughara, 8–9, 70
Wady Qena, 7
Wady Tumilat, 115, 237, 248
Wady Zeidun, 7
Wassos, 199
"Waste basket" text, 287
Water, in mythic narrative, 24
Wawat, 136, 231
Wenamun, 203
Wenis, 77
Weny, 84
Wepwawet, 27, 36, 92
Western Asia, 70, 112–14
Western Desert, 7
Western River, 2
Wheat, 5
White Fort, 39, 61, 260
White Nile, 1
Wildlife, 6
Will, 252
Wilusa, 196

Wisdom Literature, 217
Wisdom texts, 290
Work camps, 35
Workers, in Ramesside Age, 174
Work force, 67
Writing-school, 99–100
Writing school, 289

X
Xenophanes, 254
Xerxes, 260

Y
Yamkhad, 113, 126, 129
Year record, 285
Young, Thomas, XV
Yuya, 140

Z
Zagros, 125
Zakar-baal, 136
Zeus, 118